The Art of Livin

The Art of Living

An Oral History of Performance Art

Dominic Johnson

 palgrave

First published 2015 by
PALGRAVE

Palgrave in the UK is an imprint of Macmillan Publishers Limited, registered in England, company number 785998, of 4 Crinan Street, London, N1 9XW.

Palgrave Macmillan in the US is a division of St Martin's Press LLC, 175 Fifth Avenue, New York, NY 10010.

Palgrave is a global imprint of the above companies and is represented throughout the world.

Palgrave® and Macmillan® are registered trademarks in the United States, the United Kingdom, Europe and other countries.

ISBN: 978–1–137–32221–0 hardback
ISBN: 978–1–137–32220–3 paperback

This book is printed on paper suitable for recycling and made from fully managed and sustained forest sources. Logging, pulping and manufacturing processes are expected to conform to the environmental regulations of the country of origin.

A catalogue record for this book is available from the British Library.

A catalog record for this book is available from the Library of Congress.

Typeset by Cambrian Typesetters, Camberley, Surrey

Printed in China

For Adrian Howells
(1962–2014)

Contents

List of Illustrations

Acknowledgements

Being interviewed is not every person's idea of a good time. As Jean Genet (a particularly cranky interviewee) told *Playboy* in 1964: 'I'm distracted, the microphones make it hard for me to think; I can see the tape in the recorder and I start to take on a kind of politeness, not for your sake' – the sake of the interviewer – 'since with you I can always manage to get out of trouble, but for the sake of the tape that is rolling in the recorder without my intervention.' Yet all the artists I interviewed were welcoming, candid in their contributions, and generous with their time. First and foremost, therefore, I thank all the artists who consented to be interviewed. I am grateful for the time they afforded me, and the care they gave to the project. I am especially thankful to Lady Jaye BREYER P-ORRIDGE and Adrian Howells, who sadly passed away during the preparation of the book. Some of the artists also provided personal introductions to other artists: I am therefore additionally grateful to Penny Arcade and Anne Bean.

I thank Jenni Burnell for commissioning the book for Palgrave and supporting me in its development and writing; since Jenni's departure, Lucinda Knight has been a supportive editor, and I am grateful to her and her colleagues, including Clarissa Sutherland.

The labour of transcribing many hours of audio recordings was shared with Eleanor Roberts and Harriet Curtis, two impressive early-career scholars whose research assistantship I appreciated very much.

The project required international travel, and I thank the Terra Foundation for American Art for facilitating my interviews with Ann Magnuson and Sheree Rose in Los Angeles; and the Department of Drama at Queen Mary, University of London, for supporting research trips to Amsterdam to interview Ulay, and to Leicester to interview Brian Routh of the Kipper Kids.

Several scholars commissioned interviews, either live or for publication, shaping the book in important ways. Tavia Nyong'o and Robert D. Campbell at New York University invited me to interview BREYER P-ORRIDGE at New York University in 2007. Eirini Kartsaki, Brian Lobel and Rachel Zerihan commissioned me to interview Adrian Howells, for publication in a co-edited special issue on one-to-one performance. Adrian Rifkin commissioned me to undertake a live interview with Ron Athey at Iniva in 2012, which provided the transcript for the second part of the version published here.

Sections of four interviews have been published previously. In each case, I have written a new introduction. An earlier version of my interview with BREYER P-ORRIDGE was previously published as 'Positive Surrender: An Interview with BREYER P-ORRIDGE', *Contemporary Theatre Review*, 22.1 (2012), 134–45. An earlier version of Part I of my interview with Ron Athey was previously published as 'Perverse Martyrologies: An Interview with Ron Athey', *Contemporary Theatre Review*, 18.4 (2008), 503–13. An earlier version of my interview with Julia Bardsley was previously published as 'The Skin of the Theatre: An Interview with Julia Bardsley', *Contemporary Theatre Review*, 20.3 (2010), 340–52. An earlier version of Part I of my interview with Adrian Howells was published as 'The Kindness of Strangers: An Interview with Adrian Howells', *Performing Ethos: An International Journal of Ethics in Theatre and Performance*, 3.2 (2014), 173–90. I am grateful to the publishers Routledge/Taylor & Francis and Intellect for permitting me to reproduce these interviews in revised forms.

As noted, several parts of the interviews were published in *Contemporary Theatre Review*. I thank my colleagues on the editorial team – particularly Maria M. Delgado and Aoife Monks – for encouraging me to undertake critical interviews and to consider them valid and potentially valuable as scholarly research.

Introduction

The art of living is not one I have mastered. Neither is such mastery of a type one might ever seek, straight-faced, to profess. *The Art of Living* consists of interviews with artists who have, to differing extents, and with various intensities, made performance the basis of a life, turned their bodies or lives into works of art, or sought to cultivate performance art as a grammar to articulate the possible dissolution of sensible boundaries between art and life.

Performance art, in the provisional oral history constructed here, resembles an all-encompassing medium, or anti-medium. This encircling of art and life by performance can be idiosyncratic, excessive, subtle or rigorous. Outside the mere tactic of becoming a living sculpture, or speaking autobiography, performance artists have, variously: remodelled their bodies, through surgery, body modification or anomalous daily practices; become polymaths, folding every practice of their life into the continuous endeavour of artistic becoming; extended the duration of performance actions well beyond conventional limits, to last many months, or years; or found other means to expose the interior workings of their creative, imaginative, emotional, sexual or medical lives. In each case, such practices have exceeded – drastically or subtly – many more conventional aesthetic alternatives, such as to represent the intimate mechanics of a body or a life through memoir, poem, confession or song. The cumulative action of *living* (one's) art – an exacerbation of merely doing or making art – and the art of its refinement, is questioned by the performance artists I interviewed, as if to reinvent the life from whence a work springs, and to provoke a story – a possible history – of such endeavours.

The praxis of blurring art and life is a familiar theme in art history. For Peter Bürger, the early twentieth-century avant-garde attempted the 'sublation' or merging of the previously distinct categories of art and everyday life, in order to redesign the politics of artistic production. 'When art and the praxis of life are one,' he writes, 'when the praxis is aesthetic and art is practical, art's purpose can no longer be discovered, because the existence of two distinct spheres (art and the praxis of life) ... has come to an end.'[1] While for Bürger, this strategy subsequently becomes untenable after Modernism, artists and theorists have persisted in mapping new sublations of art and life. Foremost, perhaps, the artist Allan Kaprow explained the need for 'art that tends to lose itself out of bounds', particularly through live performances, installations and participatory events that would enable 'a return to the point where art was more actively involved in ritual, magic, and life'.[2] In 1958, Kaprow famously encouraged this introduction of life into art through the appropriation of new materials and effects: 'An odor of crushed strawberries, a letter from a friend, or a billboard selling Drano' – and a litany of smells, signs, objects, actions, sounds and inevitable visions – 'all will become materials for this new concrete art', namely through his Happenings.[3] The philosopher Arthur C. Danto coins the term 'unnatural wonders' to describe contemporary artworks that obliterate or confuse the gap between art and life, redefining avant-gardism in terms of 'the way monsters bridge the boundary between humans and animal'.[4] The metaphor grounds the freakish brilliance of art, not in a supernatural, metaphysical sense, but by affording anomalies a bluntly material status, trafficking monsters, and art, alike, into the pedestrian topographies of life.

The artists interviewed in *The Art of Living* are each engaged in *the work of a lifetime* – not towards an individual masterwork (there are no more masterpieces), but – to cultivate a continuum of practices in performance (and proximate media) that might extinguish the borderlines between a life and its creative labours. Ulay has remarked, for example, that performance was a means 'to choreograph [one's] whole existence. The work will restructure itself through how we live.'[5] The neo-avant-garde or postmodernist project, beginning in the late 1950s and reaching its zenith in the 1960s and 1970s, involved bringing life (or *non-art* objects and materials) into art, for example through collage or performance-installation, typified by Kaprow's Happenings, or the combine paintings of Robert Rauschenberg, which modernised and in some ways replayed the inaugural avant-gardist strategies of Marcel Duchamp's 'Readymades' by transplanting or collaging found objects onto painted canvases. In a parallel campaign, artists trafficked art into life, through public interventions, pop-up events, and do-it-yourself artworks, epitomised by the agitprop performances of Joseph Beuys, and the games- and instruction-based artworks of Fluxus artists like George Brecht and Yoko Ono. Both tendencies functioned as technologies for overcoming the aesthetic autonomy associated with Late Modernism, in order to achieve what poet John Berryman proposed as an art that 'not only expresses the matter in hand / but adds to the stock of available reality'.[6]

Apiece with yet beyond these neo-avant-garde counter-traditions, performance art is often engaged in the praxis of turning one's life – both body and subjectivity – into the stuff of art. This account of the aesthetic imperatives of performance art might risk sounding final or triumphal. However, the gesture towards the praxis of blurring of art and life also includes failure, insignificance, invisibility, boredom and subjection to the ravages of time (and age), among its dizzying remit of effects. So, while the performances discussed throughout *The Art of Living* often exemplify the art–life continuum, live art and the liveness of performance, here the broader conceit of their historicisation aims to provoke an emphasis on the *lived* nature of artistic practice, including its production and reception. Throughout the collective *corpus* sketched by the interviewees, we encounter the recurrent difficulty of distinguishing between an artist and her or his performed persona – particularly, here, for Penny Arcade, David Hoyle and the Kipper Kids, for example – and we confront performance depicted not simply as a formal commitment, but as the ontological ground for a revolutionised way of living. This might actively counter the frequent habit of historians and journalists alike to see performance art as voguish frippery, portentous nonsense, affectation or opportunism. Performance art emerges as a means of testing *how to live* – to live more fully, more atypically, more perversely or more effectively than one might do without the sustaining practice of performance.

A history of the art of living

How, then, might we write a history of such variously excessive, striking, and anomalous practices of performance art? A particular history emerges when a chosen set of coordinates, including activities, personages, events and genealogies, is privileged, affirmed and reaffirmed. A deceptively simple question arises as the basis of any critical historiography: what alternate history – or *counternarrative* – is available when one tracks a new genealogy through a different set of historical points of reference? What new historical narratives, and conceptual conclusions, might be affirmed when a new set of stories are made available? Such questions afford the organising principle of my approach to constructing a history of performance art, and hence, to interviewing, from the imperative to commence the present project, to my selection of artists, to the model of the interview I deployed, to the questions I asked.

Any history, like any body, requires itself actively to be differenced. The result of the published interviews, as a collective whole, suggests a novel premise for a differenced (though partial) history of performance by artists. The cumulative effect of these transcripts of encounters with artists – which is to say, with primary sources of information, alternatively schooled theorists and walking archives – lays the groundwork for an alternative theory and history of performance after 1960. Between 2007 and 2014, I interviewed 12 artists or groups (14 people in total): Penny Arcade, Joey Arias, Ron Athey, Julia Bardsley, Anne Bean, Genesis and Lady Jaye BREYER P-ORRIDGE, Adrian Howells, David Hoyle, the Kipper Kids (Brian Routh and Martin Von Haselberg), Ann Magnuson, Sheree Rose and Ulay. Each artist has been active for over twenty, thirty or forty years, and some are a generation younger than the more senior artists interviewed in the earliest parts of the book. Therefore, the book does not track a direct lineage or genealogy from one artist to another, and so on, nor does it give a full image of a scene, a period or a school of performance art. Rather, an oral history such as this one gives a series of close, detailed accounts of moments in the development of diverse but interrelated practices and styles across nearly a half-century of innovative practices in performance. Each individual artist I interviewed, regardless of relative age or youth, exerts massive influence upon peers and younger artists (including and beyond the others gathered here), by historical precedence and cultural seniority. Together, they enable a history of performance that privileges non-traditional genealogies, definitions and possibilities for performance art. The interviews were an opportunity for each artist to address their practices in performance – less to explain, validate or qualify her or his work, or practice, or process, than *to give an account of oneself*, and thus to establish the social milieu of one's creative and intellectual emergence, and the conditions and effects of artistic practice.

The oral history of performance art constructed in these pages – one among a multitude of such histories that may (and should) be constructed – considers a range of research problems or intellectual imperatives. These include: individual influences, contexts and origins, including artistic and extra-artistic ones; the blurring of art and life, and the aesthetic implications and subjective or psychic costs of this strategic confusion or sublation; the performance artist as auto-didact; subcultural or anti-institutional models of schooling, training and apprenticeship; the complexity and idiosyncrasy of artistic process, which is generally post-studio and anti-rehearsal; affect and emotion, including déclassé categories such as shock, disgust, laughter and fiasco; alternative spaces of performance, including artist-run venues, public spaces and clubs; and club performance and cabaret as a hidden genealogy of performance; collaboration, in terms of its enabling promise, and its discontents; the perceived relevance (or otherwise) of terminologies and categories; and repetition, documentation, re-enactment and re-performance.

What is performance art?

The task of giving a concrete definition of performance art is decidedly thorny. As the archetypical anti-form, or post-medium, any definition quickly constrains the seemingly intrinsic fluidity and flexibility of performance art. Many of the interviewees address the problem of taxonomy, including self-definition and formal classification. Many share a common uncertainty or hesitancy about naming, particularly in relation to performance art, and some have devised their own terminologies. Anne Bean, for example, prefers the term 'life art', while Genesis BREYER P-ORRIDGE aspires to 'living art'. Ulay enjoys the slippage between *performance/perforation*, and seizes on the critical neologism 'performative photography'. As such, despite the well-known, basic, categorical resistance of performance art to precise definition, using the term at all may threaten to contain the work described in these pages.

Nevertheless, working definitions abound. In 1970, Vito Acconci gave an account of performance art – one as good, at least, as any – when he wrote:

> If the artist is a performer, in action, his presence alone produces signs and marks. The information he provides necessarily concerns the source of information, himself, and cannot be solely about some absent object; the transformation pertains to the general relationship of the individual to what is transpiring.[7]

Gendered pronouns aside, his thesis usefully entertains the function of a general rule for the way performance operates. Performance art necessitates the appearance of a performing body, experienced by an audience as material, present and apparently immediate – even when (or precisely because) it is mediated. The audience might be a solitary or social body existing in the same given time and space as the performer; or the audience can be a distant one, receiving the performance as a transmission across time and space, through photographic, photo-magnetic, textual, oral and other traces.

The meaning produced in the performance, for Acconci, *necessarily concerns* the artist, whose performing body is the prime vehicle of signification. While extraneous information – context, history, a script or score – will be operative, the performance tends to privilege and prioritise effects of signification that accommodate directly the materials (bodies, objects, language, technology and space) that are visible or sensible in the performance. Therefore, the production of meaning depends upon a chemistry between the body of the artist, the materials in play and the audience – sustaining, while differencing, the conventional relation between text, reader and context. Acconci's formal definition does not directly politicise performance art, but it points to the political potential of the actions and encounters that the form produces or incites.

Genealogically, performance art – and its weird sisters, live art and body art – is typically characterised by its double articulation in disciplinary terms, namely its push-me-pull-you relationship to visual art and experimental theatre. Its negotiation by artists and scholars tends to reiterate and celebrate its debts, and wrestle with its active (sometimes churlish) refusals. We might also add to this familiar double-articulation a broader range of *multiple* articulations, including the tension between performance art and *subculture*, and other 'low' cultural histories, staged recurrently in the interviews that follow. *The Art of Living* shows that since the late 1960s, and in the slow rippling-outwards of its aftermaths, until the present day, innovators of performance art departed from their prior fixation upon the isolated and formal considerations of visual art, and forced contact – *by way of performance* – with a diversity of time-based forms, including theatre, film and music, and beyond.

The oral history of performance art shows that the work of aesthetic origination was often done in relative isolation. Yet each artist also drew from the *Zeitgeist* of personal empowerment and do-it-yourself creative entitlement, which was often tied to subcultural and countercultural developments, including activist, agitprop and countercultural activities in the 1960s; feminist and punk aesthetics in the 1970s; queer and AIDS activism, New Wave vaudeville and midnight aesthetics in the 1980s, and other techniques for countering the vehement commercialism of the decade; and industrial, post-AIDS, queer and cyberpunk cultures in the 1990s. *The Art of Living* desublimates and revives such extra-artistic influences, and the intermedial innovations they prompted, including the appropriation of club performance, music hall, cabaret, stand-up, improvisation, collaboration, music, drums, dressing up, drag, tattooing, surgery, body-hacking, sadomasochism, fetish, drugs, crime, theatre and other surprising technologies for reorganising the social fabric of art. This reorganisation persists as a secret history, or barely repressed ideal, for the development of performance in the 1970s, and intensifies in subsequent decades, reaching a fever pitch in the 1990s.

Scope and structure

It would be a platitude to say that the artists I interviewed *matter* – to history, to culture, to me – and that each is important in their own right (*pace* Nietzsche: 'And then some mischievous little bird flew past him and twittered: "What do you matter? What do you matter?"'[8]) In part, each artist matters in her or his *anomaly*. The anomaly is an exception to every rule. It is singular. Each is its own best (and only) example. While comparisons and tentative groupings can be made, a gathering of anomalies constitutes no authoritative series. A history of anomalies is necessarily a discontinuous, selective and even arbitrary series. Such a claim, of course, gives rise to problems at the level of defining scope, and rationalising one's criteria for selection and (tacit?) exclusion.

I interviewed artists who are established in their seniority in terms of both influence and age. In terms of the latter, I interviewed artists around the age of 50 or over. In terms of the former, each artist is an *éminence grise* of performance art, a subcultural icon representing one in a series of cultural outposts. Their authority is conflicted. Each demands respect and adulation from peers, cultural inheritors and audiences, yet is wilfully (and sometimes stubbornly) *confirmed in their marginality*. Their marginality is partly self-avowed, but also conditioned by tacit or explicit refusals to adapt or adjust to curatorial trends, the art market, commercialism and other cultural vogues, which they abandon, question or torture, in fidelity to their own values and experiences.

The breadth of artists included here is necessarily partial, or incomplete: I have abandoned comprehensiveness for *depth*. A specific limitation is the fact that, with the notable exception of Ulay, the majority of the artists I interviewed live and work in the UK or the USA. Despite this parochialism on my part, the interviews with Anne Bean, Ulay, the Kipper Kids, Julia Bardsley, Ron Athey, Adrian Howells and others range across Europe more broadly, as many of the artists regularly present work in other countries to their place of residence, by nature of the material conditions of festivals, commissioning and touring. Nevertheless, the main focus of the publication is on Anglo-American performance art contexts, partly due to my own research specialisms, and limited by travel and resources. Regardless, this has the unfortunate effect of undermining the importance of historical and emergent genealogies of perform-ance art in other major international locales, for example in Eastern Europe, Central and South America, Africa and East Asia (especially China).

Despite my task of selecting artists who are in some ways exem-plary for a (Anglo-American) history of performance art, many of the same artists would balk at my implicit conferral of iconicity, influ-ence and historical priority, which their suggested exemplarity might imply. Anne Bean refers to all art history as 'custodianship', for example, and Ulay lays bare the project of historical recovery, even if sympathetic, as a project in 'intellectual capture'. Both remarks are acute, and describe the sense of containment or predation that may accompany the attention of scholars of art and performance, however well-intentioned or sensitive such attention (including my own) may wish itself to be.

In terms of the structure of *The Art of Living*, I have ordered the interviews in a more or less chronological fashion, according to the decade or period of each artist's emergence. This is, of course, a tenta-tive chronology, as many of the artists have undertaken serial emer-gences, hiatuses and resurgences. Reading through the interviews in the order they are presented, here, will give an impression, however, of a series of historical contexts, twists and turns, revelations, responses to perceived dead ends, and so on. They can also usefully be read at random, piecemeal, or in reverse order. The book concludes with information on additional resources, for interested readers to continue the labour of critical discovery each interview might hope to initiate or foster.

On method: oral history and qualitative research interviewing

Why interview artists? Why value their voice and speech? Mike Kelley argued the need for artist-critics, encouraging other artists to take up the labour of productive critical discourse about art – their own, and that of their friends and peers. Such a doubling or crossing of intellectual activities, between the practical and the theoretical, begins to corrode what he terms the 'outmoded' but still-dominant 'division of labor between those who make art and those who interpret it for the masses'.[9] A prolific artist, writer and interviewer, Kelley demanded that artists disturb the stratification of power between, on the one hand, the critic, theorist or historian, who retains the privilege to record one's interpretations of art, and on the other, the producer of art who tends to labour in silence. Seeking information about art *from the horse's mouth* – inducing the artist to speak, and recording (and to some extent reordering) their speech – helps to upset this one-sidedness in the distribution of the right to describe, account for, or historicise art.

Since its invention in the mid-nineteenth century, the interview has become a staple research method for journalists, as well as for novelists, filmmakers, playwrights and other creative practitioners. In the arts and humanities, scholars use the interview as a research method to differing extents, and with varying levels of methodological reflexivity. It is a crucial tactic for questioning the tendency towards critical distance that intervenes between the historian and her topic of study, as oral history reminds the historian that one's 'sources' are responsive, empathetic and resourceful – and frequently able *to talk back* to one's interpretations.

In tone, method and scope, *The Art of Living* is indebted particularly to four existing oral histories of performance in book form: Nick Kaye's *Art into Theatre: Performance Interviews and Documents* (1996); Maria Delgado and Paul Heritage's *In Contact with the Gods?: Directors Talk Theatre* (1996); Linda Montano's *Performance Artists Talking in the Eighties* (2001); and the most recent publication, the first volume of Heike Roms's *What's Welsh for Performance: An Oral History of Performance Art in Wales* (2008).[10] Moreover, additional context is provided by a number of oral history projects online, including the *Archives of American Art Oral Histories Interviews* project, which includes but is not limited to interviews with performance artists; and the University of Girona's encyclopedic *European Live Art Archive*, for which interviews with over sixty artists have been conducted on video.[11]

Interestingly, the authors or conveners of these and other collections rarely reflect in depth on interviewing as a research method, or
on the processes of preparation, transcription and editing of interview materials.[12] Exceptionally, Marquard Smith's *Visual Culture
Studies: Interviews with Key Thinkers* is prefaced by a scholarly engagement with the interview's viability as a qualitative research method
well suited to the discipline of visual studies. For Smith, the interview
is able uniquely to respond to visual studies, as *'a living methodology'*
and a sensibility, or *'intellectual attitude'*.[13] Interviews may be singu-
larly sympathetic to the 'new political situations, ethical dilemmas,
historical documents, conceptual turns, and the new objects, arte-
facts, media, and environments' that constitute the empirical ground
of contemporary critical thought.[14] Historian Paul Thompson notes
this resistant quality when he describes oral history as 'a breaking of
the boundary between the educational institution and the world'.[15]

The production and collection of research interviews in *The Art of
Living* is conditioned and enabled by two methodologies: *oral history*,
as a socially engaged historical method that seeks to introduce new
evidence from below (or alongside) official histories; and interviewing as a *qualitative* (as opposed to quantitative) research method in
the social sciences. The former provides the present project with a
politics, and the latter, its *method*. At times, moreover, the individual
chapters might undergo slippages into the artist's interview (a
distinct genre of conversational text, which nevertheless constitutes
a kind of research-based interview).

In the 1960s and 1970s, oral history developed as a recognised
model for collecting new historical evidence. In the 1980s, Paul
Thompson argued that oral history might seek to displace the
authoritative and oppressive historical records garnered from 'the
chronicle of kings' and other signifiers of influence and bias, towards
a *history from below*; his method of collecting evidence in the form of
oral testimony invited fellow historians to divert their attention
towards *lumpen* or otherwise voiceless constituents – women, children, indigenous peoples, prisoners, the insane, labourers, artisans,
and so on – towards 'a history of a local industry or craft, social relationships in a particular community, culture and dialect, change in
the family, the impact of wars and strikes', and other minor and
subaltern histories.[16] Thompson's arguments also extend to *elite* and
professional respondents (as opposed to *everyman/woman* respondents), and may still sustain the same anti-authoritarian principles.
Through oral history, as a *grassroots* or otherwise resistant practice,

the subject of an interview – the 'respondent' – is empowered as a 'narrator', 'tradition-bearer', and 'witness', and endowed with the privilege to speak as an expert on a history to which they were party.[17]

In oral histories of art, this materialist–historicist imperative is far from inevitable. While some collections will seek explicitly to archive new voices, others reiterate dominant art history, retaining its distributions of knowledge and power; for example, in David Sylvester's excellent but staid collection, *Interviews with American Artists*, Sylvester undertook 21 interviews, yet all but two of his selected interlocutors are men.[18] For Sherna Berger Gluck, the political (and implicitly revisionist) imperatives of oral history is nevertheless well suited to evidencing women's life experiences, social relations, creative activities and work. Women's oral history of a social formation can enable 'the validation of women's experiences; it is the communication among women of different generations'.[19] Hence, oral history has sometimes been deployed, against the grain, to construct histories of women in art and performance.[20]

A historiographical approach to oral history – that is, reflexive attention to the practices and protocols of one's critical methodology – brings important questions, concerns and provocations to the fore concerning the value, veracity and efficacy of orally derived historical documents. As David Henige writes, 'If we agree that history is not so much a record of the facts of the past as it is a series of accepted judgements based on carefully considered probabilities, then we must concede that historians themselves play a major role in determining *how the past will look to the present.*'[21] As an example of this diversion of the function and content of history, by way of oral history, the artists I interviewed generally have been enthusiastic about using the interview, in part, to memorialise and archive the work of their peers. This works to populate the expanded history with the lives and labours of friends and collaborators who have been variously misremembered or suppressed in scholarship. Many of the interviews therefore include episodes in which artists celebrate and reanimate the work of peer (and often late) artists, including Joey Arias on Klaus Nomi, Anne Bean on Paul Burwell, Adrian Howells on Leigh Bowery, David Hoyle on Bloolips, Ann Magnuson on John Sex or Sheree Rose on Bob Flanagan. The living artist is therefore a portal or window on to a frequently untouched archive of performance. This is one of the many virtues of *sitting at the feet of artists*, or what Paul Thompson describes as the prime virtue of the oral history interview, namely 'tapping the river water at the sea's mouth'.[22]

As distinct from yet intimately related to oral history, *qualitative research interviewing* bequeaths a set of sociological tools for reflecting conceptually upon apparatuses, techniques and tactics that affect how and with what effects one conducts interviews. According to its terminologies and protocols, I undertook 'semi-structured depth interviews', acknowledging a shift away from *structure*, with reference to the uniformity of questions across interviews in a given project; and a foregrounding of *depth*, such that the process encourages the interviewee to make sense of and respond to questions.

Whether the interview is *autobiographical* (prompting narration of life experiences and historical thoughts and feelings) or *topical* (gathering positions from interviewees around a topic or theme), the respondent is prompted to engage in what Tom Wengraf calls *hypothesis-formation* and *theory-rectification*.[23] The two terms emphasise a collaborative commitment, between the research-led interviewer, and the informed and engaged interviewee, towards explanation, argument, autobiography, active narrativisation, entry into discourse and revision. For Wendy Hollway and Tony Jefferson, two question models are necessary: *narrative questions*, whose typical form begins with 'Can you tell me about ...?'; and *theory prompts*, which commonly begin with 'why ...?' or 'how ...?'[24] Implicitly, narrative answers and theorisations support hypothesis-formation and theory-rectification, respectively – and sometimes interchangeably.

Semi-structured interviews are researched and partly scripted, with room for follow-on questioning and extemporisation. Only a number of questions need be determined in common across all interviews – ordinarily, for the social sciences, across a *sample* or stratified *quota* selected for interviewing – and only a portion of questions will be scripted for each individual interview. Wengraf demonstrates that a qualitative research approach is formally adequate in its design – it has both structure and depth – if it includes: clear purposes, a conceptual context, research questions (as distinct from interview questions), methods (including and in addition to interviewing) and validity.[25] *Validity* refers to the applicability of the research findings provided by the data; in *The Art of Living*, validity might be understood as the extent to which the material arising from the 12 interviews can depict, support, construct or challenge a given or dominant history of performance art.

The scholarly literature on qualitative research interviewing provides detailed instructions for the activities that follow the encounter, namely transcription and editing. Following its protocols, my own process of transcription began with a verbatim transcript – transcription *version zero*. The verbatim text was then edited for sense, including the removal of repetitions, non sequiturs, culs-de-sac, hesitation sounds, stutters, and verbal tics. The more substantial process of editing and redrafting involves preserving the elegance of casual speech, and recovering the eloquence that is sometimes lost in the transposition of spoken words to the page. I specifically chose to present the interviews as written texts, rather than as recordings on audio or video that could be archived online or on DVD, as the text enables a much higher level of collaborative editing and authorial intervention, thus ensuring a compelling yet legible – and perhaps authoritative – resulting document. Competent editing requires fidelity to the spoken text, yet takes certain liberties: remodelling and reshaping the structures of sentences; enhancing or accentuating the flow, intonation, precision and sonority of the words and phrases laid down in the transcription; and the suggestion or staging of irony, sarcasm, jokes, laughter, pauses, physical gestures, singing and other enigmatic or non-verbal textures of speech that otherwise may be 'lost in transcription' (to borrow Pierre Bourdieu's phrase).[26]

As in all areas of work and life, *fidelity* is tendentious. Editorial interventions can overwork or disfigure the mediated record of a live encounter. Hence, my course of action has been to require artists to approve my edited transcription, and to provide opportunities to refine, amend, remove or add words to clarify the written content. Artists responded in a number of ways: a few made no changes at all; a few requested substantial additions and rewrites; and the majority made small but necessary interventions throughout, to enhance the legibility, lucidity and sense of the text. Each response was valid and right. The resulting texts lay the ground for a vast new grammar of formerly unknown rituals, and the recovery of a lost cuneiform of obscure gestures and thoughts. These ciphers emerge to speak of lives and languages that must, finally, and forever, be distinguished. The revival of the new aesthetic currency – a remarkable but unmarketable semaphore of signs and scenes – reveals more than a cumulative method to the madness of performance art. The persons gathered in these pages speak as if to give last rites to a culture on the brink of new, full life.

Notes

1. Peter Bürger, *Theory of the Avant-Garde*, trans. Jochen Schulte-Sasse (Minneapolis: University of Minnesota Press, [1974] 1984), p. 51.
2. Allan Kaprow, 'The Legacy of Jackson Pollock' (1958), in *Essays on the Blurring of Art and Life*, ed. Jeff Kelley (Berkeley and Los Angeles: University of California Press, 1993), pp. 1–9 (pp. 6–7).
3. Ibid., p. 9.
4. Arthur C. Danto, *Unnatural Wonders: Essays from the Gap Between Art and Life* (New York: Farrar, Straus & Giroux, 2005), p. x.
5. Chrissie Iles, 'Taking a Line for a Walk: Interview with Ulay and Marina Abramović', *Performance Magazine*, 53 (April/May 1988), pp. 14–19 (p. 18).
6. John Berryman, 'Olympus', in *Collected Poems 1937–1971*, ed. Charles Thornbury (New York: Farrar, Straus & Giroux, 1989), pp. 179–80 (p. 179).
7. Vito Acconci, 'Some Notes on Activity and Performance' (1970), in Jennifer Bloomer, Mark C. Taylor and Frazer Ward, *Vito Acconci* (London: Phaidon, 2002), pp. 88–92 (p. 88).
8. Friedrich Nietzsche, *The Gay Science*, trans.Walter Kaufmann (New York: Vintage, 1974), p. 261.
9. Mike Kelley, 'Foreword: Utopia is a Space Outside the Market', in John Miller, *The Ruin of Exchange and Other Writings*, ed. Alexander Alberro (Zurich: JRP/Ringier, 2012), pp. 7–10 (p. 8).
10. Nick Kaye, *Art into Theatre: Performance Interviews and Documents* (London and New York: Routledge, 1996); Maria M. Delgado and Paul Heritage, *In Contact with the Gods?: Directors Talk Theatre* (Manchester and New York: Manchester University Press, 1996); Linda M. Montano, *Performance Artists Talking in the 80s* (Berkeley and Los Angeles, University of California Press, 2000); Heike Roms, *What's Welsh for Performance: An Oral History of Performance Art in Wales* (Cardiff: Trace/Samizdat Press, 2008).
11. See *Archives of American Art Oral Histories Interviews* at http://www.aaa.si.edu/collections/interviews [accessed 09/07/14]; and the *European Live Art Archive* website at http://www.liveartarchive.eu [accessed 09/07/14]. Roms's *What's Welsh for Performance* has an online presence; see *It Was Forty Years Ago Today* ... at http://www.performance-wales.org/it-was-40-years-ago-today/oralhistory-introduction.htm [accessed 09/07/14].
12. However, performance scholars have explored oral history as a methodology elsewhere, especially by attending to examples of 'oral history performance'. See Della Pollock, ed., *Remembering: Oral History Performance* (New York and Basingstoke: Palgrave Macmillan, 2005).
13. Marquard Smith, *Visual Culture Studies: Interviews with Key Thinkers* (Los Angeles and London: Sage, 2008), p. xi; original emphasis.
14. Ibid., p. x.

15. Paul Thompson, *The Voice of the Past: Oral History*, 2nd edn (Oxford: Oxford University Press, 1988), p. 11.

16. Ibid., p. 8.

17. Ibid., p. 199.

18. David Sylvester, *Interviews with American Artists* (London: Chatto & Windus, 2001).

19. Sherna Berger Gluck, 'What's So Special About Women?: Women's Oral History', in *Women's Oral History: The 'Frontiers' Reader*, ed. Susan H. Armitage with Patricia Hart and Karen Weathermon (Lincoln and London: University of Nebraska Press, 2002), pp. 3–20 (p. 5).

20. See Andrea Juno and V. Vale, *Angry Women* (San Francisco: Re/Search Publications, 1991); Zora Von Burden, *Women of the Underground: Art – Cultural Innovators Speak for Themselves* (San Francisco: Manic D Press, 2012); and the online project *Performance Saga: Encounters with Women Pioneers of Performance Art* at http://www.performancesaga.ch/ [accessed 09/07/14].

21. David Henige, *Oral Historiography* (New York: Longman, 1982), p. 129; emphasis added.

22. Thompson, *Voice of the Past*, p. 265.

23. Tom Wengraf, *Qualitative Research Interviewing: Biographic Narrative and Semi-Structured Methods* (London: Sage, 2001), p. 4, n. 2.

24. Wendy Hollway and Tony Jefferson, *Doing Qualitative Research Differently: Free Association, Narrative and the Interview Method* (London and Thousand Oaks, CA: Sage, 2000), pp. 35–7.

25. Wengraf, *Qualitative Research Interviewing*, p. 57.

26. Cited in Steinar Kvale and Svend Brinkmann, *InterViews: Learning the Craft of Qualitative Research Interviewing*, 2nd edn (Los Angeles and London: Sage, 2009), p. 178.

I   The Escape Artist: An Interview with Ulay

Ulay is iconic – but elusive. Since his earliest works in the late 1960s, he has accrued no signature style. He is nomadic in his use of forms, and peripatetic in his life. He remains strangely enigmatic. In our interview, conducted in Amsterdam in March 2014, Ulay stresses the key principles of his aesthetic convictions, first articulated in a manifesto titled *Art Vital* (1976):

> No fixed living space
> Permanent movement
> Direct contact
> Local relation
> Self-selection
> Passing limitations
> Taking risks
> Mobile energy
>
> No rehearsal
> No predicted end
> No repetition.[1]

Ulay stresses the immediacy of performance, and the sensory and intellectual density of the encounter with the body of the artist engaged in a planned but precarious score of actions. It passes over into an intellectual distaste for 'cosmetic' approaches to performance, and re-performance or re-enactment, and a suspicion of other practices of dilution or capitulation to markets, conventions, and vogues.

Ulay has consistently embraced extremity, and conceptual purity, through performances, actions and *performative photography* projects, which have pushed his corporeal, psychic and interpersonal experiences to a kind of breaking point, in pursuit of images and encounters that manifest his belief in the proper singularity of aesthetic knowledge. The landmark manifestations of this praxis, as discussed in detail below, include: a pioneering project using tattooing and cosmetic surgery, namely a skin-graft to remove a purpose-made tattoo in 1972; his theft of Hitler's favourite painting from the Neue Nationalgalerie in Berlin in 1976; as well as art/life projects, including living in drag for over a year; and attempts to invoke a crisis in the ontological distinctiveness of performance and photography.

Ulay occupies an important place in the received histories of performance, primarily through his legendary collaborations with Marina Abramović in the 1970s and 1980s. These included a series of experiments into extremity and form in the spartan *Relation Works* (1976–79); and culminated in the exemplary art/life project, *The Lovers – The Great Wall Walk* (1988), both described below. His provocative and conceptually rigorous solo works, both before and after his eight-year relationship with Abramović, have rarely been discussed and historicised – eclipsed, perhaps, by his subjugation to the phenomenon of Abramović's mass-market celebrity. Indeed, Maria Rus Bojan writes: 'the rumor circulated ... that he had ceased to exist as an artist after his collaboration with Marina Abramović. But nothing could be further from the truth.'[2]

By referring to him as an 'escape artist', I seek to foreground the curious ontology that accompanies an artist on the run – Ulay on the lam from the laws of culture. Of the great 'Self-Liberator', Harry Houdini, Adam Phillips writes: 'If you are defined by what you can escape from – your country, your language, your poverty, your name – then you may forever need to seek out situations to release yourself from.'[3] For Houdini, this strategy found literal form, in public attempts to break out of chains and ropes. For Ulay, with his life of allegory, his sights are set on exceeding more inscrutable limitations. His great escape has been to evade history, national identity, critique, categorisation and epistemological closure – the concatenation of restrictions he terms, below, 'intellectual capture'. Artist and sage, human sacrifice and criminal, *Ulay is still at large.*

Dominic Johnson: *You've said that 'aesthetics without ethics is cosmetics'. What does this statement mean to you?*

Ulay: When I first said 'aesthetics without ethics is cosmetics' – 20 or 30 years ago – people were very irritated by it. I decided to become an artist in the 1960s, and I was discontented with myself, with society, and with art. My generation was beginning to create an *anti-aesthetic*. We were reacting against Late Modernism, which entirely privileged a certain model of aesthetics. The 'pope' of Late Modernism, Clement Greenberg, thought art had universal values, and that a particular work, like Jackson Pollock's *Blue Poles* [1952], could be aesthetically perfect and transcendent.[4] I didn't like this idea at all. This idea of aesthetics is 'cosmetic'. If you work as an artist and you produce works – with your body, directly, and without any other media involved – then what is the carrier, beyond aesthetics? Well, it's *ethics*. I thought performance was a great vehicle to include ethics in artistic expression.

If I look around today, aesthetics has become corporate, cosmetic – art has *anaesthetised* our fuller sense of the aesthetic. We're numbed. Aesthetics are no longer grounded in reality. Today, more than ever, ethics must play an important role, and art can no longer afford to exclusively deliver formalist aesthetic commodities.

DJ: *One of your key early works was* There is a Criminal Touch to Art *(1976), in which you stole Carl Spitzweg's painting* The Poor Poet *(1839) from the Neue Nationalgalerie in Berlin. Can you describe this action, and how it came about?*

U: I had no plans at all when I arrived in Berlin in 1976. I went there to accompany Marina [Abramović]. She did her final solo performance of the 1970s, *Freeing the Body*, at Künstlerhaus Bethanien in Berlin. It was part of a series of related works, *Freeing the Voice*, *Freeing the Memory*, and *Freeing the Body* [all 1976]. I assisted her on the last two, recording the video and taking photographs. While we were in Berlin, I was very attracted to the Neue Nationalgalerie. In the basement, I found a gallery of mid-nineteenth-century German Romantic painting: the Biedermeier period. To my surprise, I saw *The Poor Poet* by Carl Spitzweg. It's a classic Romantic painting, and it shows a poet lying in bed, with an umbrella to catch water leaking through the roof, and he's writing, filling piles and piles of manuscripts with poems. He's burning his manuscripts to warm himself and dry his wet boots. It reminded me of book burning. Among a few others, *The Poor Poet* was Hitler's favourite painting. Hitler was a house painter, and a Sunday painter. Spitzweg was an amateur painter too – a pharmacist by trade. When I was at school in Germany in the late 1940s, I had a textbook, and its only colour image was a reproduction of *The Poor Poet*. That tells you how iconic the painting was for German identity in that period. Everybody identified with it. When I saw it in the Neue Nationalgalerie, I thought if I got my hands on it, *hell might break loose*. I decided to steal it. (See **Figure 1.1**.)

Figure 1.1   Ulay, *There is a Criminal Touch to Art* (1976), film still from the Berlin action. Gelatin silver print, 20 x 25 cm. Series of 18 works. © Ulay. Courtesy of the artist and MOT International, London

What else could I do? Education at the art academy in Berlin at that time was pretty backwards. Performance was out of the question, as were video, photography and installation. They were still only teaching traditional forms: painting, sculpture, and graphic art. Kreuzberg is now a hotspot, but at that time it was the Turkish ghetto. Künstlerhaus Bethanien hosted ateliers for foreign artists in residence throughout the German academic system, and it was very popular, especially among Americans. So I drew a triangle on a map: I'd touch the Academy of Arts; I'd touch the painting in the Neue Nationalgalerie; and I'd touch Künstlerhaus Bethanien. Then I'd leave the art-world context for the secularised environment of the Turkish migrant worker, to make a point about the difference between their living conditions and the safety of the art world. I wrote a 14-line statement explaining exactly what I planned to do, and why.

There were two other people involved. Mike Steiner had a video gallery in Berlin, mainly focusing on women artists, and he 'produced' the action. He invited a documentary filmmaker for

German television, Wilma Kottusch, to film the action. The problem was that we couldn't find a cameraman. 1976 was a dangerous time to be in Berlin. People were nervous after the arrests of Baader-Meinhof, and there was a strong terrorist threat from the *Rote Armee Fraktion* [Red Army Faction].[5] Nobody wanted to take the risk of being involved in my action. We finally found a cameraman, Jörg Schmidt-Reitwein, and he demanded a car with a driver, and insisted that he would only film from inside the car, in case he needed to escape. He had worked with Werner Herzog, so he knew how to make films in difficult circumstances.[6] It was filmed, and I was given a copy on video. I never had access to the original film.

The action took place on 12 December – the twelfth day of the twelfth month – 1976. It was a Sunday. On the Saturday, I sent my 14-line statement to the press. I knew they wouldn't open the mail until Monday, by which time the action would be over. I had made photographic reproductions of Spitzweg's painting – one about two-and-a-half-metres wide, and another smaller. On the Sunday, I began my action by hanging the reproduction over the entrance of the Academy of Arts, to seal it shut. I went to the Neue Nationalgalerie. Entering the building, I went downstairs to the Biedermeier gallery, removed *The Poor Poet* from the wall, ran upstairs, and out the emergency exit (the other doors were sealed when the alarm went off). I left the building with the painting under my arm, and ran to my van, which I'd left with the engine running. I stole the painting using my hands and feet – no technology, no assistance, nothing. I knew I could do it. Marina filmed me inside the museum on Super 8 (she hid the reel inside her boot so that it wouldn't be confiscated), and Jörg followed me in his car, filming the rest of the action.

I was living in the van with Marina at the time. It was an old Citroën French police van – an anti-symbol of the Paris uprisings in May 1968, which I had painted black. I drove away from the museum, but I knew the van was so recognisable that I couldn't drive it to the third point in my triangle. Berlin cab drivers listened to the police radio, and if they received a signal they could identify me or block the roads. So after a short drive I parked the car on the outskirts of Kreuzberg, took the painting, and ran, ran, ran, through the snow, all the way to Künstlerhaus Bethanien. I pinned a small colour reproduction of the painting to the front of the gallery, and then continued to the Turkish worker's home.

I had chosen a Turkish family at random, and visited them before the action. I told them we were shooting a film (which was true), and asked if we could bring a cameraman to shoot in their home. They agreed. I left them in the dark about the details, so they wouldn't be investigated or interrogated by the police. The only time that Jörg left the car was when I brought the painting into the living quarters of the Turkish family. I took another painting down from their wall, and replaced it with *The Poor Poet*. Outside, I called the police from a phone box, and the director of the museum was invited to see the painting in its new setting. He arrived with the police, saw the painting in its new setting, and retrieved it. I was arrested. That was the whole action.

The response was incredible. First of all, the boulevard press went wild. One newspaper printed a front-page article that read 'Left radical steals our most beautiful painting' [in the original, *'Berlin: Linksradikaler raubte unser schönster Bild'*] and the reporting went on and on. When I received the videotape of the action, I added some elements, including my reading of the 14-line statement at the beginning. I also added a montage of newspaper clippings about the theft (there were many). The resulting film is still screened in festivals and museums. After nearly 40 years, it's still evergreen. Young people like it especially. They seem to find it funny.

DJ: *Did you identify with the 'poor poet' in the painting in some way?*

U: I identified simply by way of my German-ness. I'm less concerned with the actual painting. It was a symbol. I was born in a bomb shelter in 1943, in Solingen, a small German steel-producing city that was completely bombed out in the war. I left Germany in 1968, with good reason: I had an identity problem. I needed to deal with my German-ness. I wanted to *irritate* it, and I did it best by stealing Germany's favourite painting.[7] I did it by bringing Turkish misery into a discussion about contemporary Germany. I'm not a political artist. I never was. But the kind of art I have done – and still do – lends itself to political critique. I tried to avoid thinking about the action too much. I just did it.

DJ: *I was thinking about the context of the 'art criminal' as a trend in the repudiation of the politics of art, more specifically.*

U: When I gave the action the title *There is a Criminal Touch to Art*, I meant that the action itself would be deemed a criminal act. Indeed, I was prosecuted. I had to face justice. I surrendered to it. When the museum director and plain-clothes policemen came to the apartment in Kreuzberg, I made them certify the painting was undamaged.

Vandalism was not my intent. There are art *destroyers*, and there are others, like me, who give a second value to existing artworks by temporarily *misusing* them. I remember when the Barnett Newman paintings were destroyed, and when someone spray-painted the *Guernica* in the Museum of Modern Art.[8] Their actions were radical, but I disagree with vandalism. I loaned or borrowed the *Poor Poet* – without permission, of course. My action was conceptual – I added an additional value to the painting.

However, I certainly carried out a criminal act. I was, at the very least, a thief. And it's a strange thief who surrenders. I was put in prison, and in German law, after 24 hours you have to face a judge. The prosecutor had a long list of charges, and I realised I could face a long sentence. I was released on bail and returned to Amsterdam. Three months later there was a court case, which I didn't attend. I was convicted and sentenced to 36 days in prison, or a fine of 3,600 Deutschmark. *I chose neither.* A year later I was travelling with Marina from Amsterdam to Agadir, Morocco, and we had a one-night stopover in Munich, where I was arrested. Friends helped me get the money together, and I paid the fine.

DJ: *What precedents enabled the action to be understood as a work of art? The action strikes me as a classic avant-garde project – an intervention into the authority of the museum.*

U: Firstly, I did not see the action as an artwork – in the beginning, at least. The title was *There is a Criminal Touch to Art*, so I referred to art, and I also marked the art institution – in the forms of the museum, academy, and gallery. I knew the reactions would be tremendous, because I had touched a *holy* painting, but it took about six months before any art magazines acknowledged it with images and critical writing. Before that it was only newspapers, and at first they were unwilling to accept the action as a work of art.

It's not up to me to declare the action a work of art. Doing so was not important enough as a motive for doing the action. I succeeded in doing it, and that was all that mattered to me. But you're right when you say that it now looks like an avant-garde action. Well, I'm glad. I never called myself an avant-garde artist, but you could place the action in that context.

DJ: *Can you tell me about your relationship to art education?*

U: When I became an artist in the 1960s, I was an autodidact. I enrolled for a year and a half in the art academy in Cologne [from

1969 to 1971], and I studied photography, though there wasn't a department of photography. I was advanced in my work. I taught other students about photographic printmaking. After about a year and a half, the professor of painting said I should leave the academy 'before it spoiled my good character'. He thought I was ready to leave. So I did.

I like to teach. I had a professorship in Germany for six years [Karlsruhe University of Arts and Design, 1999–2004], and I demanded from my students, not necessarily that they study performance, but that they make at least one public performance. A painting can't hear, can't feel, can't smell. But when you make a performance, you turn yourself into an art object – the only sensitive, sensible art object there can be. You start to understand how people understand you, and how they consume the art object. Performance is important for any artist.

DJ: *What was your first solo performance?*

U: Well, my earliest experience of live performance was in collaboration with a famous Dutch jazz ensemble, the Willem Breuker Kollektief (*Red Venus*, Middelburg, Netherlands, 1974). I taught them to perform beyond blowing a horn on stage. But my first solo performance was *Exchange of Identity* [1975], at Galerie het Venster, in Rotterdam.[9] I integrated photographic media, performance, and the audience. I wore white slaughterhouse overalls and a white mask. I didn't want to be identified. On the wall, I had a box, about two metres high, filled with photographic linen. Opposite was a Polaroid camera installed on a tripod and connected to a flashlight. Beside it was an epidiascope – an old-fashioned kind of projector that projects a positive image from an object. In the performance, I asked a person from the audience to stand against the wall. I tore down a huge piece of photographic linen – 1.27 by 2 metres – and they'd stand as flat as possible against it. I'd take a Polaroid photograph, which triggered the flashlight. The flash exposed the light-sensitive emulsion of the photographic linen. The person returned to the audience. I had a bucket of developer, another with water, and another with fixative, and I applied the chemicals to the linen with a sponge, to develop the image by hand. A photogram would appear. A photogram is a very ghostly image, but it would show perfectly the silhouette of the missing person. Then I would process the black-and-white Polaroid, insert it into the epidiascope, and project it life-sized onto the photogram. I'd stand in the empty silhouette, dressed in white, and the image would be visible when it was projected onto me. I walked slowly outwards towards the projector, so that the image became smaller and smaller, until it disappeared. I repeated it for about five other people from the audience. The problem is when you mix developing chemicals with fixative you get tremendous amounts of ammonia, so the smell in the room was unbearable, and people started to leave pretty quickly. That ended the performance.

DJ: *How did your early Polaroid experiments come about?*

U: In the beginning I focused on what I call *identity research*. After the Second World War, my father got very ill – he had been drafted into *both* wars, and he was heavily asthmatic. He died when I was 14. My mother disappeared into her solitude, and had no contact with the outside world until her death. I had no brothers, no sisters. I never met my grandparents, nor knew their names. From the moment I became an artist in 1968, and I left Germany, I questioned my own identity. I used myself as a subject for my investigations.

My use of photography developed as I had a good relationship with the Polaroid Corporation, from 1969 to 1971. I asked for their support. I guess they thought, 'Why not?', and they gave me free cameras and film. I made what I called *intimate actions*, or private performances. I'd pose in front of the camera in ever-changing moments, manipulating myself with make-up, clothing, piercing, tattoos, transplants, and so on. I questioned the idea that a photograph is a truthful representation of a person's identity. From 1969, I took photographs of myself – *excessively* – not only changing my physical appearance in front of the camera, but also integrating the identities of other people, especially marginal folk – transvestites, transsexuals, and 'freaks'. I mostly made black-and-white images. Black-and-white photography *suggests*, while colour photography *concludes*.

DJ: *Can you tell me about the relationship between performance and photography in your practice, for example in* Fototot *(1976)?*

U: We tend to draw a line between photography and performance. Performance requires the attention of an audience, or a spectator. In the intimate actions, I performed for my mirror, and for the camera, which became my audience. That brought photography and performance together, for me, and the line between the two became less clear. Rather than make explicit distinctions between photography and performance, I prefer to use the term *performative photography*. Over the years, I took thousands of photographs of myself. I could be a woman, a man, half-and-half, a hermaphrodite. A person's identity can change for photographic purposes at least ten times a day. The possibilities were endless. I was like Sisyphus. It was useless. Senseless.

So, eventually I said to myself, OK, I draw a line *here*. This led me to make *Fototot* in 1976. It's a great word – it means *photodeath*. I mounted an exhibition at De Appel, in Amsterdam, which was more or less a white cube gallery, and I hung nine large photographs, each about 100 by 80 centimetres, over three walls. They were hung high, above head height, so the audience wouldn't throw shadows on them. I used a yellow-green light, like the one used in a darkroom for black-and-white printing, and there was just enough light for the audience to orientate themselves. They came in and we closed the entrance. They looked at the prints, and I switched on very strong halogen lights aimed at the three walls. In 15 seconds, the photographs faded to black rectangles. It was literal photodeath.[10] I was cutting my ties to photography and stepping into the space of performance. The question is: Where is the photographic image? There was a perfect gelatin silver image, and, all of a sudden, it turned black. Where did it go?

After that, I got much more involved in live performance. Shortly after *Fototot*, I did a performance, *Fototot II* [1976] based on the same questions.[11] (See **Figure 1.2**.) It was at a small gallery called Bayer Kulturhaus in Wuppertal, Germany, where I showed a little exhibition of Polaroids from my identity research. Outside the gallery was a very rough garage space, with a truck parked in it. I wanted to do a performance in there, not in the gallery (that's my anti-aesthetic sensibility at work again).

I had a mirror cut to the proportions of my standing body. I wore a mirrored chrome helmet and a chrome mask, too, and I stood as a mirror in human shape. In front of me, flat on the floor, was another mirror – a rectangle of similar proportions. I was beside the truck. As the audience were lit, they could see themselves reflected perfectly in my body (the mirror). I moved slightly to the left and slightly to the right to pick up the panorama of spectators, and slightly forwards and backwards. It's nasty to look in a mirror when it's moving. The people became annoyed, or agitated, but continued staring. After about 15 minutes, I let myself fall forward, glass on glass, and sandwiched the image of the audience. The mirrors smashed.

Figure 1.2 Ulay, *Fototot II* (1976), performance documentation from Bayer Kulturhaus, Wuppertal, Germany. Gelatin silver print, 30 × 40 cm. © Ulay. Courtesy of the artist and MOT International, London

I wasn't really worried about getting cut. However, if you fall down flat onto a surface, most likely you'll try to put your hands out in front, to break your fall. If I did that, the broken glass could have slit my wrists. I didn't trust my reflexes, so I asked someone kindly to tie my hands behind my back. I got cut anyway, though [*laughs*]. My head snapped back and I cut the underside of my chin, near my throat.

DJ: *It strikes me that you often proceed by destroying existing aesthetic languages before rebuilding them.*

U: Without destruction there is no creation. But did I really *destroy* anything? I may have *refused* certain ideas, or conventions, by questioning photographic identity, or by asserting the ephemerality of photography. I don't think these activities are necessarily destructive. I moved from photography to performance because the body is the medium *par excellence* – not because I sought to destroy photography.

DJ: *Despite the longevity of your practice as an artist, you've avoided a signature style. What's at stake in this circumvention?*

U: I'm not sure I *avoided* a signature style. A signature style just isn't my cup of tea. I never do one thing at a time, but, rather, many things at the same time. That's how I function. In terms of which media I use, I'm very project-oriented, and I try to find the most appropriate medium with which to present an idea. With each work, I'm concerned with what, whom, where, when, and how – and then I conceive the work that suits my solution to the problem. My approach is conceptual, even if it doesn't always look like it. Therefore, with any work, style isn't important.

DJ: *You were literally nomadic for many years …*

U: I still am.

DJ: *You've also been elusive in the sense that you've evaded art history to some extent. Thomas McEvilley described you as having a 'secretive' relation to art history, and that you remain 'untheorized'.*[12]

U: Tom [McEvilley] was correct. He was my best and oldest friend. He passed away last year, on 2 March 2013, and he was the person who wrote the most about me (and about Marina also). He was a great mind. The nomadic sensibility is not exactly escapism. *I do not want to be tracked down.* I prefer anonymity. Nomadism, anarchism, discontent, aesthetics with ethics – these are all crucial values for me.

DJ: *Are you suspicious of art history itself?*

U: Yes. In the 1970s, performance was not popular. Art historians were lazy. They'd sit in their studies and write. Most critics were the same. They would go to a gallery or to an archive, where they could study a work that was static, and have access for as long as they liked. Performance is more challenging for academics and critics. It's ephemeral, so if you don't seek it out, you have to rely solely on other people's interpretations. Performance mobilised critics and academics. But, you know, as artists, we can't get around one thing: *interpretation is always the last word.* There was a time when there was a lot written about my work, especially with Marina. In the best cases it was really carefully researched, and well written. At other times, it was bullshit. This is normal. I give credit to the great writers who took time to think about my work. But I've never worked for the benefit of art critics or historians.

I use its vocabulary, but I am not oriented towards art history. I want to remain difficult to catch – and art history is an instrument of *intellectual capture*. I believe I have made history, in a small way – but I really don't care. It's not what I've worked for.

Look at me. I'm nothing special. Everything I have is portable, minimal, simple. I wouldn't think of living like Marina. We're opposites. She wants to be an art star. I do not. I don't criticise her for her ambitions. But stardom is not for me.

DJ: *How do you feel about different terminologies that have been used to describe the work you've made: performance art, live art, body art, and so on?*

U: On the whole, the question of terminology is not very important to me. As a non-native English speaker, I prefer the word *performance*. I like its proximity to *perforation*. In the 1970s, with our avant-garde attitudes, we attempted to perforate institutions, including museums, not to become a part of them, but to allow them to *breathe*. But, come on, performance has become accepted within museums – especially re-enactments [*he groans – we laugh*].

DJ: *What are your thoughts on re-enactment or re-performance?*

U: I have seen a couple and in each instance I walked out, because I don't see a reason for re-enactment. If Joseph Beuys or Vito Acconci make a performance, and then 40 years later another artist tries to remake the performance, I don't think it's useful, or acceptable. Today, audiences do not have access to Beuys's live work, but so what? You don't have access through its re-enactment either. It's a different work. From 1970 to at least the 1990s, performance was subversive. With a few exceptions, it was difficult for performance to take place in museums in the 1970s – it wasn't feasible for me – or for Vito Acconci, Joan Jonas, Stuart Brisley, Charlemagne Palestine, Dennis Oppenheim, Terry Fox, each of whom I admire very much (to mention only a few). Suddenly, after the 1990s, performance became legitimated. Classical ballet, classical theatre and classical music are all re-performed, or re-enacted, continually. In this city, at any time of the year, perhaps, you can hear a re-enactment of Mozart's *Don Giovanni*, or whatever, for the hundred-thousandth time. It worries me that performance, which was once subversive, is becoming part of the same cultural agenda. There's money in it, of course …

DJ: *Is it the apparent authenticity and immediacy of the original act of performance that you're eager to preserve?*

U: One of the beautiful things about performance is it is an oral tradition. In the 1970s, in my performances, as well as for many others, there were usually very few spectators. When performance involves

violent or *auto-aggressive* acts, self-mutilation, and so on, the spectator must remain a spectator – he or she accepts that someone is mess-
ing themselves up in front of them, but is asked not to intercept,
interfere, or otherwise make it stop. It's a very strange model of
perception. But spectators were so touched by these performances
that after they left, they talked. The newspapers became interested in
performance. When they heard we were cutting ourselves, or sewing
up our lips, it would have sounded spectacular and sensational.

In my performances with Marina, there were often only 25 to 50
people present. This was normal for many of the important works we
know about from, say, 1970 to 1980. Today, thousands or millions of
people know about us. This grew by word of mouth, and now our
documentation travels on *YouTube* and other digital media.
Knowledge circulated about performance by a ritual, oral tradition,
and I found this to be so beautiful, to find your work in someone's
mouth, enabling the ritual. The few who were there explain the
event – it's a first-hand interpretation, which enables a second-hand
interpretation, and so on, including mis-interpretation, re-mis-inter-
pretation, re-re-mis-interpretation ... This is how an artwork becomes
legendary, and it's very rewarding when you're subject to an oral
tradition of history. It isn't the same when an institution gives an
iconic status to a performance by staging a re-enactment.

DJ: *One of your most compelling early projects, known mostly through
gossip or hearsay, is* GEN.E.T.RATION ULTIMA RATIO *(1972), which
employed tattooing and cosmetic surgery. I've seen photographic documentation of the work, but I'd be interested to hear about your process.*

U: Before I started making Polaroids in the late 1960s, and was flirt-
ing with the idea of making performances, I wrote poems, mostly in
the form of aphorisms. I was triggered to write by popular science
publications. At that time, the new science of genetics, microbiology,
and gene manipulation seemed threatening, like a time bomb. I
wrote aphorisms about ethics, prompted by this context, and later I'd
print them over Polaroids. But I also wanted to be an avant-garde
artist, which is to say I wanted to expose the art market. So, I
conceived a project which would involve getting a tattoo, then
removing it with a skin graft. I had a tattoo made by an artist called
Tattoo Peter [Pier de Haan], who had one wooden leg, and worked in
Amsterdam's red-light district. I wrote 'generation ultima ratio',
inserted a T between 'gene' and 'ration', and dotted either side of the
E and the T. Part of the phrase comes from a French anarchist slogan

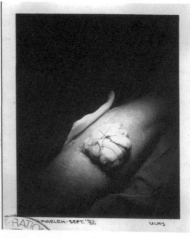

Figure 1.3–1.4 Ulay, *GEN.E.T.RATION ULTIMA RATIO* (1972), Polaroid type 107, 10.8 x 8.5 cm. © Ulay. Courtesy of the artist and MOT International, London

'ultima ratio regum' ['The Last Resort of Kings and Common Men']. It was tattooed onto my forearm, along with a crest.

Shortly after getting the tattoo, I located a plastic surgeon who worked in a hospital in Haarlem. I showed him the tattoo and asked him if he could remove it. He asked me why I had done it if I wanted it taken away – and I replied that I had done it *precisely* to remove it, and to preserve it. He thought it was a crazy idea, but agreed to do the procedure. I made an appointment, and four weeks after the tattoo was made, the transplant took place. I brought a 4- by 5-inch Polaroid camera, which was placed on a tripod behind me. They gave me a local anaesthetic, just on the arm that was being operated on. A nurse assisted the surgeon, and another nurse assisted me, changing the film for each shot (see **Figures 1.3–1.4**).

[*He shows me the location of the former tattoo; the patch of skin, more or less square, is lighter, shinier, and hairless.*]

The surgeon cut a rectangle around the tattoo, here, and peeled away the skin. The tattoo was rather deep. You have three layers of skin, and he had to cut very deep to remove all of the ink. As you can see in the images, it looked awful, because when you remove the skin, the *meat* underneath lifts up a few millimetres higher than the skin. It looked disastrous [*laughs*]. The surgeon then removed the thin upper layer of a section of skin on the underside of my forearm, here, and transplanted it where the tattoo had been, stitching it all the way around. He placed a large piece of cotton on top and tied it on, to squeeze the meat back in, and to encourage the skin to heal correctly. The scar is barely visible now, except that there's no hair.

I put the tattooed skin in formalin to preserve it, and after a year I took it out, and stretched, air-dried, and framed it. There is an expression, *to bring your skin to the market*, which means to sell yourself. I wanted to bring my skin to the *art* market. Why would I do this to myself? Well, another slogan of mine is 'If you must, you must.'

The series of Polaroid images is called *Tattoo/Transplant* [1972]. I gave a beautiful set of prints to Henk 'Hanky Panky' Schiffmacher at the Amsterdam Tattoo Museum, where they are on permanent display. He agrees that it's one of the first instances of the use of tattooing in contemporary art.

DJ: *Like the theft of* The Poor Poet, *both works take the blurring of art and life up to and beyond a certain limit, into extremity. Why is extremity so attractive?*

U: You mean, why did I have to make it so difficult for myself? I'm not exactly a conceptual artist, and neither am I exactly a political artist, but I have a certain temperament. After the war, I learned to take certain measures, in order to make things *move*. I've never sat in solitude trying to force art out of me. I never had a studio. I've always just found a context, and then *pushed* it. If I was a conceptual artist, I could have just drawn a clock on a wall, instead of killing myself in front of an audience. It would have been much easier. The minimal conceptual artists, like Joseph Kosuth, were great, and they were very much appreciated – but they took it easy. Art *is* easy, anyhow [*laughs*].

DJ: *One of the most challenging projects you undertook was* The Lovers – The Great Wall Walk *(1988), made in collaboration with Marina Abramović.*

U: I tell you, the *Great Wall Walk* was quite an undertaking. I'd do it again tomorrow. It was unbelievably beautiful – just walking, walking. It took us six years to get permission from the Chinese government. During those six years of planning, Marina and I travelled a lot, and we'd tell people we were going to walk the Great Wall of China, and that Marina would start at one end and I'd start at the other, 5,000 kilometres apart, and we'd walk for three months each, until we met in the middle. It was an epic idea. Conceptually, it was a success even before we started walking. And afterwards, the idea was picked up by others – Don DeLillo writes about it in *Mao II*, for example.[13]

DJ: *How different were your experiences of the walk?*

U: Marina and I were both involved in the preparatory period. But the walk itself was the only collaboration we did in separation – in this case for a long time, around 90 days. But when we were walking, our experiences were somewhat similar: we both had to *conquer* the wall. It was an experience of hardship, but a beautiful one. The one major difference was the topography of the wall. I walked the western part, which is on the periphery of the Gobi Desert. Marina walked the eastern part, which is mountainous. I'm a desert dweller. I walked through sand and earth. Marina comes from Montenegro, so it was appropriate she walked the mountains, from the sea, over rock and stone. But in effort, in overcoming the distance, I think our experiences were similar.

The irony was that after we each walked towards each other for 90 days, simultaneously – in total that's half a year of walking – we met, and we departed, and that was the end of us. We walked 5,000 kilometres to say goodbye. It would have been easier to take a plane [*laughs*].

DJ: *Evidently, the* Great Wall Walk *could not be rehearsed. But more broadly, you are adamant that performances should not be rehearsed. Why is this?*

U: Firstly, historians refer to *The Great Wall Walk* as a performance, but I don't see it that way. Performance requires an audience, and no one was watching us – apart from controlling bodies from the Chinese authorities, who did not perceive the walk as a work of art.

In our manifesto, we wrote, 'No rehearsal. No predicted end. No repetition.' Why? Working with Marina, in the 1970s and 1980s, every performance was driven by a concept. We never rehearsed, and we never repeated a performance. It has remained this way for me. With each performance, I start a process, and declare my body as my medium. The moment the performance is about to happen I step into a space of my own physical and mental construction, without knowledge of the experience. The setup is virginal in a way. I'd carry the concept between my ears.

Of course, the violent performances – what I call *auto-aggressive* performances – you can't rehearse. Through repetition, such actions would become pathological. As an artist you can do anything once.

Nobody called me or Marina crazy. But if you repeat an auto-aggressive action, you start to seem pathetic – or pathological, and you seem to demand a different kind of response or reading.

DJ: *Ordeal is key to your early works.*

U: I kill my body before it kills me. I had an ordeal recently. I was diagnosed with mantle cell lymphoma stage IV in 2011. It's a very aggressive kind of cancer – a cold-hearted cancer – that spreads through the whole lymphatic system, and it was in 80 per cent of my bone marrow. I was given heavy chemotherapy, starting in July–August 2011, and then post-chemo treatment, which I finished recently. Now I'm clear. I made a film called *Project Cancer: Ulay's Journal from November to November* [dir. Damjan Kozole, Emotionfilm, 2013]. It's not released yet, but we made it during my heavy chemo period, shooting in New York, Berlin, Amsterdam, moving around, working all the time. Dealing with cancer was definitely an ordeal, but it was also *filmotherapy*.

DJ: *The* Relation Works, *especially, depended on training and discipline. Did you find that there was a relationship between ordeal in performance and the personal ordeal of surviving cancer?*

U: Yes. The fact that I have been a body artist did a lot of good, in terms of the way I dealt with illness, physically and mentally. I did not allow myself to be sick. Without chemo I would have lived another six months to a year. I was never horrified by this idea. I continued to work.

By making performances, and by living through the ordeal of cancer, I know that what I have done to my body has made me more resilient. 'What does not kill me makes me stronger', to quote Nietzsche.[14] When I was ill, my body had already been conditioned by *experimental situations*, and remembering the strength I had gained allowed me to deal with cancer, physically and mentally. It's a strange association to make, I know, but I believe it. Every third person will be personally affected by cancer, in some way in their life. I'd like to do something to explain, in a constructive way, my unique self-help programme – that is, how I dealt with cancer without total surrender to oncologists.

DJ: *Pain has been central to many of your works, solo and collaboratively. Is pain a side effect, or is pain an object of direct consideration in your performances?*

U: Often, Marina and I were asked: 'Did you feel pain?' I always flat-out rejected this question. I'll tell you, in some of our performances we were really black and blue from our physical confrontations. But pain? No. I really *didn't* feel pain. When I stitched my lips together [in *Talking About Similarity* (1976)], I asked a doctor friend if he'd give me a shot of anaesthetics in my upper and lower lips in the performance, so I wouldn't express pain in front of the audience. But injecting an anaesthetic would be as painful as putting a needle through my lips. So I pierced my lips without anaesthetic, and there was no blood, and no pain.

In the 1970s, pain was really out of the question for us as a topic for consideration or discussion. Marina's solo performances before 1976 were unbelievably hard. Some of our *Relation Works* were very challenging. The unwritten rule in our work was that regardless of whatever either of us can bear, which can differ of course, we would always stop before the performance became *pathetic*. It was not our idea to make people empathise with us, or with our pain.

But you asked me whether or not I made an 'object' of pain. That's a good question. I think I have an ability to switch off – it has to do with control, but also 'mind over matter'. I was made for this, in a way. The least spectacular piece Marina and I did was our series *Nightsea Crossing* [1981–87]. It was a trivial set-up: a long table in a space, with a man and a woman sitting at either end, absolutely motionless, silent, watching each other, fasting, and under observation. We did 22 performances, and each lasted from one to 16 days. This seems obsessive to Western audiences: being inactive, silent, and non-communicative seems negative. Fasting is easy, and silence is easy, but if you sit for seven hours each day, absolutely motionless, under observation but not moving, your body rejects this situation totally. It is excruciating, first in your ass, then your shoulders, and your neck. We trained in Vipassaná meditation, twice, in Bodh Gaya, India. We learnt to massage ourselves without any movement, and to master pain without any expression of discomfort. Through meditation, you learn to identify bodily sensations and turn them into an object of scrutiny, which you let go. So we had a technique. *We made our pain into a mental object.* The mind doesn't like to be trapped. If a child tries to steal something, and you see them, they feel terrible. It's the same with the mind. It doesn't like being caught out.

DJ: *In your early Polaroids, from 1971–72, you use bloodletting as a technique, for example by cutting the line of a high-heeled shoe against the skin of your foot, using a box-cutter.*

U: I'd call it a Stanley knife ...

DJ: *OK, a Stanley knife. In another photograph from the same period you slice your fingers and paint with your blood on a tiled wall. Is pain also unimportant in these early works?*

U: No. It was a different kind of examination. Those works were very much about personal suffering. I was suffering the loss of a beloved person. I was trying to express my *emotional* pain, in Polaroid – to her, to a particular person in this case. The method I chose was unorthodox. The emotions hurt much more than the physical cutting. It didn't hurt. I mean, *I was hurt*. But the action itself was peanuts ...

DJ: *In those works, then, there is a direct response to an emotional experience through an act of wounding. The work sounds cathartic, or therapeutic. I can imagine it would be uncomfortable to think about the later works as therapy – it's an unfashionable, or critically inconvenient reading.*

U: First of all, who creates these limits? I can only talk about *myself* (and it's not my favourite subject [*laughs*]) but I do think my work has been therapeutic. Mentally and physically, if you engage in demanding types of performance, the mind and body are united. The mind doesn't like to lose control, and the body doesn't like to be confronted, so it's a very tense union, and the slight separations feel very strange. But you are the master. You have to do exactly what you set out to do, according to the initial concept. At the back of my mind, I always asked myself, how is it possible, to do dangerous or aggressive things to myself, and to always get away with it, to survive it – even without pain? It's an *attitude*, and I find it therapeutic. It has helped me a lot in civilian life.

DJ: *In the 1970s, you explored transvestism and transgendered identities, through photography, but also by embedding yourself within a milieu. What brought about this project?*

U: My curiosity.

DJ: *What did you learn from your curiosity?*

U: I lived as a transvestite for a little less than two years, around 1973–75. There were two kinds of people I spent time with in that period, transvestites and transsexuals. Transvestites and transsexuals met together in a bar just across the bridge from where we are now [the Grachtengordel, Amsterdam]. They were mostly hookers. I wanted to be accepted in that environment, and they really learned to like me, and I liked them very much.

Being in this group of people, I explored my female anima. That brought me to the point that I dressed as a woman in public, and in the bar, and adopted a female persona as my natural appearance. I was also fascinated to find that I had such ambition. I went for it. I made myself into a beautiful girl. There was a woman who lived around the corner, and men would visit her from out of town – doctors, engineers, whatever – on a Wednesday night, and she would dress them and make them up to go to the bar. I found that fascinating.

I took a lot of photographs of myself in this period. Other transvestites would visit me and we'd take photographs together. Transsexuals were much stricter about photography, but once we became better friends it was less of a problem for me to carry my camera. It was fascinating. Thrilling, actually.

I kept it up until the identification ceased to be interesting, around the time I met Marina, and I started to get more into *rough stuff*. When I met Marina in November 1975, in Amsterdam, she was interested in what I was doing, and I showed her all the identity-research photos from my gender-crossing period. She liked them tremendously. I think it was part of the decision-making process that led to us working together. Ours was a male/female collaboration, but from the beginning we venerated the figure of the hermaphrodite and the union of male and female. As long as that way of thinking worked, we got along fine. When our ideology fell apart, we also started to fall apart. But I think that my experience with transvestism had a great influence on our collaboration in the *Relation Works*.

DJ: *It also strikes me that the thirteen* Relation Works *often stage a battle of wills. A work like* Relation in Space *(1976) could be read as a commentary on gender disparity, or social conflict more broadly.*

U: From the very beginning, the general title of the series was *Relation Works*, so this emphasised the question of relationality. We worked with, and demonstrated, traumatic fears about relations. I think any relationship – male/female, male/male, female/female – will resemble a traumatic experience. We were thinking about this, and we wanted to explore the anxieties and difficulties that come with relationality, and especially those that usually do not get represented.

For Marina, the work also had a competitive dimension. You said 'battle of wills'. I've never heard that phrase, but I like it very much. In our collaborative works, there had to be two wills at work. I was not the master of her will. I could have *influenced* her will, in a way that was positive or negative, constructive or destructive. We shared one agenda for each work, but she had to generate her own will, and I had to generate my own will. Often, it did look like a battle of wills. I think, partly, that the work has so much success – even though, for many people, our performances were extremely uncomfortable – because audiences recognised something in them. Who is willing to show the *worst* parts of their relationship? We did. And others could identify with what we showed them. They shared in our fears, our reservations, and our relationship in general.

A 'battle of wills', yes. I like that. But not a *triumph* of the will [*laughs*].[15]

DJ: *I am interested in the rapid succession from one performance to another. For example in 1977, you and Marina made eight works – including two in June alone. There was an incredible pace of working, and yet there's a striking clarity to each work. Can you tell me about your process in the* Relation Works?

U: If you claim to do performances, you need an audience. In that period, especially 1977–78, we were a sensation, so we were invited frequently to perform, in alternative spaces, but also galleries, museums, biennials, and so on. We didn't repeat works, so we made new performances at a fast pace.

In terms of process, we did not conceive performances in isolation. When we got an invitation, the curator would ask for the title, what we'd need, what the work would involve, the space we wanted. To all these questions, we'd simply say: *No*. This was never a problem, but it's unthinkable now. In 1979, for example, we were invited by the Sydney Biennial, and they paid for our flights, our accommodation, and so on. The costs would have been very expensive for two artists from Europe, and the risks were high, but they brought us without any knowledge of what we'd do in our performance. All of our works in this period were conceived like this, 'on location'. We would arrive a few days before the performance was scheduled to take place, we'd find a space, and develop a unique concept for the situation. It seemed to lend a greater sense of authenticity to the work, because it stemmed from the experience of a collective mentality, in that city, in that space, at a specific time. This informed what you called the 'clarity' or simplicity of the work.

I was more or less 'in charge' between 1976 and 1980, and I wrote the performance scores. I was very Beckett-oriented. Samuel Beckett was my master, and this probably influenced the simplicity of our work. Later on, from 1980 to 1988, Marina took greater charge of our collaboration, and the work became much more spectacular, more theatrical.

DJ: *In the 1970s, it seems like theatre, or theatricality, was a dirty word for visual artists. What did theatre mean to you in the period?*

U: *Nothing.* Theatre was irrelevant. There was some good theatre at that time – there was the Living Theatre, Jerzy Grotowski, and Tadeusz Kantor, for example. These were excellent theatre-makers, and their thinking, operating, and conceptualisation was equivalent to that of performance artists in a visual art context. Theatre wasn't even a 'dirty word' for us. It was simply non-existent.

DJ: *What are your current interests in relation to performative photography? I saw a show of your recent works in London, which involved new large-scale Polaroids and photograms, for example.*[16]

U: In the 1990s, I was the only European artist who had access to a gigantic Polaroid camera in Boston. There are two large Polaroid cameras, which produce 22-inch by 40-inch and 40-inch by 80-inch images. I worked with the largest one. Polaroid is fixed. I wanted to push it. I would have loved to continue working with Polaroid, without a doubt, but Polaroid went bankrupt. There isn't much Polaroid film around any more, and the chemicals aren't the same. I was at a studio in New York a couple of years ago, where there is still a 22-inch by 40-inch Polaroid camera. I took seven large Polaroid photographs of glasses of water – they're very minimal, and very difficult, technically. I also took a self-portrait photograph of myself crying.[17]

Analogue or 'wet' photography is my second skin. It's mechanical, chemical, and optical. I'm technically able to make skilled images – but that's not my interest. I continue to experiment, even if it's not popular with museums (which are hardly spaces for experimentation). In my series *Berlin Afterimages: Flags for the European Community* [1994–96], I worked with the phenomenon of retinal negative afterimages. That is, if you look at a red spot on a wall for some time, when you close your eyes you'll see a green spot – the afterimage is transposed into its complementary colours. It's part of our neurophysiological make-up, but it's ignored. I used photography to simulate it, by printing negative images of flags.[18] There's still so much more left to explore in analogue photography.

I'm working on new works with large-scale technology, including the photogram. I also want to make a series of portraits of perform-ance artists, like a *Last Supper*. I'll continue with analogue photogra-phy, to stretch its limits one more time.

DJ: *It sounds like performance continues to be vital. What's your current relation to live performance?*

U: I am still flabbergasted by the idea of performance. Why? I'm *too young*. I can't make the auto-aggressive work I made in the 1970s, any more, and the identity issues I worked with are no longer important enough for me. I would like to move in the direction of Butoh, and the grotesque – *but only when I'm unable to*. That would be interest-ing. Classically, a performer is always in good shape. I would like to show inability, and make performance more humane.

I have withdrawn from live performance, for the moment, but I have been thinking of how to substitute the body. I came to water. The body is more than 70 per cent water. The brain is 80 per cent water. If you Google 'water' you get 30 million references in less than a second – so you better learn to swim. I created an online project, the *Earth Water Catalogue*, to archive artists' views on water, with artworks from around the world.[19] I want the catalogue to change our perception of water. Water is not sexy. In the West we have it in plenty, but the lack of it in other parts of the world is deadly. I want the artistic community, in a collective enterprise, to picture water and make it more appealing, to bring about new ways of thinking about water. I've made installations using water, and these are archived on the website. It's all for the *love* of water.

DJ: *It sounds like an activist project. Are you happy with the designation 'activist'?*

U: No, I would call myself an *artivist*.

Notes

1. Ulay and Marina Abramović, 'Relation Works: Performance texts by Marina Abramović and Ulay', in Thomas McEvilley, *Art, Love, Friendship: Marina Abramović and Ulay – Together and Apart* (New York: McPherson, 2010), pp. 49–55 (p. 49).
2. Maria Rus Bojan, 'Breaking the Norms: Poetics of Provocation', in Maria Rus Bojan and Alessandro Cassin, *Whispers: Ulay on Ulay* (Amsterdam: Valiz Foundation, 2014), pp. 20–47 (p. 21).

3. Adam Phillips, *Houdini's Box: On the Arts of Escape* (London: Faber & Faber, 2001), p. 11.

4. Clement Greenberg, '*Partisan Review*, Art Chronicle: 1952', in *Art and Culture: Critical Essays* (Boston, MA: Beacon Press, 1961), pp. 146–53 (p. 153).

5. After a guerrilla campaign from 1970, Andreas Baader, Ulrike Meinhof and others were arrested in 1972, prompting an escalation of terrorist attacks until the 'German Autumn' of 1977 (a series of kidnappings, assassinations and aircraft hijackings).

6. Schmidt-Reitwein was the cinematographer on 17 of Herzog's movies, including *The Enigma of Kaspar Hauser* (1974) and *Heart of Glass* (1976).

7. *Irritation* is sometimes used as the title of the film, to distinguish it from the live action.

8. Gallerist Tony Shafrazi vandalised Pablo Picasso's *Guernica* (1937) with spray-paint in the Museum of Modern Art, New York in 1974. In 1986, Gerard Jan van Bladeren knifed Newman's *Who's Afraid of Red, Yellow and Blue III* (1967) in the Stedelijk Museum, Amsterdam. In 1997, he returned and attacked Newman's *Cathedra* (1951).

9. See Thomas McEvilley, *Ulay: The First Act* (Ostfildern: Canst Verlag, 1994), where the performance carries the more complicated title *Null Identity for the Possible Adoption of the Other*. See note for Plate 23.

10. The performance was reconstructed at the Museum of Modern Art in Ljubljana in November 2012.

11. At the time of presentation, *Fototot II* was titled *Im toten Winkel*, which McEvilley translates as *In the Dead Angle* (see note for Plate 21 in *The First Act*). The original title also translates – perhaps more neatly – as *Blind Spot*.

12. Thomas McEvilley, 'Ulay and Photography', in *Art, Love, Friendship*, pp. 229–37 (p. 231).

13. See Don DeLillo, *Mao II* (London: Vintage, 1992), p. 70.

14. Friedrich Nietzsche, *Twilight of the Idols, or How to Philosophize with a Hammer* (London: Penguin, 1990), p. 33.

15. Ulay refers to Leni Riefenstahl's derided pro-Nazi propaganda film *The Triumph of the Will* (1934).

16. *Ulay*, MOT International, London, 16 October–30 November 2013.

17. The series is *Sweet Water, Salt Water* (2012). In *Project Cancer: Ulay's Journal from November to November* (dir. Damjan Kozole, Emotionfilm, 2013), Ulay explains that chemotherapy made his eyes water continuously.

18. See Thomas McEvilley, 'Flags for the European Community', in *Art, Love, Friendship*, pp. 159–61.

19. See Ulay's *Earth Water Catalogue*: http://www.earthwatercatalogue.net/ [accessed 12/06/14].

2   # Hiding in Plain Sight: An Interview with Anne Bean

Anne Bean's work is unfailingly diverse, precise yet untamed, and chameleon-like. It can be profound or funny; industrially robust or well-nigh immaterial; delicate or magisterial; glacially slow or fleeting. The commencement of her 'life art' project began early on. From the age of 12, Anne Bean set herself the project of writing letters to her adult self, to ensure she would become, in years to come, the artist she might will herself to be.[1] In the 1970s, and afterwards, Bean would sustain this aesthetic principle of long-term performance actions, drawn out over months and years, which seek to integrate the practices of art and life.

Born in Zambia (then British Northern Rhodesia), Bean's conflicted identity as a white, Jewish woman in colonial Africa seemingly conditioned her orientation towards individuality, ritual and fabulism – eccentricity, even. As her friend Chris Millar recalled in 1983, Bean 'tells me she how she swam in the crocodile-infested waters, only thinking of the swim and not the danger or the lack of it. She was making a Universe which didn't incorporate the possibility of being eaten by crocodiles.'[2] Her practice has retained this alchemical admixture of process, danger and creative world-making. She left Zambia to study in South Africa, and then in Reading, England in 1969. She has been resident in the UK ever since, where her project of daily universe-building has continued for 40 years and counting.

Anne Bean's oeuvre is principled yet uncategorisable. Performance predominates, alongside works in sound, drawing, video, installation and sculpture, frequently emphasising the live, durational and performative qualities of a given form. She has categorically refused to adopt a signature style, such that her practice is held together by its dissonance, as well as by a number of sustaining imperatives: her commitment to the refusal of technique and its accrual; the use of basic, poor or extra-artistic materials; making strange our sense of time, memory, language and the body; and pushing artistic concepts and forms to breaking points. Her recent, long-term project, described below, in which she moved to a new town, chosen by chance, abandoned her personal history and took up a new identity and name – Chana Dubinski – demonstrates her commitment to these lasting principles. The personal, artistic and theoretical effects are breathtaking in their extremity.

A seemingly self-reliant artist of idiosyncratic and hermetic means, Bean is also a prolific collaborator. As discussed below, her most profound collaborative groups have included the proto-glam art-pranksters Moody and the Menstruators (aka The Moodies); the Bernsteins in the 1970s; her celebrated work with Richard Wilson and the late Paul Burwell as Bow Gamelan Ensemble in the 1980s; and politically salient alliances with women in areas of geopolitical conflict, such as PAVES. Collaborations with other major artists include those with the Kipper Kids, Paul McCarthy and Stephen Cripps.

Despite all these achievements, Bean has figured marginally in histories of performance. This is perhaps the case for many important artists of her generation working in performance in the UK, including Rose Finn-Kelcey, Rose Garrard, Shirley Cameron, Monica Ross or Carlyle Reedy. However, as Bean explains in the interview below – conducted in London in May 2014 – her enigmatic or elusive quality is due in great part to her explicit attempts to go under the radar of historical and critical awareness. She refused to allow her work to be documented for several decades, and disengaged from the critical reception of art, leaving her work to percolate, untouched and unmarred by scholarly custodianship, with the ambition of not being 'part of an art-historical way of seeing', as she puts it. More recently, Bean has begun to allow her work to breach the horizon of visibility. That said, for the inquisitive witness, her interventions, experiments and sometimes-madcap occupations have been there all along, fizzing and popping at the edges of cultural perceptibility. As suggested by the title of this interview, Bean has long been *hiding in plain sight*. The effects of her surfacing ought to shake the historical edifice of art and performance to such magnificent ruins.

Dominic Johnson: *Performance has been vital to you since your earliest works in the late 1960s. What continues to draw you to live performance?*

Anne Bean: In the 1960s and 1970s, performance was part of the *Zeitgeist*. I got into live performance from being involved in sculptural practices. For instance, in the late 1960s I was working with equilibrium: balancing my own weight and mass against another weight and mass, on a pulley system, and other sculptural pieces like that. I recognised that the process of doing this kind of work was much more pertinent to me than the resulting objects themselves. I appreciated the feeling of working something out in time and space.

For me, performance has been a very permissive space, and an individual territory. In the late 1960s, I'd just arrived in England to study fine art at the University of Reading. I came from South Africa where I'd studied fine art at the University of Cape Town as a *very* traditional discipline, strictly concerned with life drawing as a basis for the development of artistic skill and technique. It was so at odds with the living situation of apartheid in South Africa at that time. You couldn't have a more ridiculous tension between the strictly traditional art practice, which was apolitical, and the horrendous, toxic situation one was living in. It emphasised the *privilege* of the prevailing model of fine art, the ridiculousness of it all. I thought, 'What am I doing here?'

I started to do actions in 1969. I didn't realise these were 'performance', but looking back I thought of them as visual protests. On 'white only' [*Net Blankes*] benches, for example, I would paint parts of my body with black paint, like the palms of my hands, or half of my face. I would sit on these benches and think: how much of you must be white, and how much black, in order to be allowed to sit here. I was fascinated by how strange colour is, as a theory and a political concept – it's very much a 'fine art' question in itself – and I tried to figure it out in visual terms. This notion of 'white', in that context, was at the very best *surrealistic*, and at the worst, completely off-the-scale fascist, which was precisely the type of nation state one was living in. What does one do about it, as an individual, and as an artist – and in this situation, as a white person, and therefore part of the perpetrators?

I think it became more and more apparent to me that, as an artist, I got most excited in terms of present-time interaction, shared exploration, collaboration, witnessing, and all the 'edges' between. When I arrived in England in 1969, I found Joseph Beuys, and learnt about *social sculpture*, which was an astonishingly prescient idea.[3] Rita Donagh, who was teaching at Reading, really made us look at what art was for, and to interrogate its function. That moment of the early 1970s was a really crucial time, poised between modernism and postmodernist thought.

DJ: *In a statement inside the cover of your book* Autobituary, *you ask: 'How does one operate as an older artist, especially when one's original nomenclature – performance – is outmoded, even redundant'?*[4] *What do you mean by that?*

AB: It's to do with the term *performance*. In some ways it's just a prob-lem of semantics and terminology, but in another sense, the word is all we have. It seems to me that performance – and especially the term *performance art* – is becoming more and more historical, as terminology. I don't think the space performance occupied in the 1970s is still valid. That space is, maybe, being occupied by some-thing else now, and it doesn't need as much *custodianship* as it might have done before.

I don't have any real beef with the term *live art*, but it is much more of a catch-all territory than we would ever have acknowl-edged when I came to performance. At that time, among those of us making performance, there was a shared consciousness about anti-materialism and anti-commodification, a shared sense of real-ity. In some ways I think those early performance positions are no longer viable. As an 'older artist', I can see that a lot of performers can be a bit holier than thou in terms of *keeping the flame alive*, even though the context has now changed considerably. Fundamentalism in a radical context is still fundamentalism. I think as an individual, one can sustain something of that ethos, but it has to come from a very particular and renewable place, and it is very difficult to sustain.

DJ: *How did you respond to formal education at Reading, both as a student of new media or expanded forms, but also as a woman?*

AB: When I arrived in England in the late 1960s, it felt *utopian*. I was completely bowled over that one's inner life could be expressed and shared, and I'd found a tribe of people that I felt very at home with. That pressure of the political situation in South Africa – being a white South African, and all the privilege that entails – it was an incredible burden. I'm not saying we were victims, too, but we were abused by the system in terms of what we were seen to stand for. You almost become overwrought by impotence, just by the fact that you are associated with a history and a politics, both of which were toxic. So, in England I found what felt like a radical questioning of *everything*. There was far more of an overlap between art and life. I felt a strange inner *at-home-ness*.

I was very conscious of the political issues around gender and women's rights, which were very much in the air at the time. However, I was also aware of coming from the politicised situation in South Africa, and I didn't want to jump into feminism, as a new political discourse. Particularly, I didn't feel at ease with the more extreme edge of women's issues, namely separatist politics. I found that very hard to deal with, again, in terms of the South African situation, and what separatism implied in that context. Finding different women's movements, and solutions, where each disagreed with the other, it was difficult to know where to identify. Coincidentally, last week, at the Live Art Development Agency, a number of women who were artists in that period joined together to talk about those issues.[5] It was wonderful, 45 years on, to see that in some way, looking back, from extreme to more centrist views on the positions of women in society, they all contributed to recognising inequalities, and being aware of suppression and dominance. Things have shifted, and all of those different feminist movements, including the extremes, have come together in a strange mélange, culminating in a recognisable shift towards social change.

DJ: *Your concept band* Moody and the Menstruators *(1971–74) emerged from your period at Reading. Can you tell me about that project and what your imperatives were?*

AB: It's strange that it has become memorable as a 'project', because it was meant as a throwaway gesture. In a light-hearted, irreverent way, we were looking at gender, cross-dressing, identity, love songs and the ridiculousness – but also the wonderfulness – of *who or what one could be*. It was the corny meets the sublime. We were experimenting with how to position oneself. I was living in the same house as Rod [Melvin], who was the pianist with Moody and the Menstruators.[6] The first night we played publicly was with Roxy Music – it was their first gig, too – and it quickly seemed to take on much more significance. People loved it, basically, and we loved doing it.

We were asked to do other things, like going on tour with Pink Floyd, and both Malcolm McLaren and the artist Barry Flanagan wanted to manage us. The doorway was open to Moody and the Menstruators *taking over* one's practice as an artist. We started to be well known, particularly in galleries, and it was very interesting to me that what we were doing was accepted as a fine-art practice in certain situations, as well as crossing the border into so many other contexts, including pop music. I'm reminded of Marshall McLuhan's idea that context or medium is a substantial aspect of the message. Where does one position oneself? This strange hybrid piece could be seen by so many people in different ways. We could do a *Spare Rib* benefit and be seen as 'right-on' feminists, even perceived as a lesbian collective; we could be seen as very powerful and strong, and yet on another night, in a different context, we would be seen as ironic cabaret. Firstly, it was able to move between all these different contexts, and secondly I started to see it as just one part of myself, among many others, and I recognised that one *can* work across different modes and contexts.

I started to think, in terms of myself, how one positions something like that with other artistic concerns. I don't know if I would have articulated it quite like this at the time, but I began to ask if performing with the Moodies was part of one's *work*, or part of a social situation, or part of a politicised situation, or just a fun, party activity. I was doing it with absolute passion and conviction and the media played the game in terms of coverage – but at the same time we were commenting on the absurdity of this 'pop' structure. Where did it fit? That was very interesting to me, as it was a way of asking, again, *who and what am I?* And yet at the same time I have a continuous need for *non-definition*.

How one is seen as an artist is often rather limiting, in terms of being associated with just one mode, or style. I started to become much more interested in the fact that, individually or collaboratively, one can be in many, many different situations, and still feel *authentically oneself*. People could be very critical and say the Moodies were merely light, or not very thoughtful, but humour and lightness was very much part of the work, and its ability to transmit itself. But in the end it just became much bigger than I ever thought it would – or wanted it to, actually – to the point that I began to wonder if it was actually *sabotaging* my ideological concerns.

DJ: *The Moodies seemed to embrace theatricality. Where did theatre fit into your concerns more broadly as an artist?*

AB: At that time at Reading – in the late 1960s and early 1970s – there was certainly an overlap between performance in the visual arts, and what you might call experimental theatre, yet other more traditional theatre didn't seem relevant. I was close friends with Alastair Brotchie, who was – and still is – centrally involved in 'Pataphysics. We read Alfred Jarry, performed his *Ubu* plays, and looked at other Dada performances. We went to Paris a few times to look into its history. I was interested in Tristan Tzara, and I did a visual production of his play *The Gas Heart* [1921], in a gasworks. I was excited about strange hybrid forms of theatre and other kinds of performance. However, while Jarry and Tzara's theatre seemed to come out of visual practice, the kind of theatre that was on at the time in London seemed completely 'other' to my interests.

DJ: *I think in that moment, in the British context, describing performance from a visual art background as 'theatrical' was sometimes a slight?*

AB: Yes, that's true. In the early 1970s, I started to work with the Kipper Kids, who had just left a theatre conservatoire, East 15. There were very intensive talks about 'performance' and 'theatre', and yes, to be described as 'theatrical' was very much a slight, as you put it. I was terribly aware, though, that whenever you found a radical practice, immediately there were rules and prohibitions attached. I've always felt, if nothing else, one ought to *escape the rules*. There would be endless talks about that dichotomy, between experimentation and orthodoxy. It was very much a time when the sublime and the ridiculous were not allowed to coexist. I've always felt, and continue to feel, that they *really do* coexist for us as human beings. It goes back to what we were talking about in relation to women's movements: the early 1970s was a time when rules were being applied to oppositional practices. I just wanted to run away from it all. If I look back, I can align myself in various ways, and I have done so, loosely, with different groups, from time to time. But I've never seen myself as *centrally* located in any single context. I celebrate to this day that I haven't.

DJ: *From the 1970s, until at least the 1990s, you were invested in singular events that couldn't or wouldn't be repeated. What was at stake in non-repetition?*

AB: The principle of non-repetition of works was concerned with – to put it in very over-abused terms – being 'in the moment'. I was committed to performance as an action that took place *in the now*, such that an audience could share what was happening in a present time and space. The fact of witnessing was a crucial and intrinsic part of the work. This led me to become more and more interested in sound as a liberating force. Visual objects and actions are material, whereas sound involves freeing up aesthetics from material reality, from the production of commodities. In the mid-1970s at Butler's Wharf, where I had a studio, I met Paul Burwell, who was a drummer-artist, and experimented extensively with the overlap between visual and sound-based art.[7] We would make improvised music, sound pieces and experiments, pretty much every night.

The kind of work I was making often couldn't easily be repeated. For example, I had a drum kit in my studio in Butler's Wharf, which I connected to lights, and I wired metal drumsticks to a car battery. When I drummed, and completed the circuit on the edge of a drum rim, or on a cymbal, the battery would light up one of several small headlamps, so that different rhythms would strike up different shadows. You could throw the light around the room and light up your own performance. The drum kit was lit by its own lights within its own rhythms. I was playing shadows as opposed to playing sound. It was a very satisfactory piece for me, a 'breaking through'. You could *see sound* and *hear shadow*. After meeting Paul, I went further into sound.

DJ: *The Bow Gamelan Ensemble was also important to your investigations of sound.*

AB: Yes. Paul and I formed the Bow Gamelan Ensemble with Richard Wilson in 1983 (see **Figure 2.1**). Richard had a studio in Butler's

Figure 2.1   Bow Gamelan Ensemble, *Six Hour Concert*, performance (Rainham Reach, Thames Estuary, 1984). Channel 4 commission/After Image. Courtesy of Anne Bean

Wharf, too, and we did a lot of boat trips along the Thames into the Bow Back Rivers, Bow Creek, Pudding Mill and also out into the Thames Estuary to places like the astonishing Maunsell Forts [decommissioned military sea towers], which we subsequently used for performances. You might see a welder under a bridge, and the bridge would light up, and you would hear loud crackling noises. The sound of that would be amplified by being under the bridge, and the shadows would be amplified in the darkness. Lots of these images and soundscapes fed rapidly into our visual and sonic awareness. We were terribly excited, and didn't quite know what to do with it but we continuously threw around ideas that finally led into an evening of new musical instruments at the London Musicians Collective, which was the beginning of the Bow Gamelan Ensemble. We worked in the physical and felt aspects of performance, and of *seeing* sound. Our sound was acoustic, in that there wasn't a mysterious black box out of which sound emerged, or any synthesised sound at all. Richard, Paul and I went on to make huge sonic landscape interventions until 1990.

Later works of mine fulfilled this fluidity between the seen and heard, like *Radiant Fields* [2000], in which I used thermal imaging to visualise the changing shapes of sounds, such as the heat produced by the breath blowing through a conch shell, or handprints on tablas, or gas burners playing through metal and glass pipes, creating mournful harmonies as the air was disturbed by the heat, and the pipes dramatically changed colour within the thermal reading. Centrally I was aware of acoustic and visual perception as wavelengths that we perceived through our limited spectrum range and I wanted to point to potential greater insights and *insounds*. I worked with other interplays between the sonic and the seen in several performances using tape-recorders or record players, which involved either burning, washing, drowning, sawing, swinging, hammering or smothering the recorders while they played, to interfere or tamper with and disrupt the original recordings. Similarly, with my own voice, while I spoke or sang, I manipulated my lips with clips, or poured substances like honey down my throat, or ate chillies, or used cling film over my face and mouth to challenge the quality of voicing (see **Figure 2.2**).

DJ: *You were resistant to documenting your performance actions in the 1970s and 1980s. Can you describe your relation to documentation?*

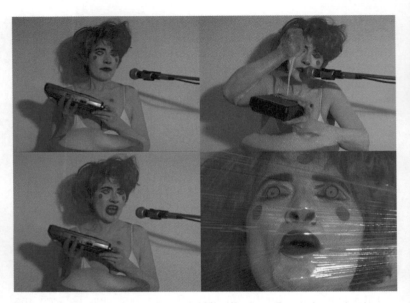

Figure 2.2 Anne Bean, *Fever* (1999), Shadow Deed from *Autobituary*. Photographs by Chris Bishop. Courtesy of Anne Bean

AB: If I look back to an early performance, I sometimes think I'd love to see the work again, and I'm pleased when somebody brings me a photograph from those years. That seems contradictory, because, at the time, documenting my performances just wasn't relevant to the development of what I was doing. In fact, I felt that documentation was a distraction, and a suppressant and inhibitor of being, of core responses, as it pushed one's awareness into collusion with a potential gaze from the future, away from now. My refusal had to be *stated*.

Going into the mid-1970s, it became apparent that performance artists became more and more invested in producing iconic images, which could sometimes be seen as more important, and more effective, than the live performances. For me, this limited how artists went about their work. The framing of the image, where a performance took place, how a performance was enacted, the context, the photographer being given the prime position within it – this was often dictated by documentation, and to me, at the time, it seemed to take away from the immediate audience–performer relation I valued most.

In one way, it's kind of ridiculous for me to be saying all this, because the Moodies was a different beast: it was over-photographed, and had little to do with being 'in the moment'. But, it was satisfying for me to uphold those very different beliefs, and to be able to feel that *one was allowed to be contradictory*. I've always been aware that these are games we make up, with invented rules. We make agreements in order to have coherent ways of playing together. These games are often profound and provocative, but they are not absolute in any sense. I try not to be judgemental, but there were a lot of judgemental qualities at the time. I think it's what happens when you are struggling through to your own manifesto, or ideology, or whatever you want to call it. At times, one does have to make some sort of statement, and it is allowed to be contradictory. I want to keep challenging myself, which means having an inner devil's advocate, which provokes me into taking a stand.

DJ: *I was wondering about works you did come to repeat, for instance* Death to Grumpy Grandads, *which you returned to in 2002 after its original performance in 1973. What was at stake in returning to it?*

AB: *Death to Grumpy Grandads* was performed by a group called Bernsteins, who were a loose group of fine art students, mostly from Reading University. There were seven of us: Brian Routh and Martin Von Haselberg [the Kipper Kids], Peter Davey, Chris Millar, Malcolm Jones, Jonathan Harvey, and me. We did lots of very different pieces about trying to come together as a collective, from very different positions, and how those positions can join up, if everyone can work together in a satisfactory and fulfilling way, even though coming from very different outlooks and perspectives on art. That was a fundamental tenet of being together. In one way, it was a questioning of the idea of taste, and also it had to do with the extensions and deepening of friendship. We acquired an old building in the East End in 1972, a semi-legitimate squat. We spent a lot of time there, asking what we were trying to do, philosophically and conceptually. One night, one of the women living in the house, Jill Jones, wrote a line across the whole kitchen in lipstick: 'death to grumpy grandads'. We were reading Gurdjieff and Ouspensky, and thinking seriously about being and doing, wakefulness and mindfulness.[8] She made her own provocation. We laughed. We jumped from a deep introspective looking into shared laughter.

In 1973, we tried it out as an action, *Death to Grumpy Grandads*, which involved attempting simply to laugh together for an hour, or more. The laughter was hopefully authentic but it didn't necessarily have to be; if it died out, we restarted with some kind of ham acting, and pushed it to another level, and then natural laughter would re-establish itself. For me it was a very satisfying piece, as we were looking at situations where performance, authenticity and theatricality meet. We had a very small audience but they literally became part of the piece as they inevitably laughed along with us. The separation of 'audience' and 'performer' was broken down. Being 'in the present' was simply unavoidable, because laughter is a very 'present' and shared action. As far as the sound element was concerned – without being too grand about it – it became quite symphonic in terms of being very loud, and emphatic, and then dying down into nothingness, quietness for a bit, and then hesitantly, all the voices coming back in, to rise and fall again.

Decades later, around 2001, the Whitechapel Gallery telephoned me and said they were planning *A Short History of Performance* (Part One, 15–21 April 2002), and were restaging performances from the 1960s and 1970s. They asked if I would suggest an iconic piece of mine that I'd like to restage. I have a real difficulty with the word 'iconic', and I don't like the idea of having a *signature* performance. I said I'd think about it. I decided that if everybody who did the original *Death to Grumpy Grandads* was available, that would be a lovely way, thirty years later, to be in a room together, and we could see where we could go with the piece, and what extra layers we could find. Of course, in a way it couldn't be repeated because it would be so different in terms of context, and age, and history. It felt like an apt piece to have done because it was inevitably about communication on a different level. Of course, we didn't have a single photograph from the first performance in 1973, just our memories of it, which were quite different between us. I liked that. So, a very threadbare Sunday afternoon in an old chemist's shop in the East End of London some time in 1973 became this piece in the Whitechapel Gallery as part of *A Short History of Performance*. I felt fine about that. It worked well and was terribly moving. At the Whitechapel, the laughter became almost hysterical, on the edge of tears. The audience joined in. It was emotional. They say sometimes at funerals people start to hysterically laugh. There's a terrible closeness between hysteria, anguish, terror, the feeling of mourning, and the ridiculousness of it all.

DJ: *How do you feel more broadly about laughter as an audience response to performance?*

AB: Well, a lot of early British performance – including my own – embraced laughter, whereas in Europe that was very much a *no-no*. In the 1970s, the Kipper Kids and I came to know Hermann Nitsch and Günter Brus [two of the four Viennese Actionists]. We would drink together and find ourselves in hilarious situations, but in their performances, humour and laughter were not acceptable. In a way, even though Vienna Actionism was attempting to get closer to reality through performance, their distance from laughter struck me as not very 'real'. Theirs was a very serious, holy space – but, strangely, laughter was not a part of it.

Meeting Paul [Burwell] and working with him, I found there was a great seriousness in the improvised music world, too – but Paul was really irreverent and provocative. Whilst he also took on board a lot of the important principles in music at the time, his default setting was the absurd. In the Bow Gamelan Ensemble, there was a lot of humour, including unintentional laughter. Working with, say, 50 vacuum cleaners spewing out talcum powder whilst they sung different notes from the fittings we'd put onto the outlets as they blew – it creates a very comical effect. But at the same time, if you listen to the recording, it's also a very hauntingly beautiful piece. I like that ambiguity.

DJ: *You've mentioned the Kipper Kids. Can you tell me more about collaborating with them?*

AB: We worked together a fair amount across Europe in the early 1970s. After they moved to America in 1974, I'd go to the States, and we'd do performances in punk clubs, as well as in galleries. I really enjoyed the crossover. Ironically, gallery situations were much more open than punk clubs to extreme, anarchic, outrageous situations – 'terrorising', one might call it, though I don't know if it was. The Kipper Kids and myself (and also Paul and myself, in other instances) were chucked out of clubs, or asked to leave, even though they'd said they wanted really on-the-edge, off-limits, full-on stuff. There was a club in Hollywood that literally pulled the plugs on us and told us to get off the stage. They couldn't take it. However, in galleries, doing the same performances was received in a completely different way. It was seen as a radical exploration, very primal, and the audiences accepted it, even if it was still controversial. So, I worked with the Kipper Kids then, and on and off in collaborative ways, but very much within the context of their own work. An exception was in Amsterdam [at Melkweg, 1972], where we changed the whole performance because of a dream I had the night before. During the piece, they gathered hundreds of red roses I had hung from the ceiling. They were like ghostly, impish, Butoh-esque gardeners from some underworld, bringing me these glorious bouquets, and culminating with a tea ceremony.

DJ: *You've also undertaken works where you collaborate in situations of conflict, for instance with PAVES in Kurdistan-Iraq and the former Yugoslavia. Are these actions concerned with social change?*

AB: In the early 2000s I'd started to talk to a young Kurdish-Iraqi refugee, Adalet Garmiany, about going to Kurdistan-Iraq, and helping to set up a contemporary art scene. He was very idealistic about it and I wanted to support him in any way I could, although it seemed completely unrealistic to me. In some ways it was a strange thought, to bring contemporary art into a situation of conflict, deprivation and genocide. How do you do that with sensitivity, and find some way of making a real input? And not just *using* the situation, which can often happen in art – even with the best intentions.

Finally, he got money from the British Council and after a lot of negotiation, I travelled there and began to develop a project called *MASS* [2007–08] with a women's group in Iraqi Kurdistan. These women had been directly affected by the genocide, and I spoke to them about their traditions and rituals, how they mourned, their grieving, and how they assisted each other. We spoke about the possibility of doing a work together that could be seen in a fine-art context, but which would have meaning to them. In Erbil – the capital of Kurdistan-Iraq – part of the art school is a former prison from the Saddam Hussein era. We decided to use the courtyard (where the prisoners would have exercised) as a performance arena. Kurdish national dress includes long dresses, often covered in ornate flower patterns. Each of the women brought one of these dresses into the yard, and we did a ritualised piece together, where each participant attached a dress to black helium balloons, and snipped the flowers from the fabric. When enough flowers had been cut away, the dresses were light enough to float up and over the prison walls, leaving hundreds of cut-out fabric flowers on the concrete floor. I recognised that it was a shared moment for the women, where each recognised the other's pain, and what they'd gone through. It was re-performed in various other contexts.

In terms of your question, I don't think I did anything hugely important in terms of social change, but within the lives of those women the action did make an intervention, and rippled outwards. One recognises how small changes can have a subtle significance. I met another young Kurdish-Iraqi artist there, Poshya Kakl. We spoke intensely about performance, and about her longing and yearning to do more, to find a way out of Iraq, and to share work in the world. This was very much on my conscience, and I thought, if nothing else, I really want to make something happen with her. I told her that I would definitely come back, and that we would work together. I made several actions with her in Iraq, including one in another former prison, the Red Jail in Suleymanya, where we worked together with doves in one of the cells where acts of torture were known to have occurred. We attempted to copy the dove calls, calling to each other and to the doves. We also worked in an extraordinary gallery in Suleymanya, the Aram Gallery, where Poshya's mother joined our hair together and her little sister helped; we spoke about the suppression of women, particularly in Iraq, and about art and social change.

I thought about other women I'd met, for instance Vlasta Delimar from Croatia, who does political performance interventions in the former Yugoslavian state. And Sinéad O'Donnell, in Belfast, who makes direct interventions in Northern Ireland. I learnt about a young Israeli artist, Efi Ben-David, trying to work with Palestinians in the context of the Israel–Palestine conflict. I thought it would be great to find a space where we could work together, if that was even possible, and the work became about our desire to find a way to collaborate despite all the restrictions. So, PAVES became a reality, and we recognised the performances were in some ways symbolic of a much bigger global situation, not least because of the difficulties of simply getting together as a group, on account of borders, rules and regulations, and prejudices.[9] It's an ongoing project and I feel very much that we're embedded in each other's spirits now. Again, in that collaborative situation, PAVES took on its own way of working. It confirmed the idea I've been very interested in for a long time, namely how identity is formed, and how we share it as individuals, whilst coming from very different places.

DJ: *In your solo practice, what is your process in finding the first inklings as to what a performance might entail? Where do ideas come from?*

AB: Well, I feel now that something has shifted. Where I'm finding ideas in the present is a different space, although there are overlaps with my process in the past. I would have to talk about the project that I've just been involved in during the last few years – as Chana

Dubinski – and how that's really shifted the way I look at my art practice, myself, and what I call myself. It concerns the continuum
between life and art. Instead of using the term 'live art', I tend to say
'life art'. Maybe one doesn't need any nomenclature at all. More and
more, my work comes from asking how performance comes about in
an everyday life situation. How can one seamlessly integrate one's
work into just *living*? In the piece of writing that I'm doing towards
the next piece, I'm asking whether or not what I undertake can be
classed as performance at all.[10] There's a date, a place, a title and a
time, so whatever happens there will be a 'performance' – but is that
enough? Is that simply what makes the piece? Is one's framing within
that date, place and time a kind of space-time conundrum? As one's
body is moving towards that, does one simply abrogate all responsibility, and just let that time and place simply be there? Does one
attempt – in as much as one can – to actively form that space? Is it
possible? Is it very confining or very liberating, that one simply is
there, in the space, without undertaking anything in the way of a
preconceived action? One simply carries on *being*, but because it is the
'performance' time, somehow the consciousness of everybody who is
there *shifts*. They ask, 'was she meant to be doing a performance?'
Will that shift their relation to me? Does that shift their relation to
the time and place, in which nothing has changed? So, in a way I'm
trying to work with something totally dematerialised, and that simply
concerns the only thing that pre-exists, which is time, and place.

It's not about losing one's faith in art. It's just that I recognise
more and more that art has become unrecognisable in what I am
doing. There's been an 'establishment', there's been 'anti-establish-
ment', there's been a radical edge, an alternative scene. But I always
feel unpositioned. *I choose not to take up a position.* I think of it in
terms of a person with faith. It is a leap of faith in a religious sense.
If a person with faith suddenly loses their faith, how do they position
themselves? How does their ethics and morality exist outside of 'the
faith'? I'm wondering if that's a very interesting position for an artist,
in which ethics must be taken on as responsibility to oneself. What
happens if one doesn't claim 'art' as one's process, or being, or as the
label that makes one recognisably safe or knowable in the world?
One wants to have a position in the world. It's very frightening not
to have a position. But, does it actually liberate one, by finally taking
that step outside of all positions?

Endgame has been part of the art world for over a century, and it's
a very real way of looking at the situation. But does one now actually

have to claim that space of impossibility, of the dead end, or of bankruptcy as an individual? How does one do it? Is one just playing with more endgames? Those are the ideas I'm looking at now. That's maybe a very different answer to the one you were asking for. But I can go back through my history and see very different processes, and different places I've taken inspiration.

DJ: *Can you tell me about Chana Dubinski?*

AB: Two and a half years ago, I took on a different name, Chana Dubinski, in a project that involved exploring how *not* to embody one's lived history. I left my home, and after a peripatetic period of three months and through a series of deliberate chance actions, I finally settled in a town where nobody knew me.[11] I introduced myself as Chana Dubinski, a name that relates to my childhood, in terms of having known it then as the likely Hebrew-Russian origin for the very plain name Anne Bean. Chana has no other history, as such. I shared the name through childhood with a best friend, with whom I still share this enquiry. In the town I finally settled in, I simply told acquaintances I was making a fresh start and that I had previously taught art, and had a private art practice, but that I had never publicly shown my work. I spoke about writing, drawing and painting but emphasised that I had just *lived my life*. If people asked, I'd say I'd left everything behind to form a new life. It was fairly honest – but ambiguous.

I slowly became integrated by going to various local classes, talking to people, and becoming friendly with people. I tried to be a supportive, neighbourly citizen. I started to build up a new way of being. I won a national writing competition [the Mabel Marbour Prize for Creative Writing 2012] as Chana Dubinski, with a true story about my childhood. I was asked to read it out publicly, which was very emotional for me, as I was sharing intimate, private, personal insights, but also being someone else. I found this art/life interface disturbing. I contributed to various town meetings, including addressing the Philosophy Society and the Art Society, which I found incredibly liberating, and thought-provoking, and renewing. I didn't have to refer to my own history as an artist. I felt a real calmness about simply being a human being in a very different social situation. I could be alive to the people I would meet. That feeling of consciousness that one needs to put into performance, the *permission* to be conscious with the people one's with – well, one can actually transmit it into life, quite powerfully – *almost too powerfully*. It became more and more evident to me that this was a very exciting way of living.

By being an artist one puts all one's consciousness into a particular space – a space called 'art' – and maybe one's life became a little more threadbare from doing that. Of course, the reversal is an overwhelming thing to take on. It's a *destructuring* of one's 'life art': a conscious removal of the whole edifice one has created, and the shared witnesses of that creation. I've found it almost dangerous to myself, in terms of how then one continues to have friends, relationships, family. These have been challenged by what I've done – not destroyed, but shifted, in need of being looked at again, and reformed.

When I went away, I think *I allowed myself to overwhelm my relationship to myself*, within certain parameters, over a certain amount of time. I allowed myself to ask: Who am I? Could I inhabit some other equally valid creation of being? I now feel a yearning to keep touching that strangeness, whether or not it is as an 'art practice', or a 'life practice' – but now with more insight.

DJ: *I'm thinking about Genesis BREYER P-ORRIDGE, who attempted to obliterate their identity through surgery, linguistic reprogramming, and other art/life practices. You both 'cut your teeth' in the artistic ferment of British performance in the 1960s and 1970s. Is your current work rooted in ways of thinking about art and life that took shape in that period?*

AB: It's a tough question, because part of my desire is to try to get out of that conditioning. But I do recognise that my attitude is still formed by part of the *Zeitgeist* that arose in the shifts from modernism to postmodernism, and now beyond that. As artists, we were excited by the *hidden*, but these revelatory layers of consciousness became self-conscious and brittle, and overly self-aware, almost leading to a standstill. Where does one take that now? It's very challenging for people who have been involved in performance for a long time to decide where we go in one's work, and how to take responsibility while sustaining a long-term practice. How to take responsibility socially? And how, as radical beings, does one push an aesthetic practice onwards?

A lot of artists get trapped in the *archival* mode. Each of us has a huge archive of work, whether material or immaterial, and it would take you until the end of your life to put that archive into any kind of sensible order. One needs to transmit our very exciting histories across, to others, but it's important to find ways to do it that are as innovative as the original. We can simply accept we are inevitably an archive of ourselves, and by carrying on working in an engaged and dynamic way, we can transmit our own histories, as well as our newness, our *nowness*. Every now and then an artist is able to cast off that problem. I've known Genesis on and off. In fact, my very first performance abroad was with Genesis and Cosey Fanni Tutti, the Kipper Kids, and Robin Klassnik [*The Revolutionary Spirit*, Louvain University, Ghent] in Belgium in 1973. I think what Genesis is doing with Pandrogeny is really astonishing, committed and profoundly challenging. Our work is completely different, but you can also see deep relations and similarities in some of our approaches.

DJ: *Earlier, you discussed your conviction about non-repetition.* Shadow Deeds *(1996–2005) involved re-performances to camera of 30 actions first performed between 1969 and 1974. In the DVD of fragments, you call them 'reformations'. Why reform those 30 actions?*

AB: It certainly didn't begin with any intention of a long-term project. I think what happened is that, in 1996, I was sitting on a chair, in a studio I had in Norfolk – a wooden chair with a reed base – and I strongly remembered my very first night at Reading University, in 1969, being in a room, knowing nobody, just having this suitcase of mine, sitting on a chair made of reed and wood. There was this intensity of the situation, a whole new life, having come straight from Africa and sitting in this room, in England, feeling cold, which was unusual, and everything was completely outside my reality, yet, strangely, completely inside it. There was a feeling of excitement, and fear, and potential. Then, I'd recognised that here was the chair holding me, and the wood had come from a tree, and the reeds had come from grass. I felt the displacement of this chair from its initial place in nature. I felt a strange connection to this chair, wondering what sort of forest the wood came from, and what the tree looked like, and where the reeds came from, and so on. I felt at home with its displacement. Sitting there, alone, I realised I was touching this chair, very sensually. It led me into a strange dance with this chair. I later thought of it as *falling in love with a chair*. I recognised it was taking me into very odd territory. It was encouraging me to use materials in a very different way. It seemed to be a very significant moment for me, and the experience launched me into the first day at Reading with a powerful, potent frame of mind. It was *alchemical*, in all the very best senses of the word, as a transmutation of material.

More than 25 years later, I was sitting in another chair, and I plunged back to that transformative moment. I asked myself if I could *reform* that earlier experience. I felt very present to the original feelings it invoked. A video artist friend, Nina Sobel, happened to be staying with me. She filmed it, and it turned out to be a sensitive film, a sensual engaged event of dancing with the chair. It seemed unselfconscious. I started to see these reformations not as *repeating* earlier performances, or as *restagings*, but as a way of looking at my practice *now*, and asking what's been borrowed from an earlier time, that crucial moment, for me, of the late 1960s and the early 1970s – almost a reclaiming of cell memory. So, it began, really, as a notebook of sorts, and not as a new project. My son had just been born, and that also takes one on a very different journey. I was thinking how to make a bridge backwards and forwards. It built up into *Shadow Deeds*.

DJ: *A lot of the early works could be seen as experiments. I'm thinking of, say,* The Days of Thy Youth *(1973), which you reformed for* Shadow Deeds. *How did such a work come about?*

AB: In 1973, I had just met somebody at Reading who could speak backwards, in small sentences at least. It seemed a ridiculous thing for him to have learned to do, and it fascinated me. It related to something in the air at the time: Aleister Crowley saying the *Lord's Prayer* backwards, and magic, shamanistic thought, and the Occult 'Law of Reversal'. So, my friend taught me to speak backwards. I thought visually about what would work alongside the sound. I chose to blow candles *into* flame, rather than out of flame. I learnt a small section of the *Lord's Prayer* backwards, recited it onto a reel-to-reel tape recorder, and filmed the candle action. The sound and film were put together and played in reverse. It was fun, but it was a throwaway piece in 1973. When I started working on *Shadow Deeds*, I thought I'd like to see it redone properly.

DJ: *It strikes me as an experimental mode. What is the nature of such an experiment?*

AB: It's a laboratory mode. A lot of work from that time had a 'process' base, at least as an initial jumping-off point. It was a practice of just seeing where an idea might go. I think the Bow Gamelan Ensemble was very much conceived in these terms. Paul and I lived together, and many days would be spent with whatever was in the kitchen, in true laboratory style – seeing if bacon dripping fat on to different surfaces would make different sounds, or throwing poems into a liquidiser to reform texts, or whatever, until one's whole life became a sort of laboratory. I have mostly lived my life in that mode, and it has been incredibly fulfilling. It was similar when I lived with the Kipper Kids in an old pub in Poplar, in the East End of London. Certainly, throughout my time at Butler's Wharf, every single day involved taking whatever materials were around, and continually trying out new things, from 'playing' a sinking boat moored up on the wharf and exploring the acoustic changes as the tide filled it, to heating lit-up lightbulbs with blowtorches, as each, rather beautifully, simultaneously extinguished the other.

DJ: *Another piece you reformed is* Raw/War, *originally performed in 1971. I was wondering about risk in that work, as a theme, but also specifically the risk of physical injury.*

AB: A lot of the work was probably more risky than I recognised at the time. I don't know that I thought of it in terms of physical risk. I just thought of it in terms of challenging myself, pushing myself. Other artists' practices are much more directly involved in risk, but I wouldn't identify myself in those parameters. I think it's a much more *open* orientation to risk, which concerns one's being and one's body being inseparable. But, the edges of what that means can of course be physically risky. For instance, the first public piece I did with Paul [Burwell] and Richard [Wilson] in 1983 involved them under Tower Bridge on a boat, drumming, and me swimming up the Thames from Butler's Wharf towards them, in order to work with the resounding echoes under the arches. It was the riskiest piece I've ever done, because the undercurrents swirling around Tower Bridge were pulling me under. I'm a strong swimmer but at one moment I was sucked right under the water. Sometimes risk is just a kind of *overenthusiasm*, rather than a theme one seeks to engage with directly.

In *Raw/War,* I knocked my head through sheets of glass, and I did recognise that I could be lacerated (see **Figure 2.3**). This was a piece about war, in which I wanted to experience fear. I wanted to have a direct simpatico with a fearful situation, like hiding in a building with the windows being blown in. So, there was a realisation that any of those sheets of glass could cut me quite badly. I did get cut, but I don't know if I considered what would have happened if the jugular vein had been lacerated. I'm asking myself if I would do it now. The physical risk is often an extension of the existential risk, rather than the other way around.

DJ: *The question about reforming works is an important one right now, as we are seeing a current vogue for re-performance, especially for artists*

Figure 2.3   Anne Bean, *Raw/War* (1998), Shadow Deed from *Autobituary*. Still from video recording by Lee Merrill-Sendall. Courtesy of Anne Bean

performing others' works in museum contexts. What are your thoughts on this?

AB: I think it's all down to archiving, which seems to be such an issue at the moment. I am in two minds about it. In one way, re-perform-ance *annihilates the original*. In another way, I find it does allow new audiences to have some recognition of works that happened at a particular point in history. That could be inspirational. It's very diffi-cult because work – and performance in particular – has become an academic concern in a way that it never was before. I realise that academic or critical attention pushes one into a particular space, and an articulacy that I've always avoided. Even though I might be flow-ing through this interview now, it's not easy territory for me to try and articulate. Verbalisation seems antithetical to my principles.

I don't know if I want to give up the position I had before, which was refusing to talk about the work, refusing to document it, refus-ing to align myself with anyone or anything, and refusing to be a part of that *consuming of who and what one is*. There's a black dog on my shoulder now, saying, 'Well, you're doing it now – *face it!*'

[*laughs*]. Frankly, just a few years ago I wouldn't have taken up your offer of being interviewed for your book. For a very long time, I felt I really didn't want to be part of an art-historical way of seeing. I wanted just to remain part of the *rippling-out* that had happened in performance. I know I've touched people in various ways, because they've told me, and that is ultimately fulfilling. That experiential, fugacious space is where I always felt the work should stay.

Maybe I feel far enough from that history, now, moving on to something else, that it feels like I *can* talk about my work. Maybe the fact that it has moved on far enough now means that a performance *can* be part of a history, and be seen as a museum piece, and no more. Then again, a painting is no more than the capture of incredible moments on a canvas. Anyone making a copy of that painting is going to convey something of its energy, maybe, but it's never going to have the feeling of that first, authentic manifestation. As long as that is recognised – and it has to be – then I don't feel that huge antithesis to re-enactment, to history, and to the archive, which I used to feel.

DJ: *You've described your work as a 'continuum', a singular, continuous work. What does this mean to you?*

AB: By being a continuum, art includes all the life 'in between'. It's just the truth of it. That's how the work happens, in among other practices of life. So, those moments in a life that happen to have a photograph or a bit of video attached, they are simply butterflies caught in a net. The photograph or the video does not *exclude* the enormous and much more exciting territory of what led to that moment, and how different ways of working shifted and flowed. The work, and the life, and everything in between – the *fluidity* of it – all of it is equally valid.

Notes

1. These letters, written from 1962 to 1971, are cited and discussed throughout Chris Millar, 'Profile: Anne Bean – A Portentous Event in Earshot of Braying Donkeys', *Performance Magazine*, 20–1 (December/ January 1983), 4–8.
2. Ibid., p. 6.
3. Beuys defines *soziale Plastik* (or social sculpture) as an attempt 'to enlarge the effectivity [or efficacy] of art ... to include the whole creativity of an

individual', for *'every human being is an artist'*. Joseph Beuys, *Energy Plan for the Western Man: Joseph Beuys in America*, ed. Carin Kuoni (New York: Four Walls Eight Windows, 1990), pp. 25–6, 22; original emphasis.

4. Anne Bean, *Autobituary: Shadow Deeds* (London: Matt's Gallery, 2006), p. 1.

5. On 2 May 2014, Lois Weaver, Lois Keidan and Eleanor Roberts convened a discussion between Anne Bean, Bobby Baker, Sonia Boyce, Geraldine Pilgrim, Claire MacDonald, Rona Lee and Hilary Westlake.

6. The other original members were Suzy Adderley, Becky Bailey, Polly Eltes, Mary Anne Holliday and Annie Sloane.

7. Burwell died in 2007. Bean presented a tribute to Burwell, consisting of a performance, a collage of video commissions by 80 artists and a documentary. See *TAPS and PAST: Improvisations with Paul Burwell* (London: Matt's Gallery, 2011), a DVD publication.

8. Specifically, Bean and her collaborators were interested in 'being-*partkdolg*-duty', a model of mindfulness expressed in G. I. Gurdjieff, *Beelzebub's Tales to his Grandson: An Objectively Impartial Criticism of the Life of Man* (London: Routledge & Kegan Paul, 1950). See Millar, 'Profile: Anne Bean', p. 6.

9. PAVES is an acronym consisting of the first letter of the name of each of the five artists. See their blog at http://pavescrossingzones.blogspot. co.uk/ [accessed 17/06/14].

10. At the time of the interview, Bean was preparing for a performance at Aaron Williamson's *Sculpture-Performance: Acme Artists Now* (Acme Studios at High Performance House, Purfleet, Essex, 17 May 2014). She appeared at the allocated space, a communal area outside Williamson's studio, and conversed with audience members (including me) for 30 minutes, while we drank and ate together.

11. Anne/Chana lived in Castlegate, Newark, for around 16 months. Her time there culminated in an exhibition in her cottage: *A Transpective: How Things Used to be Now* (2012). Dubinski has a website: http://chanadubinski.co.uk/ [accessed 17/06/14].

3   Boxing Clever: An Interview with the Kipper Kids

The Kipper Kids are legendary figures of performance art after 1970. From 1973 until their last performance in 2003, Harry Kipper and Harry Kipper performed transmogrifying variations on the same untitled performance. This involved a string of 'ceremonies' that parodied, perverted and made strange a range of social interactions, including a tea ceremony, birthday party and boxing match – accompanied by grunts, scatological sounds, squeaks, giggles, banter and garbled renditions of songs like the folk ditty *Roamin' in the Gloamin'*, or the Beach Boys' *California Girls*. By turns sweet, masochistic and ultraviolent, the shared persona of Harry Kipper struck an imposing presence. The Kipper Kids – Brian Routh and Martin Von Haselberg – embody the alter ego in subtly different ways, but their physical and affective dissimilarity is curtailed by their identical styling: greasepaint face with polka-dot stubble and black eyes; swimming hats or Boy Scout caps; prosthetic noses and chins; jockstraps; and ubiquitous slatherings of food and fluorescent paint.

J. Hoberman remembers a performance by the Kipper Kids at The Kitchen, New York in November 1979: 'As the evening progressed, the pair exhibited mock colostomy bags [polythene sacs of chocolate syrup, sliced open with razor blades], indulged in a food fight, mimed masturbation, and attacked each other with broken bottles, all the while fluttering their fingers, jiggling their balloon "udders", and taunting each other with baboonish raspberries.'[1] For all their visceral excess, puerility and jeering nonsensicality, the Kipper Kids are savvy in their critical gestures. For Robert Riley, their performances stage 'a symbol of the struggle between independence and conformity', and deploy 'unwarranted hostility and affectionate compatibility' as a critique of gender norms.[2] For Peter Clothier, their work is 'gross, obscene, irreverent and unbeautiful. It is a deliberate and unremitting distortion of the niceties of our social behaviour, our beliefs, our intimacies, and our art into the grotesque', suggesting a critical refusal of normative relations, emotions and aesthetic conventions.[3]

The Kipper Kids formed in 1971, after meeting in 1970 at East 15 Acting School in East London. From 1971 to 1974, they performed in the UK (where they were based) and in Europe, at universities, arts centres and theatres – and, strikingly, as part of the cultural events programmed at the Summer Olympics in Munich in 1972 (the occasion of the Munich Massacre, where 12 people were assassinated by the terrorist organisation Black September). While in the UK, they contributed to a vibrant scene of experimental artists working in rowdy, uncompromising and wild performances including COUM Transmissions, Anne Bean, Ian Hinchliffe, Bruce Lacey and Jeff Nuttall. The Kipper Kids emigrated to Los Angeles in 1974, on the advice of museum curator David A. Ross, who organised a number of events in California after seeing their performance at the Rudolf Zwirner Gallery in Cologne in 1973. They remained in the USA for several decades (Routh returned to the UK in 2003).

Their first work in the USA took place in December 1974, and was the inaugural performance at the now-defunct Los Angeles Institute of Contemporary Arts (LAICA). They cemented a profile as major performance artists in California, influencing other artists and the thriving Los Angeles punk scene. For Jonathan Furmanski, the Kipper Kids created 'the transgressive postminimal anti-aesthetic' in performance art, which gained further critical acknowledgement in the work of peers including Paul McCarthy, Mike Kelley and Tony Oursler.[4] After a number of incursions into TV and film in the late 1980s, the Kipper Kids' collaboration become more erratic, and they disbanded after a series of high-profile reunion performances in 2002 and 2003. I interviewed Brian Routh and Martin Von Haselberg separately, in Leicester and New York, respectively, in August and September 2014. Across the two interviews, they discuss their origins, contexts, anti-aesthetic sensibilities and idiosyncratic process – and narrate the excesses of their works and lives, with an emphasis on their prodigious propensities towards sabotage.

Part I: An Interview with Harry Kipper, aka Brian Routh

Dominic Johnson: *How did Harry Kipper come about?*

Brian Routh: Harry Kipper came about in Frankfurt railway station in the early hours of the morning in 1970. We had both been on an acid trip, while staying in the flat of a German psychoanalyst who was a friend of Martin – the other Kipper Kid. Martin and he started getting into a weird dialogue that got scary. For the sake of comic relief I became this very loud character, and Martin became a character, and we just couldn't stop. We walked to Frankfurt railway station, where we became fully engrossed in this rapport that we had made together. The name just came out of our mouths: the Kipper Kids. At first, we had different names – one of us was Harry and the other was Alf – but we could never remember who was who, so we just called each other Harry, and it stuck. We would be Kipper Kids in the street, in the pub, and at parties. *We couldn't turn it off.* We tried to get away from one another, even at parties, but as the Kipper Kids we were enmeshed. After that, we started thinking about putting it in some sort of theatrical context.

DJ: *What were your first public performances as the Kipper Kids?*

BR: The first thing we ever did was after seeing Gilbert and George do their first live performance at the Nigel Greenwood Gallery in London [*Underneath the Arches/Singing Sculptures*, 1970].[5] Our first gig was at Chelsea College of Science and Technology, in London, in 1971, and after that we got a gig at the Olympics in Munich in 1972. For two weeks during the Olympics, we did street theatre on a little stage that went out into the lake on Spielsstrasse. There were three of us performing, actually – the third person being a visual artist called Malcolm Jones. We just ad libbed as Kipper Kid characters. It was very easy to do. It's almost pantomime in a way.

DJ: *How did you progress? Was there an established context for your work?*

BR: The Olympics was the start of it, and we just carried on from there. In the 1970s we performed all over Europe, and in North Africa [Tabarka, Tunisia, 1973] – mostly at theatre festivals. At that time there was a lot of interesting theatre around, like Pip Simmons Theatre Group, Bread and Puppet Theatre, and the guy who put the ferret down his trousers – the Ken Campbell Roadshow; so there was a context of sorts for what we were doing. We made contacts at the Olympics, and we starting getting gigs. In the early years, until 1974, even though we were based in London, a lot of our shows were in Germany. We often had long runs – sometimes six nights a week, for up to three months, doing the same show over and over again. The contexts for our work changed all the time. We were in a no man's land, really – between art and theatre – so we often did things in pubs, nightclubs and festivals.

Figure 3.1   The Kipper Kids, untitled performance (Venice Fire House, 1977). Photograph by Roger Webster. © The Kipper Kids. Courtesy of Martin Von Haselberg

We pretty much did the same show for the entire number of years we performed. Sometimes we veered off and did experimental stuff, but otherwise we did the same piece with variations and additions. In theatres, we got into a lot of problems, partly because we always ended with a boxing match. (See **Figure 3.1**.) I'd box myself, and Martin would be the referee, and we sometimes swapped roles. My nose bleeds very easily. Of course, repeatedly punching yourself in the face and bleeding seems very dramatic, and people would walk out, or be shocked or angry. These dramaturges would insist that theatre is about pretending, not about realism. I didn't know enough about it to argue with them then, but we knew there had to be other options, other possibilities.

DJ: *What were your first works in a visual art setting?*

BR: The first was at the Rudolf Zwirner Gallery in Cologne [1973]. It was a pretty wild show. After that show, David Ross, who was a curator at the Long Beach Museum, invited us to the US. We moved to Los Angeles in 1974 and I stayed in the US for nearly 30 years.

DJ: *You said you more or less repeated and modified the same piece. In terms of process, how did the shape of the performance come about?*

BR: Up to the time we returned to Munich – a year after the Olympics – when we had a long run in a theatre [in 1973], we had been just doing any old thing, really. There was no set structure. Munich was supposed to be a two-week run, but they liked us, so they extended it. We started off in the big theatre and ended up in the little theatre across the street, and we developed the show into something much more substantial. We had a birthday ceremony, a tea ceremony, a food ceremony, the boxing match, a music ceremony where we played instruments and sang, and so on. We added more elements as we went along. During the run, we repeated it over and over, and we decided what worked and what didn't, until it felt like we had a tight performance.

We found props in the street, or in thrift stores, and incorporated them into our act. One day we found this weird dried flower sticking out of a trashcan in Germany, and next to it, a black doll with gold earrings, and a plastic gold saxophone. It was a pretty strange collection of found objects. They became props. In the birthday ceremony we had squeaking party horns, balloons, a bread roll, and identical rubber ducks that we hid behind our backs and gave each other as birthday presents. Everything we did came out of a series of suitcases – each suitcase contained the ingredients for a single ceremony. I think we decided each ceremony should come out of a suitcase because we were travelling so much. Each ceremony was like a little event in itself.

DJ: *When did the signature Kipper Kid look come about?*

BR: That came about pretty much right away – around 1972. I always drew cartoons and made comic books, and the Kipper Kids were characters I drew, with big noses and chins, spectacles, and cartoon stubble. At first we just drew dots on our whitened faces, for stubble, and painted on a little moustache and glasses. Later, I also made latex-rubber noses and big prosthetic chins. Some were particularly big. We played with it, but the basic look stayed pretty constant from the mid-1970s.

DJ: *Did you rehearse?*

BR: We never rehearsed, no.

DJ: *Were you often drunk when you performed?*

BR: Yes. Actually, the best shows were the ones in bars and the clubs – after the official show, if you like. We would get so liber-ated by the work that we'd go out afterwards and just go completely crackers. I don't drink now at all – I haven't done for a number of years. But in the 1970s and 1980s, I definitely became an alcoholic as a result of the amount of drink we consumed in and around the performances. We always had a bottle of whisky or vodka as part of the show. We were influenced by the writings of [G. I.] Gurdjieff – we just read the back covers of Gurdjieff books, rather than the actual content [laughs]. That's not strictly true, but it feels like the Kipper Kids' understanding of philosophy could only be very frivolous, or slightly shallow. Gurdjieff taught a Stop Exercise – people move around and someone says 'stop', and you'd freeze and take account of yourself, physically and emotionally – until someone released you from the exercise by saying 'enough'. So we incorporated that into the show – but when we stopped, we grabbed a cup that was hanging from the ceiling, and drank a cup of whisky each.

By the end of the show, by the boxing match, I was always completely drunk. I couldn't really feel how hard I was hitting myself, and I was always getting black eyes. After a month of doing that in Munich, during the extended run, I told Martin I couldn't do it any more. I couldn't keep hitting myself. Partly, our act was very abusive. There was a lot of self-abuse – but also abuse directed towards each other, and to the audience. That's probably why we stopped doing it after a while. It was just too much – the physical violence, but also the drinking. I'm sure it did us a lot of harm. I couldn't keep up that level of intensity over a period of years with-out taking breaks from each other – sometimes for five years. Then we'd get back together and do another performance.

DJ: *As a character or alter ego, it sounds like Harry Kipper was hard to turn off. Was that the case?*

BR: It was extremely hard to turn off. Sometimes it's still hard to turn off now. If I am in a public situation, I can instantly become a Kipper Kid. Maybe it's a way to deal with shyness or being afraid of social activities. I'm reclusive. When I lived in New York, people would ask me how I could be drunk and in character all the time. Well, yeah, when they saw me I was, but in between I was probably hiding behind the door of my apartment. I worked for the Mayor of New York, in his house, so I had to keep it together between shows. I

wasn't a Kipper Kid all the time – just periodically. But it was definitely very hard to turn off.

DJ: *Can you tell me about collaborations? You collaborated with Anne
Bean on various occasions, for example.*

BR: We did a lot of performances with Anne in the 1970s and 1980s.
We didn't do many collaborations with other artists. The only collaboration that seemed to work was with Anne. It felt like we were all
siblings or something. We were the naughty boys and she could put
us in our place. She did a show in Hamburg, as Moody and the
Menstruators, and invited us to participate. I remember she sang, and
we had to stand on stage in our outfits, with our penises hanging out
of our flies. The theatre was so outraged that they wouldn't allow us
back on stage. We also performed a dream she had, at Milkweg, in
Amsterdam [1972]. I remember the audience lying about on cush-
ions, getting stoned, and this guy saying to us, 'Oh God, what does
it all mean?' I didn't know what to tell him. It was a dream. We did
a lot of musical things with Anne in LA too, after 1974. I'd play the
ukulele and Martin would play the saxophone, both completely out
of tune. We did the Whisky a Go Go in LA, where Martin played the
bongos and I played the electric guitar – we did Velvet Underground
songs, and rewrote the words, so instead of *Heroin*, I'd sing
Haemorrhoids, in a Scottish accent. We did some other collaborative
shows with friends, for example in a group called Bernsteins in the
early 1970s.[6] But being able to collaborate with other people was
always a problem. Martin and I had such a tight connection that it
was very hard to make more room for other people to share the relationship, or enter into the conversation.

DJ: *You said that an audience member wanted to know 'what does it all
mean'. Were you thinking about the way meaning was produced in your
work?*

BR: Not at all. I wouldn't say anything we did was conscious, apart
from deciding on what props to use, and where to put them, and
how to build the set, things like that. We certainly thought through,
designed and set up these elements. We rigged pulleys that emptied
buckets of paint on us, or that released sneezing powder into the
audience. You could say a lot of it was like practical jokes. I don't
want to undermine what we did by saying it had no meaning,
because obviously it does – but we were impotent performers; our
characters were just free-flowing within a structure we had set up.

When people asked us what our work meant, I wouldn't be able to tell them. We didn't conceive of the work in order to make an explicit comment on, say, social mannerisms, or social niceties. However, a lot of it was probably connected to that, though, because we made and performed ceremonies in our work; and we did observe a lot of people, and imitate them – we'd mimic the way people communicate in secret, or as couples. But in terms of what it *meant*? It would probably be like asking Spike Milligan to explain what his work meant. It just wasn't a relevant question. We were so engrossed in being Kipper Kids that it would have been very hard to stand back and say, well, it means this or that. It definitely wasn't conceptual art, that's for sure.

DJ: *Was the objective to make audiences laugh?*

BR: Yeah, definitely. That was one objective, for sure – to make people laugh.

DJ: *I think that's unusual in a performance art context.*

BR: Yes. To be honest, I don't think we set out to be performance artists. We didn't think about our act in terms of where it fit, or what genre it belonged to. We just wanted to be the character, and we wanted to perform. We'd start a performance, get deeper into it, and build it up. Hammed it up, if you like.

DJ: *Were you ever censored?*

BR: No, not explicitly. But I suppose we had … some problems. We performed at Danceteria in New York [in 1980] and did the boxing ceremony, and I got blood all over the stage curtains. The guy who ran it didn't want to pay us, so we threatened to beat him up. He paid us in the end, but he was so angry, and obviously we'd never have been booked again. There was something about us that could be particularly upsetting for people. They often had a really hard time accepting us. Maybe it's because we were never cool.

DJ: *Were you deliberately uncool?*

BR: Oh yeah, definitely. Of course!

DJ: *What was at stake in that?*

BR: When people play it cool, they take themselves too seriously. The beginning of the 1970s was still the hippie era. It was peace, love and happiness, and people were doing performances like handing out joss sticks, burning incense, and unrolling strips of white paper. What we did was *very* different. But the whole crux of our work was that we enjoyed ourselves, and our enjoyment rubbed off on our audiences.

DJ: *You mentioned the aggressive or violent aspects of the Kipper Kids. Where did the violence come from?*

BR: Well, in my case I think a lot of it had to do with my childhood. I grew up in Gateshead in the 1950s, and it was an incredibly violent place. It was awful. I hated it. As a child, I had a very strong stutter. I was very nervous, and I was terrified most of the time I lived there. I suppose you could argue that a lot of the violence came – for me personally – out of being repressed and suppressed. Performance was a release for me, in a way. With Martin, it was different; he grew up in a very straight-laced, upper-crust and politically liberal household. For him, it was probably a way to react against that.

DJ: *The aggression was directed to the audience too. Why?*

BR: We'd frequently abuse the audience. They'd be completely covered in food and indelible paint. People would turn up with rain-coats and umbrellas in the front row because they knew what was going to happen. It was a sign of the times, I guess. Shakespeare wrote that 'conscience does make cowards of us all' – there was some element of that, as I got older, because I don't really want to be abusive towards people, or to have an audience, any more.

DJ: *Was there a sense of wanting to exceed any kind of limitation placed on the work?*

BR: Yeah, I think so. Sometimes it backfired on us. At LAICA in Los Angeles [1974], our show was disrupted. Earlier in the week, we'd been invited to CalArts [California Institute of the Arts, Valencia] as guest artists, and two students asked me if I'd be in their performance with them. The students' performance was really lame, and I got completely drunk and was spraying myself with paint and stuff. I infringed on their work. So, one of the students decided she'd infringe on our performance at LAICA. She and a male student got into the middle of our set – the boxing ring – and they kissed. It was silly. But Martin was doing the boxing that night, and had the gloves on, and he punched the man through the middle of the ring. It became a big deal. There were only a few times we were disrupted. In 1980, we opened for Public Image Limited [the band] in the Olympic

Auditorium in LA, and people didn't get what we were doing at all. People starting throwing things and spitting at us, so we started throwing firecrackers and beer cans into the crowd, and I set a fire extinguisher off on them, things like that. It was a free-for-all. I don't consider that a successful piece of work, even though it might have been enjoyable to someone watching. It was hard for me to see it from another point of view. Especially with a black eye afterwards ...

DJ: *It sounds like there's a tension between being out of control, on the one hand, and wanting the work to be structured in some way, or contained.*

BR: I think so, yeah. We had a structure, and a set, and an agreed number of ceremonies to work through. We could be out of control while still being aware of what's going on, and able to do it. You're doing the performance, but you're also outside it, somewhere else. It's almost transcendent – it was very much a cathartic ritual in that sense, and this heightened the experience. *Transcendence is a hard target to keep aiming for, though* – it's impossible to maintain. Sometimes it works, and sometimes it fails. That's where our work differed from theatre.

DJ: *Especially in the US, you performed frequently in museums and other establishment art spaces. Were you conscious of intervening into art institutions or the market?*

BR: No, not really. We were trying to cross over. We even tried to sell out. We did a couple of movies for Cinemax and HBO, like *K.O. Kippers* [dir. Miroslav Janek, Cinemax, 1988]. I remember lying in the trailer with Martin, on location in Mexico, wearing our make-up and costumes, and we were like, 'Yeah, we're going to make this movie, and we'll be rich!' But we never could, partly because we would always sabotage ourselves. It wasn't a strategy – we just couldn't help it. We would try to be nice to somebody, because they were a curator or a producer, but we would end up pouring our drinks over their head, or something. *Harry Kipper sabotaged everything.* There's a part of me that thought it would be nice to have money coming in, a bit of security, to not have to worry about making ends meet, and just do your work – and another part is hell-bent on making that impossible, because Harry Kipper would come along and just completely trash everything.

DJ: *When you mentioned K.O. Kippers, you immediately described it as a 'sell-out'. Was there more to your forays into TV and film?*

BR: Yes, I think so. Firstly, I wouldn't say I've ever really lived off my work. We did make some money when we did things for TV, but it's always been a labour of love. I've always had to go out and do regular jobs to support it. I like that in a way, because it keeps your work free from having to fit specific criteria.

K.O. *Kippers* was the first movie we made. It was actually quite good. We had a great director [Miroslav Janek], and the DP was good, too [Director of Photography, Eric Engler]. I was actually proud of that movie. It holds up as a piece of work. So that wasn't so much a 'sell-out', because we genuinely wanted to do it. We did another TV movie for HBO called *Mum's Magic Mulch* [1990], though, and that was pretty awful. Our director, Stephen R. Johnson, also directed the *Sledgehammer* video [1986] for Peter Gabriel, and we thought he'd be great because he was familiar with animation, and we saw Harry Kipper as a living cartoon. Creatively, we left everything to him, whereas with *K.O. Kippers* we had horrible arguments with the director all the way through, to get what we wanted. The result was really lame. The music was awful, too. Everything about *Mum's Magic Mulch* was awful. HBO didn't even show it. It was shelved.

I think at that point we really were thinking about selling out. We tried to. We were always interested in doing something that was more accessible. We started around the time as Monty Python [*Monty Python's Flying Circus* aired on television between 1969–74], so it felt like there could be an opportunity to reach a much larger audience. We wanted to do something artistic, and experimental, but powerful and impressive at the same time. But the production companies had different ambitions for us. HBO wanted us to be Abbott and Costello. They really didn't get what we were doing at all. So we couldn't sell out. It just didn't work.

DJ: *You mentioned solo shows. Were the solo shows just when you were having breaks from the Kipper Kids?*

BR: By 1980, the Kipper Kids had really stopped performing together actively. It sort of came to an end. We both got married, and drifted apart, and we would come together to do 'reunion' shows, in a way. I didn't want to wait around. I had to put myself out there and do things. I did solo pieces in Europe, and in California, also I did collaborations with other artists – especially when I was living in New York. I performed in alternative spaces with Karen Finley, 'The Alien Comic' Tom Murrin, Johanna Went, Ethyl Eichelberger and Eric

Bogosian, for example, and that was always as Harry Kipper, but separate from the Kipper Kids.

DJ: *The last 'reunion' show that you did together was at the National Review of Live Art, 2003. Was there a deliberate decision not to do the Kipper Kids again after that?*

BR: No, I don't think so. We just phased out. At *A Short History of Performance* (Part One, 2002), at the Whitechapel, Stuart Brisley was asked during the question-and-answer period why he participated, and he said, 'because I was asked'. I think that's the crux of it. When you become an older artist, you don't get asked to do things as much. You're not knocking down doors like when you were younger, and you don't get invited as much either. That said, I don't think I could do anything like a Kipper Kids performance again. I would never say *never* – but it would be hard for me to go out there and do it. I prefer working in the studio now.

DJ: *In your current solo studio work – video performances, and sound pieces using political speech and your own sound design – Harry Kipper seems to crop up, in your affectations, gestures and inflections.*

BR: Harry Kipper definitely comes out in my videos, and in some ways it's a reaction to the culture I live in, especially in Yorkshire [he lived in Hull, West Yorkshire, from 2003 until recently]. There's a preponderance of northern English accents in the Kipper Kids – our voices were mostly northern, I think. It was very hard for me to live in the North and not become the people I saw walking around, with the voices, and the big chins – because, you know, a lot of Yorkshire people have got big jaws. I'd travel on the bus and make a video of myself, being silly, talking to myself, and I'd revert to being a Kipper Kid. I can't help it.

DJ: *Where is Harry Kipper now?*

BR: Well, I think he's always inside me. He's always there. I think he stops me taking myself too seriously. I can be an intense person, and I know there's a tendency for me to be too solemn if I'm left to my own devices – bordering on depression. I think Harry's always there to bring comic relief to myself, especially if I'm in a situation where I can let rip, like on a train, or in a supermarket, or walking down Oxford Street. It's like that episode of *All Creatures Great and Small* [an English TV series of the 1970s and 1980s], where one of the farmers says to James Herriot [*in a Northern accent:*], 'I went to Darrowby last week, people walking on't sidewalks, I didn't know how to walk; big steps, little uns … .' In a certain situation I get lost inside myself too – but the Kipper Kid is a way out.

I used to do performances on the boardwalk in LA, on my own. I'd dress up, play the ukulele, sing, or whatever. I went down to the boardwalk and got set up. One side of my face was gold and one side was silver. I had a bow tie on, and a suit. I started performing, and I became incredibly depressed. I got the worst, most horrible headache, a migraine, and I sat crumpled on the bench with my face buried in my hands. I sat there for the longest time, and when I looked up, there was an audience gathered round me. I had to get out of there. I panicked. Harry Kipper usually helps me break through my feeling of gloom. The character is therapeutic, in a way. But there are times when I just can't do it. That was an instance right there, on the boardwalk. I just couldn't work through the stage fright, or the depression, and I just had to run away. But Harry Kipper will always be a part of me. *Always.* He's definitely someone who brightens up my day. And other people's too, I hope – that is, if he isn't pissing them off.

Part II: An Interview with Harry Kipper aka Martin Von Haselberg

Dominic Johnson: *As a character or alter ego, Harry Kipper is unique, not least in terms of sharing a single character across two bodies. Were you attempting to share an identity?*

Martin Von Haselberg: Well, Brian and I didn't have similar identities apart from when we were being Harry Kipper. We were otherwise very different in temperament, and in every other way, yet we would have this experience of synchronicity.

Brian and I met at East 15 Acting School within the first week of starting there, and we immediately started playing around with accents, and pulling faces, things like that, and we had lots of ideas. We started doing performance pieces at drama school, without really having any knowledge of prior performance art. We were thrown out – I like to say it was an experimental drama school and we were thrown out for being too experimental. The character started in Frankfurt, when we took acid together, and at the tail end of the trip we were standing in the street, at about five o'clock in the morning. We were doing different characters, and suddenly there was a palpable sense of the two characters becoming completely synchronised, so that we became utterly identical. That was the birth of the Kipper Kids.

Harry Kipper was constant. It actually became kind of a nuisance, because we would be triggered by anything – an expression, a gesture, a movement … [*MVH does a Harry Kipper face and grunt*], we'd immediately go into character. It became quite irritating after a while. After Frankfurt we travelled to Bochum and Paris. By Paris, we were getting really sick of it, but we couldn't turn it off.

DJ: *How did the first live performances come about?*

MVH: The first professional performance we did was at Chelsea in 1971. We didn't really know what to do, so we created a set and assumed that if we just stayed inside it, and did whatever we were doing, soon enough the character would surface, and we would become the Kipper Kids. That didn't really work in that instance, so we created a series of ceremonies. In a way, on stage we never really experienced the Kipper Kid as the phenomenon of the identical character – not in the way we did when we were just together with each other, when we were walking in the street or, doing things where there was no prescribed setting.

After that, I started getting us bookings. The first one was at the Olympic Games in Munich in 1972. But to get it we had to provide press cuttings and a bio, which we didn't have. I arranged for us to have photographs taken, and I had somebody else write a review of the Kipper Kids. A friend who worked in a printing press set it out to look like a review from the *Observer*. We got the gig.

DJ: *Did you find a context for yourselves when you returned to London?*

MVH: First we spent a long time travelling all over Europe. When we did return to London, we did a show in a pub called the Lamb and Flag. It was a lunchtime theatre. We had it for a week and we set up our set, and we invited the British Council to come and see it, because we wanted to get a travel grant. Naturally, being from an acting school, we applied to the theatre department. This woman came from the British Council, and she was the only audience member. We tried to cancel the show, but she said she'd come all this way to see us. So we did the entire show, just for her. Afterwards, we got cleaned up and asked her what she thought, and she replied, 'I can't be responsible for wasting the British taxpayer's money on rubbish like this.' That was the end of theatre for us. Someone suggested we reapply to the visual arts department, and they immediately gave us a grant. That moved us officially out of theatre and into the art world, which turned out to be much more interesting.

DJ: *In the exhibition catalogue for* Rituals of Rented Island *at the Whitney, J. Hoberman describes the Kipper Kids as 'pure entertainment'.*[7] *Is that accurate? Is that something that you identify with the work?*

MVH: I'm not sure of the exact implications of 'pure entertainment'. Does it mean saccharine, Disney-like entertainment? Or is the implication that there's an *edge* that's missing? If so, I reject that. There was certainly a lot of edge and a distinct sense of danger when we would do our shows, not just for the audience, but for each other, through physical injuries and things like that. We wanted to entertain but – I don't want to sound too pompous – we also wanted to *wake people up*. We did things to shock the audience – not just in the obvious ways, but through the use of syncopation, surprises, abrupt changes of atmosphere or light, or sudden loud noises. I do think we liked the idea of being more entertaining than other performance artists, especially those we subsequently saw, whose work we didn't tend to find entertaining at all. We certainly didn't want to be *cerebral*. I don't think we're capable of it anyway.

DJ: *The Kipper Kids refused conventional ways of experiencing art. Were you actively engaging with an anti-aesthetic sensibility?*

MVH: We definitely wanted to reject not just *aesthetic* conventions, but conventions of any kind. Yet what we were doing was also a kind of parody of convention – like our tea ceremony. It was inspired by the Buddhist tea ceremony, but it was also informed by the English working-class ritual of drinking tea. So much of what we did was rooted in appearing to use traditional symbols – tea, boxing, birthday parties, and so on – but we used them in the service of parodying traditional aesthetics. I think we created our own aesthetic. We would always really stringently avoid doing anything that smacked of being part of an existing movement. This probably resulted in us never really being considered part of the art world either. We always remained outsiders.

DJ: *Do you think there was an aspect of self-sabotage?*

MVH: In terms of a career – a potentially successful career in the art world – yes, we were constantly sabotaging ourselves.

Figure 3.2 The Kipper Kids, untitled performance (The Kitchen, 1979). Photographer unknown. © The Kipper Kids. Courtesy of Martin Von Haselberg

DJ: *In terms of process, you devised a set of actions and styles, and repeated versions of the same work across the career of the Kipper Kids. Can you say something about the process leading up to each event, how the repetition came about?*

MVH: We could never remember or figure out who came up with the germ of the idea for anything we did, whether it was the tea ceremony, the boxing match, or the birthday ceremony, or the silly things like the five-finger exercise, or the tightrope walk. They each arose out of being Kipper Kids together – playing about – and we would formalise them into a performance piece, into a ceremony.

I think the reason we kept doing the same performance over and over was partially to do with laziness. But another reason was an interest in seeing how the ceremonies and the performance as a whole could change over time. It wasn't exactly repetition, though, as everything we did involved improvisation. There was no rehearsal, so we were always open to opportunities to surprise each other, and we always had to remind each other what we were supposed to be doing – like, 'No, Martin, you're supposed to pick up the spoon with the right hand.'

I also found it cosy to do the same show over and over. There was something wonderfully sweet about putting on the same costume, night after night, even though it was completely encrusted with blood, and piss, and ketchup, and whatever else. I still have the same old boots, jockstraps and Boy Scout costumes we wore for every show. The Scout costumes are almost rock-hard now – they can practically stand up by themselves!

DJ: *How much freedom was there for you both to improvise? Were there any limits – even implicit ones – placed on what you could or couldn't do in performance?*

MVH: We always had a specific plan or sequence, and a specific way each ceremony was supposed to be performed. That was a kind of limit. The improvisation was often verbal. Or we'd improvise in the form of new noises, or repetitions of things we overheard in the street, or we would respond to somebody shouting from the audience or throwing stuff at us. We'd turn on the audience, and whatever resulted from those interruptions would prompt new improvisations.

The way of performing each ceremony initially came from an earlier improvisation, and became more and more polished through repetition, so that there was a right way of doing it and a wrong way of doing it. In our tea ceremony, for example, there was a right way of taking the teacup, and standing, and holding it, and addressing the little Buddha statue we used as part of the ceremony. It was like Zen archery, where there's a right way to fire the arrow at the bull's eye, and a wrong way – a wrong *attitude* or pose.

DJ: *What was the difference, do you think, between a show that went well and a show that didn't? Or is that an irrelevant distinction?*

MVH: No, it's an important distinction. A show that went well was one where everything was done correctly, and where we had intuitive timing with each other – where it *clicked*. Shows that weren't good were ones where we never got into the spirit of it, or where we didn't connect with the audience. That would happen. Strangely enough, the shows that were really good were often the ones where we hadn't seen each other for a long time. For example, we did a show at the Whitechapel Gallery for *A Short History of Performance* [Part One, 2002]. I don't think we'd performed together for more than ten years. It was a really good performance – one of the best we ever did. We came together in London after such a long time. We collected the props and everything else we'd need, and built the set, and it was as if we'd last performed it the day before. We got into the boxing ring, and it was just perfect, the timing, our responses. It was exhilarating. It was as if, across the decades, we had been practising, and practising, and the resulting performance were greater than the sum of its parts.

DJ: *What was useful about ceremonies as a structure for the work?*

MVH: Initially we simply tried to create a situation that would allow the Kipper Kid to emerge, so the character would perform the actions we had scripted. We weren't interested in constructing a narrative, so the ceremonies afforded us a structure. We could be responsive, too, as we could do smaller shows consisting of a few ceremonies, or bigger shows with all of the ceremonies strung together. But there's also something else to it, I think – when the performance went well, the ceremonies really allowed us to control the audience. We could really play the audience like an instrument. We could become very quiet and draw them in, and then suddenly startle them with something explosive. In that way, the ceremonies were an ideal vehicle.

DJ: *You pioneered the use of food and mess in performance. Where do you think the use of food and the creation of mess came from?*

MVH: It came about for a number of reasons. In 1973, we met Hermann Nitsch, one of the Viennese Actionists. We were in Munich, doing a six-week run at the Modernes Theater [in 1973]. Around the same time, we participated in one of Nitsch's ritual actions, where he used animal blood, carcasses and entrails. After that, we created a little parody and called it *Hermann*, which included parsley and ketchup. We were always interested in colour, so the red of the ketchup against the green of the parsley was a good combination, to which we added white toothpaste. Some time later, we were at Nitsch's house and his wife had cooked this wonderful dinner for us. We were sitting in their kitchen, ready to dig in, and all of a sudden, Brian started pouring the entire dinner over himself. Nitsch and his wife loved it.

After that, we added a food ceremony to our shows, and we chose foods as our materials for their colour or consistency. We'd use flour, and eggs, and tinned spaghetti, and they were chosen because of how they poured and stuck to our bodies and costumes. The food ceremony doesn't just use foods – we also used glitter, ink, and fluorescent paints, for example. We chose actions or movements that complemented the materials, whether it was twirling, or standing stationary, or pretending we were about to hit each other, or threatening the audience. To top off the ceremony, we'd squirt a tall pile of shaving foam on each other's heads, and carefully insert firecrackers, and light them – they'd explode out of the foam.

I think the way that we used food is misinterpreted as being about food itself. I don't think it's about food at all, but about the visual effect of using surprising materials. Eggs are great because they're small and contained, they smash, and they're sticky and yellow. Flour is really effective on stage – it gets everywhere and creates clouds that pick up the light – but it could just as well have been another white powder, like talc. Spaghetti-Os are good because you can see the little *o*'s in the mess, and the sauce has a deep colour and thick consistency. We'd use spinach, and cream, and cranberry jelly – but some other substance could just as well have been used instead. I don't think the emphasis on food is very useful, and unfortunately it's a misinterpretation that follows us around.

DJ: *Earlier, you said the work wasn't 'cerebral'. Were you trying explicitly to avoid being cerebral? And what kinds of cerebral processes took place regardless?*

MVH: I think we were always keen to avoid the cerebral because it meant we could steer clear of taking ourselves too seriously. We would poke fun at artists who we thought were taking themselves very seriously, and in a way that's why we were *perpetual outsiders*. We could never be taken up by curators, whose language is completely cerebral. We have remained outsider artists, in a sense.

When we talked privately with each other, we did talk about why we thought the work was significant to us, but less so in terms of what it meant, or why each aspect was important. We both have an interest in spiritual growth. So, even though the shows would be totally primal, rowdy, and maybe even stupid, in a sense we were practising a kind of spiritual ritual, to advance our own awareness. We wouldn't have made this too explicit at the time, not least because it would have looked like we were taking ourselves – and our work – far too seriously. It wouldn't have fit the Kipper Kid character.

DJ: *Were you also interested in the audience in the same way, in term of their spiritual growth? Do you think it translates to how the audience experiences the work?*

MVH: I hope so, but I don't think we really considered that, or talked about it. We were more interested in ourselves, and each other, and what we were experiencing – rather than thinking 'what might this mean for the audience?'

DJ: *What were the relations between you and other artists in the UK in the 1970s?*

MVH: From the time that we started in 1972, when we really started doing it professionally, we weren't really in the UK that much, as we did most of our shows in Europe, especially in Amsterdam, Berlin and Hamburg. And then in 1974 we went to America. We would come back occasionally, but we did very little in England.

DJ: *When you moved to Los Angeles in 1974, I can imagine relations to artists who were working there at the same time, like Chris Burden, Paul McCarthy, Johanna Went or Kim Jones. Did you find a context for yourself as an artist in LA at that time?*

MVH: You know, I have to say that we were always arrogant bastards. As artists, we never really wanted anything to do with anybody else. And if there were people we were interested in, they didn't want anything to do with us. In London, I remember someone saying we should meet Gilbert and George. When this person tried to arrange a meeting, Gilbert and George were like, 'please keep those pricks away from us'. I was drawn to Chris Burden's work in the 1970s, but he had *zero* interest in the Kipper Kids. From his perspective, I can see why. We can seem sloppy and out of control. We don't have a tightly delivered message, whereas his performances were always conceptual, distilled, and extremely powerful. For us, some things hit and some things missed, and you sort of came away not really knowing what you got from it. Brian and I kept different friends. He knew and worked with Johanna Went. I knew Paul McCarthy and Kim Jones – they never said much to me, but we had quiet respect for each other.

DJ: *You were in LA when it was an epicentre for punk. What is the relation between the Kipper Kids and punk?*

MVH: It's a relationship we hadn't intended at all. As I said, we didn't want to be part of any movement. We were considered to be part of early LA punk – we were known to be anarchic, so we fit right in. But we really didn't think of ourselves as punk at all.

DJ: *Violence is key to the Kipper Kids. Why?*

MVH: Harry Kipper is basically a violent character. We're very sweet with each other, but there's something aggressive about the character, which lends itself to our interactions. We also wouldn't take any shit from anybody. We picked on people. Unfortunately it was a little unfair. We did a show at the ICA in London [in 1974], where we sat facing each other, separated by two mirrors, so that we looked at our reflections. The only props were big earphones, little hand-held mirrors we could angle to see each other with, a rubber band for doing different things to our faces, and suitcases. Uniquely, somebody had designed a ceremony for us, and he made us two beautiful suitcases, with a bottle of Gordon's gin, a flask of tea, and an enamel mug, and we each proceeded to drink an entire bottle of gin, mixed with tea.

We became incredibly drunk, and when drunk we would become horribly aggressive. For some reason, I wandered off during the performance – I left the stage and started walking down the corridors of the ICA. The audience stayed in their seats, and assumed this was part of the mayhem of the performance. While wandering about, this little guy comes up and says to me, 'You know, you should go and sort things out because Brian is picking on someone in the audience.' Brian had a knack for always picking on the worst possible person – it turns out he picked on the only black guy in the audience, who he had started to taunt, verbally. At the moment this guy is telling me to go stop Brian, he appears next to me in the corridor, and I don't know why but we started beating the shit out of this guy. I seem to remember he was six inches shorter than us. He ran and got a policeman from The Mall, and came back with him, and was trying to explain to the policeman what we'd done to him. There we were, in heavy leather boots, jockstraps, and ballet tutus, with fake tits made of half-melons, and this little guy was trying to explain to the copper, 'these two guys here, they just beat me up!' The copper looked at him, he looked at us, we looked at each other, and we all just burst into laughter. The policeman left and that was the end of that.

It was the kind of crazy situation that was always happening to us. That kind of violence was always just beneath the surface, and I think it was always present, like a threat, in the performances. After we did our first show in Los Angeles [at LAICA, 1974], I'd hear from people years later that they'd left the show because they were terrified we were going to break out of the boxing ring and start beating people up.

DJ: *Do you recognise an erotic dimension in the Kipper Kids?*

MVH: Yes, but the eroticism is more of the *Carry On* film kind of eroticism, that typically English, Kenneth Williams kind of eroticism – 'ooh, get you', that sort of thing.[8] It's mostly fake eroticism. Real eroticism was there, but only potentially. If there was eroticism, it was always made fun of.

DJ: *You've mentioned various museums and galleries, like the ICA and Whitechapel. Is your aggression in some way directed against institutions?*

MVH: I don't think our aggression was ever really directed against an immediately identifiable target or victim. I think there's just something about Harry Kipper that would get our adrenaline going. No, I don't think it had anything to do with institutions.

DJ: *Were you ever censored?*

MVH: Not that I can think of, but we were always getting ourselves into deep trouble. I mean, to start with, we were thrown out of drama school. And we did things that backfired – a lot – so that we'd get kicked out of venues, and wouldn't get invited back. An extreme example happened at the Kunsthalle in Basel in 1974. During the food ceremony, we would always do an action with bags of flour. We would face the audience with our arms held back as if we were going to fling the flour into the audience. The audience would start ducking and squealing in fear, and then we'd turn away from the audience and cover each other in the flour. Well, in Basel we found ourselves throwing the flour over the audience. This was a fund-raising event in a museum, with an audience of people in fine suits and fur coats. Following the flour came a load of eggs, and paint, and ink. I remember this lady in a beautiful white mink coat, covered in food and ink. We were sued for that – for the dry-cleaning costs. One time in Los Angeles, we threw ink into the audience, and I got sued by seven different people, who for some reason were all wearing brown corduroy, yet didn't know each other. With each performance our potential options for venues was always shrinking.

DJ: *I know in the 1970s, and afterwards, Brian and yourself would do solo shows as Harry Kipper. How did that work?*

MVH: Well, Brian was always specifically interested in making work on his own. After the 1970s, the intense periods when we were doing shows together adds up to just a couple of years. The rest of the time was sporadic – Kipper Kids shows, and Brian doing performances by himself. I never really had an interest in doing solo performances – I did them, but mostly I wasn't happy with how they turned out. I always felt nothing came close to the experience of doing the Kipper Kids together.

DJ: *What was your relationship to making objects as opposed to making performances?*

MVH: In the 1970s and 1980s, I set up photo shoots for us outside of the performances. I also made videos, like *Up Yer Bum with a Bengal Lancer* [1976], which went to Documenta VI in 1977.[9] We each made our own wooden figures on which to retire the Boy Scouts costumes. We also did a show where Brian built a set of giant cartoon Kipper Kid figures, for a couple of shows at the Whisky a Go Go and Workshop IE [both in Los Angeles]. And we would always construct our own sets, like the boxing ring with creosote rope, in a way that I suppose would now be considered installation. The objects we used in the shows were mostly found. The only prop I can think of that was specifically made was a replacement for the little figure, Tomsit Profi, a found object that was central to the tea ceremony. Unfortunately, the entire tea-ceremony suitcase was stolen out of the back of Karen Finley's car, after a show in San Francisco. The original figurine had great spiritual value to us – *tongue-in-cheek value*, I must say – so Brian made a new figure for the subsequent shows. So we always had a relationship to objects, but it was mostly in the service of the live performances.

DJ: *Your final performance was at the National Review of Live Art, Glasgow, in 2003. Why was it the last?*

MVH: It's unfortunate. I daresay I'd do another performance immediately. I tried to arrange something just last year, in fact. I sent Brian an email and suggested that we do a performance in the studio, without an audience, just for each other. It's really exciting to face each other, to do the tea ceremony, for example and to experience the emotions – the intensity, the violence, and whatever else is happening underneath. And I think he misunderstood my email, but in any case it didn't work out. It has taken me a long time to get to a point where I know it's over.

DJ: *Lately your early documentation has been shown in major museum shows. How does the documentation works in those contexts?*

MVH: It doesn't work well, in the sense that we never made any effort to invite or be open to a cerebral interpretation of our work. We never cultivated relationships with curators, which, I'm realising very late in life, can effectively kill your career – certainly in America. I thought that when Paul Schimmel asked to include the Kipper Kids in the big survey show of West Coast art at MOCA [*Under the Big Black Sun: California Art 1974–1981*, Museum of Contemporary Art, Los Angeles, 2011–12], we would be quite prominently displayed, because we were influential in Los Angeles in precisely the period covered by the exhibition – definitely more so than Paul McCarthy, who was really not that visible at the time. And yet, when the show was mounted, we were allocated a small corner in a room shared with Tony Oursler (who was given equally short shrift) – right next to a huge room of Paul McCarthy's documentary photographs of his performances. We were also excluded from a previous show at MOCA called *Helter Skelter: LA Art in the 1990s* [1992]. That was a show we really belonged in, as it was about violence, and the dark side of Los Angeles – but we were studiously ignored. The Getty show [*California Video*, Getty Institute, 2008] was much better, and the curator [Glenn Phillips] had a better understanding of what the Kipper Kids had done.

One of the reasons we didn't achieve anything more substantial at MOCA is because Paul Schimmel [chief curator, 1992–1012] had an unpleasant experience with Brian in Houston in the 1970s. He had been invited to Paul's house and apparently got really drunk, pissed on the sofa, then lay down on it and went to sleep. Well, Paul Schimmel's wife didn't think it was at all funny, and essentially the Kipper Kids became *personae non gratae* as far as Paul Schimmel was concerned. Unfortunately, he subsequently rose to enormous prominence as a curator in LA. As I said, we had a tendency to self-sabotage. Brian blew that relationship, and I was the one who poured ink over the ladies in mink coats in Basel. I think we're even.

More generally, the way the Kipper Kids are received in institutions is always going to be limited, until somebody makes a scholarly study of what it is that we do. At the Whitney [*Rituals of Rented Island*, 2013], the installation was beautiful. The photographic documentation was installed in a boxing ring, just like the ones we would perform in. Yet when Holland Cotter reviewed it for the *New York Times*, he mentioned us only briefly, as 'the gross-out duo, the Kipper Kids'.[10] There was no deeper examination. It's typical of the way we're usually ignored by critics.

DJ: *Does Harry Kipper affect the way that you make work now?*

MVH: Yes – a lot. I made a series of works called *Floatulants* [2009], for example, which are distorted auto-portraits printed on large sheets of glassine, which are assembled into differently shaped balloons that I inflate with helium. The images on them, and in my paintings, all have the Kipper Kid sensibility. They are sort of masculine, and aggressive, and at the same time funny, and human. The character of the Kipper Kid is always with me – always ready to go on stage, and cause havoc, if there's an opportunity. When I paint, though, I'm not *actively* being Harry Kipper, but whatever I brought to the Kipper Kids I still bring to anything I'm working on.

DJ: *You worked as a commodities broker for many years. Was there a conflict between that and your work?*

MVH: I went to drama school after working in the city for two years, learning to be a cocoa dealer. When I arrived in LA, I needed a job, and came across an ad for commodity brokers. Essentially it was calling people up and trying to get them to part with their cash, and in LA it was all done over the phone, so it didn't matter what you wore, or what you looked like. But I did do a TV show in LA, for about 12 years, in which I appeared for 15 minutes every day, and talked about the markets, and gave advice about good investments. Sometimes I would shave my hair and I always wore really loud ties, and outlandish baggy suits from thrift stores – but I'd be talking really straight and apparently knowledgably about commodities. So while it seems like a clash, there was actually not much of a distinction, really. It was like a solo performance.

DJ: *Where is Harry Kipper now?*

MVH: I think Kipper Kids performances require an intense physicality, and that energy diminishes at a certain point in life. But where is Harry Kipper now? Well, he's there. He's here. [*In Kipper Kid voice, shouting:*] *It could be any moment!* I feel it now. *I could jump out of my seat and go berserk*. It's weird. Harry Kipper still has that effect on me. When Brian and I split, people often asked me, 'why don't you find someone else to do the Kipper Kids with?' But it's impossible. It's just really something that we have only with each other.

Notes

1.   J. Hoberman, '"Like Canyons and Rivers": Performance for Its Own Sake', in Jay Sanders with J. Hoberman, *Rituals of Rented Island: Object Theater, Loft Performance, and the New Psychodrama – Manhattan, 1970–1980*, exh. cat., Whitney Museum of American Art, New York (New Haven, CT and London: Yale University Press, 2013), pp. 9–24 (p. 23).

2.   Robert R. Riley, 'Concept, Art, and Media: Regarding California Video', in *California Video: Artists and Histories*, ed. Glenn Phillips, exh. cat., J. Paul Getty Museum (Los Angeles: Getty Research Institute, 2008), pp. 274–8 (p. 275).

3.   Peter Clothier, 'The Kipper Kids: *An Endless Ritual*' (1975), in *Performance Anthology: Source Book for a Decade of California Performance Art*, ed. Carl E. Loeffler with Darlene Tong (San Francisco: Contemporary Arts Press, 1980), p. 165 (p. 165).

4.   Jonathan Furmanski, 'The Kipper Kids', in *California Video*, pp. 134–7 (p. 134).

5.   Gilbert and George are notable as another example of a performance art duo that shares a single character or persona across two bodies.

6.   The other members were Anne Bean, Peter Davey, Chris Millar, Malcolm Jones and Jonathan Harvey.

7.   Hoberman, 'Like Canyons and Rivers', p. 22.

8.   The *Carry On* movies of the 1960s were a series of popular comic farces featuring Barbara Windsor, Hattie Jacques, Kenneth Williams and others delivering innuendo-laden lines in caricatured Cockney accents.

9. Documenta is a major international exhibition of contemporary art in Kassel, Germany. In 1977 it was curated by Manfred Schneckenburger, and included Harry Kipper (as opposed to the Kipper Kids).

10. Holland Cotter, 'Nothing to Spend, Nothing to Lose: "Rituals of Rented Island", Performance Art at the Whitney', *New York Times*, 31 October 2013, p. C25.

4   Positive Surrender: An Interview with BREYER P-ORRIDGE

'Viva la Evolution!' is a key rallying cry of BREYER P-ORRIDGE, in interviews, statements and performances. The American-born artist Lady Jaye BREYER P-ORRIDGE (formerly Lady Jaye Breyer) was a formative influence on downtown performance, as a member of Blacklips Performance Cult (with Antony Hegarty and others), and a co-founder of the House of Domination (with Marti Domination) at Jackie 60, a legendary New York club night. Since the late 1960s, Genesis BREYER P-ORRIDGE (formerly Genesis P-Orridge) has relentlessly inserted new strategies into the horizon of art and popular culture. As a founder of the British performance group COUM Transmissions, the art/music groups Throbbing Gristle and Psychic TV, and the spoken word project Thee Majesty, Genesis BREYER P-ORRIDGE has been at the forefront of British cross-disciplinary arts for four decades, and pioneered historical cultural innovations such as industrial music and body modification in the 1970s, acid house in the 1980s, and most recently, the figure of the p-androgyne.

Notoriously, the artists forwent their public identities towards a new collective subjectivity, namely the 'Third Being', a p-androgyne – or positive androgyne – that goes by the collective name BREYER P-ORRIDGE. Over a series of operations, beginning in 1999, BREYER P-ORRIDGE used cosmetic surgery, tattooing and other body modifications towards a corporeal translation of the cut-up technique of William S. Burroughs and Brion Gysin. In *Breaking Sex* (1999–2007) the two artists underwent a series of surgical procedures, including breast implants, chin, cheek and eye augmentation, dental operations and facial tattooing. *Breaking Sex* was an attempt to physically manifest 'the third mind', a concept Burroughs and Gysin invented in the 1960s to invoke the possibilities that arise from a blurring of subjective limits through a technical approximation of collage through writing. As Gérard Georges-Lemaire writes:

The Third Mind is not the history of a literary collaboration, but rather the complete fusion in a praxis of two subjectivities … that metamorphose into a third; it is from this collusion that a new author emerges, an absent third person invisibly and beyond grasp, decoding the silence.[1]

BREYER P-ORRIDGE followed, to the letter, this merging of subjectivities at the expense of a single authorial voice, producing the 'pandrogyne' (or 'p-androgyne'), a fleshy incarnation of the 'third mind'. They provocatively enacted Burroughs and Gysin's abandonment of inviolate works and artistic ownership, 'a magical or divine creativity that could only result from the unconditional integration of two sources' – in this case, the mirroring of bodies through surgical interventions.[2]

The following interview with Genesis and Lady Jaye BREYER P-ORRIDGE was conducted live at the Centre for the Study of Gender and Sexuality, New York University in April 2007. Our conversation was the keynote address to *After CBGB: Gender, Sexuality and the Future of Subculture*, a symposium that explored the possibilities for subcultural practice in an age of quickening and intensifying processes of gentrification, containment and commodification. However, their threats to traditional unities of biography and subjectivity were consolidated in disturbing ways when Lady Jaye BREYER P-ORRIDGE died, suddenly, of heart failure later the same year. During our editing process, Genesis BREYER P-ORRIDGE wrote:

Since Lady Jaye dropped her body on 9 October 2007, we dropped using 'I' in favour of 'we' to signify Lady Jaye's continued presence in our body and personality, as well as her ongoing presence in the Pandrogeny project – not just a nostalgic presence but a dynamic one as we continue to create works we co-created and proposed using photographic and other biological materials.[3]

The artists refer to themselves with traditional first pronouns in the dialogue below, but asked that I refer to them in the plural in this introduction; Genesis BREYER P-ORRIDGE also identifies in the plural in the posthumous prologue. This is not simply a methodological burden, but a sign of their insistent refusal to allow others to assimilate them and their artistic practices into convenient systems of scholarly production and critical reception.

In their innovations across the art/life divide, BREYER P-ORRIDGE explain how their *Breaking Sex* (1999–2007) complements and extends earlier solo and collaborative practices, towards new and challenging realisations in the cultural politics of live art and performance. They discuss their own perceived relations to 'Live Art', and a preference for using the terminology of 'Living Art', tying *Breaking Sex* and earlier works into the merging of art into the praxis of life.

Prologue by Genesis BREYER P-ORRIDGE

We suppose we have exaggerated a few things in terms of this project, but that's what you do – can do – in a work of fiction (thinking of Lady Jaye's life seen as a resumé). One of the first strategies Jaye proposed to me was after I complained about the tedium of doing countless repetitious interviews for different media, because of the imposed separation of literature, music, performance, art and life. S/he suggested that, instead of retelling the same story and anecdotes *ad nauseam*, that we make up different conflicting answers each time we were interviewed. Through SELF-editing, cultural, social and economic pressures and intimidations alone all lives become fictional and that is before neuroses, ambitions, paranoia and mental idiosyncrasies become part of the mix. So, as all identities are fictional, active co-authorship of our Pandrogenic narrative is an essential strategy.[4]

Dominic Johnson: *How did* Breaking Sex *come about?*

Genesis BREYER P-ORRIDGE: At the beginning of *Breaking Sex* and Pandrogeny, Lady Jaye and I saw it primarily as an incredibly romantic thing to do – to want to become each other, to look like each other. So the very first thing we did that was more or less permanent was I got two tattoos on my cheek – beauty spots matching Lady Jaye's – and she had one removed on the other cheek, so that we were beginning to make our faces superficially more the same. Then she got the shape of her eyes surgically changed so they were more like mine, and got her nose worked on to make it like mine. Lady Jaye and I both got breast implants three years ago on Valentine's Day 2003 and we woke up together in the room where you come back from being under the anaesthetic, and we held hands, and as I looked down I found myself saying, 'Oh, these are our angelic bodies.' I found it really interesting that I could go to sleep and when

Figure 4.1   BREYER P-ORRIDGE, *Untitled* (2006). Photograph by Laure Leber.
© BREYER P-ORRIDGE. Courtesy of the artist and Invisible Exports, New York

I woke up I would not recognise the person in the mirror in the same way. (See **Figure 4.1**).

I'm just a basic heterosexual, which confuses people because it's much less common for heterosexuals to be transgender. And I'm not fully accepted by the transgender community because they don't understand why it would be an art project. We really are investigating the idea of evolution. We're challenging DNA and refusing to accept it as the programming that controls our biological life. I am a p-androgyne – a positive androgyne. A hermaphrodite by choice. Pandrogeny is a suggestion or strategy for the survival of the species. In some ways all the different projects – even the music – are about challenging the status quo in order to change. I think change should be inclusive of other people, not exclusive.

DJ: *You've often discussed your relation to William S. Burroughs, Brion Gysin and Derek Jarman, for example. How important is it to connect yourself to histories of cultural experimentation?*

GBPO: People feel a kinship with what BREYER P-ORRIDGE have been doing in our various incarnations. It was the same for me when I was young in the 1960s, and I'm sure for Lady Jaye in her time. There are certain people, certain movements, usually suppressed ways of seeing the world, different ways of perceiving reality that shine like beacons because they contradict everything that's being pushed into you by the so-called normal world. I went to a very authoritarian British school that actually had a statement in their manifesto that said that art was not a real subject – parents were expected to be glad that teachers didn't waste their time teaching us anything to do with literature or art. For whatever reasons I'm perverse and that made me want to look at literature and art as much as I could. So there was an attraction to previous manifestations of rebellion, I think. If you feel rebellious against the status quo you look for commonality with other rebels. You seek them out. You ask them what it is that they're trying to say and find out if you can say something similar but in a more contemporary way. So that's how I very luckily got to know William Burroughs, Brion Gysin and Derek Jarman very early, in the period between 1969 and 1971.

Burroughs and Gysin have been highly influential to us, particularly in relation to the practice of the 'cut-up'. To liberate the word from linearity, they began to cut up texts and, incorporating random chance, reassembled both their own and co-opted literature *to see what it really says*. They referred to the phenomena of profound and poetic new collisions and meanings that resulted from their intimate collaborations as the 'Third Mind'. This was produced with a willingness to sacrifice their separate, previously inviolate works and artistic 'ownership'. In many ways they saw the Third Mind as an entity in and of itself. It's something 'other', closer to purity, or essence, and the origin and source of a magical or divine creativity that could only result from the unconditional integration of two sources.

DJ: *Literary experimentation was clearly very important to you. But how has your work been influenced by the history of performance in the UK?*

GBPO: We began working with performance in 1965 in Solihull, Warwickshire, with Dadaist street happenings like *Beautiful Litter*.[5] We scattered small cards with evocative words written on them all over town, inside cafés, bookshops, and so on, and in the street. As any curious person picked up the words, they were creating a haiku-like poem. Picking up all the cards also 'wrote' a long poem, but one that nobody would ever see or hear complete. In 1969 we joined David Medalla's Exploding Galaxy in Islington and it was there that we were mutated by the rigorous aesthetics into entirely new ways of seeing what art could become.[6] We founded COUM Transmissions in 1969 as well. Initially alone, later with John Shapeero and, as time went by, more and more people became involved to varying degrees of engagement. COUM Transmissions began to flourish in Hull in 1970–71 creating unsolicited street-theatre happenings. These actions got noticed and we began to receive Arts Council bursaries and grants. We added pages to *Groupvine* [magazine] and as a direct result COUM began to be invited to participate in a lot of the arts festivals that flourished then. We met Roland Miller and Shirley Cameron who were very supportive of our early, somewhat shambolic events and actions. We met the John Bull Puncture Repair Kit, the Welfare State and Jeff Nuttall and the People Show during the early 1970s. We were generally surprised how many of these people were art-school lecturers with very academic approaches to performance art – as it had only just been dubbed. Almost all of these groups seemed to have a pretty theatrical bent to their works with, it also seemed, a diminishing ratio of improvisation or happening. Because we were heavily involved in mail art – and through that, Fluxus – our influences were more conceptual and ironic.

As time progressed we dug deeper and deeper into taboo, transgressive actions, sexuality and gender roles, primarily with Sleazy [Peter Christopherson] and Cosey Fanni Tutti.[7] We all had the good fortune to avoid art college, so our evolution was based almost entirely upon our own communal explorations together sexually and our lengthy discussions about boundaries of all kinds. Who delineates them? Who benefits from social norms? Is there a valid reason for government intrusion into the privacy of our individual physical bodies? An artist's right to choose how they use and abuse their flesh was an important issue. Towards the end of COUM Transmissions [in 1976] the work was almost entirely about gender roles as we tried to destabilise them.

DJ: *Performance is clearly an important methodology. Do you find the term 'live art' relevant or useful as a description of your work? If not, how would you describe your practice?*

GBPO: If you said 'Living Art' we might be comfortable with that as a term. By changing 'Live Art' to 'Living Art', more levels and flexibilities of meaning are aroused. Living Art implies some form of being alive as opposed to dead. The art is active and filled with potential and still evolving. From the artists' perspective it clarifies an important distinction for BREYER P-ORRIDGE, namely the insistence that we are living art constantly without any separation between the creation of art objects, installations, films and any other useful medium available, and what are normally seen as 'domestic' activities in daily living. Art, we believe, must be all-inclusive and 24/7, with its prime motivation embedded, no matter how obliquely, in every action or product. That motivation is a positive evolution of the human species: a transcendence of current economic, social, sexual, and religious mores. When you consider transsexuality, cross-dressing, cosmetic surgery, piercing and tattooing, they are all calculated impulses – *a symptomatic groping toward the next phase*. One of the great things about human beings is that we impulsively and intuitively express what is inevitably next in the evolution of culture and our species. It is the Other that we are destined to become.

It is important to point out that whilst we continue to develop and document performances (primarily through Sigils [*magickal* drawings], Polaroids and video), these are almost exclusively enacted in private. We use self-created rituals to see how deeply we can explore the neurosphere (the consciousness and the chemical brain), the endurance levels of our bodies and minds, and their threshold for restriction and physical limitations of our bodies. The goal is not to produce aesthetically satisfying artworks but to try and retrieve the diaphanous waves of potentially new information to explain questions such as: Why are we here? What other states of being are there? What is the true nature of time? What other dimensions and locations might exist beyond our limited consensus reality? Pandrogeny includes every means of perception, so 'Live Art' would be inaccurate, misleading and far too constricting a term for BREYER P-ORRIDGE.

DJ: *You each bring very different histories and experiences to the project of* Breaking Sex. *Can you each say something about the preparations that enabled you to tackle such complex and provocative material?*

Lady Jaye BREYER P-ORRIDGE: Although our backgrounds are very different, Gen and I share common early childhood experiences. When we discussed our early life quite soon after we met we realised that sharing these similar experiences caused us to perceive the world in a certain way. As an extension of that some of the same artists resonated strongly with us – Marcel Duchamp, Pierre Molinier, Hans Bellmer, Stelarc and ORLAN spring to mind. Like getting hit over the head, you find something obscure or suppressed and it seems like a truth, and you ask how it could have escaped you for so long. Not all of our life experiences have been the same, naturally – we're from different generations, and from different countries, but that in many ways helps our work. It would not be a work of the Third Mind/Third

Being if we saw everything identically. Sometimes our views will contradict each other, like an exception that proves the rule. Our work isn't parallel sometimes, but rather perpendicular, and forms a greater whole that covers a lot more territory.

GBPO: Jaye became very active in the downtown New York scene and alternative theatre. Do you want to mention that?

LJBPO: A lot of the work that I did when I was younger drew certain parallels to Gen's work. Had I known about Gen's work – had I been a little more worldly and sophisticated – I might not have done some of these things, knowing that they had already been done in the 1970s! But I felt a need in myself to explore certain things, and when I started reviewing Gen's early work I realised it expressed similar ideas to what I was feeling at the same age.

DJ: *To return specifically to the Pandrogeny project, one of the most striking tensions in the work is that although it may seem at least superficially to be monstrous or horrific, on a much deeper level it demonstrates an investment in romance. Can you say something about the collision between monstrosity and romance?*

GBPO: At the very beginning before we were committed to being with each other for a long time, one of the very first times we actually met in New York I stayed at Jaye's apartment – we were still just good friends – and one of the first things she did was dress me up like a little doll, in a very androgynous way.

LJBPO: It was a green crushed-velvet Betsey Johnson catsuit.

GBPO: And a little leather skirt, with Fluevog shoes that you bought me especially.

LJBPO: Only the best.

GBPO: Only the best. So there was an immediate resonance between us that was never discussed at the beginning, where we began to blend. From then on we playfully started to cross-dress with each other, and play with the idea of looking similar and not taking on traditional roles. When we got married on Friday 13 June 1995, we intuitively – without a great deal of discussion – swapped gender roles. I wore a white lace dress and nice white and black shoes, and Jaye wore skin-tight leather trousers, motorcycle boots, a leather vest over her naked torso revealing her breasts, and a moustache. That was the first step – *a deeply romantic urge to blend*. The mutual orgasm can be a transcendent experience where two people seem to become one. Another way you can have that experience is to create a baby, which is again two people becoming one. We didn't want to have a baby, but we did want to create a new being that represented the two of us, so we took each other and started to analyse how we could play with that sense of *positive surrender*, and create a new dynamic being. That's where the more considered artistic side began.

DJ: *Would you say that* Breaking Sex *is a utopian project?*

GBPO: Yes. When we began *Breaking Sex* and as it developed into Pandrogeny both of us saw it as primarily a process of and for our own liberation from any gender or identity expectations or social conditioning. The central energy was our deeply romantic love for one another. Inevitably, as performance artists and creators who see no separation whatsoever between our daily life and the concept of 'art' we channelled our responses and observations back into our practice, and integrated documentation into exhibitions via sculptures, assemblages and photo works overlaid onto collages of original Polaroids generated by our experiments and rituals. A core part of our collaboration was always endless discussion and dialogue back and forth about the effects we were noting on ourselves, and the expanding implications we felt we were exposing.

In 1971, Burroughs charged me with a task: 'How do you short-circuit control?' We came to feel that control was ultimately inseparable from information and in turn recording devices, from prehistoric – or pre-*Astoric* – cave paintings to the Internet to the archaeological residue recorded within the earth itself. Control, we concluded, resides biologically in and as DNA. The gender, shape, medical flaws and longevity of individual existence are pre-programmed to a large extent by DNA. We speculated that DNA itself might be the primary life form on earth, with our species as host organisms that unwittingly enabled the continuity of DNA. We saw DNA as a limiting mechanism of human existence. To contradict, interdict and deny the DNA pre-programme of our physical unfolding became both a part of our agenda personally and a symbol of our absolute rejection of any and all imposed evolution. So we began mutating towards an hermaphroditic logo of our rejection of DNA. As we became more comfortable as a Third Being – by, at least conceptually, obliterating obvious physical and gender differences – we discovered another layer of meanings and possibilities released by our project. (See **Figure 4.2**). When you refute the control of DNA we

Figure 4.2 BREYER P-ORRIDGE, *Topless Poor-trait* (2008–10). C-print on Plexiglas. Photograph by M. Sharkey, reprocessed by BREYER P-ORRIDGE. © BREYER P-ORRIDGE. Courtesy of the artist and Invisible Exports, New York

felt you can begin to embrace a rejection of any limitations to the mutability and possibility for evolution. BREYER P-ORRIDGE have come to view the physical body as simply raw material. 'A cheap suit-case for consciousness', as Lady Jaye says.

We support all surgical or genetic advances towards self-designed futures. Why not hibernate in order to colonise space, for example? Grow gills to swim underwater? Fur or feathers as fashion acces-sories? Central to all these various speculations was the collapse of binary systems into redundancy. We believe that as one becomes the author of one's own physical and social narrative by inclusivity instead of exclusivity, as you excise oneself from either/or, black/white, Muslim/Christian, male/female, and so on you can become aware of similarities, commonality, and eventually perceive oneself as part of a 'HumanE Species'. A world-embracing mutation and radical evolution will more naturally assign resources to the most advantageous aspect for the well-being of the entire species. This is a very brief explanation of our thought process: from union through and as love; to union as a demonstration of change socially; and eventually towards the union of an entire species perceived as one fully integrated organism with no limitation on any level of biological mutability. Self-designed personally and socially in prepa-ration for the next phase of humane evolution. The colonisation of space. The human body is not sacred, it is a tool with a conscious-ness. There is no reason to believe or assume that this is our finished state. This is, to BREYER P-ORRIDGE, a 'larval', initial state of being at a crossroads. We believe, with Pandrogeny, that the means of perception can be seized and become limitless, leading our species into being an inclusive, integrated organism on a threshold of unimaginable and miraculous achievements. Hence we say, 'Viva La Evolution!' Utopian? Absolutely.

DJ: *How does the political emerge from this particular sense of the utopian? I'm reminded of Burroughs's statement that 'paranoia is having all the facts', where a political statement emerges from blurring the bound-aries between two opposites: the positive and the negative, loaded and neutral, romance and monstrosity.*

GBPO: Burroughs also said that if there's a situation that makes you uncomfortable, or feels threatening, look for the vested interest. Well, we felt very uncomfortable in the stereotypical roles we were assigned, in terms of gender and being biologically present. We wanted to expose the deliberate conditioning and the push towards emotional, economic and creative inertia, which serves the purposes of globalised culture. The last thing that the great corporations would like is to have a new species erupt that's based on the absolute rejection of everything inherited at birth – identity, body, social position, gender, race, humanity – a new species that has the right and the means to erase everything we were given and rebuild itself. That's where the political emerges.

LJBPO: Today I was talking to Gen about the story of Marduk and Tiamat. It's the first recorded story of how mankind was created – a Sumerian narrative about a pre-biblical god who conquers the dragon Tiamat who represents femininity, chaos, nature and wilderness. The other gods made Marduk in the figure of a man, and gave him the power to create the world – including the first city and the first civilisation – and the power to rule its people. So the very first creation story is based on control. There's an extension of the story that says humans were put here to serve gods and to serve kings, and fill their storehouses with grain to give them wealth. I would find some kind of change refreshing at this point.

GBPO: Gender infuses every cultural system and is a very important aspect of reassessing what it is to be present, to feel that you're alive in any particular consensus reality. Yet people often confuse gender and identity too easily. Identity is something that begins from the moment you're conceived, while you're still inside your mother's womb. Before you even come out there is the influence of relatives you've never met, whom you may hate when you do meet them; all these things that your parents want to have happen; even their friends have investments in what you're going to be; and it just gets worse from then – school, peer groups, you're a boy so you have to hang out with the boys and do boy things, and so on. The key point about this structure is that it's fictional. If it wasn't you making all those choices up to the point you become fully self-aware, perhaps around puberty, then you've had the story of your identity written for you – a narrative written by someone else. That's just not acceptable. *Everyone should have the absolute right to be the person who writes their own story and creates their own narrative.* To give it away or to let it go through laziness is a tragedy. That's how we're controlled, because we let those stories become the warp and the weft of the fabric of society, and then we're stuck. So a process of deconditioning is incredibly important if you want to rebuild your own identity and write your own story.

LJBPO: It's difficult of course, because our culture doesn't accept change, and if you were to reject everything, all your family's wishes and all their dreams for you, they would be hurt. We're controlled by guilt. We don't want to make changes that will make other people love us less or not accept us.

GBPO: I'm sure everyone knows about that. Everyone has to go through it over and over again. Well, there are very simple ways to change your identity. Change your name. The name is the first way that other people exert power over you. If you change your name you take on a huge challenge. Neil Megson thought he could make an artwork that was an extension of Andy Warhol's idea of the super-star, and consciously create a character as an art piece, which was Genesis P-Orridge. *But Neil hasn't been seen since 1969.* Gone. Subsumed.

LJBPO: And the character wasn't just Genesis. If I look at what's left of the archive, all the photographs, there are hundreds of different characters that all have very distinctive personalities and represent different ideas. Sometimes they lasted for ten minutes and sometimes they lasted for a few years. It was so wonderful to see an artist who had so much to express.

DJ: *Finally, I think it's clear from the amount of exhibitions and perform-ances that you are working on right now that there seems to be a moment for your work. I'm interested in the conditions that make the reception of work possible, but I'm also intrigued as to whether you think there's a future for subculture. Why is this the moment right for* Breaking Sex *and the emergence of the pandrogyne?*

LJBPO: In one of your earlier questions you used the word 'monstrosity'. In the past twenty years, broadcast media and adver-tising have become so sophisticated that ever since punk all these manifestations of subversive culture that young people especially are attracted to have been taken from the streets and repackaged, and sold back to them. Everything is a potential product, and I think that for some people we are just a little too raw and a little too hard to look at. It's going to be very hard to put our work in a box, place a little ribbon on it, and sell it. I think that's exciting because what we are working on isn't a commodity. How can you sell individuality? It's not the kind of individuality like 'I want to be different like every-body else', where a subversive style is defined for you, along with where you should go, the type of people you should hang out with, the shops you should purchase your clothing at, or the kind of music you can listen to. What we're doing is much more abstract than that – you can't pin it down as easily because it covers so many bases.

GBPO: There are two lines of thinking that I'm pondering. One of them is quite simple, which is that Pandrogeny, as a word, is uncluttered by any specific connections to gender, sexual orientation, or sexual preference. It's a very gender-neutral word. But it's also a very clear declaration at the same time. At the very least it gives a lot of different people a chance to discuss issues to do with the survival of the species, the way that culture is working, and the changes that are happening to the way people view their bodies. If Pandrogeny does nothing else but open up debate by becoming a word that can be rebuilt from the beginning to represent a much more non-aligned view of things, then that would be important.

The second way I can respond to your question is that we're in an age where people are still driven by prehistoric genetic codes. To put it simply, when we were all running around naked trying to catch slow-moving animals in prehistoric times it probably came in very useful for the male of the species to have the fight-or-flight reflex in his genetic code, in order to hunt and survive. Without that primitive drive we wouldn't all still be here. We then discovered weapons and tools that helped us to kill some of those slow-moving animals, including each other. We got very excited when we learnt we could make tools, and slowly but surely over thousands of years we built this incredible, miraculous, technological environment. People can pick up little boxes and talk to somebody at the other end of the earth, they can fly, they can be in space looking down. But nobody's been bothered to check on our behaviour and move it along at the same rate. We're still genetically prehistoric. So we're in this horrible situation of a futuristic technological environment and a prehistoric band of clever apes ready to destroy each other because their behavioural responses are so polarised from the world they live in. It's an incredibly dangerous time. Dualistic societies have become so fundamentally inert, uncontrollably consuming decreasing resources and self-perpetuating, threatening the continued existence of our species and the pragmatic beauty of infinite diversity of expression. In this context the journey represented by Pandrogeny – and the experimental creation of a third form of gender-neutral living being – is concerned with nothing less than strategies dedicated to the survival of the species.

Pandrogeny went from that deep romance that you mentioned into a discussion about identity and how it's made. That led us to realise that really the ultimate question is: evolution or not. That makes it a very volatile and exciting concept for us, which contains the seed of a discussion about survival. That's why it's resonating – people instinctively are seeing Pandrogeny as a door they can pass through in order to talk about their fears:

And then you want two
See if you could
Go right through
A thick brick wall.

Notes

1. Gérard Georges-Lemaire, '23 Stitches Taken', in William S. Burroughs and Brion Gysin, *The Third Mind* (London: John Calder, 1979), pp. 9–24 (p. 18).
2. Genesis BREYER P-ORRIDGE, 'Excerpts from a Dialogue with Dominic Johnson', in *Everything You Know About Sex Is Wrong: Extremes of Human Sexuality (and Everything In Between)*, ed. Russ Kick (New York: Disinformation Press, 2005), pp. 345–8 (p. 345).
3. Genesis BREYER P-ORRIDGE, personal correspondence with the author, 2011.
4. Genesis BREYER P-ORRIDGE added this paragraph as a prologue in 2011 during the collaborative editing of the transcript.
5. This section was also added in 2011, hence the shift from 'I' to 'we' in the use of personal pronoun. The grammatical shift remains to indicate the flexibility of the artists' ways of identifying.
6. See Guy Brett, *Exploding Galaxies: The Art of David Medalla* (London: Third Text Publications, 1995).
7. Sleazy would go on to create the band Coil with John Balance. Sleazy died in 2010, bringing the itinerant reunions of Throbbing Gristle to a close. Cosey Fanni Tutti is an artist, former porn actor, and a pioneer of industrial and electronic music; she was a member of Throbbing Gristle, and records and tours as Carter Tutti (with Chris Carter).

5   Slave to Love: An Interview with Sheree Rose

Sheree Rose is best known as the collaborator and partner of Bob Flanagan, and as the sadist mistress to his supermasochist. Their collaborative performances, photographic works, videos and installations are notorious in their physical and emotional extremity. Flanagan's life and works were organised around attending to his experiences of the genetic disease cystic fibrosis (CF). She worked in an inspired and tireless manner to record his illness, and both to document and instigate his idiosyncratic coping mechanisms, primarily through sadomasochism (SM). He infamously conceived of sadomasochism as a means to 'fight sickness with sickness', as if to combat the symptoms of chronic illness with defiantly perverse, 'sick' sex play. Rose was constitutive to this project. Together, Flanagan and Rose conspired to invent thrilling new tortures for Flanagan to withstand, and recorded these in an unprecedented multimedia project. From 1980 to 1996, their performances, especially, were renowned for bringing their private sadomasochistic practices, in all their erotic and thanatological excess, to broader audiences, beginning with subcultural crowds, and quickly including art audiences. The gruelling, prize-winning documentary film *Sick: The Life and Times of Bob Flanagan, Supermasochist* (dir. Kirby Dick, 2003) brought Flanagan and Rose's life project to greater mainstream reception.[1]

While overwhelming in their intimacy, and sometimes horrifying in their manifestation of *amour fou*, their collaborations were also notable for their perverse hilarity. The comedy of their performances – largely imperceptible in photographic documentation of their performance actions – depended upon Flanagan's signature goofball style, and Rose's deadpan, relentless cooperation. Rose is also an amusing interlocutor, partly on account of her radical openness, and, more provocatively, her poker-faced recounting of the many ordeals Flanagan happily submitted to, in the name of love.

Flanagan's posthumously published journals show him to be funny, and droll, but also deadly serious, and pensive, especially as death approached, and the burden of dying took its toll on him, and

Rose, and their marriage. In the midst of their dark days, when they were being investigated once more by the Christian lobby, on 21 June 1995 – in the course of its attacks on the National Endowment for the Arts (NEA) – Flanagan found the humour in his and Rose's situation, writing in his journal, 'the Christians are after us again, using us as examples again of offensive art supported by the NEA. ... Blasphemer! Too bad there's no inquisition. Too bad there are no more lions.'[2] This is typical Flanagan, in his ability to find perverse laughter in a sticky situation, by enjoying the threat of punishment, here promised not by his wife, but by Jesse Helms, bogeyman of the culture wars. In his writing, Flanagan holds court. However, in his performances, photographic works and installations, his wit and wonder are channelled through Rose, cooled by her contributions and orchestrated through their collaborative process. As Flanagan wrote, in his last months, 'She keeps saying she's going to give it all up when I die, which is ironic since I wouldn't [have] gotten involved in all this art crap if it weren't for her.'[3]

Rose cohabited Flanagan's signature style, sometimes as a foil, and accentuated his kinks with her own sadomasochistic credentials. Suffice to say, she has never been a mere sidekick, or assistant. Her prior practice as a punk-scene photographer enabled her to frame and visually direct Flanagan, whose public output before 1980 primarily involved poetry, comedy and spoken word – and his luxuriant but private erotic life. With key works such as *Wall of Pain* (1981–92), described below, Flanagan and Rose blew open the doors of the SM closet, and established an influential presence in commercial galleries and museums. This led to their major touring exhibition *Visiting Hours* (1992–94), which famously included Flanagan receiving guests in a hospital bed.

Across all her work, Rose is profound in her attempt to do away with decorum, tact and conventional evasions and disguises – particularly in relation to sex, love, pleasure, pain, disease and death, and significantly in the uncomfortable connections she manifests between, say, love and death, or sex and pain. In the interview below, conducted in Los Angeles in January 2013, Rose depicts the life she shared with Flanagan, and explains how making art emerged as a way of life.

Dominic Johnson: *When you met Bob Flanagan, you were already working as a photographer. Can you tell me about your approach to photography at that time?*

Sheree Rose: Bob and I met in October 1980 at a party for Beyond Baroque, a literary arts venue in Venice, California. I was photographing, but I wasn't doing it professionally. In 1977, I left a conventional marriage, and decided I wanted to radically change my life – and I did so by becoming involved in the punk scene. I went to my first punk concert and saw the band X, and the Go-Gos. The music was wild, and people were wearing purple hair, tattoos and piercings. It just spoke to me, and it got me into a different mind-set. I was excited by the visuals of the scene – how people looked and what they were doing – so I started capturing that, in a do-it-yourself approach to photography. I wasn't a formal photographer, and hadn't trained. I just loved taking pictures.

DJ: *You began making performances for camera with Bob in 1981, and live performances from 1984. What brought you to performance?*

SR: First of all, Bob was a very interesting person visually, and I was fascinated by his looks. When he told me he had cystic fibrosis, he said he probably wasn't going to live for more than two years. He introduced me to SM, and things I didn't know anything about at that point, and I wanted to do everything I could to keep his memory alive. I started photographing him, and recording everything we did together. (See **Figure 5.1.**) Besides being a poet, he was also a stand-up comedian, and he liked to sing in front of people, so he already had a following as a performer. My initial reaction was that I just wanted to document him and his work, and I thought it would be a two-year project. I didn't think of myself as a performer at that time. But we were a partnership. We did everything as a couple.

Bob already had a long history of doing things to his own body, and I quickly became an active participant. It grew out of our interest – and mine especially – in bringing SM out into the open, and moving beyond SM being something people did in the bedroom, but didn't generally talk about. Performing seemed like something we should do. One of our earliest performances was at Dennis Cooper's event *Poets in Performance* [July 1984], at Beyond Baroque – a venue Bob was closely affiliated with as a poet. In our performance, Bob stood in a plastic wading pool wearing little black panties and a hood on his head, and holding a sheaf of papers. It looked like he was reading his poetry, but he was making it up as he went. Some of the SM things we did at home were funny – we'd play with food, and I'd force him to eat weird things – childlike things, actually, so we brought these

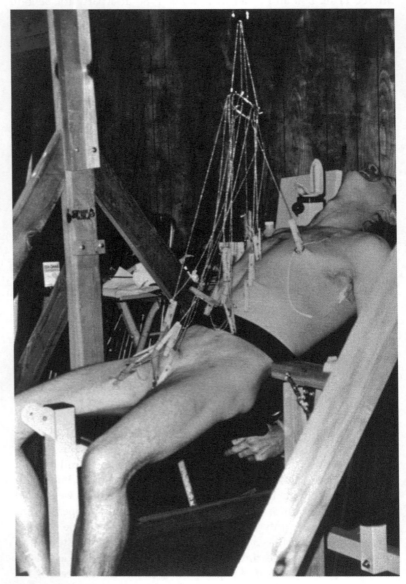

Figure 5.1 Bob Flanagan and Sheree Rose, untitled domestic performance (c.1983). Photograph by Sheree Rose

actions into the performance. We'd had a Fourth July party and there was all this extra food left over – jars of pickles, baked beans, all kinds of messy, icky stuff. As Bob was reciting his poetry, I started putting food all over his body. People hadn't seen anything like this at a literary arts event. It wasn't necessarily SM, but it was definitely a situation in which he was submitting to me. The audience went crazy. I was hooked. I saw how much fun it was to bring out the humour in our SM activities, and to reach a broader audience. He was the star. I was never the star in any of this. If he was the magician, I was his assistant – that's how I saw my role, especially in the early years.

DJ: *In an interview, Bob says, 'I never wanted to call myself a "performance artist". I just went out and did these things from an honest place.'*[4] *What was your relationship to performance art at the time?*

SR: At this point we weren't performing in art spaces, and I don't think we knew much about performance art in those days. We didn't call it that. Bob had been a performer for a long time. He had been a Groundling, and many of the other people around him went on to become the *Saturday Night Live* cohort, but he got too sick to really give it his all. But he didn't consider himself an artist until later.

After we started the Los Angeles chapter of the Society of Janus, we started doing SM demonstrations. We focused on the eroticism, and our performances continued to grow out of our SM activities for some time. Later on I think our activities and performances became more refined, especially as our audiences grew to include art and mainstream audiences.

DJ: *As your work progressed, photography became more important to your collaborations.*

SR: Yes. One of the very first pieces we did together was *Wall of Pain.*[5] I hogtied Bob in our living room and set up a range of around 20 implements. I would whip him, or hit him with an implement, and at the moment of impact he would press the remote shutter release and the camera would take a picture of his screaming or grimacing face. We made 36 different shots. It was originally printed as a grid of small images – about 18 by 24 inches, with each image the size of a contact print – but it was later blown up much larger as *Wall of Pain*, as a major part of *Visiting Hours*, where each picture was pinned to a wall using hypodermic needles. So the photos were originally done for ourselves, but many years later we adapted the piece for an art audience.

DJ: *Were your visual art works – the photographs and objects, for example – generally made without a view to how they would be presented?*

SR: Yes. For many years – in the 1980s – we made work for gatherings of the Society of Janus. One of the first performances we made specifically for an art audience was for RE/Search Publications in 1989. I had been taking pictures of Bob, but also other people in the scene. Before RE/Search published *Bob Flanagan: Supermasochist*, they published a chapter on me in *Modern Primitives* – an interview and a number of my photographs of piercings and tattoos (including some of Genesis P-Orridge, and his wife at the time, Paula).[6] Bob and I did a performance called *Nailed* [1989], at the launch party of *Modern Primitives,* which took place at Olio, a small club on Sunset Boulevard in Los Angeles.[7] That was our 'breakthrough' performance. It was the first instance we designed a show around our private practices that wasn't necessarily erotic.

I had done a few things earlier though. Around 1981 or 1982, Bob had started working as a piercer at The Gauntlet, which was the first and only professional piercing studio in the world at that time. It was rare to have photographers around, but because people knew Bob and me, I was allowed to bring my camera around. Around 1986 I made a video called *Needles and Pins*, documenting the work at The Gauntlet. I thought of it more as a documentary than a video-art piece. In the 1980s, the tattoo and piercing cultures were separate – there wasn't much of a crossover. The piercing industry was blossoming, and people who would never have got pierced before were starting to experiment with it, so the video is really a relic of those days. It was shown at an art gallery in Chicago, called Feature, and at a film festival – but it didn't get very widely shown. It's quite a humorous piece. We were keen not to make our work too serious and ponderous – it was much more light-hearted, and that really was our approach to popularising SM and our other practices. That was my political intention – not to be an artist, really, but in some sense to normalise the sexual practices we were invested in, to lessen the prejudices against SM, and to show that SM was not scary, but could be enjoyable.

DJ: *To what extent do you think your work depended on Los Angeles as a context?*

SR: Bob and I were both LA people. The LA scene took off – partly through our chapter of the Society of Janus, which started with about

12 people but grew to 700 people in the late 1980s. We also performed quite regularly in San Francisco, where we had good friends, but LA felt like a more open-minded city. We held events at big public dance halls, which gave us free rein to have SM parties. There was little or no interference from police. New clubs were opening like Club FUCK!, and the lines were beginning to blur between SM, the art world, and the music or club scenes. They could all coalesce, and I don't know if that could have happened in other cities. It did happen in New York, for example, but it seemed more narrowly focused.

DJ: *How important was friendship and community to the development of the scene and your work?*

SR: It was very important. We were very good friends with the Beyond Baroque people, but Dennis Cooper was probably the biggest influence on us, and on the whole scene. He's a writer, of course, but he also did programming. He brought in a lot of cutting-edge poets from New York, for example, and his involvement in LA poetry extended a scene that was otherwise pretty parochial. He had parties at his house where he would bring together artists, musicians, filmmakers, poets – and people like us who were somewhere in between. Collaborations often happened because we were friends. For example, Jon Reiss was a mutual friend, and he directed Bob in the music video for *Happiness in Slavery* [1992] by Nine Inch Nails, which was one way Bob was acknowledged in a broader cultural sense.[8]

Mike Kelley was also important for us. Bob and Mike had an improvisational band called Idiot Bliss [with Jack Skelley and Alec Duncan].[9] Mike's ideas about art complemented ours, and a number of works came about because we were friends. For example, we were in a series of photos Mike made in 1990 – I'm in the background and Bob is in the foreground, and we are rubbing our crotches and asses against stuffed toys. Bob looks like he's covered in shit – actually, it's chocolate syrup.[10] We also made a video called *One Hundred Reasons* [1991], which is probably the piece of ours that has been shown most widely. That came about because we invited Mike to give a reading at an event to celebrate our tenth anniversary. He had a poem called *One Hundred Reasons*, listing imaginary names for paddles. As Mike read this poem, I spontaneously spanked Bob with a paddle: one spank for each of Mike's hundred reasons. We then re-performed it as a video piece, which is closely framed on Bob's rear end, and it became something of a phenomenon.[11] After that, I also did a project where I photographed one hundred spanked asses, which has been shown in part a few times – but I hope to show the full series of all one hundred together.[12] Again, many of these things started in private – in clubs or at parties – and then changed or expanded to become something else.

Through working with Dennis Cooper, we had a show at LACE [Los Angeles Contemporary Exhibitions] called *Leather From Home* [1984]. Dennis gave us the title, and in the performance Bob writes a letter to his mother describing a girl he's met who does all these wonderful things for him – funny things that sound sweet but are very suggestive – and this is followed by the two of us performing a series of SM actions together. The performance got LACE into a lot of trouble. But it was another bridge for us, between SM and art spaces, and we used it to develop other performances. Venues got wind of our work and started inviting us to perform. One thing I should say about our art career is that I can't think of a single time where we sent off a proposal to a venue. News about us spread by word of mouth, and people who were interested asked to hear our ideas.

DJ: *Your work at venues like LACE led to opportunities to work at major museums.* Visiting Hours *is particularly compelling because it took place in two major museums. How did it come about, and did you have to negotiate any problems with the venues?*

SR: We were offered a show at the Santa Monica Museum of Art, and we came up with the idea for *Visiting Hours*. The relationship between sex, SM and childhood was an interesting starting point for us – CF is a childhood-onset disease, and Bob had spent so much time in hospitals as a child, and as an adult. In Santa Monica and New York [*Visiting Hours* travelled to the New Museum], the shows were very popular, and had thousands of visitors. The only real problem we encountered was with the *Supermasochist* photograph – the only image that actually showed Bob's penis. It was about sexuality, but it didn't show sex *per se*, and the exhibition wasn't pornographic in any way. Police came on the opening night in Santa Monica, and watched me suspend Bob – but they laughed about it and left. In New York the museum was more worried about Bob dying during the show, but I don't remember them being so concerned about the content. They required letters from Bob's doctors, and an insurance policy. We had the New York Fire Department set up the rigging for the hoist so it was perfectly safe, and we signed liability waivers. Both museums put up signs to inform visitors about the imagery. But they never prevented us from doing anything.

DJ: *Were you ever censored, directly or indirectly?*

SR: Well, our performances were never censored *per se*.[13] However, Senator Jesse Helms did raise questions about us in a letter to John Frohnmayer in 1989, who was Chairman of the National Endowment for the Arts (NEA) at the time. Helms wanted to know if 'comedian Bob F.' and I had ever received funding from the NEA.[14] However, we hadn't received NEA grants, and at that time our performances took place either in private or at venues that were not directly funded by the NEA. We didn't know any of this was happening until a reporter from the *LA Times* put in a request under the Freedom of Information Act, and found out that Helms and his Senate committee had investigated us and our work. This was frightening to us at the time, but Bob said that they could try to arrest us or censor us, but we shouldn't change the way we live our lives. I liked his attitude.

DJ: *Bob said that his use of SM was an attempt to 'fight sickness with sickness', locating his rationale in relation to his own experience of cystic fibrosis. What was your own relationship to SM?*

SR: In the 1970s I was involved in the feminist movement. I had been a relatively typical housewife – married with two children, and teaching in a school. I was interested in other things like communal living, as many people were in the 1960s and 1970s. Through SM, Bob offered me an opportunity to enter more fully into my feminist ideal of breaking down the structure of traditional marriage. Instead of the man being the dominant partner and making all the decisions, I wanted to stand this cliché on its head, and create a situation in which I became the arbiter of all the decisions that were made in our relationship. I wanted to control everything. And I wanted to do that inside and outside the bedroom, and beyond the underground, and I found I could achieve this through SM. So Bob would 'fight sickness with sickness', and I had my own agenda. (See **Figure 5.2**). I had been socialised to be the submissive partner in a marriage – and I am not a submissive person.

I wanted to show our lives to the world and say: Here is a different model. I was influenced in this by feminism, but also by the gay and lesbian rights movement. My brother came out in the late 1970s, and I learnt about gay politics, which I had not really known about before. And one of the revolutionary things about SM in that moment was that it brought together lesbian, gay and transgender

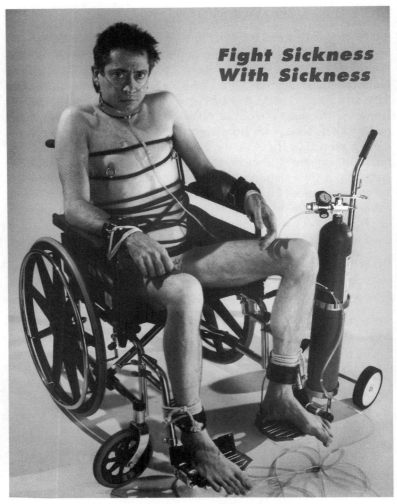

Figure 5.2 Bob Flanagan and Sheree Rose, *Fight Sickness with Sickness* (1994). Photograph by Sheree Rose

people, and straight people – the only thing we had in common was that we were into SM, and we didn't want to be ashamed of that. Our genders, even our politics – none of that really mattered.

Bob was destined to be a star. Often people say that Bob was a submissive but he dominated everything in terms of our work. The fact is that's not true. In an SM relationship, only the dominant is empowered to decide. That's my feminism. It certainly isn't everybody's definition of feminism, but it was my version of a feminist approach to SM. We had a friend who was a professor of human sexuality at a college called Orange Coast College, and Bob and I would do a lecture there every semester. Bob had a Prince Albert [piercing] in his penis, and a ring in his guiche [perineum], and I would lock those together and keep the key around my neck. I'd tell the girls we could control men's sexuality. I even went on Sally Jesse Raphael's TV show saying the same kinds of thing. Our views didn't exactly take off [*laughs*], but we were unique, and we were always very open in what we said and did.

DJ: *You drafted and signed a 'slave contract' together. Can you tell me about this?*

SR: The slave contract was influenced by Leopold von Sacher-Masoch's *Venus in Furs* (1870), where Severin signs away his rights to his mistress Wanda.[15] In fact, we had more than one contract. We had time-based contracts and they were equal in the sense that at the end of the term both parties could talk together and say this is what I like and this is what I don't like – and renegotiate the conditions. At first we had short-term contracts, but eventually these contracts became open-ended, and stated that Bob would become my slave for as long as he lived. I also had slave contracts with other people. At that time I had a missionary zeal for telling people who were getting married that they should only do so for three months – not for life – and if the first three-month contract worked out well, they might remarry for another six months, and then a year, and so on. I thought the short-term contract was a great way to revolutionise marriage, but unfortunately that was another one of my ideas that didn't catch on [*laughs*].

DJ: *SM also engages with contracts in the informal or social sense, by requiring or facilitating negotiation, consent, and unwritten 'terms and conditions'. How did your work stage SM as a 'social contract'?*

SR: Although I was the dominant partner, and Bob was the submissive, we always negotiated what we would and would not do to each other, in private and in performance. In *Visiting Hours*, for example, a key part involved me suspending Bob by the ankles periodically throughout the duration of the exhibition. From the perspective of the audience, it might have looked as though Bob was lying in the hospital bed and he'd be mysteriously drawn up to the ceiling, like an object. In fact, he would give a signal to a video camera, and I'd receive the signal and start pulling him up. He was sick. I was controlling his movements, but there was give and take. I wasn't going to suspend him whenever I felt like it, or surprise him without his consent. We incorporated negotiation into everything we did.

We also involved aspects of negotiation with audiences in some instances. We felt the need to do so after *Nailed* at Olio, in which people in the audience fainted. I had a slave tied to a cross, and I bound her breasts. I took a scalpel and cut around her nipples, which were very prominent and tight. I had done this several times before, and it bled slightly, and it looked beautiful. But because I had bound her so tightly this time, as I cut her the blood started gushing out from the increased tension. It was too much for the audience. From that point on, we tried to do the more challenging images at a remove. Much later, Bob wanted to hammer a nail through the head of his penis. It was something he had done once before in private, before he met me, but for the performance, we decided he wouldn't do it directly in front of an audience, but for video.[16] I was an audience of one. We thought it might be too much for a live audience – so we certainly had some feelings about how and when we should implicate an audience in what we were doing. One of the last pieces we made was called *In My Room* [1996]. Bob was in a hotel room and people were across the way in another hotel room, watching through a window. It was voyeurism to the nth degree, but they were hardly forced to look. We didn't impose images upon them.

We also involved audiences in encounters that weren't as explicit. One of the aspects of *Visiting Hours* that was very popular was the re-creation of Bob's hospital room in the museum. We had a chair by his bed, and at first I would sit in the chair. However, during the run of the show – which was eight hours a day, for two months in Santa Monica, and for four months in New York – I couldn't always be there, so people would sit down and start talking to Bob. He would engage with them in very intimate conversations, as there was usually no one else listening in. When that person would leave, other brave museum-goers would take up the seat and talk to Bob too. He had a steady stream of visitors, and they told him all kinds of private things. This was consensual – people weren't required to sit with him, and if they did choose to sit by him, they didn't have to talk. We were always very aware of the complicity of the audience.

DJ: *SM is an interesting space for thinking about and figuring themes that are intangible, or that resist representation – for example trust, responsibility, care, commitment and consent. What have you learnt about these themes?*

SR: In the autopsy scene [in *Sick: The Life and Times of Bob Flanagan, Supermasochist* (2003)], I choke Bob. It was influenced by the movie *In the Realm of the Senses* [dir. Nagisa Ôshima, 1976], which I saw before I met Bob. The two main characters in the film experiment with sex, and in one scene she chokes him while they are having intercourse – almost to the point of death. In the end of the movie she does actually kill him. We didn't want to go quite that far, but we did incorporate choking into our lovemaking, and it was very erotic. Bob had to give himself over to me, and trust me that I was going to be careful enough to give him a powerful erotic charge – he trusted that I was not going to kill him. That to me was a delicate activity, because we were playing with life and death. When you're choking someone you should use a wide bathrobe belt or similar cord, without knots – and in everything we did we tried to be as careful as we possibly could. Some of this, though, is dangerous, of course – and that is part of the erotic charge – but it was always consensual. Accidents did happen to people we knew who were less careful. The couple in *In The Realm of the Senses* don't know when to stop. Trust is very important, as someone is placing their life in your hands – when you're pulling the cord tight – and you have to take that responsibility seriously.

DJ: *Can you tell me about training or the accrual of knowledge in SM, and in your development as a practitioner specifically?*

SR: SM is a folk order of knowledge. Before Bob and I got into SM, it was mostly a practice belonging to lesbians and gay men. There were some books available, and people would give demonstrations at parties, showing others how to do things safely; for example we might show each other how to tie somebody up, and what knots to use, where you could whip a body safely, which parts to avoid. These demonstrations became an important part of our work, especially in the Society of Janus. We developed a project called *SM 101*, where we gave safety lectures on basic skills, but also taught people the more esoteric practices, like branding. A lot of the information is handed down, like folklore, from those who know by experience, or from being taught by others, and it's passed on to people who are interested in learning. The club setting was important – in the beginning we knew everybody in the scene, and we knew we'd be safe as the necessary information was available. At parties there would be a dungeon master or mistress, who could keep an eye on things: if you were being tied at the wrists, the master/mistress could step in and suggest a different kind of knot, or make sure you knew that you can't tie your arms above your head for too long. The parties were fun, but they were also a learning process.

DJ: *Does your work valorise hardship? How do you feel about your work being described as hardship art, or ordeal art?*

SR: We never saw it like that. No matter what we did we were explicitly interested in the erotic component. Bob didn't want pain for its own sake – to put it plainly, he wanted pain because it made his dick hard. The point certainly wasn't to become stars. Bob was so creative, and he brought out my creativity, so we sought out opportunities to develop our private practice as performances. I think that calling us 'hardship artists' or 'ordeal artists' forgets the importance of love, laughter, conversation and poetry in everything we did together. Bob had a great sense of humour, and talking was always a part of the work – unless I had him gagged.

DJ: *In your collaborations with Flanagan, humour is clearly present. For example, in* Nailed, *it's absurd for him to play Leonard Nimoy's kitsch rendition of* If I Had a Hammer *and then nail his scrotum to a board. Yet humour is often written out of accounts of performances that deal in some way with pain.*

SR: I agree. Having fun with your body, or having fun with sex, is very important. At the very least it counters the old-fashioned idea that the only way you can have sex is the missionary style, in the dark – which many people still do, probably. Sex is *funny*. Hopefully sex is hot, but there's a whole lot more to it than just climax. Being human, we fart, piss and shit, and those things can be a source of humour. Religion and other conventions often separate our spiritual and cognitive experiences from our physicality, but the recombination of these things can have interesting effects – sometimes it's frightening or disgusting, but at other times it's funny. I saw Ron Athey performing at clubs in the early 1990s, where he'd give himself an enema – it's taking the most private, dirty, disgusting thing you can do, and showing it to strangers – and I would laugh hysterically.

Layers of modesty and respectability shield us from the humour, but Bob and I were interested in recognising the pleasure in things that were otherwise hidden, unfamiliar or shameful. In *Nailed*, there's a section where Bob opens his robe and there's a ten-pound weight hanging from his balls, and he shakes the weight. It was hysterical. Is it disgusting or horrifying that he could stretch his balls? No. It's *interesting* that he could do that. Not every man could or would do it. But essentially it's a funny thing to do with your body. There are limits, I suppose, but it's through humour that we assert our humanity, and our commonality with others.

DJ: *How would you describe Bob's sense of humour?*

SR: First of all, nothing was sacred. Bob was a naturally funny person, but he was dealing with disease and the prospect of death on a daily basis. He saw the world as absurd. He had spent a lot of time growing up by himself, in bed, and his outlook developed as a survival mechanism, so as not to take matters of life and death too seriously. He used black humour, but it was honest, almost childlike, and very disarming – not cynical laughter, but a way of lightening up even the most outrageous or extreme things, so that they seemed bearable. Bob was definitely a unique personality.

DJ: *Can you tell me about the relationship between suffering and laughter?*

SR: When you experience intense pain you're opening yourself up, and you might not know what emotion will erupt, or whether you will laugh or cry. Bob experienced pain all his life, and he had to find a way of dealing with it. He did that through humour. He was also a counsellor at a summer camp for young people with CF – in *Sick,* he parodies Bob Dylan by singing *Forever Young* as *Forever Lung*. He gave those kids so much – it wasn't just for himself. He had a lot of compassion, and to this day I am still in touch with some of the kids from his camps, who are adults now, and who still remember him so fondly. So he's not just the guy who put a nail through his penis. He was so much more than that.

Before 1980, there wasn't really a context for disabled people to talk about suffering, disease and death – in art or more broadly. There certainly wasn't a space for humorous responses. Bob was able to create that. We all know we are going to die, but we don't usually have to think about it every day, the way Bob did, or the way that other people with terminal illnesses do. We didn't think it was funny that he was going to die. But he didn't think being ill or being close to death made him a freak. I think he showed that it was one part of the human condition. If we can laugh at it, so much the better.

This was difficult in the eighties. After around 1983, a lot of beautiful young people we knew started dying, and AIDS took a lot of the humour out of death and dying. AIDS was a scourge – not just for the people who were dying, but also to the prospect of sexuality freed from any concerns other than self-expression, which was a value we had worked towards.

DJ: *In your solo and collaborative works, I think one of your key achievements is to make the viewer feel that something we know becomes defamiliarised. One of the specific transformations that you seem to achieve is the defamiliarisation of romance.*

SR: We were in San Francisco one time – Bob was reading his *Slave Sonnets* – and Kathy Acker told him, 'You and Sheree are the most romantic couple I know.'[17] Kathy Acker understood us, and she was well placed to see that a deep romantic connection can be kind of scary.

A lot of people couldn't believe we were together for so long and yet were always so in love. This was in some ways illusory – it wasn't just that he was submissive and I was dominant: we were like any other couple in that we fought, and we had our problems, but there was a romantic aspect to us that was larger than life. Even though we had obstacles – he was so sick, and I was older than him – we had this amazing love story, which influenced people. I hope we gave others the courage to do things they might not otherwise do.

We certainly did unique things to each other and called it *love*. I'd put him in a cage and leave him there for 24 hours; or tie him up under my house and feed him through a tube. Love can come in all kinds of strange and unusual forms, and there doesn't have to be one rigid definition of what love or romance looks like. Bob wanted me to castrate him after he died, and to save his penis. We talked about it a lot. He was very attached to his penis and wasn't going to be able to use it any more. I would have, except for the fact that he died in a hospital. He died in the afternoon, and the hospital staff sent me, my rabbi, and Bob's body down to a room, where I practised some rituals. I washed him, shaved him, cut him, and took some photographs, and this was an amazing experience. I had cut him many times before, but it was different to cut into his dead flesh.

We were an unusual couple and we were very much in love. Instead of diminishing each other we made each other more – we were a couple that was more than simply the sum of its parts, which was transcendent. It's been seventeen years since he died, and I still think about him almost every day. I still talk about him as if he's here. I feel him and his influence, still.

DJ: *I'm interested in your solo works since Bob's death. A key piece is your inflatable sculpture,* Bobballoon *(1996). How did the piece come about?*

SR: Bob died in January 1996, and the sculpture was commissioned and shown in Japan in August of the same year. There was a major international exhibition in Tokyo, to open an exhibition centre called Tokyo Big Sight, and the curator asked a mutual friend for suggestions for international artists, and my name was put forward.[18] They originally wanted material from *Visiting Hours*, but I was interested in doing something new.

If you drove along the freeway in Los Angeles you'd see huge inflatable vinyl figures on the tops of automobile dealerships – gorillas, dinosaurs, and different fantastical creatures. I thought something like that would make a wonderful tribute to Bob. He was certainly a larger-than-life character. He was the Supermasochist! Also, Bob had wanted to make a series of six-foot-tall inflatable 'punch-me dolls' for *Visiting Hours*, but it never came about. When I was given the opportunity to make something on a really grand scale, it seemed like a good opportunity to bring the two ideas together. The shape was based on a photograph I had taken of Bob in a black leather straitjacket and a ball gag. I enhanced the penis quite a bit though, which he would have loved! The venue in Tokyo was at least 50 feet high, so I made the *Bobballoon* 20 feet high – with a four-foot erect penis that's pierced underneath, tattooed round the base, with a big steel ring in the tip.

I didn't tell the curator that the penis would be visible. In Japan there are Shinto festivals devoted to the phallus, but there was still some anxiety about the piece. I was asked to cover up the penis so I fashioned a kind of sumo-style loincloth to drape over it. I removed the covering after a day or two, and it wasn't an issue. The piece was very popular, and over a hundred thousand people visited it over ten days. For me it was a beautiful – and *funny* – tribute to Bob. I've showed the *Bobballoon* in LA a few times since. The last time was at an exhibition in 2011, where I installed it outside the gallery on Sunset Boulevard – drivers honked their horns as they passed by.[19]

DJ: *Tell me about your* Corpse Pose *series.*

SR: When I perform, I am aware of the audience, and I like to draw an audience in. In the *Corpse Pose* pieces, I use a yoga position called *Shavasana*, where you still your body, lowering your breath and your blood pressure to as low a point as possible. In the first version I was laid out on the *Gurney of Nails* [1992]. Bob and I made the gurney [topped with a sheet of plywood studded with 1400 steel nails facing upwards] for *Visiting Hours*, and Bob would lay on it occasionally during the show. In the first *Corpse Pose* performance [Country Club, Los Angeles, 9 September 2011], I wore a white robe and lay on the gurney for 45 minutes in the *Shavasana* pose. In the second version of the *Corpse Pose* [Human Resources, Los Angeles, 27 January 2012], my breasts are bare, and an assistant invites the audience to put wax, flower petals, feathers, or other materials on my body. In the latest *Corpse Pose* [Coagula Curatorial, Los Angeles, 25 August 2012], I worked with a young artist called Michael Griffin who paints my body. I'm naked except for a hood. Mine is an older, female body, and I feel brave being naked. Partly I'm trying to invite the audience to consider what it feels like to view me as if I am dead, and to touch, paint, or otherwise interact with my body – to be gentle with it, to accept it. For me, it's cathartic. I'm obsessed with death, and as I get older it gets closer and closer. I'm thinking of rituals in which dead bodies were tended with red ochre, or other processes. It's a subtle interplay. Some people feel able to do things to my body, and others do not. I'm completely passive in these pieces, and vulnerable, and people are very tender in their interactions with my body.

The works relate in some ways to a piece that Bob and I made called *Video Coffin* [1994], which was included in the second version of *Visiting Hours* [New Museum, New York]. A coffin is set up as if in a funeral home, surrounded by flowers, and decorated with etchings of bullets, a switchblade, a scalpel, a hammer, and other instruments. Inside the coffin there's a monitor with an image of Bob's face where the head of the corpse should be. When you approach the coffin, and step onto a mat, you activate a camera and the monitor switches to display an image of your face. Around the coffin an epitaph reads, '*quod tu es, ego fui, quod ego sum, tu eris*' ['what you are, I once was; what I am, you will become'], and the work stages this fact. In both pieces, the audience hopefully gets something out of the experience, and so do I.

DJ: *In your descriptions of your body in the* Corpse Pose *performances, I'm reminded of your interactions with Bob's body shortly after his death. I am* *also wondering about the difference between your submissive role in the solo performances, and your dominant role in collaborative performances.*

SR: I like the idea of giving up control in these performances. It's new for me, but I appreciate the experience of being passive. In my own work – and as I'm getting older, and preparing for death, maybe – for some reason I don't need to be dominant. It's not something I would have entertained earlier, especially with Bob, where he was always acted upon, and I was always the actor. I agree I'm taking his place in a way. I am thinking about the last time I saw him, after he died, and he was laying on a gurney. In a way I am both re-enacting his death and previewing what my own death might look like.

DJ: *I've been moved by your current collaborations with Martin O'Brien, who considers (in his words) 'how to be a CF suffering body artist in a post-Flanagan era'.[20] There are clearly similarities and differences between Bob's and Martin's experiences, and between your relationship with each collaborator. Can you describe some of these tensions?*

SR: There are similarities between Bob and Martin, including their body types. CF makes you thin, so they resemble each other physically – but also, Bob was 27 when I met him, and Martin is also in his twenties. They're both interested in using their bodies as an avenue of expression, whereas many other people with CF try to hide their bodies or their experience. Martin is interested in endurance, and shows that he can do amazing things with a 'flawed' body. There are connections, but Martin and Bob have different motivations. Bob started doing SM because it was sexually fulfilling for him, and this is not the case for Martin. Martin isn't a masochist.

There's a clear difference in my relationships with Bob and Martin in that with Bob our activities were erotic, although my sexual fulfilment with Bob wasn't necessarily related to whether or not I could cut or whip him. Our performances were never overtly sexual or pornographic, but whatever we did together on stage or in private would be incorporated into our sex life. As a gay man, Martin's relationship to me is not sexual, it's something else, and this is made more pronounced by the age difference between us. There's something maternal in my relationship to Martin, which I felt very strongly when I spanked him that first time in London.[21] (See **Figure 5.3**.) I think I'm always expressing a love/hate aspect in my relation to Martin, like the ambivalence of a mother to her child, who loves but also resents him – these feelings are heightened

Figure 5.3 Martin O'Brien and Sheree Rose, *Action* (*Access All Areas*, A-Foundation, London, 2011). Photograph by Manuel Vason

when the child is a sick child. I don't have incestuous feelings towards Martin!

When I met Martin we had an immediate connection that was almost spiritual – and I do feel Bob's presence when I do things to Martin in performance. In the last performance [*Regimes of Hardship III*, Performance Space, London, 2012], I specifically did things to Martin I had done with Bob – the slave contract; shaving, painting, and mummifying him; throwing food on him; and forcing him to cross-dress – these were all the things I had done with Bob 20 or 30 years ago in difference contexts, some in performances and others in our private lives.

DJ: *Patrick Califia writes that '[if] you have decided why you will hurt, and for what purpose, and for how long, you are no longer a passive victim; you become a hero completing an ordeal'.*[22] *Do you agree with that sentiment?*

SR: Absolutely. Bob and Martin are given permission to be who they are, and to be triumphant in their identities – not afraid, or pushed into a corner – and people are in awe of that. Bob's persona was the Supermasochist. He was never a victim. He was taking control of his life, but in a passive state. Similarly, Martin does what I tell him to do, but he gives himself to me voluntarily. Both collaborations, and both relationships, depend upon a contract between equals.

Notes

1. *Sick* won the Special Grand Prize at Sundance in 1997. Rose objects to the film, and distances herself from it. Her conflict with Kirby Dick relates to his reneging on an agreement to be present at Flanagan's death; the lack of clarity concerning the reproduction of her archival film; and his exclusion of Rose from the touring and promotion that accompanied its release in 2003. On the controversy, see Simon Hattenstone, 'Love Hurts', *Guardian*, 13 February 1998, p. 2.

2. Bob Flanagan, *The Pain Journal* (Los Angeles: Semiotext(e), 2000), p. 72.

3. Ibid., p. 153.

4. Andrea Juno and V. Vale, 'Interview Three', in *Bob Flanagan: Supermasochist* (San Francisco: RE/Search, 1993), pp. 66–83 (p. 80).

5. It was first shown at Dennis Cooper's event *Writers Who Make Art* at Beyond Baroque, Los Angeles, 1982.

6. See Andrea Juno, 'Sheree Rose', in *Modern Primitives: An Investigation of Contemporary Adornment and Ritual*, ed. V. Vale (San Francisco: RE/Search Publications, 1989), pp. 109–13. Genesis and Paula P-Orridge are profiled in a separate interview in the book, pp. 164–81.

7. In *Nailed* at Olio Flanagan *described* himself nailing his scrotum. It was subsequently performed at the Southern Exposure event at Project Artaud, San Francisco in the same year, and in this revised version – also called *Nailed* – he sewed up his scrotum using a needle and dental floss and hammered several nails through the skin. The revised version of *Nailed* was re-performed several times, including as a SM demonstration for the Threshold Society (formerly the Society of Janus) in 1989. See Flanagan's detailed description in Andrea Juno and V. Vale, 'Interview Two', in *Supermasochist*, pp. 30–63 (p. 62).

8. Flanagan was also commissioned to perform in other music videos at the time, namely Danzig's *It's Coming Down* (1993), also directed by Jon Reiss; and Godflesh's *Crush My Soul* (1995), directed by Andres Serrano.

9. Jack Skelley remembers of Idiot Bliss: 'We had no repertoire. All the songs were completely improvised on the spot.' Flanagan and Skelley were also in another band, Planet of Toys. Jack Skelley, personal correspondence with the author, 8 August 2014.

10. Rose refers to the black-and-white photograph *Manipulating Mass-Produced, Idealized Objects* (1990); and the sepia photograph *Nostalgic Depiction of the Innocence of Childhood* (1990).

11. See Bob Flanagan, Sheree Rose and Mike Kelley, 'One Hundred Reasons', in Mike Kelley, *Minor Histories: Statements, Conversations, Proposals*, ed. John C. Welchman (Cambridge and London: MIT Press, 2004), pp. 204–6.

12. The entire series has since been shown as Rose's solo exhibition *100 Reasons*, Coagula Curatorial, Los Angeles, 26 April to 24 May 2014.

13. Nevertheless, movies involving Rose and/or Flanagan – including *Happiness in Slavery*, *It's Coming Down*, and *Sick!* – were censored on account of their participation. See Steven Allen, *Cinema, Pain and Pleasure: Consent and the Controlled Body* (Basingstoke: Palgrave Macmillan, 2013), pp. 46–7.

14. The letter (7 November 1989) inquired about the funding status of Rose's 'video work featuring genital piercing/photography of tattooing, piercing, sacrification [*sic*] combined with a provocative bondage & discipline bloodletting ritual', and Flanagan's 'emotional presentation of his autoerotic scaffold'. The letter is reproduced in Linda S. Kauffman, *Bad Girls and Sick Boys: Fantasies in Contemporary Art and Culture* (Berkeley: University of California Press, 1998), pp. 28–9.

15. Wanda reads her slave contract to Severin: 'You have no rights and therefore cannot bring any right to bear. My power over you must be unlimited. … You are nothing and I am everything.' See Leopold von Sacher-Masoch, *Venus in Furs*, trans. Joachim Neugroschel (Harmondsworth: Penguin, 2000), p. 51.

16. Flanagan describes his first (botched) hammering of a nail through the glans of his penis in Andrea Juno and V. Vale, 'Interview One', *Bob Flanagan: Supermasochist*, pp. 10–29 (pp. 21–3). Although he got the nail in, he subsequently missed and landed a second heavy blow on his penis.

17. See Bob Flanagan, *Slave Sonnets* (Los Angeles: Cold Calm Press, 1986), a book of powerful and funny poems written in homage to his relationship with Rose.

18. The exhibition was *On Camp/Off Base*, Tokyo Big Sight West, 10–19 August 1996, part of *Three Urban Art Projects: Encountering the City of Hope*.

19. Bob Flanagan and Sheree Rose, *The Wedding of Everything*, at Country Club, Los Angeles, 8 September–10 October 2011. It was more recently shown at Beyond Baroque, Los Angeles on 26 December 2013, where the sculpture was overinflated, and burst.

20. Martin O'Brien, 'Action with Sheree Rose', in *Access All Areas: Live Art and Disability*, ed. Lois Keidan and CJ Mitchell (London: Live Art Development Agency, 2012), p. 92 (p. 92).

21. Martin O'Brien invited Rose (and Ron Athey) to mentor him towards his commissioned performance for a disability arts programme called *Access All Areas*. O'Brien made a two-day durational performance called *Mucus Factory* (A Foundation, London, 4–5 March 2011). At the close of the performance, on the second day, O'Brien and Rose collaborated on a spontaneous performance involving spanking.

22. Patrick Califia, 'The Winking Eye of Ron Athey', *Speaking Sex to Power: The Politics of Queer Sex* (San Francisco: Cleis Publications, 2002), pp. 357–64 (p. 361).

6 The Designated Mourner:
An Interview with Penny
Arcade

Penny Arcade is the designated mourner of the New York underground. She decries and laments the loss of its ethos, and the material disappearances of its denizens.[1] Her life's work, as a performance artist, activist and community elder, has involved mourning the loss of individual people, including artists lost to AIDS, drugs or poverty, which, cumulatively, claimed so many of her generation. She also mourns the minor histories threatened with extinction by what she calls 'cultural amnesia', a tendency of cultural neglect conditioned by gentrification, political apathy, certain strains of stupidity, and the perceived decrepitude of scholarly cultural history. Her homages are not simply mournful, but funny, biting and loving. In her statements in performances and in daily life – at best an arbitrary distinction – she revives counter-traditions that other artists and scholars might undervalue. Gripped by lives, practices, scenes and histories on the brink of secession from collective memory, Arcade seeks to remind her audiences that the precedents that give her succour may be precarious, or unsafe, but they are not 'already over'. There is still a flicker of life in those lingering legends yet.

The content of Arcade's monologues include wry and often hilarious social commentary, memoir and pointed recollections recounted as forewarnings of imminent cultural decline, post-Beat Downtown philosophising, and blasts of critical invective. Customarily, her performances will also be studded with gem-like aphorisms tossed off by the stars of her personal pantheon – especially Jack Smith and Quentin Crisp, whose mentorship she earned and coveted.

Penny Arcade arrived in New York City in 1967, aged 17, after a stay in a convent-run home for wayward girls in rural Connecticut. After Borstal, she was inducted into a different institution of sorts, namely the theatrical underground of New York. The next two decades involved radical cultural apprenticeship in Andy Warhol's movie-making (namely in his and Paul Morrissey's *Women in Revolt* [1971]), John Vaccaro's Playhouse of the Ridiculous, Judith Malina's Living Theater, Hibiscus's Angels of Light and Jack Smith's demented orchid lagoon. Her performances are wordy, and they are also adept in their theatrical staging, in her use of lights, costume (and pointed states of undress), character and video, no doubt informed by her extensive work with the pioneers of experimental theatre in New York.

In recent years, Arcade has consolidated her attachment to the marginalised legends of New York by co-founding (with Steve Zehentner) the Lower East Side Biography Project, an oral-history video programme committed to 'stemming the tide of cultural amnesia' by interviewing underground artists (and other 'individuated' persons, as she calls them), who are yet to be accorded their proper dues in official histories of art, performance, film or literature.[2]

Penny Arcade is a talker. Words are her key medium, and she has an easy, funny, acute and verbose handle on her métier. In September 2013, I arrived at her apartment on the Lower East Side to find her standing on the kerb, berating – in sisterly but stern terms – a neighbour for her cultural neglect of an elderly painter who lives in Arcade's building. I stood by, and as her acquaintance sidled off, Penny slid seamlessly into a monologue, schooling me in her own particular brand of streetwise instruction. As we entered her apartment and settled at her kitchen table, she continued to talk, and I nodded, smiled and laughed. Finally, after about ten minutes, suddenly incredulous at my passivity, she said, 'Why aren't you recording this? You're missing all this excellent material.' I whipped out my recorder, not realising the interview had already commenced long before, on the street – without the need for my questions. I pressed record. Hence, the transcription below begins mid-stream, to preserve my impression of her verbose indefatigability.

Penny Arcade: ... and I said to her, 'you cut down the *tree* because of your *mural*?' We are on the Lower East Side in New York City. A painter living in my building is 89 years old. He's been in this neighbourhood since 1945, and he's really distressed. He likes to sit at his kitchen table and look out at a tree. Now the tree is gone. She said, 'Oh, well, I didn't realise that.' The tree was in the way of her mural by a famous German painter. I asked her, 'Do you know how many painters live in this neighbourhood? You had to bring a painter from *Germany*?' Couldn't you find a painter on the Lower East Side to make your mural? You are contributing to the erasure of history!'

We're in an era that's been steadily building since the 1980s, where mediocrity is the sought-after quality in art. The politics of art run on a high-school cafeteria hierarchy. Where art was a scene of outsiders, it's now a scene of insiders. So, the whole downtown art scene is just one clique after another. Older artists, who perhaps didn't have relationships with other artists or with the designated art world hierarchy, or, nowadays, have nothing to do with the not-for-profit hierarchy, are being erased from history. I was an outsider. It was hard for art-world insiders to understand my work, mostly because they didn't actually come to *see* it. Just hearing about it was too much for them. I suppose the word they use for me is 'provocative', but I don't think I do anything merely to provoke. I've always just tried to tell the truth of situations, as I see it.

DJ: *Are you talking about a generational divide?*

PA: Yes, at least in part. There was an event called the Brooklyn Commune about two months ago. I guessed it was going to be a bunch of 40-year-old academic artists who no longer get funded as emerging artists, and are pissed about it, but I thought I'd check it out. One of the speakers started making work ten years ago and is already touted as a 'legendary performance artist'. The artist did a 'performative conversation' with a tax consultant. She passed out the budget for her latest work – a budget of $186,000. This artist has been funded *up the ass*, ever since she started making work. She said if she didn't continue to get funded, she'd have to stop making work. I looked around the room of a couple of hundred artists under 40, and no one laughed, or even rolled their eyes. They were gripped by this artist's dilemma. My natural reticence (which people do not believe I have) prevented me from doing what I wanted to do, which was to throw myself on the floor, scream and keen, and plead: 'No! You can't stop making your work! Your work has already cured cancer! And brought peace to the Middle East! Don't stop now, please!' People just swallowed what this artist said. There wasn't a raised eyebrow in the entire room.

I think about people like Carolee Schneemann, who – between 1992 and 2000 – was put in limbo as a '1960's artist'. When Marcia Tucker was putting together the *Bad Girls* show at the New Museum of Contemporary Art, she told me the show was inspired by seeing *Bitch!Dyke!Faghag!Whore!* [1990]. I asked why Schneemann wasn't included, and she replied that she wasn't doing a show about the

1960s. I said, 'but Carolee Schneemann is *still working!*' At a fundamental level there's a profound hatred and misunderstanding of
what being a *generative artist* means. Being a generative artist is being
somebody who creates work out of a kind of psycho-spiritual connection with themselves. This was very apparent in the 1980s, where
everybody was very distinctive. A Penny Arcade show was different
to a show by Deb Margolin, which was different to one by Split
Britches, Frank Maya, Bina Sharif, Holly Hughes, Tim Miller, John
Kelly, Karen Finley, and so on. Everybody had their own style and
content, and stood out in stark relief from each other. Then in the
1990s, people started taking from other people's work, and in the
2000s that expanded, and now people are just re-creating and re-
enacting the work of others, because they don't have any time to
really go through the difficult process of being a generative artist.

Being an artist has become an identity. It's no longer a particular
activity that one actually does. 'Performance artist' is now simply a
catchphrase for someone who doesn't do anything in particular. I
don't even know why anybody wants to become an artist. I've never
really understood that. I never saw it as a choice.

DJ: *You have an antagonistic relation to the art world, including both the
commercial art world and the Downtown scene.*

Figure 6.1 Penny Arcade, *Bad Reputation* (P.S.122, New York, 1999).
Photograph by Bob Gruen. © Bob Gruen: www.bobgruen.com

PA: I have spoken out about hypocrisy and what I see as outright lies. My relationship with some art factions has been antagonistic because I speak out rather than just go along to get along. Believe me, this does nothing for me personally except maintain my self-respect. By 1986, I had been performing for almost 20 years, but I wasn't embraced by the new art-school-educated Downtown art scene because I wouldn't play the Warhol Superstar role. It had become a middle-class scene, whereas I was from a more rugged, class-conscious artistic background. Also, most people were very young, just out of school – and I was ten years older.

It's very hard for me because I want to be liked. My conflict is that I'm a people-pleaser, an abandoned, homeless kid who wants accept-ance – and yet my intellectual position does not allow me to kiss ass, or to compromise in order to get what I actually need as a human being. So when I have the experience in all my performances of something transformational happening, for me and the audience, it's not a feeling of *grandeur*, it's a sympathetic feeling. I'm willing to be a martyr, to sacrifice myself for the betterment of the whole.

Perhaps it's my own fault in some ways, but I haven't done a full-length work in New York since 2002 – except for one work-in-progress, *Old Queen* in 2009. I've only done one-offs, or club work at Joe's Pub, and places like that. I've been hosting Earl Dax's perform-ance club Pussy Faggot!, which I'm devoted to, where I do a lot of improvisational stream-of-consciousness audience orientation, with social, political and historical content. I also participate in other people's work. I've achieved a lot, but I'm not really in a position to exercise my ability in New York. That's why my run of *Bitch!Dyke!Faghag!Whore!* in London [in 2013] was so important. I did 48 performances. Not a lot of people can do even 20 shows. I was able to exercise my ability every night, and of course I became better. This is the problem with the focus on emerging arts. Programmers leave mid-career and established artists out to dry. Sooner or later this will come back to haunt them, because not only is it disrespectful, but it also does a great disservice to young artists.

DJ: *Jack Smith was a huge influence upon you as an artist and as a thinker. What was the nature of his influence?*

PA: Within a few weeks of arriving in New York in 1967, I met a lot of the people I would know for my whole life.[3] I met Jack probably within a week of arriving. I just walked around all the time, and kept seeing him, this very bizarre-looking figure. I met him on St. Mark's

Place, on the corner of Second Avenue and 8th Street, where I also met Harry Smith and Taylor Mead, and countless other people. The streets were populated by these creatures. I was told, as a 17-year-old, that Jack had Robert Rauschenberg and other artists ripping up linoleum around the city, while Jack screamed 'Linoleum is the enemy!' He was a force, an intellectual force – extremely brilliant but completely unschooled.

Jack influenced me in many ways. His audiences weren't there to see a performance. They were there to see Jack Smith. In the 1960s, everybody performed all the time. It was a way of entertaining your-self and entertaining your friends. But it wasn't self-conscious. It wasn't like everybody was 'on' all the time. It was a way of mediat-ing your own personality. We didn't have any model for the kinds of people we were. We were freaks in the real sense that we were not normal. We were pegged as not being normal, in school, and by our families, and we were here in New York being not-normal together. So it was as if we couldn't communicate in a direct, emotional way, so we lived in a fantasyland, the way that people do when they can't really face reality. The first person Jack enrolled into his perform-ances was Maria Antoinette Rodgers, from the Playhouse of the Ridiculous. She was a Mescalero Apache, and an amazing creature. She couldn't really say lines, but she was phenomenal looking and a true presence, and she was in a lot of Jack's midnight performances at his loft on Greene Street. Jack was fundamentally influenced by John Vaccaro. Vaccaro was in Jack's early films, like *Normal Love* [1964], and they worked together collaboratively in Jack's first performances; then Jack made posters and costumes for Vaccaro's early plays. They influenced each other. After 1967, after working with Ronnie Tavel's plays, Vaccaro would have a script, but never follow it. He would make his performers – he never called us actors – practice active meditations on a script. You'd be given a sentence, and Vaccaro would drain all the meaning from it. We would work around this improvisationally for hours. That's also what Jack started to do in his own midnight performances from 1968.

Jack would scream at the people on stage, and at the end of the performance he'd scream at the audience: '*Get out, get out! I don't need you any more!*' Performance was an escape, and it's the same for me. For example, I knew that I was going to be doing this performance the other night, and I'm so wrapped up in another project that I couldn't think of anything I wanted to do. They had me on last, and all the time I'm sitting there I'm panicking, thinking: What am I going to perform? I have nothing to perform! In the end, the whole thing was about survival, it wasn't about self-expression. I was trying to do monologues in my head, trying to remember stuff I'd written, and then suddenly it was time for me to go on stage. I thought that for self-preservation the only thing I could do is be completely in the moment, completely at risk. That was Jack.

There would be a struggle, where Jack couldn't really focus – it wasn't really about creating artwork, that wasn't the goal. The goal was to alleviate some pressure – not in a therapeutic sense, but on a deeper metaphysical level. I really saw that when I had a huge fight with him because he wanted me to come and sew every day. I went one day. He wanted me to come again, but I had huge blisters on my fingers from him making me sew with a thin needle through six thicknesses of fabric. When I refused to come and sew the next day he was furious and told me I couldn't go to his performance that week at the Pyramid. I tried to explain, by saying I had to work for money, to do my laundry, to make a performance of my own. He screamed at me on the phone: 'No one is that surrealistically busy!' So I wasn't going to the performance, but everyone said I was crazy, that I *had* to be there. So I go to the performance shrouded in coats, hiding in the back. I'm sitting there frightened he's going to see me, feeling ashamed because he asked me not to be there – and I take that seriously. And he comes out and his first line is 'So you didn't want to sew!' I'm thinking he's seen me, and I'm freaked. But he didn't see me. It was his segue into the performance. Everything that's going on in his life becomes the performance and it doesn't really matter what he's talking about because he's just using it as a way to alleviate the pressure by transforming it, to somehow travel through his anxiety. In my opinion, in order to be called art there *has* to be a transformation. Art is alchemy.

I don't think I copied him though. I just have the same mental problems he had [*laughs*]. The other side of feeling different and weird and awful and alienated is feeling special. Healthy balanced people do not become performers. They don't need to. By the early 1980s Jack could barely go to other people's performances. In 1982, I was in Hibiscus's last show, *Tinsel Town Tirade*, and Jack came to see it.[4] Of course he had absolutely no interest in Hibiscus, to the point where he wouldn't even boo him. But Jack came to the play every night. He combed out my wig backstage and whispered to everyone that I was a genius. I portrayed Andrea Whips in *Tinsel Town Tirade*.[5] Jack had known her and was impressed by my ability to become her so seamlessly in the show.

By 1983, every time Jack went to a performance he would disrupt it. He couldn't tolerate what he saw as everybody being fertilised by him, ripping him off, when everybody *should* have been helping him. Now that I have feelings like that too, [*laughs*] and I have had those feelings since I was about the same age he was when he died (he was 57).

When I came to New York in 1967 there were three art stars: John Cage, Jack Smith and Andy Warhol. But Jack was a bigger name than Warhol for the underground, even in 1967 (and probably until about 1971). Warhol didn't have the same cachet yet, because at that time cachet could only be earned. You couldn't just be hyped into it. It used to be 'the people's award'. Cachet was a grass-roots thing. But Jack turned his back on being an art star. I think Jack thought it was his choice and that he could go back. Many of us think that if you have success at one point in your work you can return to that public awareness of your success and reclaim it. The fact is you can't – and I think that is a tragic reality, especially for an artist like Jack Smith. By the time I came back to New York in 1981 and was living here full time again, Jack, and Jackie Curtis, Peter Hujar, Paul Thek and many other influential artists had been relegated to the past by the careerism that had entered the art world. They had been giants in the 1970s, but by the time I got back, they had been swept aside, as the art world and art history consigned the concept of *lineage* to the trash heap.

DJ: *Jack Smith told you to give up the 'horrible realism' in your work.*

PA: Yes [*laughs*]. In August 1989, six weeks before Jack died, I was doing a performance called *True Stories* at P.S. 122, and I made a bed for him on the stage so he could see the show. The piece included a section called 'Homage to Jack Smith', and when I asked if the audience knew who Jack Smith was, in a sold-out house only two or three people would know. Being the truth-teller I am on stage, I still had to ask that question even with Jack in the room. I steeled myself and did it.

After the show I took Jack home. I was spending many hours a day with Jack taking care of him at that time, mixing his Chinese medicine, and generally just being there for and with him at his beck and call. I arrived at his house the morning after the show (with Mitch Markowitz, who I was living with at the time), and as I was leaving, Jack exploded. He said, 'I can't believe it! You used the *blue* light!' I said, 'Jack, it's a homage to you.' He said, 'The *onions*! You used the onions!' I tried to explain, 'Jack, the whole piece is about you!' He then decided he wanted to help me. He crooned at me, 'It's not your fault. John Vaccaro ruined you!' Jack said he wanted to be my mentor. He said, 'You've got to get out of the gutter! You have to stop this horrible realism!' He said it wasn't my fault that I had been horribly misdirected, but I needed to steer my course towards an uplifting fantasy such as he employed in his work. I told Jack that he had influenced my life, but that I did a different style of work to him. I had just turned 39 and had been making my own work for four years. Jack said, plaintively, 'But I want to be your teacher.' It was a truly heartbreaking moment. I agreed that, yes, he would be my teacher and we spoke about how to proceed. Jack suggested that we would make a performance together. I agreed and said I wanted to make a piece about *denial of death*, hoping that we could make something about AIDS, and about what he and I were sharing at this moment. Jack responded 'Oh! *The Nile of Death*. Perfect! Something Egyptian!' So up until his death on 16 September, we talked about how to create this 'Egyptian' number, with my content, our shared politics, and influenced by his style of fantasy.

DJ: *What does realism mean to you?*

PA: Realism for me quite simply means that I'm somebody who has *really lived*. Few people have lived as hard as I've lived. As you get older, you start to think, 'was that all really that necessary?' It comes at a tremendous cost. I guess from the beginning my work has always been a kind of social realism. It has always been moored in non-fiction.

DJ: *You left New York in the 1970s. Where did you go, and what were you doing?*

PA: I left New York with the Playhouse of the Ridiculous for Amsterdam in 1971, and spent my twenties living many lives. Two months after arriving in Amsterdam, I left the Playhouse. For eight months I ran a shop with Rene Hammink – an artist and male hustler – and we bought Art Deco and Jugendstil stuff at the flea market at 6am and sold it at the shop in the afternoon. I moved to Formentera, Spain and made music, danced at full-moon parties, lived with the Formenteran farmers, learned their language and witchcraft and herbs, and started a school for the children of expats. I belonged to an international theatre collective in Ibiza, spent a summer in Deià, Mallorca with the poet Robert Graves and his salon, joined a

Mallorquín political puppet theatre, drank with sailors as a B-girl, whored in the back streets of Palma, Barcelona and the south of France – and all this before I was 24! I arrived back in the United States and lived in the backwoods of Maine for four years, without running water, indoor plumbing or heat. I became a waitress, belonged to a backwoods theatre collective, became a social worker for Fairfield, Maine (with no credentials), worked with destitute, white trash, was hired by the town manager of Pittsfield, Maine to run a 300-seat theatre (which the town inherited for unpaid taxes) programming 35mm films, theatre, poetry and music. I lived and toured with Peter Gallway's band as a supporter.

Ten years after leaving New York, I returned in 1981, when LaMaMa ETC and Vaccaro invited me to remount Ken Bernard's 1970 play *Night Club* for the venue's twentieth anniversary. It was the last play we did in New York before we left the city in protest in 1971. I was really kind of *stunned by my own life*. AIDS was just starting, and *Night Club* – a play about an unnamed plague – seemingly anticipated it. So, when I started making my own work I had lived a lot of life. All of this is the *lived* experience – my realism, if you will – that would inform my own work when I began to create it in New York at the age of 32.

DJ: *Can you tell me about those first solo works?*

PA: It took a really long time before I felt I could make my own work. At first I did small club performances – most performance art in the 1980s happened in clubs, rather than in theatres. The first real full-length performance I did was when I was 34 years old, at St. Mark's Poetry Project in 1984. Ethyl Eichelberger [a legendary Downtown performance artist] was at that performance and he said to Mark Russell at P.S.122, 'You have to book Penny Arcade. She's a genius.' Ethyl didn't throw that kind of word around lightly. Those first works involved me commenting on what was going on around me, and people were often pissed off by it. People didn't like to hear me talking about gentrification in 1981, which is pretty funny when I look back at it now. But when I would speak as Andrea Whips, or [drag royalty] Margo Howard-Howard, people would not be mad at me. It was removed somehow. So, my work came out of storytelling – literally, on Avenue A, stopping and talking with people, telling them about something and doing impressions of Jack or somebody. I started to realise I could do that on stage. I went to see Eric Bogosian doing one-man shows, and I realised I didn't have to write a play – which at that time was all I knew as an experimental theatre artist.

Fundamentally, what I was doing in the 1980s was what I had glimpsed as a 20-year old. I spoke to Warhol about it and he was the *only* person who thought it was a good idea for me to 'do' people I knew in performance. In the 1980s my work was more aligned with portraiture, to try in some way to recoup these people, and what they stand for in the world, which is disappearing constantly. I think it's interesting that I understood it was disappearing in 1981, even though it wasn't a conscious thing. I needed those people. Andrea was already dead. My life is a history of people dying. The punk-rock designer Arturo Vega died about two months ago, and he was about 65. This week Ronnie Cutrone died. He was a painter and a Factory person. He was 65. Today the poet and painter Rene Ricard died. He was 67 years old. Today, in my generation, 65 is the same as 95 in another generation. We have lived hard. Our week beats your year.

DJ: *How does comedy feature in your work?*

PA: Patti Smith wrote to me in Amsterdam in 1971, and she said, 'I always loved you because you could find the laughter loophole in any tragedy.' If you're going to be up close with life, the one perk you get from experiencing pain is that you also get to experience what is hysterically funny about it. There's something just so absurd about life that is quirky and weird. For instance, there is something completely funny – a *laughter loophole* – in most of the rapes that happened to me. In *Bad Reputation* I tell the story of this guy who tied my legs together, and I thought, 'Well, how's he going to rape me if he ties my legs together?' I guess everybody has those experiences. It's a way to maintain sanity. The reason why I chose *realism* was because I was just so stunned by how crazy real life is. I suppose because my early experiences were with camp – with Vaccaro, for example – everything has been a sideshow carnival. I wanted to show the ridiculousness of reality.

DJ: *What is the difference between Penny Arcade on and off stage?*

PA: There's no difference really. It is simply that on stage there is a heightened presence, one's energy field expands – that is, if you have a sufficiently developed one. I have always been thoughtful. Even as a small child, apparently I liked to have situations explained to me. In the beginning all of my work involved characters. I hid behind those characters. I didn't have a *core* emotional sense of myself until I was in my early 50s. It was there intellectually, but emotionally I had no core.

Quentin Crisp said I was a *born loser* who had become a *professional loser*. I was not the person who would quit school at 16, but it somehow happened to me. As a kid, I was not the typical 'bad girl' of the town. That label was foisted onto me, even then. I was atypical – the bad girl coming out of the library with a stack of books. I never fit in with the bad kids. I never fit into *anything*. Somebody interviewed me recently, and when it was over he turned to me and said, 'How did you survive your life?' I was stumbling around in the dark. *I dug my way backwards*. My destiny was to be who I am.

Hilton Als wrote a review of my book in the *New Yorker*, accompanied by a cartoon. This could have been a huge deal for me. But he ended up reviewing *me* – not the book, not my writing. He clearly had never seen my work, and had no idea about me at all. As soon as I read his opening line, I knew I was fucked. [*Penny finds a copy and reads it aloud*]: '*Bad Reputation* is the self-consciously transgressive title of ... Penny Arcade's book.' And, 'since when was Penny Arcade shy about rubbing our faces in her outlaw status'.[6] What the fuck does that mean? I'm not rubbing anybody's face in anything. I talk about my life. He says something about me he would never say about Courtney Love, or Madonna, who are just pretending to be 'bad girl' outsiders.

I had all these people writing to me saying what an honour it was to be caricatured in the *New Yorker*. But they made me look like someone between *Terry and the Pirates* and 1950s prison pulp. The only thing they didn't do was put a big wart on the end of my nose. I looked like an ugly witch! I am a very pretty witch! Als describes me as 'not model tall'. What does this have to do with my work? He says I'm 'hardworking and obscure'. It's true that I toiled in obscurity in the 1980s. But since 1993, I have managed to have an international mainstream presence for my work. That's 20 years. It's no small feat for an independent artist who is not supported by the not-for-profit touring world. He finishes by saying, 'She continues to critique the very world that now considers her a legend' [*laughs*]. A few weeks later I saw him at a party, and I attempted to thank him for the review. He seemed taken back by my modesty, and said 'You don't have to thank me – the book is brilliant!' I wanted to shout, '*Then why the hell didn't you write that?*' If he had done so, it might have made people want to read the book. But I kept my mouth shut. You see I am not confrontational about anything except *ideas*. That is what people have trouble understanding about me. Maybe that's the difference between myself on stage and off. In my work I use what makes me the same as other people, not what makes me different. Penny Arcade on stage is an *amplification* of elements of myself.

Someone asked me in the mid-1990s, 'Who do you consider to be a downtown icon, aside from yourself?' I replied that I've never 'iconographed' myself. I guess I became an icon, but it wasn't my own doing. Some people *do* have a hand in iconographing themselves. Many rock stars do it, by working to manifest their own vision of themselves as an icon, like Robert Mapplethorpe, Iggy Pop, Lou Reed or Nico. Nowadays it seems everyone tries to iconograph themselves first, without actually creating any work – they just copy someone else. Once on the street, I overheard myself saying – to myself – that *my relationship to my own life has been largely incidental.* I never chose anything. My life unfolded. A series of synchronistic events. The opposite of me is Patti Smith, who iconographed herself right away. Patti and I were close friends in the late 1960s – the time she wrote about in *Just Kids.*[7] When I was in Provincetown this summer, it hit me as I walked up the street. I was thinking over my life and remembering the early 1970s when I left Warhol and the New York art scene, and I thought, 'Oh my god, I out-Rimbaud-ed Patti!' I left everything to live other lives, and I came back ten years later. I didn't have a sense of myself for a long time, there was only an internal dialogue beginning at the age of five. Eventually, an icon emerged.

DJ: *When you share your survival stories with audiences, are you at risk of opening yourself up too much? Is performing ever an added emotional burden?*

PA: No. It's not a burden at all – but there is risk. I want to be a *parrhesiaste*, a personal truth teller.[8] Someone is said to use *parrhesia* and merits consideration as a *parrhesiaste* only if there is a risk or danger for him or her in telling the truth. In the act of telling that truth, a transformation takes place. For me, there *has* to be a transformation of the material. Almost everything that is in any script of mine is derived from something I once said to somebody. For instance, in *New York Values* [2002], I say, 'Downtown used to be filled with writers, painters, photographers, filmmakers, musicians, junkies, whores and weirdoes. Now it's filled with NYU students pretending to be writers, painters … .'[9] Long before it found its way into a performance, I said this to somebody in a fit of real life, and realised later, 'Oh yeah, I could use that in the show!' But if there's no transformation, it's not art. Something has to change, metaphysically. With the audience, I really feel like that's my job. I don't feel superior to them. I feel I'm at my best when I don't know what I'm going to say, even though I'm afraid. It's a form of channelling.

It's also a part of my personality. But it's hard to explain to people that *I wasn't always like this*. I grew into it. I always saw things clearly, though, and it made people uptight. I'm an *empath*, and I'm psychic, and I see and know things about people. I was never an egomaniac. I didn't have the entitlement in my life that can create that. If you have a half-page in *Vogue* magazine as a performance artist, in 1988 at the age of 37, and all your mother can say is, 'Your mouth looks like the grand canyon', it's kind of hard to be egotistical. You'd have to be a really fucking insane narcissist to withstand the amount of emotional abuse I have endured since childhood – and go on to be an egotist. I'm also not crazy, which is a big deal because a lot of people working in the arts are *fucking nuts*. They're covering up for something. All human beings feel like less. *We've all been less than we want to be*. I feel a great freedom in saying that. I performed eight or so ten-minute performances this weekend, and people kept coming up to me saying, 'Thank you for making me feel something.' Wow, how bereft are we? Look at an artist like Ron Athey. He makes people *feel* something. I think Ron's audience can often be people who really don't feel *anything* otherwise, and they need to experience something that fucking intense to feel anything at all.

It's interesting to me that my work operates on an intellectual and emotional basis. I'm kind of emotion-phobic myself – it's part of survival – so my emotions always go through an intellectual process, although in performance I can convey really hardcore emotions to people. So many horrible things happen to me. I was already 46 or 47 before I understood that those horrible things didn't happen to *everybody*. I thought everybody had the same horrible life experiences as me! At the same time, I didn't *identify* with the horrible things that happened to me. I think from the very beginning of my life I saw myself as a *target*, not as a *victim*. I have very little self-pity in my emotional makeup. Self-pity doesn't work well in a survivalist context. I always see what happens in my life in a societal context, but I think that very few people can understand that distinction. I think that's how I know I'm truly sane. Some people are saner than others. Some people are more down to earth than others. I'm a very grounded, down-to-earth person but it creates problems in the way my work and I are perceived.

DJ: *I think you've been talking about authenticity – about what it means to be an 'authentic' person, and an 'authentic' performer. At times, you're clearly acting in your work. How does acting figure in what you've just been explaining?*

PA: Sometimes I can get closer to what I'm trying to portray by acting it, because it's something that's not really in my nature. Right now I'm doing this Tennessee Williams play called *The Mutilated* – Mink Stole and I are starring in it.[10] The character I play, Celeste, is *very* close to being me. I explained to the director, 'Celeste is me if I wasn't an intellectual.' All the rest is there. She's a proud person, an indomitable spirit, and vain. I'm quite vain – I'm interested in myself, my experience and abilities. I'm aware of my downfalls, my foibles, my weaknesses, and I'm very judgemental and critical about myself and my motivations.

In the case of Charlene, the prostitute character in *Bitch!Dyke!Faghag!Whore!*, I am acting. If you met her you'd recognise her immediately. With her, I instinctively know that I can use her voice, and it allows me to say things and get people to listen to things that they would never listen to if I wasn't acting. So, in *Bitch!Dyke!Faghag!Whore!* the only time I act, really, is when I play Charlene. When I do the phone girl, that's me. Those are all real phone calls. I did the phones in whorehouses a lot. As a matter of fact, I was both the whore *and* did the phone because I was very good at ferreting out the police. The little girl is me. I'm not acting I'm just being *that part* of me, which is still a very big, vital part, and very easy to tap into. That's about it. There's no other acting. My characters I act, but that is me wanting to *become* them and share those people with the world, like when I perform Margo Howard-Howard, or Andrea Whips.

Right now, we're rehearsing *The Mutilated*, and I'm very good at remembering lines.[11] I'll never say the line in the same way twice. I could have been an actress and it would have been so easy! It would have been much easier than having to generate my own material. As a child, I believed I was going to save my family by becoming an actress. Every night I would go to sleep with a lot of anxiety because we were very poor and my mother worked all the time. My grandparents raised me. We were four children all very close in age, immigrant peasant children in the 'bright promise' of 1950s America. I wasn't the only immigrant child in that town. There were other immigrant children, but they weren't Italian. The Italian children were all second- or third-generation, so they had cookies and toys. They were Americanised and we were not. When I went to school it was like being in this other culture that had nothing to do with what was going on at home. When I went back home I'd open the door and it would be like skipping six centuries. It was medieval Italy and I was a serf. I'm a displaced person from a family of displaced people. I'm always trying to heal and form some connection to something. It is typical of displaced people to easily identify with other people, or other cultures, because we are disconnected from what usually moors other people to society.

DJ: *Your performance* Old Queen *(2012) is scripted. When does the script get written, how, and why?*

PA: Through the 1980s, I didn't have scripts. My work was improvised every night in front of a live audience. I went on stage armed with only ideas. When I made *A Quiet Night with Sid and Nancy* in 1988 for Engarde Arts, the other performers didn't want to improvise, so I wrote a script for them. Then in 1991, I had to write a script for *La Miseria* because there were 33 people in it. So I wrote the parts for the other performers and I improvised my parts. For me, though, performance art is live action. Rehearsing performance art means you make bad theatre.

With *Old Queen*, I had been booked to do a work in progress at Dixon Place. It was happening in three weeks, but I was going through a divorce, and was doing nothing, and had nothing. I had done a small performance piece three years earlier at the same venue, where I became the Old Queen. It was visual, and non-verbal. I was crying a lot, because I was thinking about people who had died. The world that I come from has disappeared. I think people think they're respecting that world, but they don't respect it. They want it to be what *they* think it is. They love to worship the Goddess as long as it's not a *biological* woman. All these things are so twisted right now, and it's very *fin de siècle*. The good, the bad and the indifferent are all thrown up together at the same time.

In the meantime, I got booked in San Francisco at the Marsh. I was getting divorced and going through a hard time but I had a show to create. The day of the first performance I thought to myself, 'Jesus Christ, I still have *nothing.*' I sat down and wrote the AIDS monologue that morning and at 7pm I went on stage, and improvised it from what I remembered. Then I started to just tell stories, and people were totally transfixed by the story of how I entered into the gay world at the age of 14. I am known for developing work in front of an audience. I go on stage with the *ideas* I want to talk about, and then I find the material in the communion with the audience.

This particular time, though, we had about two weeks before the show at Dixon's Place, so I just started talking while Steve [Zehentner] wrote it down. Then he gave the material to me and I tried to learn some of it – or at least memorise the chronology of the pieces so as to not to interfere with the video and sound cues. I also memorised two of the Old Queen character's monologues. A lot more got improvised during the performances over the course of nine shows. I always say that someday I will write the script first and the press release second. Usually, though, I write the press release first. I need to find out what it is I want to talk about.

DJ: *Is there ever an instance in performance where the attempt at improvising fails? What is 'failure' in your work?*

PA: *New York Values* [2002] was a treatise on failure, long before that concept entered academic jargon. It takes so much to really attempt something, and there's a really big difference between wanting to be *good*, and wanting to be *true*. I'm talking about the chasm between those two things, where sometimes you fail. Sometimes the 'failure' is the crack in the idea you're trying to get to. That happens very frequently on stage. Something won't work, and I'll acknowledge it's not working. I'll say something to the audience about it. 'It's not working!' It's fun to tell the truth, although it hurts a little too.

In *New York Values* I talk about *the nobility of failure*, the idea that if your heart and mind are in the right place, failure is more powerful than success. Bad work doesn't involve this kind of failure. Bad work is just bad work. Failure is when you're really attempting something that's unmapped. Failure is being at risk. It can't just be something that's bad, or that lacks ability. Then the *concept* of failure is just an excuse.

DJ: *You performed a revival of* Bitch!Dyke!Faghag!Whore! *in London in 2012.*[12] *What changes did you make, and why?*

PA: I added six sentences to the show. The sentences I added were about AIDS right now, about how many new cases there are, and the side effects of AIDS cocktails, and to try to raise awareness about Hepatitis C. Over the course of the 48 performances in London I also changed an element about a relationship I had with somebody who had intimacy issues. It was so old – 20 years later I wasn't really

Figure 6.2 Penny Arcade, *Bitch!Dyke!Faghag!Whore!* (Arcola Theatre, London, 2012). Photograph by Holly Revell

interested in that any more. Instead, I started examining how I used to insist on being involved with people who didn't want to be involved with me, or I was involved with them and they couldn't give me what I needed, and then I *demanded* it from them. It happened after about six performances and then became part of the last 35 or so shows. I would say to the audience, 'I tortured perfectly nice people!' The audience were just howling, because they all understood it. *You must love me!* You have to love me, and if you will love me, I will give you my help, which you so desperately need! [*laughs*]. I was failing in being able to talk about it, but I was failing *with the audience*. Eventually it developed into a whole new monologue that had the same premise as the stuff about intimacy, but it shifted to becoming more about my inability to *want* to be in a relationship with myself. I constantly wanted somebody else to save me. I stopped focusing on the other people in my life and took responsibility for my own happiness. In our culture of coupledom that is a radical idea.

If I had my druthers, I would perform every day. That's what I love to do, and it's what I do best. It seems to be the thing I'm actually *made to do*, in that it's my livelihood and my form of behaviour. When I was 21 my friend Richard said to me, 'One day you're going to be very wise.' I replied, 'Really? Me?' [*laughs*]. I didn't set out to be who I am now, but I did set out to have the values that I now embody, which is a *fucking incredible* accomplishment.

DJ: *Is your work therapeutic?*

PA: I know that my work is therapeutic for others. Therapists have sent their clients and patients to see my work since the 1990s! It's not, however, *therapeutic for me*, because by the time I'm talking about something on stage I've already processed it a lot.

I entered serious analysis when I was 31 years old. I remained in analysis for 14 years, after which I have availed myself of many different forms of therapy. I am currently in therapy with a feminist therapist because I do fully understand now that so many of my problems stem from being a woman in a misogynist world. I do not share things in order to process them. By the time I reveal something on stage I have found a way to transform the experience into something else. But it's therapeutic to share our common dilemmas. An important element of my work is that it triggers empathy in the audience – a human ability that is being erased. Jack Smith asked, 'Could art be useful?'[13] It's the most important question. I want my work to contribute to the audience. My work triggers empathy, because I need empathy. I need sympathy and understanding. These things usually elude me in real life.

It's very hard to make 'content-based' art, because a lot of people can't stand content. In the 1980s, I asked a curator why The Kitchen wouldn't book me, and he said, 'There's too much content in your work.' Curators and venues need things to be vague so nobody gets into trouble. They think *real* art is vague. That is why they hated Jack Smith's work. It was too political, too honest that his pain was caused by society.

DJ: *In your work, is anything off limits?*

PA: I don't think so. My work assumes that sensationalism and content cannot coexist. If there is real content, there cannot be sensationalism. A provocative gesture without content is just shock. Ok, so you piss on stage. So what? You're nude. Really? You did a shit on stage? Wow. If there is not a transformational element, it's meaningless, it's inane. A real provocation leaves the theatre with the audience, and has an effect later on. Otherwise it's just shock. It's very easy to shock somebody, and it's also very easy for them to discount it. When an audience is *really* provoked, something is lodged within them and they cannot get away from it. With shock it's simply, 'Oh, you're just trying to shock me, so *fuck you*', or 'I was shocked, but now I'm not.' When something lodges inside of an audience and goes away with them, then that's a whole other arena of action.

DJ: *The Lower East Side Biography Project is very important. What drives the project, and what are its effects?*

PA: The fundamental thing that drives The Lower East Side Biography Project is what drives all of my work. I'm trying to combat the erasure of history. Everything I've learned, I've learned through people, because I didn't go to school. Oscar Wilde said 'nothing worth learning can be taught'. Most of what I've learned has been through highly self-individuated people. I wanted to reintroduce an intergenerational voice into New York, because it has been silenced. There is such a rift between older and younger artists. When you go to events in New York, the majority of people are under 30 because there is a terrible ageism at work. Old has never been younger in this city – or sadly anywhere else.

I did a pirate radio show called *Steal This Radio* for two years [1996–98] with Al Giordano of *Narco News*. In 1996, I did a fantastic interview with Sylvère Lotringer, from *Semiotext(e)*, and he was talking about everything happening *in the cracks*, now that free-market capitalism had erased the space for big movements. Moreover, Americans, as a whole, are culturally the least sophisticated people in the world.

I was performing at *Weimar New York* at Bard College this weekend, and this lovely kid turned up in drag, and I said, 'Querelle! Querelle!' He turns around and says, 'What?' So, I repeat, 'Querelle! You look like Querelle!', and he just says 'Who's that?' I said, 'Jean Genet? Fassbinder?' And he was like, 'Who?' I thought, is this really possible? It scares me. I mean, it's not *his* fault, it's part of the whole dumbing down of culture. In fact, very few people *hold the door open* to the past. That's the problem. It used to be the case that the privilege of having a connection to people that came before meant you would want *to hold the door open*. It hasn't always been: 'I'm just so fabulous all by myself.'

We keep missing people we want to interview, because they keep dying. We have no funding, and that's partly our fault too. The whole point of the Lower East Side Biography Project was to take all these highly individuated people and interview them and to let them show us how they achieved individuation. In the words of Jack Smith, 'To be in the presence of a genius for even an hour is enough!' Each interview will trigger something in you, and that's the function of the Lower East Side Biography Project. We really should be doing it full-time, or at least part-time with funding and money to go and get these people before they die. Every time you turn around some-one else dies, and they're not *making* people like that any more. Those stories are being lost. In my performance last Saturday night I said to the audience, 'I'm the *designated mourner* for a whole world that's disappearing.'

DJ: *As an audience member, what do you want when you go to see other people's work? What do you want from the encounter with art?*

PA: I want to experience a highly original point of view. I want to experience *work*. We call it work for a reason, there has to be some fucking *work* in there, *real* work. When someone is making real work, each thing they're doing is like putting together a giant jigsaw puzzle, you're part of that and your consciousness is part of that. I really believe that the audience doesn't *owe* you anything. They really don't. The current practice of a performer saying to the audi-ence, 'Give me some energy! Come on! Come on!' I say no. The way it works is that *you*, the performer, do something that amazes us and *then* we, the audience, may applaud. I don't applaud for nothing. If an artist does the same thing over and over in an attempt to make a product – even if you have a core audience who comes to see you – it's not going to have the same response the second or third time.

An artist should be generative. Art has to be a living thing! Penny Arcade Axiom Number One: Art can be product, but product can never be art.

Notes

1. See Penny Arcade, 'The Designated Mourner', http://pennyarcade.tv/ blog/ [accessed 24/08/14]. The title refers to a play of the same name: Wallace Shawn, *The Designated Mourner* (London: Faber & Faber, 1996).
2. To date, the series includes films on Betty Dodson, Mary Woronov, Gregory Corso, Herbert Huncke, Jayne County, Shaylah Beykal, John Jesurun, Jonas Mekas, Joel Markman, Tuli Kupferberg, Richard Foreman, Bruce Benderson, and many others.
3. This long response about Jack Smith is taken from an unpublished interview I did with Penny Arcade in May 2005, towards a research project on Smith. It has been introduced into the interview to expand on her discussion of her origins and influences.
4. Hibiscus (aka George Harris) was best known as the ringleader of the Cockettes, a bearded glitter drag troupe from San Francisco. The founding Cockettes disbanded in 1971, and Hibiscus left for New York, and set up the Angels of Light Free Theater in 1972. He died of AIDS in 1983.
5. Andrea 'Whips' Feldman was a Warhol Superstar known for her nutty, amphetamine-fuelled personality, and her spontaneous performances at Max's Kansas City. She committed suicide in 1972. Feldman spoke with a high-pitched, flattened, somewhat whining, highfalutin drawl, which Arcade emulates in performances including *True Stories: The Girl Who Knew Too Much* (1995).
6. Hilton Als, 'Critic's Notebook: Arcade Fire', *New Yorker* 86.4 (March 2010), 12.
7. See Patti Smith, *Just Kids* (London: Bloomsbury, 2010).
8. Arcade's understanding of *parrhesia* is influenced by her reading of Michel Foucault, *Fearless Speech*, ed. Joseph Pearson (Los Angeles: Semiotext(e), 2001).
9. The line first entered into her performances in the improvised piece *Sisi Sings the Blues* (Vienna Festival, 1996) and was added to the touring show *New York Values* (first shown at P.S. 122 in 2002).
10. *The Mutilated* was directed by Cosmin Chivu and played at the New Ohio Theatre, New York, in 2013. *The Mutilated* (1965) premiered on Broadway in 1966 alongside *The Gnädiges Fräulein* under the collective title *Slapstick Tragedy*. Mink Stole is an underground actor, best known as a co-star in John Waters's movies of the 1970s and 1980s, including *Pink Flamingos* (1972) and *Female Trouble* (1974).

11. On her role in *The Mutilated*, see Tim Murphy, 'Loud and Colorful, with Total Recall: The Performance Artist Penny Arcade, Now an Actress', *New York Times*, 31 October 2013, www.nytimes.com/2013/11/03/theater/for-penny-arcade-a-new-role-onstage.html [accessed 28/09/14].

12. *Bitch!Dyke!Faghag!Whore!* (1990) was restaged in London at the Arcola Theatre, 27 June–22 July 2012; and Albany Theatre, 15–23 December 2012.

13. 'Could art be useful' is the opening line of Jack Smith, 'Capitalism of Lotusland' (1977), in *Wait For Me at the Bottom of the Pool: The Writings of Jack Smith*, ed. J. Hoberman and Edward Leffingwell (New York and London: High Risk Books, 1997), p. 11.

7 Capricorn on Fire: An Interview with Ann Magnuson

Ann Magnuson is a polymath of sorts. She is best known as a performance artist who emerged from the Downtown scene, and a vocalist in bands – the psychedelic folk band Bongwater, and her art concept bands Vulcan Death Grip, and the Bleaker Street Incident. She has also exhibited paintings, including her *Fake Basquiats* series, and is a familiar character actress in mainstream movies and on television – all of which requires her to move peripatetically between over- and underground cultural spaces.

From 1978, Magnuson became what C. Carr calls 'a star of post-television performance'.[1] She would be a driving force of East Village and 'New Wave' performance, along with partners-in-crime such as Kenny Scharf, Kristian Hoffman, Joey Arias, John Sex and Klaus Nomi, particularly through her important work behind Club 57, Danceteria and other club performance spaces of the late 1970s and 1980s. Her performances typically involved zany characters. In the 1980s, these include her own concoctions, like televangelist Sister Alice Tully; Fallopia, the Prince lookalike; or Anoushka, the Soviet pop star. Or they were modelled on real-life personalities (usually scandalous ones), like Andy Warhol's muse Edie Sedgwick, or the Manson Family's Lynette 'Squeaky' Fromme (both performed with Joey Arias as, respectively, Andy and Charlie).

Magnuson's work is famously wild and wacky – typified for me by the Bongwater song *Dazed and Chinese* (1988), in which she sings Led Zeppelin's *Dazed and Confused* (1969) in Mandarin. However, her work is never simply comic vaudeville. Especially since the early 1990s, Magnuson's clarion call has been to remind her audiences of gentrification, and loss – especially of AIDS – and to create a utopian rejoinder, through performances, songs and other interventions that are typically kitsch, kooky and classy. For example, punctuated by a refrain of 'hello death, goodbye Avenue A', her *Folk Song* is a paean to lost friends and opportunities, and an obituary for Downtown New York. The song appears in an early version in her performance *You Could Be Home Now* (1990–93), and on Bongwater's album *The Power of Pussy* (1990). It's partly sung in Magnuson's trademark songbird vocals, or reeled off in a charging stream of acute observations and well-aimed accusations that are half-spoken, half-chanted. Glorifying death and destruction, she tells us, is no longer 'anarchist', but more likely a symptom of 'youthful brooding and sexually charged enthusiasm', which are regressive, or out of sync with the times – the times being the times they are, namely the time of AIDS, burnout, poverty and urban displacement.

Since the 1990s, Magnuson has presented cabaret-format performances, structured around songs (her own and covers), theatrical scenarios and patter. In her performance *Ann Magnuson Plays Bowie and Jobriath, or The Rock Star as Witch Doctor, Myth-Maker and Ritual Sacrifice* (2011), Magnuson explores (without irony, or parody) her love for Jobriath's music, memorialising her childhood cathexis in his glam rock excess and unabashed faggotry. Magnuson's *The Jobriath Medley* album (2012) showcases covers of songs by the glam-rock musician, interspersed with her own spoken-word memories and elegies, drawn from her live performance. She figures the sadness of Jobriath's bloated hype and sad decline, as his dreams turned to fairy dust, and in a crystalline little voice – which can turn to bluster and bombast, but here twinkles with a sensitive vibrato – her homage mourns the loss of youthful ideals, and the dimming of radical possibilities.

Our interview took place in Los Angeles in February 2013. As Magnuson explains, if her work has anatomised the material conditions of survival in a time of gentrification, personal loss and plague, her message is nevertheless a positive, affirmative one. 'A city set on a hill cannot be hidden,' she says at the end of her Jobriath tribute, 'nor do people light a lamp and put it under a bushel basket, but on a stand, and it gives light to all in the house.'[2] With her proud, delicate voice shimmering over choral orations, she ends her work with a note of wisdom borne of realism and experience, and wrought in amorous words and glamorous gestures. 'Be like her, your creator, and *create*,' she commands us, 'for you are the light of the world and must shine, shine, shine. *Shine on*, Star Children!'[3]

Dominic Johnson: *You arrived in New York in 1978. What was the trajectory that took you from West Virginia to New York?*

Ann Magnuson: I grew up in Charleston, West Virginia, doing puppet shows, theatre, music, art and dance. I was always dreaming up something, always writing. I made a little newspaper and wrote my own miniature comic books. I would cast my brother and the neighbourhood kids in shows I wrote and put on in our basement. My mother told me after President Kennedy was shot we were playing 'assassination' in the backyard (which she put an immediate stop to). I don't remember, but I don't doubt it happened. I grew up acting out stories and being creative in a lot of different ways, and my mother, who was a great lover of the arts, certainly encouraged me to be that way. In college I majored in theatre and cinema at Denison University in Granville, Ohio. I found myself in this tiny midwestern college town that was straight out of Norman Rockwell. A beautiful setting but the theatre department was fraught with frustrating politics and erratic personalities, which, actually, was probably great 'training' for the real world of show business. I was more encouraged by Elliot Stout, the film professor who also taught theatre history, than by the theatre department heads. There was one theatre professor, Calvin Morgan, a scenic designer, who was great. He took a group of us on a fantastic theatre trip to London and Prague for three weeks in January 1975. We hung out in Josef Svoboda's studio in Prague and it was amazing to experience a country still behind 'the Iron Curtain'. Experiences like those were my real education. I chose to do my junior year abroad in London in 1976–77. That was when the Sex Pistols and punk rock were erupting so it was a very interesting time to be there. Plus the Royal Shakespeare Company had an infamously stellar season then. I learned so much watching those productions. I rented a moped and just traversed every inch of London, spending every waking hour going to museums, concerts, films, and every kind of theatre from the fringe to the West End to the National Theatre. For a little gal from West Virginny I was a kid in a cultural candy store and I gorged myself on it all!

When I returned to Denison, I was part of a group of renegades who did our own fringe productions under the banner Theatre II. We did Ionesco's *The Chairs* in a lecture hall, Genet's *The Maids* in a warehouse on the outskirts of town, and I directed a Polish expressionist play called *The Mad Man and the Nun* [by Stanisław Ignacy Witkiewicz, 1923], adding a soundtrack by Ornette Coleman. I was always drawn to the wild, the wacky and the avant-garde.

In high school I was into David Bowie, Lou Reed, Alice Cooper – they were my gateway drugs, so to speak, into the land of rock'n'roll storytelling. But the earliest influence was probably Soupy Sales. He had a kids' show in the early 1960s that is best described as 'madcap Dada'. And all the variety/vaudeville-style TV shows that flooded the airwaves really informed my sensibilities, especially *The Smothers Brothers Show* and *Laugh-In*, which combined political satire with surreal wackiness. Plus watching Vietnam protesters, the Black Panthers and radical hippie troublemakers like Abbie Hoffman and the Chicago 7 creating their own style of agitprop theatre on the evening news every night. From an early age I liked the rabble-rousers, and the tricksters. Bugs Bunny was my first love. And when I discovered Isadora Duncan when I was 16, well, that sealed the deal. I wanted to live the artist's life!

DJ: *What drew you to New York, and what did the city mean to you?*

AM: The first time I went to New York was on the way back from that 1975 class trip to London and Prague. I was obsessed with Anthony Hopkins because of the 1972 BBC series *War and Peace*, and I wanted to see him in *Equus* on Broadway – so I ventured into the scary world of NYC alone ... and was promptly mugged. In my hotel room! By the maintenance man! He was sent up by the bellhop to fix my faulty heating. Well, he *said* he was the maintenance man. Maybe the two were in cahoots. I was very naïve. If I hadn't fought so hard I think I would have been killed. He pulled a switchblade on me. This was a hotel across the street from Lincoln Center, too. *Welcome to Noo Yawk City!*

I did go see *Equus* the next night. Then I scurried back to West Virginia to lick my wounds and then back to Ohio. But I'd had it with Denison. I figured out a way to spend the final semester of my senior year in New York on a work/study programme. I wanted to work at an avant-garde theatre – like Richard Foreman's Ontological-Hysteric Theater, or the Wooster Group – but I was placed in an Off-Off-Broadway theatre called the Ensemble Studio Theater. It was made up of people who had previous associations with the Actor's Studio and while it was fringe economically, they were aesthetically pretty traditional. But I learned a lot about what the Uptown theatre world was – and that I didn't want to be there. I went Downtown nearly every night, to Max's Kansas City and CBGB. New York represented danger, freedom, insanity, imagination run amok, punk rock, sex and rock'n'roll and I found all that Downtown.

DJ: *You wrote that there was 'something in the air' in West Virginia.[4] How is Charleston a context or origin for your work?*

AM: I refer to it constantly. Some shows are exclusively about it. Most of the Bongwater material was written there and was inspired by it. Home is a central issue in my work – it represents yearning, love and loss. It all begins and will probably end in West Virginia. The valley I was born and raised in was known as 'The Chemical Center of the World': Union Carbide, Dow and DuPont all had plants there. So the 'something in the air' was definitely chemical. But there is also something else, something ancient lurking in *them thar hills.* There is something mystical and spiritual and very, very weird going on in the woods of Appalachia. The Bible-thumpers and snake-handlers are part of it too. But so are the folk artists and those who just get blind drunk on a Saturday night and howl at the moon, Jerry Lee Lewis style. I certainly did a bit of that as a teenager out in those woods with my glam-rock hillbilly hippie friends. Then the madmen repent it all the next morning at church.

Charleston, West Virginia is pretty isolated and not easy to get to. Or get out of. It's quintessential Southern Gothic, but it's not quite as south as 'the Deep South' – we seceded from the Confederacy in 1863. That part of Appalachia is its own world, and the outside world only filtered in through television, pop culture and specifically rock music. You mix in Ziggy Stardust with the primal and the biblical and it becomes its own hybrid. Not to mention all the chemicals in the water tweaking the brain in some fashion.

My Grandfather Magnuson was a Swedish evangelist, and my grandmother was a strong believer. But I was brought up in a very positive, Golden Rule-following, Jesus-loves-all-the-little-children-of-the-world liberal Protestant environment. Even as a kid I was obsessed with the wilder, hyperventilating Pentecostal preachers on the TV and radio. I was fascinated by their trance states. I loved the atonal, backwoodsy gospel music, and the way the scripture was delivered with this incredible poetry and prosaic wordsmithing – plus someone was always dying of snakebites or from drinking strychnine. So how can you *not* become obsessed with that? Especially when you're equally obsessed with monster movies. Two of my one-woman shows – *You Could Be Home Now* [1990–93] and *Back Home Again (Dreaming of Charleston)* [2009] – were based on these Appalachian memories and experiences. I have an ever-present yearning for that place called 'home'.

I've also always been an intense and vivid dreamer. Those chemicals may have something to do with it. Or I was just blessed, or cursed, with an overabundance of DMT being secreted in the sleeping brain.

I am deep into Carl Jung now and am learning more about how and why these unconscious shadow worlds affect our behaviour and choices. These dreams make their way into all my work. In fact we just wrapped production on a new web series based on my dreams called *Ann Magnuson's Dream Puppet Theater*. I appear as hostess as well as different archetypes but I use these otherworldly dolls my Grandma Magnuson made to tell the stories. They're created out of old stockings, pipe cleaners, fabric remnants, sequins and intricate crochet. They are wonderfully strange looking. My grandmother was very much a folk artist, although she would never have described herself in that way.

DJ: *You started Club 57 shortly after arriving in New York in 1978. How did that come about?*

AM: I was hanging out at Max's and CBGB and I met a lot of people who I would end up being lifelong friends and collaborators with, including Kęstutis Nakas, Kenny Scharf, Tom Scully, Susan Hannaford, Klaus Nomi, Kristian Hoffman, Lance Loud (who I knew about from watching *An American Family* [1971] on TV back in West Virginia); and, a little later, others like Eric Bogosian, Joey Arias, Steve Buscemi and Lydia Lunch. (See **Figure 7.1**.) Then there were the tribal elders like Jack Smith, Jackie Curtis and other Warhol Superstars – and eventually Andy himself. Tom, Susan and I had a shared passion for so many things: from monster movies to Dada to old vaudeville, which was

Figure 7.1 Polaroid photographs of Ann Magnuson and Joey Arias, taken after a performance of *The Imitators* (Danceteria, New York, 1984). Photographer unknown. © Ann Magnuson

perfect because Tony Pastor's Opera House was just down the road from CBGB on the Bowery. That is what we first bonded over, when we all met at CBGB and decided we *had* to revive vaudeville! First and foremost I wanted to be a director of original works – I wasn't interested in putting on the usual scripted plays – and so the *New Wave Vaudeville Show* [1978] dawned on us as something we had to do.

In the Downtown scene there was only around 300 'cool' people at the most, and you ended up knowing everybody. Even if you didn't meet everyone face-to-face, you could identify them as part of the scene just by passing them in the street: you knew because of the way someone dressed, or if their hair was dyed blue-black or peroxide blonde or an unusual colour (Club 57 member Drew Straub had blue hair – a first – and it sadly got him beaten up a couple of times). It wasn't too difficult to get involved in everyone else's productions – Tom [Scully] had written a play called *Moo Goo Guide Plan*, and he asked me to be in it. Jackie Curtis was the star, and I had seen Jackie in the movie *W. R. Mysteries of the Organism* [dir. Dušan Makavejev, 1971], which Elliot Stout, my saviour film professor, had shown us in Ohio in film history class. Just working alongside Jackie made me feel like I had *made it*! We were all kinetic pinballs bouncing off each other in the crazy, dangerous, exciting pinball machine known as Downtown New York.

The *New Wave Vaudeville Show* took place at Irving Plaza, which Tom and Susan had found. This fellow Stanley Strychacki worked there and he also supervised the 'little' Club 57 which was in the basement of the Polish National Church at 57 St. Mark's Place. He asked Tom to manage the club. Tom didn't want to take over all those duties. He and Susan Hannaford preferred to curate special one-off film festivals, and they hosted a weekly event called *Monster Movie Club*. They were involved in many of the theme nights there too. Tom and Susan were cineastes of the highest order, and they programmed fantastic films, which, at the time, were extremely obscure and very hard to find. All real film. 16mm prints. Projected! Tom suggested that I manage the club as a whole and programme all the other nights and I jumped at the chance as I lived to organise. *I was a Capricorn on fire*!

My desire to be a theatre director was channelled into the club. Every night was a different night, a different piece of theatre, and we created these unusual environments – you could call it immersive theatre. We had theme parties, film festivals, tons of live performances. Jack Smith performed there. We had fashion shows, and screened old films and forgotten TV shows, the 'new' video art, underground films by upcoming filmmakers, 'classic' underground stuff – Kenneth Anger showed some of his films – and we put on 'real' plays from time to time too. We even had a lady wrestling night, a wacko prom for all of us who skipped our real high-school prom and a whole kaleidoscope of other uncategorisable stuff.

People were initially drawn into the club by an incredible jukebox filled with 45s from Tom's collection. We were all go-go dancing like the teenagers on *Shindig!*, a show we watched as little kids in the 1960s. Now we were grown up and could act out all our wildest fantasies. Like London before, the East Village was a candy store. It was a dangerous and rather scummy candy store, but that made the candy all the more bright and tasty.

DJ: *I'm interested in cabaret, vaudeville and club performances as forms that have productive limitations built into them. Was this the case for you? How are these conditions productive for an artist?*

AM: Club performance is punk rock as theatre. It was immediate, disposable, doable and affordable. At the time, nobody had any money at all, so it was really the only way we could make performances. We tried to book bands at Club 57 but the neighbours were up in arms about the noise, so we needed to devise alternative forms of entertainment, and we settled on film programmes and conceptual theatre on a shoestring budget. Many of us were informed by the Theatre of the Absurd, Dada and the Surrealists, the performance art of Yoko Ono. John Sex, Keith Haring, Wendy Wild and Kenny Scharf were all students at the School of Visual Arts at the time, and were applying their newfound knowledge directly into action at the club. John Sex created his *Acts of Live Art* shows [1981] right after learning about Hugo Ball and the Zurich Dadaists. We turned each other onto a lot of things. I told Keith Haring about my hero Alfred Jarry, whom Keith had never heard of, and Keith, in turn, taught me William S. Burroughs's cut-up method when he performed his version at the St. Mark's Poetry Project nights.

Later on, around 1982, Marc Shaiman and Scott Wittman became an integral part of the club. Marc and Scott brought in a more polished Broadway-style professionalism to the club – although it was a very twisted version of Broadway. They created their own wacky musicals and, decades later, won a Tony for *Hairspray*. When I saw them on Broadway, Scott gleefully told me, 'Ann, it's like Club 57 with money!'

A lot of the conditions were fuelled by alcohol – but mainly we were fuelled by a sense of community, and a sense of necessity. We *had* to create – or *die*! At least I had to. There was no other place to do our work, so we took advantage of the DIY method and made our own venues – rather than wait around for somebody to approve of us or give me a break. We just did it ourselves, for ourselves – in that sense it wasn't that different from the puppet shows I did in my basement growing up.

There's a sense of freedom in club performance. We bonded together and created a surrogate family, but without the interference of a naysaying authority figure. There was no Grand Poo-Bah. At the Ensemble Studio Theater the Artistic Director was very much in charge, a successor to that old school acting world patriarchy – not unlike Lee Strasberg. Uptown there was definitely more of a patriarch-run hierarchy that everyone dutifully adhered to. I was his assistant so was privy to hearing what was said behind closed doors. I would watch desperate actors and actresses come in and then hear what was said about them and I decided: there is *no fucking way* I am *ever* going to be an actor! I want to be in control of my destiny. So it's ironic that I'd end up making a living as an actress. I think that only happened because I didn't actively pursue it. I pursued my passion for the alternative and was noticed for that.

Frankly, one of the appeals of Downtown was you could reinvent the wheel. And women had more autonomy. There were strong women like Ellen Stewart at La MaMa ETC, and people like Patti Smith who took the bull by the horns and did what she wanted. Lydia Lunch was a real trailblazer too. In New York at that time there were a lot of male acting teachers abusing their power – and that just seemed like a repeat of what I experienced at Denison. Certainly abuse of power is a recurring theme in institutional theatre and academia. So I ran as far away from that as I could. Cabaret, punk rock and alternative clubs is a big 'fuck you' to authority figures. Of course much of the alternative work is going to be rougher and messier, and there might be a different ratio of success to failure, but for me the concepts of 'failure' and 'success' weren't applicable. That was the central appeal to me of Downtown New York. We didn't need to adhere to old rules and traditions. We did something new every night. If something didn't 'work' it didn't matter. You'd try something different the next night. The stakes were low so you could take endless risks. That was what punk rock was all about. Once you have a taste of that kind of freedom it's very hard to go back. That is why

Figure 7.2 Ann Magnuson, *After Dante* (The Kitchen, New York, 1981). Photograph © Paula Court

I operate like the Vietcong with the mainstream world. You pop up where you have to, do the job, grab the money then scurry back down into a series of tunnels and re-emerge where you are safe to create freely. I have been continually drawn to people who work in that vein, and to environments that allow you to do anything you wanted.

Our band Bongwater followed the same ideals, but musically. When we were recording I didn't think anybody would buy our records. I didn't think anyone was even listening. There was no Internet, no way to get this stuff to anyone except a small band of freaks, and there was never a time when I thought any of it would be played on any kind of radio station – let alone be a hit record. Not that Bongwater would've *ever* had a 'hit' record! [*Laughs.*] I just made up songs or brought in a bunch of texts and my ever-present dream journal, and cut loose. It was total freedom, and there was never a sense that the music was going to make any money. The prime motivation was to laugh, and, for me, to work out the angst. I see now that Bongwater was all about flinging the doors wide open onto the unconscious shadow world, releasing the wild things. The fact it garnered a cult following – and we actually sold records – came as a complete surprise to me.

DJ: *Why did you start to move away from New York?*

AM: Kristian Hoffman moved back to California in 1984 and I came out to visit him and perform in our sardonic folk band Bleaker Street Incident. By the mid-1980s the East Village sensibility was being co-opted by Uptown money people who were coming Downtown in their limousines. MTV was starting their commodification of Downtown artistic sensibilities. As far as I was concerned the East Village was over by 1987 – which, coincidentally, was also the year Warhol died – and it was much more exciting here in LA. I left New York during a horrible blizzard, in January or February when a really intense winter depression can sink in and I felt reborn by the California sunshine! I met artists like Jim Shaw and Mike Kelley and the alternative theatre and music scenes in LA were really thriving. Reza Abdoh was doing theatre that blew my mind! LA bands like Redd Kross and artists like Jim and Mike had the kind of sensibilities that first drew me to New York. There were cool alternative theatre and cabaret spaces in LA like Olio and the Lhasa Club where you could wave your freak flag very, very high, in the wayest-way-out part of the truly *alternative* Tinseltown. I kept my apartment in New York, but started coming out here more often.

DJ: *You mentioned Jim Shaw and Mike Kelley as being crucial for you in LA. I know this was also the case for other artists, especially in the 1980s. How did they influence you?*

AM: Partly, I was influenced and encouraged by their humour. Jeffrey Vallance was actually the first 'LA artist' I was turned onto. I really love his sense of humour in works like *Blinky, the Friendly Hen*.[5] I love the conceptual nature of the work, and his very sharp intelligence. I loved Jim Shaw's work with dreams, which I also work with, and after meeting him I asked him to do the cover artwork for the next Bongwater album, *Too Much Sleep* [1989]. Mike Kelley was hilarious, and smart, and always sticking it to The Man. I sang and improvised songs in Mike's band Supersession, which he did with other artists, using rotating vocalists. I think Raymond Pettibon did vocals directly before me. I incorporated some of my material for Supersession into the musical story I told in *The Luv Show*, including *Miss Pussy Pants*, which perfectly combines Mike's Detroit wildness and those teenage nights when I was howling at the moon in West Virginia. All these folks I met were, like me, teenage hippies, then punks, and they retained those anarchic sensibilities – rebellion against authority figures – with a shitload of wit. I'm glad they became very successful, although I know that before his death Mike was disillusioned with the art world. Success of that magnitude means you're just making art for rich people. That is what always seems to happen. It happened in the East Village, it's happening now in Silver Lake through gentrification, and the art world has been completely taken over by The Money Machine. As Dave Hickey said, everyone in the art world is now a courtier to the rich.

I think the key is your motivation. Why are you making the work? Is it to be the next Art Star? Or to give creative expression to something that simply has to come out of you? Can the two coexist? Then one must ask, where is your artwork going? There's a cul-de-sac in that gated community called Wealth, and once you get in there you're stuck, and then you're creating work only for one express purpose, namely to please and serve the Rich – and if you fall short of pleasing those consumers, you're deemed a failure. The world that delineates people into 'Failure' and 'Success' bores the hell out of me and I try to steer as clear as possible. It'll kill you. When you see it coming, *quick*, make like the Vietcong and scurry down into those tunnels!

DJ: *Do you think of yourself as an 'LA artist'?*

AM: The few times I do go to auditions, people will still think that I am only visiting LA – they're shocked that I've lived here for over 25 years. They say they think of me as a New Yorker. Is that an insult? Maybe! Or perhaps it's the ultimate compliment? I think of myself as a West Virginian, first and foremost. I remember when I first wanted to make a career in show business, you either went to New York or LA. But in the 1970s, LA was *CHiPs* and *Charlie's Angels*, and I knew wouldn't fit in, so it had to be New York. New Yorkers still like to believe there is more 'gravitas' in New York and LA is just a superficial Tinseltown but I think it's now the reverse. Since Manhattan has been invaded by *Sex and the City* hordes and run by the one per cent, it's more like what we used to accuse LA of being: status-seeking, money-grubbing superficiality. I used to write a column for *Paper Magazine* and I addressed this subject stressing the diversity of LA. It has lots of different neighbourhoods and includes vastly different elements and, hence, more options.

I recently read a quote by David Bowie about his time in LA in the 1970s, when he was whacked on cocaine – it's a singular perspective – and he was calling LA 'the most vile piss-pot in the world', full of the worst aspects of humanity.[6] I know that part of town but I make a point of not getting off at that exit. Not unless there is a damn good paycheck involved. New York City is clearly no longer hospitable to artists and LA is rapidly following suit. So I think calling someone a 'New York artist' or a 'LA artist' is meaningless, because everything is ruled by the same marketplace now. Is your god money, or is your god something else? I am excited by the homegrown art scenes in places like Joshua Tree. There is even one in Charleston, West Virginia, which excites me more than what is happening in New York.

DJ: *You're well known to some audiences as an actor in movies and TV. How and when did you start performing in these industries?*

AM: In New York around 1981 I began to get parts in 'indie' movies. I was in *Vortex* [1982] by Beth and Scott B, alongside James Russo, and he introduced me to Mary Goldberg, a top casting agent. Sergio Leone was in town casting for *Once Upon A Time in America* [1984] and I loved his films so was over the moon just getting to meet him! I wasn't right for that, but Mary Goldberg remembered me when Tony Scott came to NYC casting *The Hunger* [dir. Tony Scott, 1983]. Susan Seidelman cast a lot of Downtown people in *Desperately Seeking Susan* [1985], so I got a role in that film. Then I did Sara Driver's *Sleepwalk* [1986] – shot by Jim Jarmusch – which was instrumental in Seidelman casting me as the lead in *Making Mr. Right* [1987, with John Malkovich].

The producer of the TV show *Anything But Love* saw me in *Making Mr. Right* and offered me a regular role in the series.[7] So one thing literally led to another. I was really in agony deciding whether I should do a sitcom. I thought being on TV was 'selling out' – a notion that sounds incredibly quaint now. I remember having a long talk with Vincent Gallo about it, and he emphatically told me to take the money and run. That sitcom was smartly written and was *The Iceman Cometh* compared to the reality dreck on TV now. Nevertheless, I took a lot of flak for doing that show. But I needed money. I wasn't living on a trust fund. I had to make it entirely on my own. So the money I made from that TV show and other mainstream work was funnelled back into doing my other decidedly uncommercial work. That's worked out pretty well until recently, when the mainstream work is scarcer and it pays far less than it used to.[8] It has also become very difficult to do DIY stuff. The economic landscape has changed a lot and not for the better for artists.

DJ: *I'm interested in artists' processes. What is your process for getting from an idea to a piece of writing to a finished performance?*

AM: It generally starts with an idea. Hatching a plot. Writing. Words are usually first but sometimes it's a piece of clothing or, with music, it's a riff or a beat. Or I find an object at a thrift store, or lying by the road, and I think, 'That's art!' It's putting together the pieces of a puzzle. The pieces often come from my dreams. I want to go on a journey and I want that journey to be fun for me and for everybody else. I like to embed 'heavier' ideas in there that maybe aren't readily observable. I also like to use comedy and surrealism as the bait. The Bowie/Jobriath show [*Ann Magnuson Plays Bowie and Jobriath, or The Rock Star as Witch Doctor, Myth-Maker and Ritual Sacrifice*, San Francisco Museum of Modern Art (SFMOMA), 2011] was just such a Trojan Horse – the audience thinks they're coming to see a show about Bowie and they get the classic Bowie tunes but then we hit them with *The Jobriath Medley* encore and tell *that* story.[9] It's basically a story about success and failure, and suggests that neither of those exists except in the illusory world of currency. Bowie was a 'success' but it nearly killed him. Jobriath was a 'failure' but his story is the classic hero's journey, and we end the night with Jobriath triumphing as the star!

My process also has to do with whomever I'm collaborating with – and basically we're usually just making each other laugh. I did that a lot in the 1980s with my friend William Fleet Lively, and it was certainly the case in Bongwater (although some stuff, like *Folk Song*, was entirely mine). Kristian Hoffman and I collaborate often but right now I'm working on my own in the recording studio, with just the engineer and me. I'll bounce ideas off him but I've been writing the material alone. If I am collaborating – and theatre is almost always a collaborative art – I usually make an outline before sitting down with the person I'm working with and then create a road map as we go along. There are detours and tangents galore. It often looks like one of those spider webs when they've given the spider LSD. I used to refer to my one-woman shows as Rube Goldberg inventions.[10] I basically create them that way for my own pleasure. Thankfully other people seem to enjoy them too.

My pieces are always scripted, but I like there to be a lot of room for accidents, mishaps, spontaneity and improvisational madness. I don't perform long runs any more. I do each show a few times. Twice is usually enough for me to exorcise the demon and move on. I know that causes problems from the business end of things – by the time people might find out about a show I've already started the next project.

DJ: *An important part of my project of interviewing involves asking about other artists whose work has in some ways been excluded from or obscured within the historical record. I'd like to ask you about John Sex and Klaus Nomi, both of whom you worked with and were friends with. What was important to you about their work?*

AM: John Sex was very smart. He was a very positive can-do person. He was also a fantastic visual artist. He made great silk-screens and we used many of them as posters for Club 57 events, but John put that work aside when he discovered the unbridled joys of performing. John had a very generous spirit and a hilarious sense of humour. That was the energy we all seemed to thrive on: enthusiasm, encouragement and positive reinforcement.

Klaus Nomi wanted to be a star. John did too but in a much more carefree way. We were all living in the moment, but perhaps because he was older, Klaus didn't want to waste time. When he got his chance he ran with it, and rightfully so. Klaus made science fiction real by remaking himself into 'Nomi', a New Wave alien opera diva. John also reinvented himself, as a Liberace/Tom Jones hybrid. He also played the lead in Scott Wittman and Marc Shaiman's production of *Peter Pan*. We were all Peter Pans in a way, encouraging each other to not grow up, going on collective flights of fantasy – daydream believers who can make something out of nothing. That's what theatre is. John did it with a lot of American optimism and sparkle, and Klaus with German resolve and a devilishly charming, mischievous streak.

When Klaus and Joey Arias sang back up with David Bowie on *Saturday Night Live*, it inspired us all to shoot for the moon.[11] Unfortunately, Klaus's ambition led him into some terrible business deals right about the time he got sick. In a way, that became its own cautionary tale. When Klaus died we were all bereft.[12] I think that's when lot of us stopped shooting for the moon and set our sights on Pluto, because if you were going to die tomorrow you might as well go way, waaaay out there! So, we circled the wagons and encouraged each other to take it into overdrive. There's a snippet of Klaus on a Bongwater record, *Breaking No New Ground!* [1988]. It's an answering-machine message he left me right before he died. I began to collect them when people started dying because it was the only way I knew how to keep them alive. One day I want to make a sound installation with all the messages. I still can't listen to them though. It's too painful.

Every one of us, including John and Klaus, was bursting with the desire to shine. Beginning with the *New Wave Vaudeville Show,* where Klaus debuted his Nomi character, the environment we created Downtown provided those opportunities. In the 'straight' world we were fleeing there were so many refusals. No, no, no. We were collectively stampeding to the land of *yes* – and this is always easier to do when you're in a group.

DJ: *There are two specific works of yours that I'd like to ask you about. The first is* You Could Be Home Now *(1990–93). The performance is clearly about coming to terms with loss, mourning and sorrow.*

AM: It started with my Dad announcing he was going to sell the house we grew up in. My brother and I were pretty upset about that but we also didn't have any say in it. I created the show as a meditation on home and also to express all the feelings I was told I had to hide. That is the main reason I do any of these shows. To get the unexpressed feelings expressed.

I had started to lose friends to AIDS very early on – 1982 or 1983. Henry Post was the first one, then Klaus. My brother Bobby told me he was HIV-positive around 1986 but I wasn't supposed to tell anybody. My best friend from West Virginia told me he was HIV-positive the next year but I wasn't supposed to tell anybody. A host of other people very close to me told me they were HIV-positive but I wasn't supposed to tell anybody. This was a horrifically fearful time and there was lot of ignorance about the disease and, hence, a lot of secrecy. I was crushed by the weight of these secrets and the mounting grief as the deaths began to pile up. By the time I wrote *You Could Be Home Now* I figured everybody was going to die. I thought I was going to die. I thought: there's no reason I shouldn't have it. So it was certainly about loss. It included *Folk Song,* which ended up on the Bongwater record *The Power of Pussy* [1990]. The chorus begins with 'Hello death, goodbye Avenue A', and suggests we could die tomorrow, next week or next year, so let's make the most of the time we do have. Don't delay! Follow your bliss wherever that bliss may lead! It's only in the last ten years that I've started to shake that feeling, that trauma. I got used to seeing someone in the street and then hearing just a few months later that he had died. It was a hellish time. This all started to escalate when I got the part in *Making Mr. Right,* which was supposed to be my big break in movies. But I was in such a state of perpetual trauma and sadness that it was impossible to fully play that game. I couldn't tell anyone, outright, why I was so depressed. I was keeping so many secrets.

The reviewer at the *Village Voice* got it; he recognised that *You Could Be Home Now* was about deep sadness and loss. That was probably why a lot of the other reviewers didn't like it. Who wants to be sad? In the theatre world there are too many rules, and that show got lambasted as it didn't have a traditionally clear narrative and there was no flat-out moment where I tell the 'moral to the story'. I was interested in deconstructive approaches to theatre – the Wooster Group was a big influence, and so was the legendary Jeff Weiss, who was one of the first Downtown theatre performers I met. *You Could Be Home Now* got fantastic reviews in Toronto. Flat-out raves! And I toured it in San Francisco and Seattle, and it had a very good run in LA. But I had a difficult time with that show. It was very painful. But we did fantastically well in NYC for a show that got trounced by the mainstream critics. It was sold out, and people were scalping tickets for $300 a pop! We didn't make any money for the investors, but we didn't lose them any either.

DJ: You Could Be Home Now *is about personal loss – the loss of specific people to AIDS – but also the loss of New York City to gentrification. It also seems to be about the loss of hope, authenticity, excitement, or possibilities for the future.*

AM: Yes. I really came out of the hippie era, which itself came out of the beatnik era. We thought there was going to be an alternative way of living and it did exist for a while. But then it was co-opted by the world of currency where there are winners and losers – and you better be a winner. But I was only ever interested in the 'losers'. But now they've even turned losers into a brand.

Don't get me wrong – we all need money, not least because in this country we have to buy health insurance. I have played the game too. I own a house. I have health insurance. The freedom I had when I was doing Club 57 or Bongwater was only possible because I had an apartment in New York that only cost $150 a month. I didn't want any more than I needed, and I needed very little. To be truly free you have to have freedom from economic constraints. You can't want things. You can't have insurance premiums due.

I think the most radical thing you can do today is create something that has absolutely no commercial application whatsoever.

That's why I think someone like Genesis BREYER P-ORRIDGE is brilliant. Penny Arcade also tells the truth. Jack Smith was a true artist rebel genius kook. I worked with Jack, and would see him around the East Village all the time. Today I am mostly interested in folks who follow in their footsteps, like Heather Woodbury, Robbie D. or Shari Elf. They're creating incredibly original work on very little money, but with tonnes of ingenuity. And, of course, what Pussy Riot is doing in Russia is hands-down the most important performance work going on today.

Like all my performances, *You Could Be Home Now* was a kind of exorcism – a way to come to terms with the pain you can't express in any other way. *Rave Mom* was the same. Everything in Bongwater was too. Is it catharsis? Yes, some shows more than others. That's why I don't want to keep performing the same pieces – I experience the catharsis, then I can move onto the next thing that can be dealt with, observed, or shared. (See **Figure 7.3**.) Or changed. After this latest chemical spill that contaminated the water in six West Virginia counties – including my home town – it seems the only show worth doing now is one that addresses the crazy corruption of the coal industry.

Figure 7.3 Ann Magnuson, *Revival Meeting* (Life Café, New York City, 1982). Photograph by Laura Levine. © Laura Levine

DJ: *A series of performances for camera were published in* Paper *magazine in October 1992. I understand you were burlesquing Madonna's* Sex *book.*[13]

AM: I have done a lot of 'performances for camera' for various magazines. That was one of many I did for *Paper*. It was called *I Have A Sex Book Too*. I hadn't actually seen Madonna's book at the time. I had only heard about it, and it sounded ridiculous, so I thought: 'I have a sex book too!' It was a parody of the idea, before her book even came out. It was really just a springboard – into a different swimming pool altogether. [*AM gets the magazine from her archive.*] I told the idea to my friend the photographer Len Prince, and he came on board to shoot the series. David Hershkovits at *Paper* wrote the introductory text: [*AM reads from the magazine*] ' "I have a sex book too", she says. "It's called *Wank*. It will be sealed in latex that you have to bite off, and sold on the Home Shopping Network. It's going to accompany my album *Neurotica*." Ann Magnuson is winking again using her multifaceted talent to poke fun at the world around us.'

It was straight-up satire. Joey [Arias] played Steven Meisel and my friend Pilar Limosner did the styling for us. We also got Al Lewis involved – he played Grandpa in *The Munsters*. That was really bizarre. We were laughing ourselves sick during the shoot. Len had a big dildo that Joey was playing with at one point. Sadly, those pictures weren't published. I wore an SM mask in another image, playing the suburban housewife who ate her kids, and I did silly sexual poses with stuffed animals in another. Here I am having a gang-bang with Republicans. This one's me as Babe Wrangler, my old-school butch dyke character. I was still doing Bongwater at the time, and we had a song called *Chicken Pussy* based on a dream I had, so we did an image with a taxidermy chicken.[14] Here I am topless as the Vargas girl who gets her revenge by airbrushing away The Male Gaze. *Paper*'s deadline prevented them from finishing my concept, where the photographer is being airbrushed into oblivion by the pinup girl. That was annoying. So that piece is definitely due for a restoration!

Jeez, I was doing this stuff for free! It's kind of ridiculous, especially when you consider *Playboy* was willing to pay me to do a topless pictorial when I was on TV. But *Playboy* would never have let me do it as satire. I never thought about the future, or about the consequences of anything back then. For *Paper* it was all good clean fun. It was all an excuse to laugh, and to get the drug of endorphins going. I'm sure it's a main reason why I do any of this, for the serotonin surge.

DJ: *I want to ask you about the way you move between forms, media, sectors and venues. You're a polymath, and you are very versatile in choosing formats or venues that suit a specific project. Is that resourcefulness, or strategy? What drives your versatility?*

AM: Opportunities. Of course, sometimes I have a feeling about what kind of piece I want to do, and I will look for suitable mediums or venues to make that a reality, but by and large it has been about what opportunity presents itself at a particular moment. In the past I have turned down a tremendous amount of potentially lucrative mainstream work and I look back on some of those decisions and I am aghast! I turned down jobs because I didn't think they were 'cool' (and often they weren't), but there was only a small window of opportunity where I could have potentially made some really big money by saying yes to a lot of things I said no to. But in the world I came from it definitely was *not* cool to be rich. Even in West Virginia where I knew families with some really big coal money it was considered tacky to flaunt it. I still think worshipping the trappings of luxury is tacky. Immoral really. When I was a teenager the cool people were the ones on the fringe. Come to think of it, the original London cast recording of *Jesus Christ Superstar* was one of my first LPs and who celebrated the fringe more than Jesus? All the people I was interested in – the New York Dolls in particular – they came out of the hippie era and then created glam and spawned punk, and they were rebels.[15] The Dolls probably wanted to be as big as the Rolling Stones but I didn't know that. I just saw the anarchy ... and the lipstick. The people I liked didn't want to be successful, or accepted. You could call it arrested adolescence, and it probably is, but I've never completely outgrown that. And, of course, David Bowie moved with great fluidity between various guises and mediums so I just accepted that is what an artist is – or was – supposed to do.

DJ: *I'm interested in the frequency with which artists of your generation cite punk as crucial to one's politics as an artist.*

AM: Certainly rock'n'roll provided a particular value system for me as a youth, and I haven't really shaken it. I keep going back to the music that gave me goose bumps when I was 14 or 15, although the thrills aren't quite the same now – apparently you lose serotonin levels as you age – but there's a Pavlovian response to things that gave you a kick when you were forming your ideas about what you valued, and what you wanted out of life. Ultimately I think punk gave us all the freedom to 'talk back' when we were expected to keep quiet.

DJ: *While punk has been important, glam has also been influential for you. Is there something you value in its superficiality?*

AM: I don't think glam is superficial. I think there's something very deep and beautiful in glam music and culture. It's about theatricality, or the Vedic idea 'play and display', which is the essence of life. For me, glam was always connected to Art Nouveau, which is a very feminine energy. That was an important thing back then, considering the Vietnam War was still raging and the hawkish macho men were in serious control. Art Nouveau was concerned with emulating the explosions of gorgeousness in nature – like peacocks and birds of paradise. To me it's a celebration, a very joyful thing, and not necessarily a front or a pose, though for some it clearly was that. I also associated it with the Ken Russell movies of the time – *The Boy Friend* [1971] and *Women in Love* [1969] – or Diaghilev, the Ballets Russes, Gustav Klimt, Aubrey Beardsley, Erte.

There is a lot of hippie in my glam. But I don't put on make-up unless I absolutely have to. Truthfully, my everyday life is more macramé than glitter.

DJ: *What was it about Jobriath that excited you?*

AM: At first I was interested in the fact that his music was piano-based rock with a classical bent. I took piano lessons as a kid and loved classical music. While I was listening to Bowie and Lou Reed – *Hunky Dory*, *Ziggy Stardust*, *Transformer*, *Berlin* – or the New York Dolls and Alice Cooper, I was also listening to Glenn Gould, Bach, Debussy, Chopin and Mendelssohn's *A Midsummer Night's Dream*. I played classical records as much as I played rock records. Jobriath wove that into glam. The infamous ad for his first record appeared while we were waiting for Bowie's next album, so Jobriath simply felt like another icon to add to the collection. I loved the lush productions, and we certainly tried to emulate that in the strings on *The Jobriath Medley*. I didn't really know the tragedy of Jobriath's story at the time. Brian Eno, Patti Smith, Television and Richard Hell began to take centre stage and my tastes shifted while Jobriath faded away. When I met Kristian [Hoffman] and Lance [Loud], we'd start talking about our record collections and when Jobriath's name came up everyone knew him. We all responded to the same dog whistle. In 1996, Kristian helped me put together a show called *Pretty Songs*.[16] We got the idea to do some Jobriath tunes since he wrote the prettiest songs. That's when I learned the sad details about what happened to him and realised I had to tell his story while singing his songs. Audiences thought I made the story up. Nobody had heard of him. Artists like Jobriath gave me the freedom to allow my imagination to run wild – to be magical instead of practical – and it's my hope that our recording of *The Jobriath Medley* pays that forward.[17]

DJ: *Your performance at the Museum of Modern Art in San Francisco was titled* The Rock Star as Witch Doctor, Myth-Maker and Ritual Sacrifice *(2011). Do you channel the rock star in everything you do?*

AM: No, not at all. I channel hundreds of different personae. But the rock star has the *cojones* to get out there and say 'look at me!' That certainly sticks with a teenager still forming an identity. The rock star is the shaman who gives you permission to do certain things you might not otherwise have the courage to try. That's what art and theatre are for – so we can all be shamans. Then we can all throw a party, dance around the fire, and conjure up infinite worlds!

Notes

1. C. Carr, 'Am I Living in a Box?', *On Edge: Performance at the End of the Twentieth Century* (Middletown, CT: Wesleyan University Press, 1993), pp. 229–31 (p. 229).
2. Ann Magnuson, *Jobriath Medley* (Pink Fleece Music, 2012).
3. Ibid.
4. See Ann Magnuson's website: http://annmagnuson.com/performance.html [accessed 01/05/13].
5. *Blinky, the Friendly Hen* (1978) was a conceptual art piece in which Vallance purchased a frozen chicken from a supermarket, named it Blinky, and took it to a pet cemetery in Los Angeles, as a commentary on the meat industry and varying attitudes towards animals as pets and as material for consumption. The cemetery accepted Vallance's invitation, and undertook the burial.
6. Bowie in Charles Shaar Murray, 'David Bowie: Who Was That (Un)Masked Man?', *NME: New Musical Express* (November 1977), http://www.bowiewonderworld.com/press/press70.htm [accessed 17/01/14].

7. *Anything But Love* was a prime-time situation comedy series that aired on the US television channel ABC for four seasons between 1989 and 1992, and starred Jamie Lee Curtis and Richard Lewis. Magnuson played hip magazine editor Catherine Hughes in 50 episodes (of a total of 56).

8. However, Magnuson has continued to appear in TV series – in 2013 she acted in *The Young and the Restless* (CBS, 2013) and *Modern Family* (Fox, 2013). She also continues to appear in movies, including, most recently, playing the wife of Christopher Walken in *When I Live My Life Over Again* (dir. Robert Edwards, 2014).

9. Magnuson presented a slightly edited version of the SFMOMA show as *Bowie Cabaret* and *The Jobriath Medley* on the same night as the LA premiere of the documentary *Jobriath A.D.*, at the lesbian and gay film festival Outfest, at RedCat, Los Angeles on 20 July 2012.

10. Rube Goldberg (1883–1970) was a cartoonist who drew people operating amusingly complex machines that were over-engineered to achieve a simple action through a series of chain reactions.

11. Nomi and Arias were back-up singers and performers for Bowie's appearance on *Saturday Night Live* on 15 December 1979.

12. Klaus Nomi died on 6 August 1983, and was one of the first high-profile figures to die from an AIDS-related illness. John Sex died on 24 August 1990 from the same causes.

13. Madonna's *Sex* book (1992) featured nude portraits of Madonna by Steven Meisel with SM styling by performance artist Julie Tolentino. The book was bound in aluminium and sealed in Mylar. It was released to accompany the launch of Madonna's new album *Erotica* (1992).

14. *Chicken Pussy* was released on Bongwater's album *The Power of Pussy* (1991). Magnuson rattles off a dreamlike sequence of images and reflections, including the spoken word description of a sex scene with the obese singer from Canned Heat and his shape-shifting chicken-woman wife.

15. The New York Dolls formed in 1971, and were noted pioneers of proto-punk and proto-glam, alongside Iggy Pop and Velvet Underground. They were known for short high-energy songs with simple riffs and shouted lyrics, and their androgynous, trashy image. The band folded in 1975.

16. A CD project called *Pretty Songs & Ugly Stories* was published in 2006, retaining some of the material from the original live show. The CD was all original material, and excluded many of the covers performed in the live performance (including Jobriath's songs).

17. *The Jobriath Medley* was recorded and published as a CD in 2012.

8 The Accidental Goddess: An Interview with Joey Arias

Joey Arias has a majestic face, a boldly crafted silhouette, and *that voice*. His eyes are large black almonds, framed with colour and painted with thick long slashes of liquid black. Nowadays he wears his hair long, and jet-black, with harsh Bettie Page bangs cut in below the hairline. Over the years, the styles of Arias's costumes have changed, but for the last decade they've been stripped back to black and sheer couture, like lingerie and leather with a six-inch red-soled Louboutin stiletto heel. Arias might look classy, but, in his drag element, tends to do dirty, or be thrillingly lewd – a solicitation, a blowjob gesture, a nipple flash – seemingly just this side of drunk, and lovingly unhinged. This is 'The Goddess' at work. Then Arias opens his painted mouth. That voice!

Arias's voice is sharp, and it seems less sung that loosened from his throat. It feels royally mismatched to his playfulness, superstar realness and severely sketched silhouette. The jarring quality of that crystalline voice, pitched high, contralto, into falsetto, traffics the sound, feel and style of his totem, Billie Holiday, including her signature rasp, giving a quality of cracked glass. When Arias sings full-blooded Billie – the lover's lament, *You've Changed*, or her lynching dirge, *Strange Fruit* – the effect is uncanny. All of a sudden, he's channelling Robert Plant singing Led Zeppelin's *Kashmir*; or goes deep, to rise up into a searing, full-blown rendition of Cream's *The White Room* – both Arias classics.

Arias reinvented himself through that voice. Since arriving in New York City in 1976, Arias has been a key fixture on the Downtown art scene, first after installing himself in Fiorucci, then the hippest store in the city; and then as the collaborator of Klaus Nomi. Nomi and Arias were back-up singers and performers for David Bowie's appearance on *Saturday Night Live* on 15 December 1979, to promote Bowie's album *Lodger*, which had recently been released. Folded into Bowie's act, they thought they'd hit the big time, until they were unceremoniously dropped, likely for threatening to upstage Bowie with their visual ingenuity and street authenticity. Nevertheless,

Arias and Nomi continued to work their magic in the margins, through their club performances – as well as, intermittently, in the mainstream. For example, a report on the NBC television show *Real People* (1980) describes the 'employees during a typical day on the job' at Fiorucci, and proceeds to show Arias winking at the camera, Nomi posing, and a range of other salespeople dancing and gesturing, amid the zany sounds of the B-52's' *Rock Lobster*, and the store's fluorescent décor. 'Would you buy clothes from one of these people?' asks the incredulous reporter. 'This is my everyday look', Arias says in voiceover, as if to mitigate the strangeness of the scene, as he applies lipstick to his pancaked jawline. 'I paint my face. It makes me feel happy', he adds nonchalantly, before doing a brief robot dance to camera. Another employee adds, laughing, 'they want to be appropriate to the situation. And the situation is mad.' In follow-up shots, Arias, Nomi, painter Kenny Scharf and others do stark New Wave dances in the window, to the mostly blank stares of bemused passers-by.[1]

Since Nomi's death in 1983, Arias has continued to be a force to be reckoned with in New York, through a string of art concept bands and performance art projects in the club venues that blossomed in New York throughout the decade. These projects included the video band Mermaids on Heroin; kooky bands like Justine and the Pussycats, and the 1960s tribute act Joey Arias and the Bodacious TaTas; and theatrical skits with Ann Magnuson, including the *Imitators* (1984), in which they played Gala and Salvador Dalí, and other eccentric celebrity couplings. Arias's most recent performances include cabaret-style events, often around a specific theme. For example, *Strange Fruit* (Queen Elizabeth Hall, Southbank Centre, London, 2012) showcases his renditions of Billie Holiday songs, and has been revived regularly since 1993; and *Lightning Strikes* (Institute of Contemporary Arts, London, 2012) was an homage to Nomi, by Arias with Kristian Hoffman (Arias is also the legal executor of Nomi's estate).

In the interview below, conducted in London in October 2013, during a run of performances at the Soho Theatre, Arias explains the context of his emergence in the 1970s and his earliest works in the 1980s, through to the development of what is now his signature style, namely the elegant silhouette, crafted in large part by a long-standing collaboration with Manfred T. Mugler. Arias explains the esoteric logic of 'The Goddess', playing a delicate line between holiness and sacrilege, reverence and laughter.

Dominic Johnson: *First and foremost, the singularity of your voice is very striking in performance. How and when did you find your voice?*

Joey Arias: I've been singing my whole life. I grew up in a musical family, and I sang in the choir at Catholic school. I remember listening to Billie Holiday records, and there was something in her voice that I wanted. I didn't want to be her, but I was inspired by her sincerity, tonality and phrasing. I would sing and try to get the same feeling. In New York, I would always sing *Good Morning Heartache* to people late at night, just for fun. [*Arias sings:*] 'Good morning, heartache, you ole gloomy sight. Good morning, heartache, thought we'd said goodbye last night!' Friends would sit there, and listen, and rave about my voice.

In 1987, I was in London, as I considered moving there for good. My boyfriend Chuck Francis Smith had passed away, and I wanted to try to change my life. I was living with Jon Baker (who ran the Z model agency) and his wife Ziggi Golding. We were doing shows, and they invited me to their studio to record a song with Iggy Pop's band. They had a rock song ready for me, and I was like [*sings like Billie Holiday*] and they were shocked. They had to rethink the song choice, but they encouraged me to keep singing. So I was kind of pushed into using my voice. I sang *Good Morning Heartache, A Hard Day's Night* by the Beatles, and Madonna's *Holiday*. They thought the contrast between me and my voice was bizarre, and that it would blow everybody out of the water. That's where it started. After that I used my voice more consistently in my performances. I sang a lot of Billie's songs, and my voice got a lot stronger. I started to build up my repertoire by singing newer songs in a way that I thought she might interpret them, and that grew into the show *Strange Fruit*.

DJ: *I've heard you sing lots of Billie Holiday songs, and the resemblance between your voices is uncanny. The other night you sang Led Zeppelin's* Kashmir, *and your voice morphed into or towards Robert Plant's. However it's clear to me that you don't do impressions. It's more akin to channelling. Would you describe it this way?*

JA: Yes. Channelling is almost a spiritual feeling. It's like being a medium. I get lost. Although I get funny and out of control in performances, channelling feels special. It's not impersonation. It's almost sacred.

DJ: *Your performances often refer to or borrow from cabaret. What does cabaret mean to you?*

JA: Cabaret means a lot of different things to me. Cabaret was very popular in Nazi Germany, and it became a sort of political platform in the 1930s and 1940s, to poke fun at the situation, and it allowed misfits and society people to mix in dark and gloomy venues. But by the time people started telling me they thought I was a cabaret artist, in the 1980s, it had become a dirty word. At the time, I wanted to enter into pop, and play rock stages and concert halls, but now I really enjoy the association with cabaret. It's a home for me, where I can experiment, and try out new things. Cabaret can be intimate. You don't need a lot of money or equipment to pull off a show in cabaret. It can still be political sometimes, without me needing to wave banners and shout slogans. It's a platform for speaking to people at night when they are trying to get away from their boring everyday lives and want to experience something otherworldly. I live at night.

DJ: *I was wondering about histories and terminologies. When you perform, it's very clear to me that you do so as an artist. You're also clearly a musician, and your voice is an instrument. Do you conceive of yourself as a musician and a performance artist, or one more than the other? Is there a tension between these associations?*

JA: I think music and performance art can go hand in hand. I definitely identify as a musician. In a concert the song tends to be the most important element, but in performance art the emphasis is on the body. My relationship to one or the other is intuitive. My relationship to performance art is more complicated. I've never really studied performance art. When Klaus [Nomi] and I were working together people would tell us we were Bauhaus. We'd look at each other and be like, 'what's Bauhaus?' Of course, Klaus and I bought a book on Bauhaus and we could see the similarities between us in the 1970s, and Bauhaus in the 1920s, and that was exciting. I guess we were channelling the greats, but by accident. Sometimes you don't need to learn a history by studying it, because it's installed in you as an artist.

I saw a lot of performance art in New York, just to keep an eye on what was happening, and I read a bit about the histories of performance too. But I like to keep clear and fresh in the directions I'm going in my own work. I don't get too mixed up with the past. I don't worry too much about what everyone else is doing.

DJ: *You're a very funny performer. What function does comedy serve in your work?*

JA: Especially in the world right now – where there's so much hatred, and people taking advantage of situations and of each other – I think we need to make light of life. I don't think of it as comedy, and I don't set out to make a comedy show. I knew I was funny when I worked with Ann Magnuson, as people would laugh themselves sick. I learnt a lot about improvisation when working with Cirque du Soleil. But setting out to do comedy requires a different kind of preparation. Most of the funny stuff in my performances is improvised. I recount things that have really happened to me, although most of the audience wouldn't believe that my stories are true. I make observations, or use word play, or fool around with the audience. I'll use observations or thoughts that have come to me during the day, and talk to the audiences about stuff I've been thinking about. It's mostly quite absurd or surreal.

DJ: *How did you get into drag?*

JA: I used to hate drag. I'd get taken to drag clubs in the 1970s and early 1980s and I'd walk straight out again. I thought it was terrible – all these characters trying to be Elizabeth Taylor or Liza Minnelli. It wasn't sexy at all. It was just boring. It wasn't until I started to see people like Lady Bunny and Sister Dimension at places like the Pyramid Club that I realised it could be more interesting. I was invited to a Halloween party held by Andy Warhol for Truman Capote – I guess around 1985 – and the only way you were allowed

Figure 8.1 Joey Arias, *Strange Fruit* (Carnegie Hall, New York, 2012). Photograph by Krys Fox

go was in drag. So a couple of friends dressed me up as a super-vixen. At the party, someone asked me my name. I was in the library, and I saw a book by the Marquis de Sade, so I said 'Justine'.[2] They said 'Justine what?' I replied, 'Justine de Sade – and I ain't no hog.' A few weeks later I got a call from someone inviting me to be photographed as Justine for the cover of a drag calendar. I said no, thank you. Then they offered me £5000, and I was like, let's go for it! After I was on the cover, things started changing for me, as the money on offer tripled in comparison to when I was just performing as a guy. I'd created her by accident but I used Justine as my main vehicle – with my band, Justine and the Pussycats [also Justine and the Pussycats From OuterSpace] – until I started the Billie Holiday shows.

Lady Bunny booked me to do Justine and the Pussycats at Wigstock, and one year she asked me to do Billie, as she'd heard me sing some of her songs. I hadn't done Billie as a live show, though, so I didn't know how I was going to make it work. I had the record of *Lady in Satin* at home, so I modelled my look on the portrait of Billie on the cover. I wore a chiffon dress, pulled back my hair, and wore big gold earrings and a bit of tan make-up. I looked like her! When I got there, and sang, people were floored, and things really started to roll after Wigstock.

DJ: *What is the effect of drag in your work? For me it seems to enable a kind of high glamour in your persona.*

JA: The glamour aspect really kicked in after I started working with Manfred T. Mugler [formerly Thierry Mugler] as my director in 1992.[3] Our first project together was a music video for George Michael's song *Too Funky*.[4] Manfred taught me to stop wearing certain things, and showed me how to re-create myself as a silhouette. He thought that all I needed was a black bra and panties, and that I should get rid of everything else. He gave me a lot of beautiful clothes and we fine-tuned the 'essence of Joey Arias'. That's where glamour, elegance and chic really became my signature. As Manfred says: I'm classic and classy – and a little trashy. We found the essence of Joey Arias, and we call it the "Z Chromosome".'

When I perform, it's not really a drag show. I'm not a man in a dress. I'm a silhouette. I like to think about myself like kabuki performers in Japan. They're not drag queens. They're national treasures. They're artists. But drag has been good to me. I embrace it. There are certain artists who are made famous through drag and then don't want to touch it any more. It's a medium that has done me well, and I have to continue to don the costume, like a king or queen who you never see on the throne without their diamonds, furs and gold. I'd never perform in jeans and a T-shirt. I could probably get away with it, as my hair is long, but I want to give the audience a show. It's like at the end of the movie *Elizabeth* [dir. Shekhar Kapur, 1998], where she finally accepts her role as Queen. She cuts off all her hair, is covered in ivory paste, and becomes a virgin, a robot, a statue. 'Observe, Lord Burley, I am married to England!' I get goose bumps just thinking about it. But that's what I feel like too. It's a process I go through, and at the end, The Goddess is there.

DJ: *You were born in Fayetteville, North Carolina, and moved to Los Angeles when you were 6 years old. How has your childhood influenced your work as an artist?*

JA: I was an army child, and being from North Carolina but growing up in LA I always felt different. I hated LA. I became a rebel and I associated myself with the rebel flag of the South. I was raised on film and music. We'd go to the movies four or five times a week. I'd sneak out to watch horror movies on my own when my parents were watching television. I'd re-create what I saw in films, putting on shows for the neighbourhood kids, or play-acting. I'd cut up plastic bags and string for wigs, and make shoes out of tape and trash. I was such a strange creature – my parents used to joke I wasn't really their child, but that something had dropped me off at the front door. They couldn't stop me. Thankfully my parents were open-minded people, and they nurtured me without letting me go too far.

DJ: *In 1976 you moved from Los Angeles to New York. What did New York represent to you at that time, and did it live up to your expectations?*

JA: I'd wanted to go to New York for the longest time. My grandparents and cousins would visit from New York, and I fantasised about Coney Island, and the movie *King Kong*. I met my friend Kim Hastreiter in 1975 (she later founded *Paper* magazine). The first day I met her, she told me that after she graduated from CalArts she was going to drive cross-country to New York and that it would be fun to have someone to drive with. I told her I'd join her. We shook hands, and after hanging out together for a year I packed my bags. I'd been with an improv group called the Groundlings with Laraine Newman, and she'd left to go to *Saturday Night Live*, so I already had a few connections in New York. Kim and I drove for over a week, with a few days here and a few days there, and shoplifted – I mean thrift-shopped! – our way across America. It was the Bicentennial when we arrived in New Jersey [Sunday 4 July 1976] – and when we finally got to Manhattan it was hot as hell. I was shaking. The city surpassed my expectations. The island of Manhattan was burning with creativity, and I could feel it in my pores. Music was playing, and specifically I remember the smells, the energy and the looks. The people were so exciting to me. Within a few days I met Klaus Nomi, Debbie Harry (before Blondie became famous [in 1978]) and other New York characters. My friend Katy K. introduced me to Klaus. He was a particularly strange character. I was fascinated by him.

DJ: *What was your survival plan for New York?*

JA: I wanted to do what Manhattan wanted me to do. I had a bit of money set aside – I'd sold a lot of my clothes, and a car, just before leaving Los Angeles. So for about three months I could just live. I was running around, seeing stuff, coming and going, and partying my ass off. I got a couple of little gigs, and then I started working at Fiorucci on East 59th Street, and it was the hippest store in Manhattan. I would do whatever I could to be part of the city.

I thought I wanted to work in fashion, and the highlight was working with Antonio Lopez.[5] Antonio was an amazing fashion illustrator. I'd been a fan of his in Los Angeles, mostly from seeing his drawings in copies of Andy Warhol's *Interview* magazine. Antonio came to Fiorucci about six months after it opened, and he art-directed the window displays. I freaked out when I saw him, and stayed behind after the store closed so I could help him with his designs. He said he liked my energy. I'd visit him and Juan [Eugene Ramos] at their studio, and Antonio would sketch me. I'd go to his parties and there would be creativity everywhere.

I wanted to be involved in fashion but somehow I found myself on stage with Klaus – by sheer accident really – and before I knew it I was on *Saturday Night Live* with David Bowie [in 1979].[6] Bowie was my 'rock god'. He told me that after *Saturday Night Live* my life was going to change. That was it for Klaus and I in terms of the directions we'd choose to take, towards music and performance. People paid more attention to Klaus though, partly because he was already singing, while I was still stuck in the fashion world.

Everything is always an accident. I feel like there's a road, and I always choose the alley, or the dirt road, to get to where I'm going. I take the bumpy broken road, through the nondescript section of town, which is always more interesting than the road that's straight ahead. Maybe it's a blessing and maybe it's a curse. I don't know. Sometimes I see a lot of money, and sometimes I don't see a lot of money. I think about it and I don't think about it. The universe takes care of me.

DJ: *How was Fiorucci important to you in terms of the type of performances you were beginning to make?*

JA: I was a salesperson. I was there to sell clothes, and I was paid on commission, so the more you sold the more money you could make. The way I looked, and the way I ran around – twirling about and rolling on the shop floor – meant I'd always have four or five customers at a time. I'd see an interesting-looking person and I'd *zap* them, talk twenty-miles-an-hour, exchange numbers, get them to buy clothes, be their stylist. That's what my day at Fiorucci was like. People think I was doing performance art at Fiorucci, but that was because Klaus and I were filmed doing a one-off stunt in the window for television, and it was aired in a news report [*Real People*, NBC, 1980]. It wasn't a day-to-day occurrence, but rather a little show for the tourists. People would visit New York to see the World Trade Center, the Empire State Building – and Fiorucci. It had clothes, art, a coffee bar. Andy Warhol would be there doing a book signing, Klaus and I would be running around, and music would be playing. I'd bring the Downtown people Uptown, and I used the place as my office, or my gallery, for myself. It was a very important place for New York, but eventually it lost its cachet and had to close [in 1986].

DJ: *New York was clearly very important to you in the 1970s and 1980s. Knowing that the city has changed, and that you tour extensively, what is it that keeps you coming back to New York?*

JA: Well, I never really leave New York. I always think I'm going to move somewhere else, but I have my home in New York. Something draws me back. I was going to move to London. I lived in Berlin also, but I came back for Antonio Lopez's funeral [he died of an AIDS-related illness on 17 March 1987]. I brought my stuff back with me, expecting to return to Berlin, but I stayed in New York. There's an energy in Manhattan that calls and holds me there – a secret vibration. I'm part of New York now. I can't really leave. Times are changing, but I still love New York.

DJ: *What do you consider to be your first live works as an artist?*

JA: The first performances in which I created 'the enigma of Joey Arias' – besides those at Fiorucci – were with Klaus. (See **Figure 8.2**.)

Figure 8.2 Joey Arias and Klaus Nomi, New York, 1980. Photograph © Anne Billson

I'd had a taste of it slightly earlier with Edwige Belmore. Edwige was the punk fashion queen from Paris and I was the hippest person in New York. We were both involved in a fashion show [in 1977]. We both walked onto the runway together, and the audience went bananas. I was excited by the audience's reaction – they were screaming and carrying on. Klaus got a gig at Max's Kansas City, after he performed at Ann Magnuson's *New Wave Vaudeville Show* [1978]. Klaus didn't know what he was going to do at Max's, so Kristian Hoffman put a band together for him, and I got Kenny Scharf to join me to back them up, as policemen from Mars, or something. It turned into a show, and that was the start of it for me. It was my first onstage work with music and lights, and a few numbers. I guess this was in 1979. A lot more gigs were booked, and I found myself working with Klaus all the time for the next few years, until his death in 1983.

DJ: *Klaus Nomi is very distinctive for his alien persona. Others, like yourself and Kenny Scharf, also explored an extra-terrestrial aesthetic at the same time. How did Nomi's look come about, and what was at stake in using an alien persona?*

JA: We were very unreal looking to start with. Klaus wore strange otherworldly make-up, but his physical being underneath looked rather unusual too. He was a lot older than us. When I was 19 or 20, he was 35 or so. He was 10 to 15 years older than other people in the scene; his hair was thinning, and he was already going bald. He had a high, bulbous forehead and naturally thin eyebrows. When he got dressed up, at first he just emphasised his features by adding make-up.

Klaus was a very dramatic character. He was operatic, and sometimes a diva, but also very funny, and silly. When he was booked to do his aria at the *New Wave Vaudeville Show*, he was still Klaus Sperber, but he wanted to reinvent himself. A dancer we knew called Boy Adrian was very much into science fiction, outer space and extra-terrestrials, and Klaus and I were fascinated too. Adrian and Klaus were walking in the Lower East Side, and Adrian tore down a poster for *Omni* magazine, which was a popular new science-fiction magazine at the time. Back at Klaus's apartment, Adrian pointed to the title on the poster and told Klaus to use it for his new name. Klaus wrote out the title and rewrote variations: Omni, Moni, *Nomi*. Klaus Nomi. Do you *know me?* Adrian and I went to the *New Wave Vaudeville Show*, and the host David McDermott introduced the next act: 'Klaus Nomi'. It was the first time we heard the name spoken out loud. The music started up, and Klaus entered in his transparent plastic cape, with a little make-up, and his hair slicked back apart from a thin black fin. At the end of his aria, Klaus backed out into a cloud of smoke, and the audience went crazy.[7]

While he sang he moved in a way we'd never seen before. Our friend Boy Adrian was very beautiful, and he would do a 'mutant dance' that looked like Dynamation, the movement of creatures in Ray Harryhausen's animated movies of the 1930s, which had also been very popular in the 1950s and 1960s when we were growing up. Klaus couldn't really move well – when he danced he thought it looked silly – so he tried to teach himself to dance like Adrian. Klaus couldn't do it so gracefully, so he slowed it down, made it sharper, and did gestures with his hands and face, making simple but stark images on the stage, with little movement. It became his signature.

In 1978, Klaus was just beginning to define his look. I'd play with Klaus's image. I'd fix his hair, and we'd try different looks with his make-up. We shot slides of his face and projected them on the wall. We'd draw over the projections with pencil. The way the light hit Klaus in one of the slides made his hair look like a fin. Klaus loved it, and drew over it to emphasise it. We dyed his hair jet-black – partly to cover his bald spot – and he'd brush it up into the fin we'd seen in the slide. It was the beginning of the 'Nomi look'. A friend of ours worked at Vidal Sassoon, and after *The New Wave Vaudeville Show* she gave him a much more defined look, including the triangle cut-out above the ears, which makes the ears look pointed. The next day I went and got the same cut too. Our hairlines start far back, and with our new haircuts we started to look more and more like alien characters. We started telling people – starting with Kenny Scharf – that if you wanted to be a Nomi you had to get the haircut!

Klaus's make-up got much starker. Kenny had a show of paintings at Fiorucci, called *Fiorucci Celebrates the New Wave* [1979], and Calvin Churchman – the art director at the store – invited Klaus to perform at the launch party, as part of a campaign themed around the Bauhaus. Calvin organised a tuxedo for Klaus, and added pointed shoulders. He asked Klaus to make his make-up more black and white. Klaus wasn't convinced, but Calvin was adamant about making him look more Bauhaus. It became the iconic Klaus Nomi look, and he continued to develop it, for example by making his lips more unreal-looking. His look became monochrome, dominated by triangles. But the alien look was by mistake, really. The make-up and hair, the name, and his style of movement all came about by accident to make Klaus Nomi.

DJ: *Part of the tragedy of Klaus Nomi's death is that it happened on the eve of his great international success. What do you remember of that period in 1983?*

JA: Klaus had just received a gold record in France, and he was achieving stardom worldwide. He had gigs in Japan, and we were in meetings and doing shows in London and Paris. New material was being written for him. We did the *Simple Man* show together in 1982, but the record company decided they wanted to save money, so they made Klaus prepare for a solo tour instead. Klaus started the solo tour in Europe – it was operatic and very grand – and he got sick. By the time he came back to New York he had lost 45 pounds. We were all thin already so to see him like that was very distressing. He died shortly after, on 6 August 1983.

DJ: *Nomi didn't have time to make a huge amount of work, but his imprint on experimental culture has been vast. What is it about his work and his persona that has made him so influential?*

JA: I think people are inspired by the material he chose to sing, and especially by his personal style. When any artist passes before their time, the work takes on a life of its own. Klaus was such an enigmatic character so it prompts his audience to make up our own ideas about what the work means to us – a work like *Za Bakdaz* is wonderful even though the words themselves don't mean anything – they came to him in the middle of the night and he wrote them down, and made them the beginnings of a whole opera.[8] I hear people's stories about how he influenced them, and I always laugh because what people imagine about him never sounds anything like Klaus. If someone's impression of Klaus and his work is inspiring, it's still valid, even if it's distorted. People pick up the loose strings and make their own bow to inspire themselves.

I miss Klaus every day. I look at pictures of him and wish he was still here. That's why I'm doing my *Lightning Strikes* show [2012], which involves me singing versions of Klaus's signature songs, like *Simple Man*, or *Total Eclipse*. Kristian Hoffman put together Klaus's repertoire, so it's important that we worked together on this show. I'm not an opera singer, but I do a pretty good job of hitting the high notes. Klaus and I spent all of our time together. We were one. He put himself first though – he used to say he was Hitler and I was Goebbels [*laughs*]. But when we got together, we were like two world leaders – one from Mars and one from Venus.

DJ: *You mentioned Justine earlier. Can you tell me about your art-concept bands of the 1980s and early 1990s? You made work as Justine and the Pussycats from OuterSpace, and as Strange Party, for example, and I was wondering what you thought about your bands as art works in themselves, or about the relations to, say, the work of Vaginal Davis or Ann Magnuson, who have similarly made music as part of larger conceptual projects.*

JA: It started in the late 1970s going into the 1980s, when I did a project called Mermaids on Heroin. The idea behind Mermaids on Heroin was that beauty was being destroyed by pollution, because all the drugs being consumed at the time would end up in the ocean and affect the mermaids' looks and behaviour. It was a nutty idea, but people were mortified by the name of my band. I met Lou Adler and other music producers who wanted to get involved, but they were really put off by the title. I wanted to evoke an underwater world of beauty and glamour – but people didn't seem to read it like that. Danceteria booked Mermaids on Heroin for one night a month for a year [in 1983]. Every month was a new show: *Mermaids on the*

Run, or *Mermaids and Robots*, and so on. Ann Magnuson was involved in it with us, and Klaus too, and the B-52s. That was my first performance band. It was always a visual extravaganza. For example, the band would play, and the guitar player would drift up above the stage, as if he was swimming through water, and I would sing and add dialogue.[9] Frogs would be talking. It was crazy. It was interesting that the name of the project made people slam the door on us. Even people in the performance art world avoided us, including historians like RoseLee Goldberg. Our friends warned us that the name would stop us from growing. Whatever!

Strange Party was another band that started while I was working with Klaus. It was at the same time as Mermaids on Heroin, but it didn't last as long. I also did a project with Ann Magnuson called *The Imitators* [1984], which was a spoof on the 1960s, based on Andy Warhol and Edie Sedgwick, but played as a Sonny and Cher TV show, with surreal touches of Salvador and Gala Dalí. There was a lot of Porky Pig too. Warner Bros did a Porky Pig cartoon based on Dalí's paintings [*Porky Pig in Wackyland*, 1938]. I found the footage so we played that in the show. I'd paint through the show, and when I turned the canvas round it would be a portrait of Porky Pig.

Other artists in bands were often much more punk. I think someone like Vaginal Davis is much more chaotic and confrontational, where I'm preoccupied with beauty. I'd go and see Lydia Lunch and other performers and be really excited by what they were doing, but I always tend towards something more beautiful, crazier, joyful.

DJ: *You arrived in New York when punk was the most important musical subculture in the city. What was your relationship to punk?*

JA: I was very excited by the Ramones, and the New York Dolls, and other punk bands. The first week I arrived in New York in 1976 my friend Gabrielle invited me to see her play in a band at CBGB's. That's where I met Klaus, and Debbie Harry. I was wearing my Tarzan look – a khaki outfit with snakeskin collar boots – and all the punks were lined up in the club, wearing black. I'd say 'hi' and they'd all flinch and sneer at me. It remained that way, I guess. I'd walk around Downtown wearing gold jeans, and Seditionaries outfits from London, straight from my day job at Fiorucci. I was one of the first people in New York to get my hair dyed – at a shop called Jingles – I had it Day-Glo pink with a bright yellow spot in the middle, and sections chopped out. I tweezed my eyebrows thinner, and I looked outrageous. The punks would scream at me and throw rocks. I took to wearing a hat in the street, and I'd always have to run and hide. Other people would throw flowerpots at me and Klaus from their windows. It's funny now, but it was terrifying at the time! Where does punk stop and other styles start? We were definitely pushing the limits. I think drag became the punk of the 1980s.

DJ: *New York was changed irreparably in the 1980s by AIDS, and I know your life has been impacted by AIDS very powerfully too. Did it affect your work, though? Has your work functioned as a response to AIDS in some way?*

JA: I remember reading about 'gay cancer' in 1982. I heard that people I knew were sick, but then all of a sudden Klaus – my other half – was dying. It was very intense, and it happened very quickly. We were so young, and someone I loved was dying, like he was 95 years old. I tried to be there for him. Then other people got sick. My boyfriend got sick. My mother passed away around that time too. The 1980s were full of death. We were supposed to be celebrating: in the afterglow of *Saturday Night Live*, Klaus had found success, and the art world was taking off for friends like Jean-Michel [Basquiat], Ann [Magnuson] and Keith Haring. There was money, and success – and all of a sudden everyone was dying. We'd popped the champagne bottle, we heard the bang and felt the bubbles, but the bottle was empty. There was nothing left. We were young, we thought we had our whole lives in front of us, but we had to confront our own mortality. It was like the fire died down in New York City, and all that was left were little cinders burning in the fireplace, and all you could do was try to keep the little flecks of fire going.

We had to start to re-evaluate our lives. Susanne Bartsch created a new party at Copacabana [in 1988], because New York City was starting to be a really sad place, and we needed a new spot where we could all come together. The city had to figure out a way to party without pulling our pants down, without swallowing cum. We had to redefine fun. Why should New York go down? We dressed up. We got crazy again, but in a safer way. New York was a very sexual place before AIDS. We had very little inhibition. Things had to become sexual in a different way, which we evoked through dressing up and acting out, and through our attitude. I guess what I did with Justine, dressed in latex and acting very sensual, was a kind of protest, like it was my way of saying you could still be sexy, and still get turned on, and have a good time. But in reality, I stopped having sex – not totally, but certainly I had sex differently to how it was in the late 1970s.

I think turning to entertainment, and comedy, and a new sensuality came about naturally for me, as a way of responding to the reality of being in the middle of a crisis. I didn't think about it actively,
or set out to make a statement. If you're in a room that's on fire,
you're going to open the door and run, or throw water on the fire.
Justine came about in the right place at the right time. Justine
addressed the mood of the situation we were in.

DJ: *Throughout the 1990s, you ran a night at Bar d'O, with Sherry Vine
and Raven O. What did that involve?*

JA: I did my Billie Holiday show, *Strange Fruit* for over a year at the
Astor Theater on Lafayette Street [New York, 1993–94], and next door
was a restaurant called Indochine. I did a little number at Indochine
for their tenth anniversary or something [in 1993]. It was all decked
out in Chinese decorations, like Wigstock, and it was a lot of fun. The
owner, Jean Marc [Houmard] had also bought a bar called Bar d'O on
Bedford Street about six months earlier. There wasn't much happening
with it, so he asked if I'd want to try something there. I asked Raven to
join me and we went to look around. When we walked into the space,
it was small. There was a bar, and small wooden platform, a DJ booth,
and seating with beautiful couches. I leant against the platform, then
sat on it, and sang a song, and Raven chirped in. So we just thought
we'd try it for a night. A few weeks after, we called a bunch of friends
to come by the bar, and someone from *New York Magazine* reviewed it,
and it seemed to remind people of the old days in New York. It was like
a speakeasy, very decadent. The review in *New York Magazine* came out
on a Monday, and the following night there were two lines around the
block. The bar was mobbed. We'd do three shows a night, every
Tuesday. That was the beginning of Bar d'O. We'd also do other nights
too, sometimes three nights a week. At first it was me, Raven and
Edwige Belmore. After about four months Edwige had to go to Paris, so
we brought in Sherry Vine. Edwige never rejoined the show, so Sherry
stayed. Sherry was the comedian, and Raven would sing songs with
passion but also say the nastiest, off-the-wall stuff. I was the sexual
person, and I sang Billie songs and developed bits like the 'cock-a-
phone'. We'd also invite other friends to perform, like Jackie Beat, Sade
Pendavis, Marc Almond, Boy George, Flotilla de Barge or Lady Bunny.
The list goes on. I used to wear my hair in a certain way for *Strange
Fruit*: I'd slick it back and draw on a hairline like Billie used to wear it.
I needed a new look for Bar d'O so I put on a Bettie Page wig that some-
one had given me, to look different. The look stayed, and now it's

iconic. The nights went on at Bar d'O for ten years, until I got involved with Cirque de Soleil, and the bar closed a couple of years later.

DJ: *Cirque du Soleil's* Zumanity *(2003) is the largest production you've worked on. What was it like moving from smaller shows to your involvement in such a huge event?*

JA: I knew about Cirque du Soleil beforehand, of course. I was put in touch with Andrew Watson from Cirque when he was visiting New York, and we talked about the possibility of doing a show together. I introduced him to Manfred Mugler, and the company confirmed him to direct their next show. The concept revolved around a cabaret, and I was their first and only choice as the host. The contract would entail a year in Montreal and a two-year run in Las Vegas. I didn't want to leave New York for that length of time, so I turned it down a couple of times, and each time Andrew would say he couldn't get a green light for the production if I didn't say yes. He sucked me into the machine without me knowing it [*laughs*]. Once again it was something I hadn't planned, but it came along and I got swept into it. The next thing I know I'm in a workshop in Montreal. I didn't know what I was doing. There was no story, just a concept. There was no music, so I co-wrote a song called *Sex is Beautiful* with the musical director, and a few other songs too.

Manfred told me I had to be in drag from the very beginning of the process. I'd go to dance classes in the morning, ballet and jazz, and after lunch I'd run and change into a G-string, bra and heels. I'd let my hair down, looking like Bettie Page, put on a little lipstick, throw on a robe, and go to the workshops. From noon 'til dusk I was The Goddess! I was in Montreal for most of a year, working my ass off, and came back to New York for a month. I did Bar d'O a few more times, then left for Vegas. We put the show together over the final three months, and it became a journey of sensuality and sexuality. Who else better to host it! That journey was my whole life – but now it was being played out in a hundred-million-dollar production.[10] That's a ridiculous amount of money. A major Broadway show is expensive if it costs over $10 million. My dresses alone were worth upwards of $300,000. I worked on the show for six years.

DJ: *Did being in* Zumanity *change the way you work, or open up new possibilities?*

JA: After *Zumanity*, Manfred advised me that returning from Vegas after being away for such a long time, I should try to do only two things a year in New York, and secure bigger venues rather than the smaller clubs. It worked, as I was able to elevate to a different level after Cirque du Soleil. I also learned how to make sure the sound is right for my shows, and to make sure that the lighting is visually interesting, even for a small gig. I learned to look at venues differently. I don't need a $100 million budget, but I can make sure everyone looks and sounds right. *Arias with a Twist* was my first big show after *Zumanity*, and it was made on a penny-budget in comparison – about $60,000 – but it looked like a million dollars.[11]

DJ: *Can you tell me about your collaboration with Basil Twist on* Arias with a Twist *(2008)? It seemed to be a show that was very much guided by 'the enigma of Joey Arias', but with a different level of technological possibility than you've explored in other works.*

JA: The medium of puppetry is a whole world I had no idea about. I was a huge fan of Basil Twist, and I'd seen many of his shows. He's a master puppeteer, and it's amazing to see how he can construct and manipulate inanimate objects in performance. I'd been back from Vegas for about a month, and I spent an evening with Basil, drinking wine and talking. We came up with lots of fun ideas – I wanted to be abducted by aliens, and we imagined other scenes like going on an acid trip, and a Busby Berkeley routine around a giant cake. We drank, and laughed, and carried on coming up with ideas. He went away, and sketched the ideas into a full show, and suddenly the ideas we'd been playing with were a reality, and Basil got a budget together. Mugler was in town, so I brought him to Basil's studio to see the designs. I imagined myself running naked through Basil's world, so Manfred came on board as our artistic director. As part of his design for the piece he made a look for me where I'm naked except for sheer, criss-cross lingerie, and another dress that goes on top. So it's very much Joey Arias – but *with a twist*.

DJ: *How do you prepare for a performance?*

JA: I listen to music and choose songs. I work with musical directors, but I call the shots about what material I want to sing. I work with a manager who books venues. I don't like to rehearse for hours. I prefer the performances to work organically.

On the day of a show, ever since the days of Bar d'O, I won't eat all day. I have to be *hungry* when I go on stage. I want to be starving when I'm up there, *ravenous*. A performer shouldn't be on stage with a full stomach. You think differently when you're hungry. I think of it as a little sacrifice, a ceremony. I offer myself. I'm Ankhesenamun and Imhotep.[12] Know Thy Self. Even The Goddess has to enter with her head bowed to the higher vibration.

DJ: *What does 'The Goddess' mean to you?*

JA: I'm The Goddess. Pure energy. Pure life. The Goddess is not a diva or a queen. I was voted *Diva of the Strip* in Las Vegas, and I beat Céline Dion. I said Céline should get the award. Céline is the diva, with a mansion, fancy cars, and all the worldly objects anyone might want. I accepted the award anyway though.

The Goddess is from another dimension, an extra-terrestrial. I'm joking with you. I'm not being serious. It's a fun thought that keeps me going. The look that Manfred created for me is the personification of The Goddess. She's a hologram, invisible. She'll be dismantled and put back together, so beautifully, in *Z-Chromosome*, the next show we're making.

The Goddess is on top of a holy hill. She's Krishna. Siddhartha. She's on a mountain that goes no higher, and she's listening to a vibration. She doesn't need diamonds. She's pure energy. She is enthusiasm and inspiration.

Notes

1. See 'Klaus Nomi and Joey Arias dancing in Fiorucci windows NYC – Real People', *YouTube*, http://www.youtube.com/watch?v=G-pMwDzK8uw [accessed 17/02/14].
2. Justine is the title character in D. A. F. de Sade's libertine novel of 1791. See Marquis de Sade, *Justine, or the Misfortunes of Virtue*, trans. John Phillips (Oxford: Oxford University Press, 2012).
3. Mugler changed his name after Clarins acquired his eponymous fashion and cosmetics brand.
4. Mugler directed the music video for *Too Funky* in 1992. Arias plays the Svengali at a fashion show featuring Linda Evangelista, Tyra Banks, Julie Newmar, Rossy de Palma and Lypsinka.
5. Antonio Lopez was perhaps the greatest fashion illustrator of the 1970s and 1980s.
6. Nomi and Arias danced as Bowie sang *The Man Who Sold the World*, *TVC 15* and *Boys Keep Swinging*.
7. Nomi's aria at the *New Wave Vaudeville Show* is included in the Klaus Nomi documentary, *Nomi Song* (dir. Andrew Horn, 2004). Boy Adrian's 'mutant dance' (described below) is also included on the DVD release, as an additional feature.

8. *Za Bakdaz* is an opera Nomi was writing when he died. It is available on CD as *Klaus Nomi's Za Bakdaz* (Heliocentric, 2007).

9. Arias made a 13–minute video document in 1985. See *Mermaids on Heroin* (1985) on YouTube: https://www.youtube.com/watch?v=eNUWW34pBKQ [accessed 30/04/14].

10. The overall production budget of *Zumanity* is likely around $90 million (£54 million). See Geoff Keighley, 'The Phantasmagoria Factory', *CNN Money,* 1 January 2004, http://money.cnn.com/magazines/business2/business2_archive/2004/01/01/359604/ [accessed 19/02/14].

11. *Arias with a Twist* was a performance made in collaboration between Arias and Basil Twist, and it opened on 12 June 2008 in the Dorothy B. Williams Theatre, HERE Arts Center, New York.

12. Ankhesenamun and Imhotep are the main characters in the iconic movie *The Mummy* (dir. Karl Freund, 1932), played by Zita Johann and Boris Karloff, respectively. In the movie, Karloff's Mummy is accidentally released from a curse, and reincarnates a society lady as the doomed Queen Ankhesenamun (Imhotep's former lover).

9   Perverse Martyrologies: An Interview with Ron Athey

When one considers physical extremity in performance art, one likely thinks of Ron Athey. For 30 years, Athey's performances have urged his body up to a certain limit – that of the beautiful, the endurable or the possible. His body and those of collaborators are cut, bled, penetrated, hung, pierced, bound to the stake and slain in the spirit. He testifies, sings, shrieks, keens or speaks in tongues. His imposing form, tattooed from head to toe, is often stripped naked, or gussied up in operatic costuming.

There is no denying Athey's influence, which has been especially strong in Europe, where he continues to tour new performances and, now and then, curate events. Nevertheless, institutional acknowledgement of his practice in the US has been obstructed, arguably because of his stigmatisation in the culture wars. The enduring political fallout of the scandal, and its conservative observance by curators, has seemingly prevented some cultural institutions from showcasing his work – though this neglect has begun to wane, as evidenced by recent performances at UCLA's Hammer Museum, Los Angeles and Tate Modern, London (both 2013).

Athey's earliest works were made in 1981–82 (in collaboration with the deathrock pioneer Rozz Williams), and included bone-grinding sound experiments and visceral, bloody performances. However, his signature style emerged in the early 1990s, in his celebrated *Torture Trilogy* (1992–95). These early ensemble works derive from autobiographical material, including his childhood 'calling' as a prophet, his familial triumvirate of schizophrenic women, religious schooling in Pentecostalism, and subsequent drug addiction, subcultural education, HIV sero-conversion and illness and relative salvation. Athey writes: 'In my performance material, I am guilty of enhancing my history, situation and surroundings into a perfectly depicted apocalypse, or at least a more visual atrocity.'[1] Yet he is at pains – in the work, and in our discussion – to remind audiences that one's encounter with his work is hardly restricted to a hermeneutic game of decoding his legion autobiographical references. Rather, he provokes broader aesthetic and political frameworks through which to encounter his visual palette of body modification, bloodletting, ritual actions, fetish glamour and operatic excess. Recent works like *Incorruptible Flesh (Messianic Remains)* (2013) continue this removal of the image from its apparent reliance upon biographical sources, through the crystallisation of an *ecstatic* theatre of wordless spectacle.

Our interview was staged in two parts. Part I was conducted in London and Los Angeles in March and April 2008, and published in the journal *Contemporary Theatre Review* in 2008. It ends on Athey's notes for a major new performance series, *Self-Obliteration I–III* (2009–11). Part II was undertaken as a live interview at Iniva, London in 2012, and begins by reflecting upon the achievements of the same performance. Throughout, Athey discusses his performance practices as a staging of crisis, sexuality and the death drive, in the 'plague years' and in the 'post-AIDS' era.

Part I

Dominic Johnson: *What is your process leading up to a performance? Through what processes and techniques does a new piece come about?*

Ron Athey: My performances are usually not based on any 'issues' defined clearly in advance. I think, initially, they come out of posing a tough, philosophical question that I work through in the process of making. When making *Deliverance* [1995] right at the point that anti-retroviral therapy was becoming standard treatment, I asked: When faced with terminal illness, how does the belief and definition of healing change? Then I made a fantastical leap. This of course referred me back to my upbringing, and to experiences of pursuing miracles, such as faith healing. I'm not always consciously motivated by the horrors of the body, but the mortal tightrope feeds this tension, whether clearly at the beginning of my career, or looking back at the outrageous exhibitionism of *Solar Anus* [1998]. In that piece, for example, I thought: How to queer Georges Bataille? The image of Pierre Molinier auto-penetrating his anus with a dildo attached to his high heel really affects me, as an articulate expression of defiance. Once that's established as a source, a part of me wants to reinvent the costume before really establishing the structure of the piece. But I seem to be on a cycle of creating (for me) 'minimal' solos and grander theatrical pieces. When I find a logic, or avenues of new inspiration, these start coming to life. I also work on images through writing down dreams, and especially cognitive dreaming. This isn't an easy part of myself to reckon with, as it goes back to the insanity of my childhood experiences, but really adds flair to problem solving. I have altered other aspects of performance with hypnosis, which at this point happens almost automatically as part of my process.

DJ: *The Monster in the Night of the Labyrinth and Solar Anus are examples of the way Bataille's writings have influenced your work.*[2] *What draws you to Bataille's writings?*

RA: Reading Bataille – especially *Visions of Excess, Literature and Evil* and *The Trial of Gilles de Rais* – definitely helped me make sense of my own work. While I am unwilling and unable to pull my punches, I also experience a paranoia about what I'm unleashing on audiences. Some of Bataille's major premises as the 'excremental philosopher', and his accusations (such as his critique of conservative Surrealists in their name-dropping of de Sade), resonated deeply in me. He elevated filth to sacred status, Incestuous Mother, Perverted Priests, while completely destroying familial, cultural and societal myths. He even claimed Jean Genet was overrated! That hurt my feelings for a minute. His essay 'Solar Anus' triggered and fit my view of the magic tricks inherent in the anus.[3] But visually it was the self-portraits of Pierre Molinier from the 1970s that fed the visuals to me. Rather than fetishising a young girl's anus (like Bataille), Molinier was obsessed with his own 70-something-year-old asshole. With the required stockings and heels, he successfully transformed himself into a cheesecake pin-up figure, the look drilled in through cut-and-pasted photographs, repeat images and mandala formations.

DJ: *You've described the rectum as the 'homosexual weapon', and Amelia Jones has written that your asshole 'has its own place' in the history of visual art.*[4] *What, to you, are the cultural, political and artistic implications of the asshole? How have you explored these in different works, and to what effects?*

RA: There is a homophobic repulsion at the idea of the rectum as a receptacle for sex; or further, a more general body-phobia (that many gay men also share) of the turned-out asshole as fist-hole: punch-fucking, double fisting, dark red hankies and the elbow-to-armpit fist. (See **Figure 9.1.**) There's also the pathology of shit-eaters, a direct link to cannibalism. But more importantly, in our time, this particular hole garners more phobias for its symbolic potency as a receptacle for

Figure 9.1 Ron Athey, *Self-Obliteration I–II* (Galerija Kapelica, Ljubljana, Slovenia, 2008). Photograph by Miha Fras. Courtesy of Ron Athey

disease. Bataille's revelation is that the anus is both the day and the night. In keeping with this idea, here's a brief *assholeography* of my work. In *Deliverance*, in the 'Psychic Surgery' sequence, several metres of pink stretch banners are pulled out of my ass and draped around the central two-level set piece; an enema is then administered, and the water expelled into clear cylinders pre-filled with glitter. Later in the performance, in a section called 'Rod 'n' Bob: A Post AIDS Boy-Boy Show' with Brian Murphy, after genital 'castration' (using surgical staples) we ride a double dildo while I read a text in as calmly modulated a voice as possible. The double-dildo connection is severed with large sheers by a figure called The Icon [performed by Divinity Fudge], an act we call the second castration. In *Trojan Whore* [1995], a short solo, devised as a tribute to Leigh Bowery, I appear encased inside a stuffed lady body. The casing is cut open, and I emerge, in drag. I'm bent over, and an endless strand of pearls is pulled out of my rectum. *Solar Anus* opens with the pearl trick, followed by auto-penetration with dildo attachments on my high heels: a slow motion, penetrative can-can, modelled on Molinier. In the middle of *Judas Cradle* [2005], my operatic duo-drama with Juliana Snapper, I climb a ladder and mount the Judas cradle – a large wooden pyramid used as a 'gentler' form of torture in the Spanish

Inquisition. This is penetration with a steep learning curve. I am currently working on the second action in my *Self-Obliteration* series, *Sustained Rapture*, which will somehow capture full throttle punch-fucking.

DJ: *To some audiences, some of the sexual acts you perform may be unfamiliar, even monstrous. What is the attraction, on your part, of bringing these events to the theatre?*

RA: I do think about the experience-levels of audience, but mainly I acknowledge that it's so varied. If the audience provides the possibility of an entire spectrum of experiences, why does the standard focus attend to the lowest common denominator and privilege the inexperienced heterosexual? I think an image can unify the sexually jaded and naïve, and in the transformation become something else altogether. That 'something else' can become beautiful, like a dripping strand of pearls, but it can also be a stand-in for violation, or, in another mood, an act of defiance. What is my attraction, or drive, in exposing these actions? Honestly, *it's not a strategy of shock, but of generosity*. The image or action must be shown. Pulling one's punches may be the tradition, but I still quiver when live, real-time experience happens.

DJ: *I remember you saying Annie Sprinkle suggested that you might incorporate safe-sex messages into your performances. Her conception of sex as a form of healing seems diametrically opposed to your project, but in fact your work has often staged rituals of sexualised cleansing, or purging through eroticism. I'm thinking of the blood-washing scene in* 4 Scenes in a Harsh Life *(1994), and the vaginal douching segment in* Joyce *(2003), for example.*

RA: To provide a context for my response: safe-sex messages seemed obligatory by the latter-days of ACT UP in the late 1980s and early 1990s, so I can see that, in a narrative performance about sex, there could be space for that kind of information.[5] But I couldn't imagine including a Public Service Announcement for the betterment of the audiences for my work. Yes, sexualised cleansing acts have been staged in some of my performances, but the effect of these acts is not instructional, and they're often set in another time period: biblical, or the 1960s. I'm not sure how successful I've ever been in addressing current politics unless there's a deeply personal link. AIDS may be the exception, because it involves a complex galaxy of issues revolving around life and sex and death. But I do also reference other specific events, like the Abu Ghraib sequences in the projected video of *Judas Cradle*, or the reimagining of queer unions in the three-way wedding scene in *4 Scenes in a Harsh Life*. In these, I was able to tease out something that's more like role-playing, which resonates differently to sincerity.

DJ: *More broadly, how has living through the height of AIDS informed your practice, or indeed your outlook?*

RA: If I look through my personal photographs from that era, and see a table full of people, a small percentage of them are still alive. AIDS destroyed my world, so, how to go forward? And how to reckon with my own sickness? I still feel at odds with planning for the future. I was diagnosed HIV-positive in 1986 – a death sentence until the three-therapy cocktail [in 1996]. But by that time I had already lived ten years of that sentence, and had been through the deaths of too many friends. (Having been an IV drug-user, and being gay, I had a particularly high number of sick friends.) And idols I never met also died: the death of David Wojnarowicz devastated me. I wrote down a line, 'The Best are Already Dead', and felt this for some time. This heaviness triggered what I call the 'dissociative sparkle', which for me was manifested firstly in the grandiosity of the *Torture Trilogy*. In those three works, all the players (sick men, caregivers) recede into the paintings of Christian martyrology: my appropriation of esoterica and definitions of healing simultaneously heightened and became grim. The first part, *Martyrs & Saints* [1992] opens with Pigpen [a performer in Athey's company in the 1990s] strapped into the frame of a pyramid, having blood drawn, which refers to a dying friend's morphine hallucinations; at the end of *Deliverance* (and of the trilogy) the bodies of the three men are restrained in body bags and buried under hundreds of pounds of dirt, with wailing butch women atop the mound.

From there, it's a case of *still here in the 'post-AIDS' era* of the antiretroviral cocktail. From the living corpse of the *Incorruptible Flesh* manifestations[6] to wrestling the death drive in the *Self-Obliterations* – for me, whether or not these images are front- or back-loaded with the spectre of AIDS, it's still relevant, and representative of life: of *learning to love the monster*, pseudo-health aesthetics, and the giver of death, anal sex.

DJ: *You mention David Wojnarowicz, and I can see the links between your work and his, and why his example would be so vital to you. I wonder,*

*though, about the importance of other artists whose influence on the offi-
cial histories of performance have not been fully registered, at the level of,
say, the market or the academy. I'm thinking specifically of artists close to
you, like Lawrence Steger, Johanna Went or Rozz Williams. Can you say
something about why various artists have not, perhaps, been assimilated
into cultural histories?*

RA: Well, this is about access to information, exclusion from proper
mediums for whatever reasons, and the validity of underground
sources, such as the importance of fanzines before the Internet. *No
Mag* in LA profiled bands, and published smart political satires, did
features on custom tattooing (a profoundly new concept in 1980),
and also covered artists like Johanna Went, Z'EV and the Kipper Kids,
all of whom were very influential for me. RE/Search Publications was
available first as a tabloid, and then as serial books that documented
'industrial culture', such as Throbbing Gristle, SPK, Boyd Rice, Monte
Cazazza and Survival Research Laboratories. I believe this not only
led the curious such as myself into looking at a culture broader than
the music scene, but also changed the way my generation looked,
firstly by examining body modification in tribal cultures, and eventually the Modern Primitives scene. More intimately, it seemed like
people older than me kept their own archive. For example, I spent
weeks with a Yippie who owned a punk record store called Toxic
Shock, and he played me everything he had that could have led to
the emergence of the industrial bands: John Cage, weird Captain
Beefheart offshoots, particularly interesting bits of New Music; and
Don Bolles, the Germs drummer, collected *Alarma!* – a very graphic
tabloid of accident and murder photographs from Mexico.

Some time in the 1990s, I remember talking to Genesis P-Orridge
at Vaginal Davis's Club Sucker – a Sunday afternoon punk-rock tea
dance – on a particularly lively week, and s/he seemed to be loving
the scene, but asked, 'why punk'? Certainly that's a valid question,
why alternative Queercore went that way. I came to performance
through the music scene – Rozz Williams was my first boyfriend, and
basically lived as a deathrock woman during that time, 1979 to 1982.
His band Christian Death was largely responsible for the Goth
aesthetic, though it had not yet been named. And the next in my
'I'm with the band' moment, I was with Edward Stapleton of the *très*
intellectual synth-punk-queer band Nervous Gender; they were 15
years ahead of the techno dance scene, using synthesisers and drum
machines, and lyrics such as 'Jesus was a cock-sucking Jew from

Galilee, Jesus was just like me, a Homosexual Nymphomaniac'. Anyway, those people were *creating* – not appropriating nostalgia.

There is currently an ACT UP-era show [*Make Art/Stop AIDS* (2008)] at UCLA's Fowler Museum, that includes the stars such as Wojnarowicz, Félix González-Torres and Gran Fury, but also much more underground activist artists who contributed to zine publications like *Infected Faggot Perspectives* and *Diseased Pariah News*. This period of the late 1980s and early 1990s was one of the last issue-driven movements, and the energy, with all its rage and despair, is still palpable. Why, though, is 'timeless' art considered more valid than the ephemeral? I care more if it has at least cut to the quick at some point, as opposed to it being a piece of smarty-pants art in a vitrine for semi-eternity. Do I need to read another queer Warhol essay?

Of course the Internet and the nature of Google searches supports and dilutes the distribution of obscure information. It's not exhaustive, but I'd imagine some of my profound isolation at a younger age would have been relieved if I had known that certain artists or events existed or had taken place. It was a slow journey through books for me. Scenes can be described superficially, and again, are ephemeral, and therefore are deemed not to be of great importance, but in my life this is where creativity has been stoked and supported. That is, there are great influences on creators of work that are outside of academia. Performance created for audiences of other students rarely has the same edge as performance made for a general (even if specific) audience: it's not so easy for the latter to be masturbatory.

DJ: *To pursue P-Orridge's question: what is it about punk that is being sustained or rethought in your work, and/or in the work of artists like Vaginal Davis or Goddess Bunny? I'm also reminded of Kembra Pfahler's term 'availabism', as the desire and necessity for DIY culture. Does punk revivalism go deeper into the aesthetics and politics of punk?*

RA: Let me preface by saying I feel rebellious about this topic because I'm surrounded by friends my age who are nostalgic for that era. I'm not. I think punk is too general a term. But, other than religion and suburban ghetto life, I had no cultural references before punk. DIY is probably the most brilliant aspect of that movement. I suppose I also felt green-lighted to proudly explore anything abject as part of the 'fuck you' attitude. So being a faggot was helpful, and being a junkie gave me credibility. How this informs me now? It would never occur to me that I should hold back in my politics or aesthetic, or whitewash the work I make. I do recognise the rough, unfinished punk aesthetic in Kembra's visuals, and I don't think Vag is capable of reverence. Let's leave the Goddess in her own category.[7] If punk is the last hold-out in a slick, commodified, homogenized culture, I think I can believe in it again. But does punk continue to be a counter-balance against the hippie love thing, as well as against the system, or is it a parody of a clown show?

DJ: *As a means of approaching your performance heritage from a different, literary perspective, how and when did you discover Jean Genet, and what was Genet's effect on you?*

RA: I don't mean to be too dramatic, but Genet saved my raggedy teenager life. Isolated, post-religion, post-home-dwelling, I couldn't quite figure anything out, and I read *Our Lady of the Flowers*, *The Thief's Journal*, *Miracle of the Rose* and *Querelle de Brest*. These books resonated with me: not only the themes and antics of Darling and Divine, the dissociative hallucinations of tattoos on rough-trade objects of desire, but importantly, I was reassured by the legend of the conditions under which Genet was writing. This history validated my fucked-up queer perspective. I met Patrice Repose, the singer of the band Gobscheit, and she was a Genet fanatic. She wanted to direct Rozz Williams and me in *The Maids*, so I started studying Solange's lines (this would have been in 1981). Unfortunately, we never did our kinky Goth-industrial version of *The Maids*, but it brought me deeper under the influence of Genet, and certainly expanded my inner visions of what it might be possible to stage.

DJ: *Continuing with the thought of relations between you and other makers of performance, you worked with Reza Abdoh as a performer in his film,* The Blind Owl *(1992). Was his work influential for you more broadly?*

RA: I remember seeing a piece of Reza's in the early 1990s in the ballroom of an old hotel in the MacArthur Park region of LA. It was a live *telenovela* in Spanish, and he had brought up a pack of transsexuals from Tijuana to perform in it. I met him when he was preparing *Bogeyman* [1991], parts of which were obviously heavily researched – and partly cast – at Club FUCK! He even borrowed our theme song, by Ministry. I had never seen an insane non-narrative production with a huge budget before, and I was hugely inspired by the way he was able to structure chaos. And the three-storey set was extremely grandiose. It was his usual cast, plus the Goddess Bunny, and the mad queen behind Club FUCK!, my little sister Cliff Diller. I think I felt inspired to go large. His relationship to [William] Burroughs's cut-ups was really effective, simultaneous and overlapping outbursts configuring something new. But as physical as it was, it was still theatre. Later I saw a few of Richard Foreman's pieces, *Benita Canova* [1998] and *Bad Boy Nietzsche* [2000], and could see his influence on Reza's work.

DJ: *Tell me more about Club FUCK!.*

RA: The dynamics of a bona fide scene are intense, as in life-changing. I don't tend to think of myself as a 'scenester', but I was present and active in a series of cultural moments: ghetto gay disco (as opposed to the gay ghetto), 1977–80; the inland empire suburban and then Hollywood punk scenes, 1979–83; death rock, 1980–82; industrial culture, including bands like Throbbing Gristle, SPK, Cabaret Voltaire, 1980–84. After 1983, the LA scene returned to big fashion-scene clubs and gigs seemed kind of sad. 12–Step recovery needed to be my residence for quite some time, after 1986; this internal work doesn't fit here except that most of the foundational Club FUCK! people were also in recovery.

Tattooing was a huge part of the punk and post-punk scenes, and this identity was incredibly strong in my life, but it was more rigid, conservative and hetero then the Modern Primitive period that started properly in the late 1980s. To become a scene, to become more involved, Modern Primitives needed an evolution of the kind of heavy bodywork that takes years to acquire, a book to contextualise it, and a spokesperson – Fakir Musafar – who eventually trademarked it.[8] In 1990, Club FUCK! was a fusion of the Modern Primitive ethos at its most boiling, crossed with the rudest period of the short-lived Queer Nation activists. These tendencies were then crossed again with the most brilliant old-school gay and straight kinks. Directors like Reza Abdoh and Barbet Schroeder were there. Tired celebrities were also panting to get in: Courtney Love, Madonna, Kate Pierson, Jean-Paul Gaultier and, eventually – preposterously – even Liza Minnelli.

Club FUCK! was in a small but high-ceilinged cha-cha bar called Tobasco's, with a corner for four go-go dancers off of the dance floor. The regulars throughout the entire three years it was at that location (and valid) were myself, Cross [Athey's former co-performer], Michelle Hell [Michelle Carr] (before Velvet Hammer Burlesque but same harsh look) and Kristian White. Rotating were Jenny Shimizu, Bud Hole and Jake [aka trans-man porn star Buck Angel].

Performances were sometimes short sets by bands like Vaginal Davis's art band PME, Rozz Williams and Eva O's Shadow Project, Drance [Robert Woods and Brandy Dalton] and Babyland. There would also be a piercing or SM demonstration, by Elayne and Alex Binnie, Durk Dehner of Tom of Finland fame and myself. This is what led me back into making performance work again, after a nine-year hiatus. *Martyrs & Saints* was created there, as a series of individual ten-minute pieces. In and around our group, the 'First Family of FUCK!', the early 1990s were really the heavy time of AIDS deaths, so the project was powered by frustration, grief, anger, despair. Sexually charged, exhibitionist behaviour rattled through this group like an affirmation of life, and I'm not being wordy with the sentiments. I could suddenly dream, and feel, and fuck nasty again.

Three fags started FUCK!: Miguel Beristain, who had worked selling fashions for years on Melrose; Cliff Diller, an amazing nutty Oklahoma queen and make-up artist; and James Stone, who had been doorman at many of the fashionette clubs in the 1980s. They powwowed with us (the regular dancers and performers, plus PME) and the first Sunday night happened with a bang. The music was the launch of Chicago techno dance – My Life with the Thrill Kill Kult, Ministry, Nine Inch Nails and the like. We worked hard to keep it from being overexposed, including a 'No' to Madonna's request to have the upstairs alcove as her private viewing perch; and different door prices for non-queer or no-kinks, as another club had opened – Sinamatic – which was larger and less focused on the theme and was good for the spillover fools. Anyway, three years of sustained intensity was an awesome second wind for me.

DJ: *How was club performance important to your development as an artist?*

RA: At this point I had no real agenda to enter the art venue circuit. Encouragement came from Lydia Lunch, Dennis Cooper, Bob Flanagan and Sheree Rose – they were friends, and each had some credibility in the art world at that time, despite the kookiness or excessiveness of their work. I did an excerpt from *Martyrs & Saints* at Highways [Performance Space and Gallery, Los Angeles] in 1991 and performed the full-length version for the first time at LACE [Los Angeles Contemporary Exhibitions] with a cast of 15. (See **Figure 9.2.**) That week, word spread to New York and Chicago, and this was the beginning of my relationships with Julie Tolentino and Lawrence Steger, probably the only two people who ever had a hand in my

Figure 9.2   Ron Athey and Company, *Martyrs & Saints* (Museo Ex Teresa, Mexico City, 1995). Photograph by Monica Naranjo. Courtesy of Ron Athey

work – literally and on a mentor level – until my opera collaboration [*Judas Cradle*] with Juliana Snapper in 2004–05. Steger was a brilliant performer, writer and curator, and programmed me into Chicago art venues. Tolentino was a member of David Rousseve's dance company Reality, and she booked me into New York clubs. She was also behind pivotal early-1990s gigs like the ICA [Institute of Contemporary Arts] in London, P.S.122 in New York, the Walker Art Center in Minneapolis, Festival Atlântico in Lisbon and the Sigma Festival in Bordeaux. I was so into doing club shows that, when we performed *Martyrs & Saints* at the ICA, London for three or four consecutive nights, one night we also did a midnight performance at Fist.[9] This was the trip I also met Leigh and Nicola Bowery on a few occasions.

The tableaux format of *Martyrs* and *4 Scenes* was partly the result of creating vignettes for clubs, and by 1995 I was unsure whether the scenes might fit together or flow in a different way if, instead, I could conceive an entire 60–minute performance without relying on pre-existing vignettes. So, during the construction of *Deliverance*, I mostly stopped performing in clubs, and started doing showcases in more intimate and focused spaces. I do think I would still make a performance for a club if I was into the idea, as it's a completely different kind of reward to be able to grip a drunk, distracted audience who didn't necessarily come to see you. But it's also a pain in the ass – low-tech, usually with impossible prep conditions.

DJ: *Moving in another direction: Bernard-Marie Koltès is a French writer who died of AIDS in 1989, and a direct inheritor of Genet's theatre. Koltès writes: 'I have always rather detested theatre because theatre is the opposite of life; but I always come back to it and I love it because it is the one place where you say: this is not life.'[10] How do you conceive of the relation between theatre and life?*

RA: I don't know Koltès's work, but I immediately thought of Artaud, a closer reference for me: 'Like the plague, the theatre has been created to drain abscesses collectively … . The theatre, like the plague, is in the image of this carnage and this essential separation. It releases conflicts, disengages powers, liberates possibilities, and if these possibilities and these powers are dark, it is the fault not of the plague nor of the theatre, but of life.'[11] Artaud is referring to a heavier, sacred form of theatre when he concludes that this emerges from the practice of living. I don't know if Koltès believes that theatre is dependent on fantasy, or indirect because it's reduced, symbolised and stylised, but thinking in terms of the theatre (rather than, say, writing a novel) may not, for me, be a choice. I would hope it could accurately convey and, better yet, explore internal/external themes. Theatre is a broad and messy category; unlike Koltès, though, I am in no way talking about plays. I have my own schisms in terms of determining what to stage. Because many of my concepts are developed from autobiographical situations, I think I'm giving 'realness'. But actually, in my intent, I'm doing something more akin to channelling.

DJ: *How would you define 'realness'? It reminds me of the term 'butch realness', and in that sense it seems interesting, in that it is more concerned with the performance of sexual identity than simply, say, an opposition between 'reality' and 'fakery'.*

RA: When I say 'realness', I mean a sense of being anchored, something with weight; not fantastical in origin, and definitely not strategic or polite. Again, overly sincere life and death topics reign. Action-wise, what started as piercing can be categorised as SM play, but live anal penetration in a non-sexual setting is blatantly not fakery, putting the very 'real' roots of homophobia on the table. 'Realness' can be used in layers, something 'real' – that is, not faked – nevertheless standing in for something fatal. Or in reverse, as in the spontaneous bleeding I've been exploring in the *Self-Obliteration* actions, real infected blood becomes unreal for its lack of explanation: this lack de-martyrs the act.

DJ: *Can you tell me about the* Self-Obliteration *series, its concerns and how you see these works developing?*

RA: I see this topic as a purgatory of sorts – zeroing in on it rattles me. So I'm not predicting a solution or resolution to your question. The series is not literally about suicide, and also not a metaphor for destroying the ego, but creates an aggravated, suspended state. Again, like much of my work, it's backed up by heavy life experiences: I attempted suicide a number of times between the ages of 15 and 25, and that will always stigmatise me. A brand of shame is applied to didactic self-destructions, but I've experienced a fuller range of revelation within that dark place. It can be a final act of strength, rather than a vortex of un-medicated depression. Somehow these thoughts started brewing after I explored what it means to be an Ecstatic, as a through-line in my research. I've always had a tendency to trance out, to have audio hallucinations, or visions. How lucky for me to be born into a radical Pentecostal family of five schizophrenic Scorpio women.

In other pieces I've explored the vocal and movement aspects of these experiences, but the Ecstatic identification reaches from birth to my current performance practice, coming from within myself. So if I let my psycho-neurological system run wild within a framework – in *Self-Obliteration I*, that being a wig, five needles and two sheets of plate glass – could this happen with minimal action? The glass scene came from *Incorruptible Flesh (Perpetual Wound)*. Identifying myself, the decomposing post-AIDS survivor, with the eternally gaping and unhealing wound of Philoctetes, the glass was used as a barrier to press my nasty gash against the fresh wound I inflicted on your body, as a young Neoptolemus figure run through a *Pink Narcissus* filter [a reference to the film by James Bidgood, 1971]. This is followed by an action on the floor where I shuffle the two sheets of bloody glass over my supine body: a sick frenzy, then holding a pose, and back to a display as a living corpse.

In *Self-Obliteration I: Ecstatic*, without the interplay of the blood from two bodies, I found pleasure in an emotional distance from the traumatised body, and a fusion of stigmata and glamour. Pinning the opening look (a shiny long blonde wig) to my scalp are thick needles, hidden under the wig cap. So the unpinning act of removing the wig causes profuse bleeding from unexplained head wounds before my face has been revealed. Masquerading as a blonde and sliding two bloody glass sheets over my body like guillotine blades – this feels like a stand-in. I create an excuse to convulse this living 'dead' body. I give out an improvised vocal that is either a death rattle, or perhaps just fucking weary.

Self-Obliteration II: Sustained Rapture came about when images and a litany of words came to me in a dream, and I concluded that my deepest desire was to rupture to obliteration in an ecstatic state, specifically through hard sex. Is this a revelation? It did startle me that the destructiveness of my sexual fantasies has not changed since puberty. I don't believe dreams are always prophetic, but I appreciate that these images can come from a well-lubricated source. In the mornings as a child, my grandmother discerned my dreams with a lap full of interpretation books. She encouraged cognitive dreaming, so many of my dreams were on repeat-play until the desired outcome was finished or changed.

I dreamed that I was facing off a man, and I was talking. I remembered the sound pattern but not the words. I was delivering a relentless litany. So I wrote to the man this was directed at, and then the dream repeated itself, but this time the words hung in the air with form, like ectoplasm. The content, what I heard myself saying with urgency and brutal flourishes, was more like a manifesto, calling for me to abandon convention, emotional safeguarding, and complacency, in order to build a deeper love. This came to sex with no boundaries, a willingness to literally have no limits in the interaction of animalistic sex. This idea of intense pleasure ramped up to full throttle – would I be able to stop before the death drive at the brink?

Part II

DJ: *We left off by talking about your plans for the* Self-Obliteration *series. You've since staged and refined these works. Can you tell me about the works?*

RA: As *Self-Obliteration I-II* developed, I asked myself why I keep presenting myself as if I were dead, or more specifically, as a sexualised *living corpse*?[12] I was at a place in my work where I no longer wanted to make something in response to an issue. I wanted to see if I could make a performance using objects or materials that don't mean anything to me. The wig isn't drag. The glass is and isn't a vitrine. All the actions are articulated in the moment, based on the mood rather than choreography as such. The very last performance was on the day of my fiftieth birthday, on 16 December 2011, in New York. In that particular performance I achieved what I've been trying to achieve for 30 years, which is to move beyond performance through the event itself. I fell into a state where I no longer even understood that the audience was there, or what was happening to me. I lost my mind, and time, space, and boundaries seemed to drop away.

DJ: *There seem to be two ways to think about sexuality, broadly speaking: first, what you might call the 'Pollyanna' view, in which sex and sexuality can achieve a social good, as vehicles for freedom, liberation, personal fulfilment and truth, which is politically radical but only in the most idealist fashion; and another approach, the daemonic perspective, which sees sexuality as a force for disruption, a thanatological imperative that can tear apart the subject, and even reconstitute social relations, but always in a monstrous, alien or terrifying manner. I associate you, of course, with the latter. Why do you find yourself drawn to one over and above the other?*

RA: One of the benefits of being longer in the tooth is that I was lucky enough to have sex in the 1970s. It was a more exhibitionistic era, and it was sex-positive, before polite versions of gay sexuality started to appear. Street prostitutes were everywhere in Los Angeles in the 1970s; the sex workers were amazing, fashion-show wise, and very visible, lined up along Sunset Boulevard for miles. The male hustlers were one block up, along Santa Monica Boulevard. I saw public sex as a statement, above and beyond pleasure. I learnt that being overtly gay, overtly sexual, can be used as a weapon. When HIV came along, in the 1980s, I thought there was nothing to lose. Everybody died, including practically everyone I admired, and it seemed like the only people left alive were mediocre. Everybody died, and the mediocre people took a bigger seat of power, because suddenly there was space for them. *What a crappy world.* The community started to self-police. The *nasty girls* stopped being nasty – and I mean this in terms of queer men and women – they became monogamous, had babies. But not all of us want to make work for a child-safe world. I'm not willing to give up a certain dimension of my imagination. The *daemonic* side of sexuality that you're talking about, well, it also has to do with seeing sex and death on a continuum. The images are married together in my imagination. It's morbid, but it's not simply titillation. I've spent a life under that cloud.

DJ: *You've said before that you've seen your work reinvented at key times in your career, for example in the 'plague years' of the mid-1990s, and again in the 'post-AIDS' moment, after around 1996. In what ways do you think your work has undergone important shifts over the years?*

RA: Before AIDS, blood could be used as a material – think about blood in body art in the 1960s and 1970s. In the 1980s and 1990s, everybody's blood was read in the context of HIV. Now we're back to blood equals blood. I lived with the *death cloud* from 1985 onwards, so I read my body very much through the lens of death and dying. It was a busy time for dying. As Diamanda Galás said, 'There are no more tickets to the funeral.'[13] Now I'm 50, and healthy, and there's a Frankenstein cure of sorts, so my attitude towards the image has had to change periodically over the last few decades. Moreover, I've never really resided in the art world, so I've been forced to find different spaces for my work – clubs, galleries, alternative venues, festivals – and moving through these contexts and learning how they work tends to change your attitude to making.

But throughout, I have understood my palette, and I've refined it in terms of my conception of neurology. That is, there is something scary about blood because it's so close to us, all the time – your nose could start bleeding at any moment, or you catch your skin and it would bleed. When you're in the audience at a performance that involves bleeding, or penetration, you get sweaty, your skin gets greasy; nobody's aroused, apart from a troll or two, but your pupils dilate, you fidget, and your heart beats faster. The content of my work might change, but my palette of effects stays consistent.

DJ: *A transformation takes place when your work is presented through the mediation of video. Perhaps it's the flattening of the image or the coldness of the medium, but showing your work on video seems to brutalise the image, making it more difficult to bear than in live performance. Why is this the case?*

RA: It's something to do with the concentrated or forced gaze that video demands. Video drags you right down to the action, and ignores everything else outside the frame. The action becomes more brutal because it's reduced to sight and sound alone, instead of all the responses an audience member might have to other stimuli, like the feeling of being among other people, or distractions, or the atmosphere in the room.

DJ: *You're quite persistent in your use of autobiography as material in your performances. How do you feel about readings that strip away this context and read the work in other ways?*

RA: Well, I'd say it *has* to be read in other ways. I use autobiographical references, and images, and so on, but I don't apply a narrative in the way I might if I was writing a memoir. I carry the images and events at a *cellular* level, in the sense that it's coded into my design, as living flesh. The content isn't really available to the audience, because it's obscure in this way, but also because it's presented visually.

DJ: *In our earlier interview, you mentioned the term 'dissociative sparkle'. What does this term mean to you?*

RA: Imagine impending doom, in which the world is getting darker and darker, and your experience is compressed, and suddenly a mirror ball lights up and starts rotating, or a drag queen shimmies in a sequined dress. Dissociative sparkle is that *split*, where intense pressure makes something explode, in a glittering, oddly captivating manner. (See **Figure 9.3**.) I suffer guilt at how heavy and morbid my work can be, so there needs to be a moment of release, or clarity, amid the carnage, to offset the horror of it all. In the *Torture Trilogy*

Figure 9.3 Ron Athey, *Incorruptible Flesh (Messianic Remains)* (Performance Space, London, 2014). Photograph by Manuel Vason

pieces, for example, everyone is bled out, strung up, cut up and fucked, and is eventually dead and buried – but in the middle of it all, I'll put in a disco scene, or squeeze out an enema of glitter stars, or Divinity Fudge dances in sequins, as The Icon pierced with crystals [in *Deliverance*]. That's dissociative sparkle! It's organic – it's not abstract, or contrived, or a 'what the fuck' moment. Our communities are special, because we find surprising responses to deep oppression. A speck of glitter emerges. It's very different to being happy and glittering. The sparkle works differently when it's paid for in a certain way.

DJ: *Is camp relevant too?*

RA: Camp is a parody of a parody. We have a lineage of camp. Camp is a mask, a façade of silliness with a surprise underneath. The surprise is sometimes nasty! It's not always happy. In that way, it can be political, and it can be disturbing. Look at John Waters's earlier films, like *Pink Flamingos* [1972]. He nails that fucked-up aspect of camp. I am interested in camp, but I'm nervous of it as a terminology because it's one of those words that have been completely exhausted by academia. It's like the word 'failure'. It's so overworked that it's no longer relevant. You can't take a word and talk about it back and forth for ten years and expect it to remain productive. No one's really *shooting for failure*. It's just an odd situation something else can be born inside. I think camp is similar in that way.

Like dissociative sparkle, it's also a tactic. You have to interrupt the morbidity to shape the rhythm of the piece, and to make the imagery and the atmosphere bearable. I think some people might think I'm gunning for total visual onslaught against the audience, but actually I'm always *feeling out the contours of the spectacle*, in the planning, and in the performance itself. When I'm performing, I can try to speed up and slow down the intensity, and I can figure out when an action needs to be stilled, or when it has to lift, while keeping the rhythm and the intensity organic. It can go quite far out, for sure, but I think I'm mostly in control. The birthday performance of *Self-Obliteration* is one instance, though, where I went out farther than I expected, and I started to freak out about whether or not I could even come back.

DJ: *The title given to us for this event employs the word* exorcism.[14] *Is exorcism a concept you relate to?*

RA: I'm not entirely comfortable with the idea of exorcism. It is too tied up with the *myth of catharsis*. This myth seems to suggest that my childhood and adolescence were so fucked up that by making this work I'm *working through it* in performance; or, the story goes, AIDS was so horrible, and the grief and loss was so disastrous, that I dealt with it by making performances. This is inaccurate – neither myth works for me as a grand solution. If anything, I'm cycling through the pain and grief in the performance, visualising and embodying it, again and again, and making the loss *more difficult* to bear. The images produced in the work are monstrous beyond what is possible in everyday human experience, bringing the dark parts of experience to life in fantasy form. It's not as simple as purging the experience so that the artist can feel better.

DJ: *So you're not exorcising personal demons?*

RA: No, not at all. My work is not about direct address. There's no confessional dimension. If there are moments, it's just as punctuation, or as something to allow me to spin on my heels. If anything, I'm exorcising cultural and social demons. You have to understand the context of when a particular work of art was made – it seems to be the case, very much so, for my *Torture Trilogy* works, for example. This talk of exorcism takes us away from the historical situation in which a work is made. Look at another artist's work, like James Bidgood's *Pink Narcissus*, which straddles the historical line before and after the legalisation of gay porn in New York. The film embodies the kinds of fantasies made necessary by the censorship of homoerotic imagery. It's unfair to criticise the film for being too nelly, or campy, or fantastical, because those qualities are necessary in that specific time and place. If we return to my own situation in the 1990s, living in a community that was literally dying, the extremity of my response makes more sense. It's too neat to think of this as simply exorcism, or catharsis. I had to take a stand, and the stand I took was brutal. We also forget that in that moment, my audiences were split down the middle, between body modification enthusiasts, and queer/AIDS activists. There was a sprinkling of general art crowd people too.

DJ: *What about channelling? This seems to circulate in and around exorcism, and you mentioned it in the previous interview.*

RA: Yes, it's relevant, although I wouldn't know how to define channelling. Performing isn't acting, but in the heat of performance, *I know I am not myself.* Maybe channelling is a good way to explain the difference between acting and not being myself. I'm certainly not interested in trying to be myself on stage. This is part of a bigger issue around what kind of embodiment I think I am trying to invoke in performance. I must say, I would *never* want to make the kind of work where I come on and say, 'Hi! I'm Ron Athey. I have AIDS, and I'm angry!' I hate that kind of work. It's not me – I want visual bloat, operatic extravagance, and excess. I want to be bigger than myself on stage.

Similarly, why is it that I won't rehearse? What do I gain by not knowing how to move through an action? Look at *Self-Obliteration*. If I watch the early versions on video, I see I'm nervy, on edge, but I seem confident I won't drop the sheets of glass while I shuffle them over me. I've no reason to be confident. I don't know how the glass will move, or if I can hold them firmly when my hands are bloody, and I see and hear glass hitting heavily against glass, and I don't know how hard they need to collide before they'll break. I'm jinxing myself now, but I've never broken the glass. It could be a disaster if I dropped them, or shattered the sheets in my hands, not least because the audience is a metre away from me, at eye level – but I hold them and move them as if I know how, as though in a trance.

I think of that situation – inhabiting the performance – in relation to channelling. Something irrational is happening in the action, which I am in control of, but without good reason. I don't want the process to sound too mystical – although José Muñoz liked to call me a 'spooky lady' [*laughs*].[15]

DJ: *One of your unique characteristics is that you seem to revel in the debased or déclassé concepts that attach themselves to the wound. You lay claim to pathology. What do you achieve by this, and what are the costs of doing so?*

RA: I don't think there is a cost. Sure, some people have become very prickly about these topics, for example I was criticised by SM practitioners, who said I was inviting 'mentally ill' people into the community.[16] I wasn't even part of that community. The attempt to distance the wound from the meaty ideas that circulate around it concerns art as commerce, and *whitewashing* the difficult aspects of performance. If I can convince you that my blood has nothing to do with AIDS, nothing to do with manifesting self-hatred (my own or that of society), and nothing to do with Christian guilt, and its obsessive and crazy representations of the body – if I can convince you that my blood simply and exclusively signifies the colour red, then my *life force* doesn't mean anything. When you watch me bleed, you watch the life force actively draining from my body. It's emotional. It's not a conceptual exercise. As I said before, it's neurologically strange. You can sometimes smell the blood, the metallic tone dispersed in the air. It taps into an audience's own pathologies. I don't know what each person brings with them to the performance, or how the image burrows its way into their brains. Admitting there is a range of complex ways the work makes meaning doesn't equate to saying I know how audiences will interact with the work. Blood, to me, suggests witness, penetration, sadness, narrative. By saying blood can signify redness, but it's also inseparable from a rich and scary *mess* of significations, I'm simply being more generous, more honest.

You said 'debased'. Talking about pathology, and admitting this as relevant to the work – even my 'rudeness' when it comes to talking about performance in ways that might offend other people – I don't see this as a *debasement* of performance. Really, I'm admitting that performance is sacred. I like the formality of performance. That's why I don't enjoy casual work, why I hate 'smart' work. Why be glib? How can you take the piss? I guess I see art and performance through quite a *churchy* lens. Why lie about where things come from? The histories and complexities, including the implications that make us nervous – all this is deadly serious to me, even though I can allow laughter into my treatment of specific issues and images. The practice of performance should line up with what we actually think and feel, outside of art, in our life experiences. I think this is the point of activist art, like Gran Fury, or feminist art like Carolee Schneemann, Gina Pane or Ana Mendieta, from whom I've learnt so much; and it's an urgent principle for artists who are my beloved peers, like Franko B, Kembra Pfahler, Guillermo Gomez-Peña, Annie Sprinkle or Bruce LaBruce. They're each very important in their own rights, but their work taps into an energy force that is relevant, and meaningful. These artists aren't interested in *faffing* with concepts in a museum. This infects all my interests in the history of art. If I see a painting, I'm generally a bit blasé, but when I see a photo by Pierre Molinier, for example, and I know the history of the man behind the work – taking pictures of his asshole, in a mono-obsession that lasted his whole life – well that confusion of the life and the work gives art a rhythm that I find provocative and sustaining. I don't believe at all that a work of art has to exist in and of itself.

I just want to be honest. I don't think an artist's work is more valid or more interesting if you strip away their biography, or pathologies. It's the same for my work. It has to be. Otherwise it's just whitewashing, which suits nothing so much as the demands of commerce. I'm not interested in whitewashing. I don't have anything to sell.

Notes

1. Ron Athey, 'Deliverance: The Torture Trilogy in Retrospect', in *Pleading in the Blood: The Art and Performances of Ron Athey*, ed. Dominic Johnson (Bristol and London: Intellect and Live Art Development Agency, 2013), pp. 100–7.

2. Co-curated by Athey and Lee Adams, *The Monster in the Night of the Labyrinth* was an evening of Bataille-inspired performances at the Hayward Gallery, London, on 3 July 2006, organised alongside the large-scale exhibition *Undercover Surrealism: Bataille and Documents*.

3. Georges Bataille, 'Solar Anus', *Visions of Excess: Selected Writings, 1927–1939*, trans. Allan Stoekl (Minneapolis and London: University of Minnesota Press, 1985), pp. 5–9.

4. Amelia Jones, 'Holy Body: Erotic Ethics in Ron Athey and Juliana Snapper's *Judas Cradle*', *TDR: The Drama Review*, 50 (2006), 159–69 (p. 159).

5. ACT UP (AIDS Coalition to Unleash Power) is an activist organisation founded in 1987, which responded to government inaction at the height of the AIDS crisis, and used direct action and creative protest to provoke changes in medical healthcare, federal support of medical research, and legislation.

6. *Incorruptible Flesh (Work in Progress)* was performed with Lawrence Steger at CCA (Glasgow) and Galerija Kapelica (Ljubljana), in 1997. Steger died of AIDS-related pneumonia in 1998. *Incorruptible Flesh (Dissociative Sparkle)* was a solo durational performance, presented at the National Review of Live Art (Glasgow) and Artists Space (New York), in 2006. *Incorruptible Flesh (Perpetual Wound)* was a collaboration between Athey and Dominic Johnson at Chelsea Theatre (London) and the Fierce Festival (Birmingham) in 2007. *Incorruptible Flesh (Messianic Remains)* premiered at Stanford University, California, in the summer of 2013.

7. Kembra Pfahler is a performance artist, best known for her art-concept band the Voluptuous Horror of Karen Black. Vaginal Davis is a performance artist and no-budget filmmaker, and the creator of homocore zines in the 1990s such as *Fertile LaToyah Jackson*. Goddess Bunny is a disabled transsexual punk cabaret performer, and she appears in Joel-Peter Witkin's macabre photographs, and the cult movies of John Aes-Nihil.

8. See *Modern Primitives: An Investigation of Contemporary Adornment and Ritual*, ed. V. Vale (San Francisco: RE/Search Publications, 1989).

9. Fist was a monthly club night run by the promoter Suzie Kruger. It was a public sex and fetish event, and hosted performances by major artists, including Athey, Franko B, Leigh Bowery, and others.

10. Koltès, cited in David Bradby, 'Introduction', in *Bernard-Marie Koltès: Plays 1* (London: Methuen, 1997), pp. xv–xlvi (p. xv).

11. Antonin Artaud, 'Theatre and the Plague', in *The Theatre and its Double*, trans. Victor Corti (London: Calder & Boyars, 1970), p. 21.

12. *Self-Obliteration I-II* are shown together, as two parts of a single performance. *Self-Obliteration I* has been shown alone; and parts I-II have been shown with a third part as *Self-Obliteration I-III* – only once, at National Review of Live Art, Centre for Contemporary Arts, Glasgow, in May 2010.

13. The track *There are No More Tickets to the Funeral* appears on Diamanda Galás's album *Plague Mass* (1991). Galás writes: 'And on his dying bed he told me / "Tell all my friends I was fighting, too, / But to all the cowards and voyeurs: / There are no more tickets to the funeral".'

14. Part II was conducted live as 'Exploring Exorcism Through Extreme Performance: Ron Athey and Dominic Johnson in Conversation', at Rivington Place/Iniva (Institute of International Visual Arts), London on 29 March 2012.

15. José Esteban Muñoz was an influential performance studies scholar, and a foundational theorist of performance art by queer artists of color. He died on 4 December 2013.

16. This criticism was levelled at Athey in London in 1994, during *4 Scenes in a Harsh Life* (Institute of Contemporary Arts, London), at a roundtable on SM and censorship.

STORIES

BOOKS · GIFTS · CAFÉ

1716 SUNSET BLVD
LOS ANGELES CA
90026

T 213 413 3733
F 213 413 3737

STORIESLA.CO

10 The Skin of the Theatre: An Interview with Julia Bardsley

Julia Bardsley is masterful in her staging of bodily reinvention. In her performances, she transforms herself through prosthetics, brilliantly detailed costumes and stylised performance. In her spectacular, uncanny performances, Bardsley's body is endlessly phantasmagorical: it sprouts horns, emerges from a sequinned chrysalis, grunts in the darkness, or coddles the gold-leafed corpses of hares. Throughout her work, Bardsley explores the troubled agency of a body bound into perpetual change, and potential catastrophe. When she turns her stare towards pleasure – as in her current *me_(i)dea room* series (2011–present), which explores the neurology of female orgasm and the crypto-science of alchemy – the effects are startling and unnerving. Anterooms that contain sculptures, pinhole photographs and drawings, created in the process of developing her live works, generally accompany her performances. The intense atmospheres of her theatrical worlds often involve special effects and video projections, and sound environments created with her long-time collaborator, the iconic British composer Andrew Poppy.

Bardsley's work as a director in the 1980s and 1990s informed her spectacular aesthetic, and particularly conditions her reliance on persona and elaborate costuming. From 1985 to 1989, she devised productions for dereck, dereck, the theatre company she co-founded with Phelim McDermott (later a co-founder and Artistic Director of Improbable). As Joint Artistic Director of the Haymarket Theatre, Leicester (1991–93) and the Young Vic Theatre, London (1993–94), Bardsley directed highly experimental adaptations from the Western canon, including Federico García Lorca's *Blood Wedding* (Haymarket, 1992) and Émile Zola's novel *Thérèse Raquin* (Young Vic, 1993).

As Bardsley explains, her frustration at theatre's institutional limitations led her to abandon her directing career, towards an auteur practice derived from European avant-garde models and fine art practices. This required aesthetic strategies that formally mirror those of live art and performance art – although, as she notes, the alignment with the latter was more happenstance than calculated. Bardsley is best known for *The Divine Trilogy* (2003–09), a series of three spectacular and disturbing performances exploring disaster, horror, prophesy, esotericism and disease. Bardsley invents catastrophic personae, including the morbid, suicidal jester of *Trans-Acts* (2003), the toothless, hare-lipped soothsayer of *Almost the Same: Feral rehearsals for violent acts of culture* (2008), and an evangelical, yellow-eyed cowboy of the apocalypse in the final instalment, *Aftermaths: A tear in the meat of vision* (2009). In the latter, Bardsley stirs up her audience with glossolalia and enraged commandments to touch her glowing wounds – red panels of light stitched into her cowboy costume – accompanied by sick sidekick personifications of the four plagues from *The Book of Revelation*.

Ever the shapeshifter, since *The Divine Trilogy* Bardsley has innovated further, discarding the (theatrical) convention of the touring performance altogether. Instead, she uses the space of live performance to work through tasks, processes and states in carefully structured but singular and ephemeral installations. For example, in *me_(i)dea laboratorium* (King's College, London, 2013), Bardsley appropriated the Medea myth as a starting point to transform a former anatomy museum into a laboratory, in which the function of the orgasm was explored, imagined and transformed through performance, sculpture, live drawing and creepy couture. The work will not be repeated. Rather, each manifestation of the project requires a different set of gestures, objects and situations. Each distinctive performance in the series is modelled on the pre-existing conditions of the site, and the new developments in her ongoing research.

In this interview, conducted in London in December 2009, Bardsley considers the key themes, techniques and strategies she has developed. She discusses her influences and processes, and her peculiar scenographic interventions, including the use of gridded spaces, and the effects of her movements across – and beyond – theatre, visual art and performance art.

Dominic Johnson: *What do you find interesting in theatre?*

Julia Bardsley: For me, theatre is interesting when there are two things happening. You enter a world of fantasy and wonder, and you are transported in a magical sort of way. As an audience member and a maker, what I am after is a sensation that bypasses the intellectual and hits somewhere else. I don't want audiences to sit back and be detached. I am interested in a physiological sensation. At the same time, I want to see the workings of the theatre, in a way that doesn't undermine the fantasy.

DJ: *When you were Joint Artistic Director at the Haymarket and Young Vic Theatre, how did you bring those two elements together in the productions you directed?*

JB: A lot of the time I was taking well-known texts, like *Macbeth*, which is relatively familiar territory for many audiences. Because it's familiar, they perhaps don't really listen to it, or fully experience the text. *Macbeth* is an incredibly extreme piece of work, and at Leicester [1993] I wanted to comment on the nature of the theatre space, the arena of the theatre as a place of violence, where the performers or actors are under the control of the director. I placed myself, as director, in the role of performing the witches, so that the theme of destiny in the play related to the director's control over the space of the theatre and the performers. The battleground was the battleground of theatre. Simultaneously, I wanted the audience to enter the fiction as well, by creating moments of wonder and transformation. I extended the temporal qualities of the theatre. Usually in theatre there is a comfortable time that events take, so the murder of Lady Macduff – I had her being drowned – went on and on and on, until it went beyond 'proper' theatre time. The mechanics of the theatre – the lights, the rig, the scenery itself – was an imposing force, so that they became visible, acting on the performance space. The theatre itself became the place where ideas, emotions and violence were being played out. So I have always been interested in the meeting of those two elements, the fantasy or the fiction, and the reality of actors on stage and an audience in the real space of the auditorium. At Leicester, particularly, I was interested in bringing this challenge to audiences who perhaps hadn't had that experience in the theatre.

DJ: *How did you become disenfranchised with the theatre, if that's what happened?*

JB: I think I did become disenfranchised. The institution of British theatre has a particular history, which is based in literature. What I was seeing from Europe, especially from Poland, was a type of theatre that wasn't purely literary, even though language was a part of it. I saw something else, where a person working in theatre could be seen as an artist, unlike in the British theatre scene where a director is seen as some sort of careerist. If you were a British director, it felt as though it wasn't legitimate to do other things as well – make installations, for example. It felt very limiting. I really admired artists like Tadeusz Kantor, who was devising and performing in his pieces, but was also a sculptor, where his sculptures informed his performance work. I experienced a kind of suspicion and resistance in my desire to explore ideas and expand the notion of what theatre could be. I wanted to be a theatre artist, and it seemed very difficult to do that within an institutional theatre environment. The restrictions are partly economic. If you are running a building, the main imperative is to make the books balance, and that has a very negative effect on creativity and experimentation.

DJ: *Did you feel that there were specific institutional limitations on departures from the text and from a literary model of theatre?*

JB: Not in Leicester, because I actually had a fantastic time there, and I did some work that I am very proud of – quite extreme work for a regional repertory theatre. Problems arose more in London, where the controlling structures of the institution started to dictate what I could and couldn't do artistically. They were more clearly horrified about a director tackling a text from the theatrical canon, and doing some sort of interpretation of it, even though I don't think the interpretations I was doing were particularly radical. But there's a sense that you are not allowed to touch these sacred cows, which is mad really, as it is only material, and up for grabs. My production of *Hamlet* (*Hamlet?*, Young Vic Theatre, 1994) was a celebration of theatre – that was my interpretation of the material – but in some quarters it didn't go down very well, because they thought I wasn't being reverential enough to the text, even though I was trying to do what I thought was a careful reading of the text, trying to understand the material itself rather than what the play has come to mean.

DJ: *How did you make the transition from the institutional space of theatre into a different space?*

JB: I just totally stopped making theatre. I say I *retired* from the theatre. I thought: I'm not going to do it any more under these circumstances; I want to make theatre but on my own terms. I did lots of courses: printmaking, jewellery, metalwork and woodwork, and entered a studio-workshop environment, without any real idea of where it would lead. While I was printmaking, I started to think a lot more about objects and their presentation, which led to the solo installations *The Error Display: a presentation of remaining* (Alternative Arts Projects, London 1996) and *Punishment & Ice Cream: ruminations on the rod and the cone* (Central School of Speech and Drama, London, 1999). I also explored film and video. I made my first film, which was a 16mm project called *Snow* [2000], based on a short story by Ted Hughes. The story is about visual perception and seemed to be a good starting point for thinking about what film is – starting from the idea of light through the projector. I stopped thinking about performance and started working much more in visual art, until I got a Nesta Fellowship (National Endowment for Science, Technology and the Arts, 2001), which meant I had three years of support with no prescriptions about a final outcome. It was a fantastic opportunity to ask questions about myself: What am I? What do I do? What is my relationship now to theatre? It was through that process that I came to the realisation that I am many things: a photographer, performer, theatre-maker, sculptor and video artist. (See **Figure 10.1**.) It's fine to be all these things, but I had a problem with it for some reason. It's as if you need to fix on one role, but it's the ideas that should tell you what form to work in. The ideas will tell you they need to manifest in one medium or another.

DJ: *At what point and to what extent did the discourses and histories of live art and performance art become useful?*

JB: At the time I didn't think about it in that way, but in retrospect I can see that the context of live art is incredibly generous, particularly in terms of the people who are involved in that arena. Suddenly a dialogue about form, ideas, process and serious critical analysis – elements that have always been part of fine art discourse – were here naturally applied to performance. In the theatre it sometimes seemed that you were just making shows in a few weeks, and then you would put them on, and then you started the next show. There was no real space or precedent for having dialogues with audiences or other people working in the theatre, no real desire to have conversations about its place in a wider cultural context or the directions it was moving formally. I stumbled into the live art scene, really through Nikki Milican [Artistic Director, National Review of Live Art, Glasgow], who had seen the work and has given a space for it over the years [2002, 2005, 2008 and 2010].[1] People within live art seem so alert and curious but also enormously generous with their time

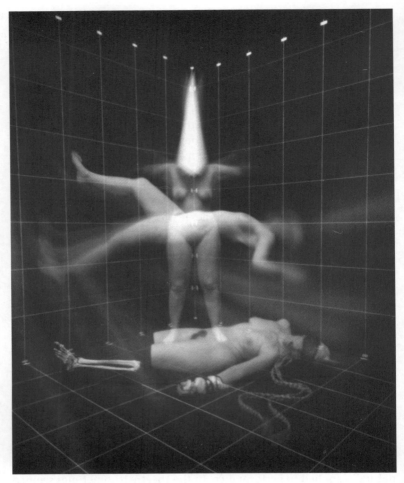

Figure 10.1 Julia Bardsley, *Sleepwalker* (2004), from the series *Dunce (Sad Eve) Nine Places of Hurt* (2004). Pinhole photograph. Created as part of *Trans-Acts* (2003–7). Courtesy of the artist

and commitment to the work and ideas. I had never had that kind of dialogue before and I found it extremely stimulating, and very supportive. But it was never a conscious move into that territory.

DJ: *Another aspect of live art that is very useful is the fluidity of relations between the UK and Europe, in terms of the festival circuits, which comes back to your earlier point about the insularity of the theatre.*

JB: I think the festival circuit is vital. When I was working in the theatre everything was so isolated. You worked on your own production and didn't really brush up against other works or other people. The European festivals that I have been involved in have all been incredibly stimulating, and have actually been the place where I've met UK artists. That was how Robert Pacitti [Artistic Director, Spill Festival of Performance, London] saw *Trans-Acts*; we didn't know each other, and it took a foreign festival to bring us together. The first Spill Festival [2007] was a really wonderful context for *Trans-Acts*, because Robert didn't mind talking about theatre – he didn't set up an antagonistic relation between live art and theatre. For someone like me who came from the theatre, I could have felt like an interloper, but the context was totally supportive.

I also met other artists through the festivals circuit. For example, through Spill I met Kira O'Reilly. I was already really fascinated by Kira's work, particularly her work with animals.[2] From the outside it would seem that our work couldn't be further apart. Kira's work deals with the real, and I deal with the body in a totally artificial way – everything I do is artificial and constructed, and deliberately *not* real. So when she came to see *Trans-Acts* I was very nervous, because I was putting spikes through my tongue using fakery, whereas she uses real wounding in performance. I was worried she'd feel I was belittling her way of working. The next day we both attended a symposium as part of Spill, had lunch together, ended up not going back for the afternoon session, and spent the rest of the afternoon talking, realising that we had much in common, even if the outcome of what we do is very different. Her friendship continues to be really important to me and how I see my work.

DJ: *You have used animals in your own work, from the taxidermy hares in* Almost the Same *to the pantomime horse in your recent collaboration with Andrew Poppy,* Improvements on Nature: a double act *(2009).*[3] *Could you say something more about your use of animals?*

JB: I remember when I was very little we had a German shepherd dog, and she gave birth to 11 puppies. My mum and dad ran a café at that time and there was an upstairs room covered in newspaper, and the dog was there with all the puppies. I must have been about three, and I would nuzzle up with them while they were feeding, and I remember the smell of the milk and their fur, their sweet breath. So there is a connection with the animal, a sense of missing my animal side. Through culture and socialisation you are not allowed to access

Figure 10.2 Julia Bardsley, *Almost the Same: Feral rehearsals for violent acts of culture* (2008). Photograph by Simon Annand. Courtesy of Julia Bardsley

that animal nature. I think I feel that restriction quite keenly. *Almost the Same* was an opportunity to explore that feral and uncultured side – *a healthy chance to howl*. (See **Figure 10.2**.)

DJ: *Many of your pieces seem to explore that tension between fantasy and the visceral, where a flight of fancy gets pulled down to a horror of the body.*

JB: Yes. I think performance is always about a tension between those two poles: the glitter, glamour and beauty of diamonds, fur, leather – our adornment with skins, cultured, tamed and appropriated from nature – and the real meat of what it means to be an animal, the blood, shit and piss, which retains its own sort of pleasure, the mucky, dirty side. I am pulled between the sheen and gleam of the surface and the shit on the underside – the meat being turned inside out. I like the coexistence of those two textures. There's something very exciting about it.

Almost the Same came out of the very animal experience of a miscarriage I had in rural Portugal. It's the most primal, feral, visceral experience I've had. It was a bodily process that was happening, over which I had no control. It was like I was both outside of myself and simultaneously truly being my physical, animal self; watching and experiencing the phenomena of the meat that we are, the meat that we produce inside our bodies and the amount of meat that can be expelled. Similarly, later, when I was in the development stage of *Almost the Same*, I did three days of durational performances at the Camden Arts Centre [in 2008]. On the last day I ended up spending two or three hours dribbling and spitting into a bowl, and I was amazed at how much stuff the body can generate. Where does it come from, and how is it possible for the body to generate material like this? These are physical things that you don't have conscious or cultural control over, that remind you of the *meatiness* of the flesh, of your insides, and your organs at work.

DJ: Aftermaths, *the final instalment of* The Divine Trilogy, *explores the idea of apocalypse. Can you explain what that concept means to you?*[4]

JB: I was interested in apocalypse as a celebration, as a revelation, or what it is to reveal, which is what theatre is, to see and to show. The spectator is there to see something revealed, in the same way that an autopsy is an opportunity for seeing inside the self. For me the apocalypse is about spectacle – vision in all its connotations, including prophecy (which is what the *Book of Revelation* is deemed to be) and other ways of seeing, where the imagination is an inner eye. *Aftermaths* is all those things thrown together, tying up apocalypse, carnival and celebration – a Bacchanalian idea of apocalypse as letting go, release, to get to somewhere that is ecstatic. I've been looking back and thinking, in a sense, how I failed to reach the level of ecstasy I intended for that piece. I've been to gigs where I have danced for hours – like Underworld [the British techno-house band] at the Roundhouse [2008] – where I was totally transported but inside something, and felt so released, and free, and out of my body. I wanted that to happen for the audience in the theatre in *Aftermaths*. I don't know whether it is the conventions of theatre that tame that experience, or there weren't enough people crammed together, or the material is not familiar enough to bring the audience to an ecstatic state. Either way, achieving that feeling of transformation is quite a task. People become familiar with music by having it in their homes. They can listen to it again and again, and a particular type of music will therefore belong to a particular moment in your life. Gigs draw on shared memories, but the audiences that come to the theatre are much more disparate – there's no ecstatic commonality in the sense you get at a gig.

DJ: *Your work often involves a sense of the magical and the occult – for example the use of sacred geometries and obscure equations in* Almost the Same *– and perhaps cults, which your work also flirts with.*

JB: Yes. I would still love to do something where the audience was really transported, and where we reached an ecstatic moment together, because in a sense that is the ritual of theatre, a group of people coming together towards a unique experience. Jim Morrison of The Doors talked about gigs as a secular ritual where everybody was working towards some sort of ecstatic state, which music can do in a way that is much more difficult for performance. There must be ways to do it but I haven't tapped into them yet.

DJ: Almost the Same *and* Aftermaths *are striking for the ways you create different configurations for audiences. For example, in* Almost the Same, *you begin the performance in the seats, with the audience on the stage in a triangular formation, and then physically move the audience from the stage to the seats, and then back again, transforming the set into an exhibition.*

JB: Sitting in the seats can be quite passive, both intellectually and physically. The lights come down and you become anonymous, so I like to highlight the mass, as well as the body of the spectator. I am specifically interested in what it means to be an audience in an auditorium, and the configurations of theatre spaces – the wings, backstage, the gods – the physical shape of the theatre. If you have these conventions, it's not just a case of accepting them as conventions, but of using their power to try and find a way to alert an audience to the fact that they *are* an audience, as part of a mass, and as individuals who have an effect on the performer and the performance.

DJ: *Do you feel that, as a theatre artist, you have a responsibility towards 'audience development'? What is your response to this terminology?*

JB: It's a difficult phrase. Audience development relates to funding criteria. I am not sure I have any responsibility for creating the context through which theatres garner new audiences or find the younger generations who will come and see the work. In a sense I'm not sure that's my role. Obviously I want people to see the work and I know that if they did – even if it's not something they would normally come to – they would get something out of the experience. The audience is crucial, because without it you don't have a work. That's why I concentrate on alerting the audience to their responsibility within the piece, by making sure they know they are part of the work. I'm not talking about audience participation in the crude sense, but without the audience there is only actions and lights and sound. Theatre needs that meeting of the public with what has been private. The work happens when those two things come together. It's in the public performance that I start to understand what the piece is about, because until then I am just working with material. The audience starts to shape it, to make sense of it, because the performer's concentration works in a different way in front of an audience, and something else starts to occur in the space. In some ways I hate audiences [*laughs*], because they don't always concentrate very well. I don't mind disruption, or heckling – I've had to deal with that quite a lot, even in conventional theatre. When I did *Macbeth* we had lots of people shouting out, and leaving, which great because it meant that they were really feeling something, even if it was something negative.

DJ: *This might be a generalisation, but live art that draws on theatre often seems polarised in its relations to audiences, between a desire for alienation and a desire for easy participation. On the one hand there is an attempt to withhold pleasure, and, on the other, an urge to love or support an audience. I think your work intervenes in that polarity.*

JB: I have a tendency, though, of trying to please an audience too much, or of over-narrating the work. I try to knock it out of myself. Coming from a narrative or storytelling tradition it has been very hard to get away from guiding an audience through a piece, which, in a way, only appeals to the intellectual level. Now I am much more interested in giving them a physiological experience. By offering elements that do have a structure, but one that is buried, the audience have to piece together what is offered. Starting with *The Divine Trilogy*, especially after *Trans-Acts*, and definitely in *Almost the Same*, which was closest to what I wanted to achieve, I've begun to deliberately avoid helping the audience in that way, to pull away from my own explanatory tendencies.

DJ: *What kind of an audience member are you?*

JB: Terrible [*laughs*]. I can concentrate very well, but I don't like being amongst other people. As an audience member, I find the presence of other people really annoying. I'm quite intolerant!

DJ: *In terms of what you have described as your tendency to guide audiences, do you feel that you enjoy or appreciate being guided through other artists' work?*

JB: No, I don't enjoy it at all. I'd much rather that things were just offered and left hanging in the air, so that I have to work hard to make sense of it and understand it. I'd much rather the experience of not knowing. That's what I go to the theatre for, for something totally unexpected – not shocking, necessarily, but the experience of something *other*. I get this from Simon Vincenzi's works, which are utterly uncompromising and resist any temptation to explain. His works reach a place beyond the intellect that is totally compelling, without me understanding how, by appealing to something dark and indistinct.

DJ: *Can you tell me about your process of making? Where does your initial idea come from, and how do you develop it to the finished performance?*

JB: It doesn't usually begin with one single idea, but four or five that are swimming around, including something that is happening at the moment, politically or socially, or something I have read, or an image, or a flavour of an atmosphere, or just a desire to explore materials. I'll spend a couple of months reading and make notes, pursuing the ideas separately without knowing how those four or five disparate things might eventually come together into some sort of whole. It's very important that they stay discrete, so they don't get watered down, and keep their individual strength. When I transcribe my notes I'll start to see how some of the ideas cross-fertilise, or make marriages in some sort of way. I'll start doing some drawings, including maps of the space, configurations of the audience, and general ideas about how the conceptual work can be translated into a spatial dynamic. This phase involves processes of translation, so that the work doesn't remain at the level of concepts but will begin to move into questions about materials, space, shape or bodily forms. I also start making objects as well.

Although I find the process of research exciting, you can get so bogged down in reading that there comes a time when you have to move out of your head and into your hands. I start gathering the lexicon or vocabulary of materials. Will it be fur, wax, honey, gold leaf, bones, plastic? What tones might they be? As I begin to make objects, I simultaneously start to sketch out a visual score, to understand how the piece will work temporally – what sections there might be, their tenor, how one section might move into another. The piece then starts to take shape, to become more concrete, and I can get garments and set elements made. Parallel to that, I have conversations with Andrew [Poppy] about the sonic dimension, which is incredibly important for me. Without that, the performance wouldn't work, because the sonic space holds everything. Andrew will work on his own. I usually won't listen to anything and he'll only see a few things that I am working on. Towards the end of the process, Andrew will play through the material he's generated and we'll start to place it in the project score. The objects that I have made will often end up in an exhibition or installation, as a precursor or epilogue to the performance, to allow the audience a way into what I have been thinking about during the process. The objects might not necessarily appear in the piece, or be clearly connected to it, but they will have participated in the thinking process. That has always happened – even when I was in college I would provide a prologue by presenting the objects I had made. The receptacle of the theatre isn't big enough to contain everything I want to do and say, so the work tumbles out into different forms, and has to be expressed in some other way like sculpture or installation.

DJ: *Do you rehearse?*

JB: In the conventional theatre, of course, a director will work with the cast for weeks to reach a cohesive interpretation of a text, but one of the most fantastically revelatory aspects of solo performance is that you can almost dispense with rehearsal. To me this is a total joy, because I really *loathe* rehearsals – the idea that you have to find cohesion before the work is presented to an audience. For me, performance is about non-cohesion, the coexistence of elements that don't necessarily fit together, but when put together make another world that has meaning, over which the creator/performer has no control. Not rehearsing is about relinquishing some of that control. Of course, I still set up a structure, and there are fixed elements, like the video, but within the structure I am free to do whatever I want. The audience will accept what you offer them as belonging to the work, and read it as what was intended.

DJ: *How much will a piece change or develop during a run, for example the parts of* The Divine Trilogy?

JB: They change in a fantastic way. Except for *Trans-Acts*, I haven't performed them nearly enough to know fully what the performance is. Certainly with *Almost the Same* and *Aftermaths*, I feel that they have just started. The piece really grew when I did a run of six performances of *Almost the Same* in an old veterinary training hospital in Lisbon [Kanart 2008]. It felt very different to the first performance in Glasgow [National Review of Live Art 2008], where I wasn't really *inside* it, whereas now there are sections where the physical quality of the performance is very extreme. I reached a point where I understood much more clearly the differences between the three sections 'Nigredo', 'Rubedo' and 'Albedo', and the different qualities of the personas in each part. I felt much freer in the performance, and Andrew did live mixing of the sound in response to what I was doing in the space – or he would try something new and I would respond to that. Marty [Langthorne, the lighting designer] would follow the developments with the lights, freewheeling a bit. The performance is more clearly live, happening in the moment, even though there is a base structure. This way of making, performing and developing the work has been a revelation and a source of creative liberation for me.

DJ: *How do you review the process, and the work itself? Do you work with the documentation in order to develop a live piece, or to review the results?*

JB: I try not to review video documentation in that way, because the third eye makes me self-conscious of my performance. The way that the performance feels, and the response of the audience, is never registered on video, so that documentation will always be infused with disappointment. I think the reviewing process happens while I am performing, because with each new presentation of a piece, with a new audience – especially if I am doing two or three performances a day, like in *Trans-Acts* – what tends to happen is that you find something new and can implement and develop it immediately in the next performance. Almost naturally, I also shed things that don't work. A section will start to morph, through accumulation and shedding, as the reviewing process happens in front of the audience.

DJ: *Is stage presence a useful term for thinking about your work?*

JB: Stage presence isn't a term I would use. I prefer to think about *quality of concentration*, because I think any performer who has stage presence is really working with points of concentration. That's what I understand from performance – a quality of concentration that occurs when a performer focuses on something internally, and that informs the quality of the external presentation.

DJ: *Do you therefore not believe in stage presence, in terms of the ability of a body to attract and keep an audience's attention, in a way that is open to scrutiny but seems almost magical? Ron Athey talks about 'psychic weight' as the way in which a body can wield its experience as it presents itself to an audience. In your performances – especially* Almost the Same *– there is a sense that your body captures and holds attention, in an almost 'mystical' way.*

JB: Stage presence is key to performance if you are asking an audience to stay with you, watch you, and be with you. But although the power to hold people might lead to a seemingly mystical reading of the body in the space, I think it is achieved through practical means. It's a combination of, as you say, 'weight' – the history and experience of a body – and the performer's concentration with the action that is being undertaken. This is not necessarily concentration on the thing itself. Sometimes powerful concentration – and in turn its effect on an audience – can come from focusing on thoughts, or other internal elements the audience isn't aware of. Audiences are acutely aware of being transfixed, or drawn to watching – they don't need to know what's motoring that action, as long as the concentration exists. Without that concentration, the performance is flabby. It evaporates because there is nothing holding it. With a lot of live art, which is often action-based, and concerned with rarefied space and action, those qualities of concentration become even more important, as there are less trappings – music, environment, lights, set, costume – to support the body. Kira O'Reilly's work is very interesting because she has a very particular and acute quality of concentration.

DJ: *Perhaps persona is more important than stage presence?*

JB: Persona emerges from the release of not being yourself, or of simultaneously being yourself and other. I always say, perhaps flippantly, that I wouldn't ever go on stage without a wig. The wig is a mask that gives me permission to do things that I would never do as my bare self. So I prefer using a persona, instead of the theatrical idea of taking on a character, because persona is much less anchored, more fluid and ambiguous than a fixed character. Persona enables me to take an aspect of myself, which is then pushed in a different or more extreme direction. The baseline is that the persona is a version of me, and in the pieces I often reveal myself, Julia. This returns to my earlier point about the suspension of disbelief, where the audience will engage with you as a persona but, underneath, always knows the fact of who you are and that the persona is a fiction, a construct. I like to maintain a tension between those two identities.

DJ: *Two scenographic techniques that recur in your work are grids – on floors or on walls – and scrims or screens between the performer and the audience. What's useful about these?*

JB: The grid has a very practical function. Historically it is has been used to demonstrate optics and perspective in painting, and to show scale. I use the grid as an anchoring device, to fix something. In *Foolish Suicide Attempts* [2003] or in the black-and-white pinhole photographs, both from *Trans-Acts*, the grid is a fixed point across which the action takes place. Without it, the movement that happens over the photograph wouldn't register in the same way. The grid relates to the audience's point of view, the fixed place of the camera. The pinhole photos are taken over very long exposures – eight minutes long, divided into sections. You open up the aperture of the pinhole camera and photograph the grid for one-and-a-half minutes, and then close the aperture. The grid remains on the image, and anything you photograph afterwards – the movement – is layered onto the fixed point of the grid, because the image making happens in-camera. In *Improvements of Nature*, we build a grid at the back of the space over which the movement of the pantomime horse can then register in the darkness. It is also connected to honing down the space – in forensics, 'walking the grid' is a term for surveying the crime scene, noticing all the details within a fixed square or rectangle of ground. At primary school we were taken on field trips where we placed a metre-square ruler on the ground, and you noted everything that existed within your square of the grid. In the same way in the theatre, the grid acts as a framing device.

I'm very interested in containers, the box, or the display of things – not even necessarily what's in the box – but how something is displayed or presented. The container or the box works to contain the scattering of the objects that I carry out in performance. A grid prevents the scattering from being arbitrary, but instead registers the location of things. The scrim is also practical. In *Almost the Same* I wanted to include video, but I didn't want the tyranny of the white projection screen at the back of the space. The black gauze allowed me to integrate the video into the piece as a cohesive element. I also didn't want the information in the video to be simply a light source – even though that can be interesting as well. The gauze becomes a surface where the pre-recorded performance coexists with the live, but where one doesn't dominate the other. Anywhere there is black in the projected image will allow the live presence in the space to show through behind the gauze, and you get a strange, hallucinogenic state, where the audience can't quite understand what is the projected image and what is live. It's a pantomime technique – characters are lit behind gauze to create a sense of wonder. It's an old trick from the theatre, but it allows me to include video, and have a dialogue between a persona I'm performing live and another persona that has been pre-recorded.

DJ: *In* Almost the Same, *the gauze is then lifted to allow the audience to pass through the division between the two spaces. The gauze becomes a skin between the audience and the performer – a skin that breaks.*

JB: The gauze does function like a skin – a skin between me and them. It alerts the audience to a division or containment, creates an alertness that the audience is against the performer. The ritual of performance is almost *gladiatorial*. There's an expectation that the performer will give the audience whatever it is that they need, something to take them out of themselves, a revelation, but the performer can never quite live up to the audience's expectations. There is a scapegoat mechanism to the theatre, the crowd versus the individual. In *Almost the Same* it was important that there was a confrontation at the beginning between the audience and me. They're in the performance space and I'm in 'their' space. In the end there is an invitation, which is a way of demonstrating that the theatre is a construct, and that we are all in this together. I can lift the veil and take the division away, reopen the stage and invite the audience into the once sacred performance space. We're ultimately not separate – we're the same, and we're in the theatre space trying to sort something out together, and that's why we congregate in this ritual of witnessing performance. I don't know why else we would do it. Why do you go and see performance?

DJ: *I agree with you that it's the allure of a tension between letting go and being allowed into the machinery of the theatre. That's why there is something deeply unsatisfying, for me, in naturalistic theatre, where failure in the machine is smoothed over, or ignored as mere embarrassment. Live art often seems to call into play its own impending failure.*

JB: That's why I am drawn to live art, and feel very at home in it as an arena. The prospect of things falling apart, and of trying to get to the place where we are on the edge of total incomprehension, but still holding on – there's something life-affirming in that situation. The theatre is a safe space for witnessing failure. We should embrace failure, and accept that it is part of the process, and part of our selves. Maybe we can see mortality as the failure of life. If so, I think the arena of art is the only place to explore and to witness this.

Notes

1. The National Review of Live Art (NRLA) was the longest running festival of performance art and live art in the UK, and celebrated its thirtieth anniversary in 2010, before its forced closure in 2011.
2. Bardsley refers to O'Reilly's performances using animals, such as *inthewrongplaceness* (Home Live Art, London, 2004), a one-to-one action in which the artist dances with the cadaver of a female pig; and *Falling Asleep with a Pig* (Cornerhouse, Manchester, 2009), in which the artist cohabited in a gallery with a live pig for 36 hours.
3. *Almost the Same* is the second instalment in *The Divine Trilogy*, and was presented at: City of Women Festival, Ljubljana, Slovenia; Queer Zagreb, Croatia; Chelsea Theatre, London; KANART, Lisbon; and NRLA, Glasgow (all 2008); and at Laboral Teatro, Gijón, Spain (2009). *Improvements on Nature* was made in collaboration with Andrew Poppy, and commissioned by Chelsea Theatre in 2009.
4. *Aftermaths* is the third and final part of *The Divine Trilogy* and has been presented at Laban, London (2009) and NRLA, Glasgow (2010).

11   You Made Me Love You: An Interview with David Hoyle

David Hoyle speaks his mind (that's putting it mildly). Since the early 1990s, he has been the *enfant terrible* of the British lesbian and gay scene, and a force to be reckoned with in performance art, first as The Divine David – in clubs, visual art events and on television – and, since 2006, by his given name. The Divine David was infamous on the club scene in Manchester in the 1990s, as well as in residencies at venues like the Royal Vauxhall Tavern and the Institute of Contemporary Arts in London. His guerrilla drag – excessive make-up, ostentatious costuming and mannered performances – was also readily recognisable to viewers of late-night television at the end of the decade, on account of his strikingly original series for Channel 4, namely *The Divine David Presents* (dir. Bernadette O'Brien, Allied Forces, 1998) and *The Divine David Heals* (2000). In the latter, a typical episode includes Hoyle doing a provocative striptease and expressive dance routine to *Follow Me* by the transsexual Europop diva, Amanda Lear. Hoyle's audience consists of a dozen or so 'elders of Ivy Lodge', the octogenarian residents of a rural retirement home in Haxby, England. It is painfully funny, and not a little dubious – although the ethical quandary of his intervention is assuaged by his post-show discussion (also televised) with the ladies and gentlemen in his audience, over tea and biscuits. 'Are you a very affectionate person?' one participant asks. 'I try to be,' Hoyle replies sardonically, signing autographs, 'but it gets me in trouble sometimes as I'm quite drawn to animals.'

In Hoyle's more recent performances, at stake is the fact of his political commitments, and his unremitting obligation to provoke us in our assumptions about the true and the good. His pronouncements are incisive, surprising, funny, outré or shocking. They are sometimes contradictory, even offensive. His most outrageous insights in performance emerge at the crescendo of a rush of thought, or otherwise merely as an aside, or quip, thrown in to add frisson, realism and colour to a song, a lurid or tragic anecdote, a confession, a gag or an invitation to intimacy with particularly attractive members of his audience; the profound shock of his insights is often strategically deflated by adding the trademark phrase, 'I'll leave it with you'.

Reading through the transcript of our interview, conducted in London in April 2014, Hoyle tells me he feels he may have given me an impromptu one-to-one performance. This rings true. Two nights after recording our interview, I saw Hoyle perform (at a club, Vogue Fabrics, in East London), and I was struck by how some of his concerns in the interview – the abolition of gender, boycotting men, the 'cancer' of the bourgeoisie – emerged as points to riff off in his performance. Of course, he sang Judy Garland's traditionally plaintive *You Made Me Love You*, too – in his barbaric warble, and uniquely, here, to the accompaniment of a MRI scanner alarm, which screamed through the bunker-like space of the venue. The slippage of content across interview and performance confirms that he prepares for live performances by thinking up a storm – becoming 'tightly coiled', as he puts it – ready to unfurl with explosive intelligence in the moment – be it on stage, as planned, or in other social encounters leading up to the event, for example in our interview.

In performance, and in the interview, below, Hoyle is unnervingly unguarded. 'I suppose there's some self-mythologising here', he discloses to me, over the phone. In part, the mythology he weaves concerns the murky borderlands between his on- and off-stage personas, and his avowed uncertainty as to whether art or life takes priority over the other. Hoyle explains his emergence into performance, and maps the rise and fall of The Divine David. Throughout, he is forthright about his politics, particularly his sexual politics, his thoughts on the construction of gender, gender disparity, and how these inform the style and content of his work. Hoyle's words, when written down, miss the fruity particularity of his tone in performance. However, the interview should be framed by a plaintive statement he gave in a performance in 2008, offered after a particularly brutalising improvised monologue: 'I'm leaving you with some little thoughts that I hope will chew away at your fucking brain stem tonight', he tells us. '*And I'm doing it motivated by love.*'[1]

Dominic Johnson: *My first question is about the epithet 'kill all authority'. It's one of your slogans.*

David Hoyle: Yes, it's a catchphrase. Instead of 'shut that door' – *kill all in authority.*[2]

DJ: *It's a catchphrase, and it's instructional. Does it typify your politics in performance?*

DH: Well, it's a nice throwaway line to use about throwaway people. The ones in authority, I believe, have access to power bases that we know nothing about. It brings out a lot of paranoia in me. I suspect them of being self-interested, and more concerned with control than liberating and freeing us. To me authority is a control mechanism. It needs to go. I think of Shelley in *The Mask of Anarchy*, telling us 'ye are many, they are few', and I agree we *should* 'rise like lions after slumber'.[3] This caste of people in authority – maybe this is almost slightly Stalinist of me – but they should be *liquidated*. They're of absolutely no benefit to society, especially to a society that hopes to progress. They have an inherent conservatism, which isn't a million miles away from fascism, in order to control us – and there's billions of us – they really can't afford to have billions of freethinking people. Most of what we've been told is a lie. We all need empowering, and to be encouraged to have more confidence in ourselves, and less in what we're told. I like to think that's my responsibility.

Sensitive people will spend most of their adult life either in therapy, or trying to sort themselves out, often through drink, or drugs. Basically, you have to try to jettison all the lies and the shit that you were told as a child. That seems to be the definition of contemporary adulthood in the twenty-first century. We will spend the whole of our adult lives trying to deprogramme ourselves, to achieve not so much mental equilibrium, but a semblance of freedom or empowerment. I think to a greater or lesser degree, most of us are petrified by our potential, in terms of our own personal expression and potential freedom. It sounds hippie, but there is only love and human potential. The rest is distracting bullshit.

DJ: *Listening to you, I'm struck how what you say in performances clearly reflects what you believe, and what you think and say outside of perform-ance. What are the differences between you, now, and on stage?*

DH: I think I'm a very different person in so-called 'real life'. I think you can get so far into performance that it's at the expense of having a life. Penny Arcade writes about this in her 'Letter to a Young Artist'. Penny has taught me a lot. I think, like me, she has 'street' realness. I recognised what she'd warned against: your whole life can be subsumed into performance, to a degree, so that you don't have any time to actually live, or to garner new experiences.[4] I think that's happened to me. I wanted my life to be my art, and my art to be my life. It seemed like the right thing to do, but when you arrive at that point where you've actually achieved this, you think: *Oh God, what have I done?* Have I commodified my life? Have I made a product out of my experiences? What I have I done? (See **Figure 11.1**).

Figure 11.1 The Divine David, aka David Hoyle, performance, mid-1990s. Polaroid photograph by Jay Cloth

Recently, I've woken up to the fact that my *modus operandi* has been to do shows in London, or in other cities, and go home to Manchester, and then live in a depressed state of suspended animation until the next show. In between performances I'd just close down as a person, and barely function as a human being. I was just living for performance, and nothing else. Now I'm trying to open my life up to new experiences, outside of performance. I feel that my life is a lot more enriched as a result. I recently bought myself a washing machine, and that's opened doors [*laughs*].

DJ: *It's difficult to talk about your work in terms of specific pieces. You do seemingly self-contained events sometimes, and you don't repeat works, but I think of your work as a continuum – a life's work. Do you think of it that way?*

DH: Yes, I do, because performance is what I've done with my life. I'm very fortunate, in as much as I can be creative 24/7. I'm getting older – it's almost like I can smell the interior of my own grave ... As a consequence of that, I paint more, express myself more. I never used to enjoy writing, but I write a lot now. I'm determined to try to tell my truth, which I realised is an ever-changing truth. I continue to grow older and become bolder in my thinking, but I'm still a work in progress.

I have made my life into a performance, really, and vice versa, rightly or wrongly. I wouldn't advise it for everybody, because there's a big price to pay, and it's especially hard for beginners. If you turn yourself into a living specimen of art, personal relationships become almost impossible. It has been a lonely life for me. If you are a *costume performer*, it can confuse people. They know you've got external genitals, but you've worn a dress, which they think is a 'female' identifier, therefore they have to neuter you, and make you a non-sexual entity. To think I am sexually potent, and manifested in such a baffling way, *beyond gender* – that would be too scary.

DJ: *In terms of what you were saying about the lack of a distinction between art and life, receiving criticisms of one's work can be difficult. How do you take criticism?*

DH: I can do without it. If you're going to criticise me, I hope you're going to criticise David Cameron, too, and I hope you criticise George Bush, and Colin Powell. I hope you criticise Tony Blair, and Henry Kissinger. If you're going to criticise, choose your fucking target. A well-intentioned performance artist is not the most pressing target for criticism – so *get a grip*, or go to Beachy Head and do us all a favour.[5]

DJ: *In your performances you use what you've called 'anti-drag'. Why?*

DH: I dress up, but in a way it's a bit of a red herring. I think for people like myself, if I wasn't dressed up and creating a bit of a *visual*, then maybe what I'm saying might appear dogmatic and high-handed. I think drag sweetens the pill. It makes it less preachy. But, of course, I am interested in transcending or destroying gender. I don't believe in 'cross-dressing'. Cross-dressing suggests that some garments inherently have a gender, and that you need the complementary genitals to wear this particular garment. Well, that's nonsense. If you don't believe that a garment has a gender, then you can't be cross-dressing, can you? I think that a garment is literally just a piece of fabric cut in a certain way. I don't think it signifies anything. I mean, we were born naked, so whatever you put on your body should be of no significance.

I like to open my shows by saying: 'Good evening ladies *unt* gentleman, and all of you clever enough to have transcended gender.'[6] We're all just humanoid organisms. We might have biological differences, but they're insignificant. I don't have any great investment in the fact that some people have internal genital organs and other people have external genital organs and a fleshy tube to piss through. Big deal. I don't think people should be at each other's throats on account of genitals, or what we do with them. The more we obsess about our differences, the less inclined we'll be to unify – to work out who our true enemies are and destroy them. Because we're not *each other's* enemies. We're just *collections of cells*, with a finite amount of time on this prison planet. We're here for a nanosecond in terms of the ever-unfolding, infinite universe. So, don't get your knickers in a twist, and don't take yourself too seriously.

DJ: *A specific issue you seek to address in performance is the conservatism of gay culture.*

DH: Yes, very much so. I think gay culture has entered an era of conformity, or what I call *neo-orthodoxy*. I think the main problem is the priority of the individual at the expense of the communal. I mean, being 51, I'm very fortunate that when I was young – here we go, *in my day* … – if you were gay, you'd go on demonstrations for gay rights, but, quite automatically, you'd also be allied to the anti-apartheid movement, and you'd go to fund-raising events by Lesbians and Gays Support the Miners. So, being gay was inherently political. I liked the fact that all these different protest movements were interlinked and mutually supportive. We marched for our rights, but for other people's rights too. That ethos is gone now. When I've complained about it, young people have said to me, 'Well, you didn't march for me', or 'I never asked you to do that.' They believe their freedoms were created as if by magic.

We have to be very aware of *the cancer of the bourgeoisie*. My friend, Gerry Potter – the poet and pop-cultural commentator – speaks very eloquently about what he perceives to be the *bourgeois Zeitgeist*, which of course is wholly apolitical.[7] It's neoliberalism. It's indifferent to suffering, and has no interest whatsoever in creating a valid, grown-up sense of unity. It's childish self-interest, and a conscious reluctance to grow up, and to connect with other humanoids. I'm very proud of my past, when it comes to protest and demonstration. Unfortunately, young people are more prone to becoming *ciphers of the mundane*, and walking, talking examples of the banal.

DJ: *Are your performances a kind of activist intervention?*

DH: Well, I think performance is an emotional response to the world as I perceive it, and also there is a psychological component. I would say that to a certain extent, life in contemporary society can drive you insane. But I ally myself to a kind of activism too. I'm fully conscious that we live on a revolving planet of perpetual war, where there seems to be no hope of a ceasefire or a truce. I think the most damaging entity on this planet isn't politics, nor religion – it's *men*. Humanoids who *identify as men* are my enemy. I think they're weak, obedient and hypocritical, and they will always do what they're told. If men are instructed to join an army and kill, like little sheep they will. And yet, we put these men on a pedestal and regard them with qualities they don't have. There's no strength in killing. There's nothing heroic about doing what you're told. So, I now see humans who identify as 'men' are pathetic, cancerous, old-fashioned, dangerous, and an absolute obstacle to the progress of society. Gender is a performance, and I find men's acts unconvincing. It's been very liberating for me to realise this, because I've always been feminist, and now *I no longer desire men*. They don't do anything for me at all. Do I need to look at another ego-driven, apolitical, bourgeois waste of time? I don't feel any erotic charge from looking at these parasitical things. They make me think of bacteria on a petri dish. They are a disease. I'm very into Valerie Solanas. The *SCUM Manifesto* [1967] makes a lot of sense.[8]

DJ: *What you've just been saying is serious, and at the same time you have a sense of humour about your argument.*

DH: Well, I am from Blackpool …

DJ: *We'll come to that shortly …*

DH: It has three piers, you know.

DJ: *OK. You laugh a lot when you're performing, and when you're speaking – even, or especially, when you're saying something outrageous. How would you describe your laughter?*

DH: Hysterical laughter.

DJ: *And why do you laugh when you're performing?*

DH: Well, I used to work on the cheese counter at British Home Stores, so whatever I'm doing now always feels funny in comparison. I had a sense of purpose once! When I came back from my hiatus, for *David Hoyle SOS* [2006], I was advised by Sarah Frankcom [who directed the show] to go out and enjoy myself, and that people will want to see me enjoy myself. It was great advice. Plus, sometimes I hear myself and what I'm saying and I just think *'what?'* The surprise makes me laugh.

DJ: *Laughter is an important way your audience engages with you. You demand 'total fucking silence', but you always excuse riotous laughter. Why do you think people laugh?*

DH: What I do has a lot of ingredients in it, from Northern pub-and-club dimensions to performance art and political ideas. Sometimes laughter is just a reflex, but it can also give you thinking time. What would the alternative be? I don't want to be in a situation where I'm performing in stony silence, and everybody's stroking their chin and being earnest. Laughter is very powerful. It's cleansing, and it's a kind of social glue.

I don't like the idea of the isolated performer, and the obedient, mute audience. I think we're all in it together. If you are doing anything as a performer, it's as a conductor of energy. You're *orchestrating* the energy that happens as a result of us doing something communal – which is *outside* of that which is ascribed to us, and that which *they* want to pollute our minds with. So, we're creating these oases of cleansing, and clarification, and empowerment, hopefully, outside of imposed orthodoxy. Laughter, I think, is very defiant. It's beautiful. *Let there be laughter.*

DJ: *You always sing. The songs I've heard you sing a lot are* You Made Me Love You, Maybe This Time, *and* Where Have All the Flowers Gone? *Why sing? And why those songs?*

DH: Why sing? Why not? Believe it or not I used to be a choirboy, and then my voice broke – admittedly into a million pieces. But singing – again it's another communal activity. I hope it might inspire people to let themselves go. You don't have to know how to sing properly. It's a bit like that Morecambe and Wise sketch, when one accuses the other of playing the piano incorrectly, and Eric Morecambe says, 'I *was* playing the right notes, but not necessarily in the *right order.*' My repertoire is a bit limited, and my interpretations are somewhat avant-garde. I say I only know two songs all the way through, and that's *You Made Me Love You,* and *Maybe This Time* from *Cabaret.*[9] The choice of songs is important. I think we all know what it is to yearn, and to want.

I think singing *Where Have All the Flowers Gone?* is a double-edged sword – it's political, but it's also tongue-in-cheek. It was written by Pete Seeger, and it's associated with the anti-war movement, but personally I like the fact that Marlene Dietrich got hold of the song. I like how she bravely turned her back on her own country, Germany, during the war. Her interpretation of that song, to me, is a masterclass. It's that mixture of genuine, sincere, anti-war politics, with camp and artistry. She might not have a technically excellent voice, but I would rather listen to Dietrich's intelligent interpretation of *Where Have All the Flowers Gone?* than some warbling personage who might hit every note. All three songs are camp, of course. I don't shy away from that in my own renditions. I think camp is very powerful, and it's an effective tool in getting really hideous information across to an audience. Again, perhaps it's like how I package myself, by softening the harsh edges with a little bit of *maquillage* and – dare I suggest it – an *outré* costume.

DJ: *Collaboration is important to you. What do you draw from collaboration?*

DH: Yes, it's very important. When I was The Divine David I worked a lot on my own. I can genuinely say *that way madness lies.* When you're not collaborating with anybody, you might feel you're in control, but it's a very lonely place to be. I don't think it's mentally healthy at all – for me at least. It's too much pressure. Working with sensational people has definitely enriched my life, personally and professionally. Collaborators keep you on your toes, and we can learn from each other. I've always enjoyed working with Bourgeois & Maurice, for example, and we might end the night by singing *The Power of Love* together: [*sings*] *'Cause I'm your lady* ... You know, nobody really gets into it at first. *And you are my man* ... It makes a nonsense of gender, it's very liberating, people are in hysterics. *Whenever you reach for me* ... It's a mess, we're dying with laughter, falling into each other. *I'll do all that I can* ...

I tend to work with friends. I've worked closely with photographers, like Lee Baxter and Holly Revell. Nathan Evans has directed me in many of my performances in more conventional theatre spaces. Thom Shaw contributes to lots of my recent shows; he'll do my make-up, and often performs as his village-hall character Pam Lustgarten, from the Women's Institute. Pam is very interested in the history of art and homosexuality, and likes to regale us with stories of her experiences in fertility festivals in the Gambia. Ashley Ryder is a frequent collaborator. He's a porn performer and director, and we made *Uncle David* together [dir. Gary Reich and Mike Nicholls, Peccadillo, 2010]. I've done other movies recently too – I just finished filming for *Set the Thames on Fire*, written by my friend Al Joshua. I also learn a lot from collaborations with people I meet through performance. Recently, I was an artist-in-residence in Copenhagen, at Warehouse9 [in 2013], and I had the pleasure of performing with Jesse Kleemann, an incredible Inuit performance artist from Greenland. Greenland is a colony of Denmark, so we talked about Danish imperialism, in front of a mostly queer Danish audience. It was very challenging, to put it mildly.

I think some of us are looking for family. If you've been told you're eccentric yourself, and you meet with and can commune with other eccentric people, then it's like birds of a feather, isn't it? You think: Thank God I'm not the only *loony*. Or thank God I'm not the only one whose soul and spirit is deeply insulted and hurt by the nonsensical world we're living in, which only makes sense to one per cent of the population. The rest of us are little more than slaves. The Pharaohs are still in control.

DJ: *In tension with that yearning for sociality, you're also caustic and acerbic in your performance style. You eject people from your audience, for* *example if they're not paying attention, or if they talk and disrupt the performance. I think some might find it cruel.*

DH: I don't think it's cruel at all. Not only will they be thrown out of the venue, they are invariably refunded. If I'm feeling really generous, I may chuck in some money for a taxi. What's important is the expediency with which they are dispatched from the situation. A little bit like a child who's going into the naughty corner: Fuck off, go home, and think about what you've done. Learn to join in, or top yourself, but either way do it in *your* time, not mine, and certainly not in my audience's time. We've all got more work to do than deal with one fool who's terrified of original thinking.

DJ: *When you throw people out of pubs and clubs, you'll often remind them that they 'haven't just wandered into a regular boozer'. What are you reminding everyone about the space?*

DH: Well, I think in that circumstance they probably take a look at me and apply the traditional hierarchical structure: i.e. there's the white, able-bodied male, with his fit, symmetrical body, and he's at the absolute top of the pyramid, and then it's 'minus' figures all the way down. The more 'feminine' you are, the less points you're worth. So, they probably take a look at me and think: Well, he's in drag, he looks feminine, therefore I'm more important than him, he's at the bottom of the pyramid, and I've got more power than him. I'm there to remind him: *No, you don't*. No. You do not have more power than me. (See **Figure 11.2**.)

DJ: *How important are audiences?*

DH: It wouldn't be a performance without the audience. It would be like singing in the bath. Audiences are very important. To me, they're family. I live on my own. I can be quite a lonely character. So, to me, a performance is a celebration. I just can't get enough of the audience. I talk to them constantly, I ask them questions, and I like to pull them onto the stage and paint their portrait.

DJ: *You have a very hardcore fan-base, who seem to* need *your work. What do you think your audience seeks from your performances?*

DH: Well, I look at it this way, Dominic – and *I am looking at you with X-ray eyes* – as a punter I would attend one of my shows in the hope of meeting somebody like you. That does go on. A lot of people tell me they're in relationships with people they met at my events, or

Figure 11.2 David Hoyle, *Gender Trouble* (Limerick Dance Space, Limerick, Ireland, 2014). Photograph by Gerard O'Donnell

happenings, or get-togethers, call them what you will. I'm really pleased about that. If you are critical of society as it's presented to us, then you'd be inclined to go to one of my shows, and then you're bound to be in the company of like-minded people. I'm proud of that.

DJ: *What's your process? How do you plan, or prepare?*

DH: I'm an autodidactic mess, I imagine. If something interests me, then I research it. I'm always fixated on what's going on in the news – at the moment I can't stop reading and watching videos about the centennial of the First World War, and I'm particularly obsessed with following the conflict in Gaza. I'm interested in information, and I love reading. I think that's what we all do isn't it? We expose ourselves to different kinds of information, and then we regurgitate it in some way. So I read until my eyes have nearly dropped out of my head, and I begin to feel like I'm a coiled spring. A lot of what I do is improvised and spontaneous. It's about speed and reaction. To be able to react in a nanosecond means you have to be pretty tightly coiled. Maybe I'm blessed by being what's euphemistically termed *highly-strung*. It keeps me on my toes.

In the dressing room before I go on, I always remark to the people I'm working with that I've no idea what I'm going to say when I get on stage. That's always true. That will be five minutes before the show starts, and it's pretty terrifying. It's nerve-racking, but I think it's my duty to be nervous, because I care about what I do. This might sound, dare I say, vaguely *pretentious*, but when I'm on stage I regard myself as a *conduit of spirit*. I do actually believe that I'm guided by spirits not of this world. They're free of physical being. They're free of the bodily prison. They don't have genitals or genders. I think we're pure energy housed in an organic organism, and I try to channel that energy when I speak, or sing, or perform *abstract shapes*.[10]

DJ: *Are there times in a performance when improvisation – or being a 'conduit' – fails?*

DH: Well, you're in a better position to say, as an audience member. But it can go either way, I suppose. It can seem to fail when I don't get a response. I might comment on it if the line of thought I'm following seems to fizzle.

DJ: *In performance is anything ever off limits as subject matter?*

DH: No, it shouldn't be. No.

DJ: *Why?*

DH: Because if you're guarded about content, you run the risk of employing ridiculous phrases like *inappropriate*, which represents a way of thinking that I loathe. Anyone who says something is inappropriate should have their head yanked backwards by their hair, their throat cut, and their body thrown in a skip. We need to be able to talk about everything and everybody. There should be nothing we can't touch on, imagine, or discuss.

DJ: *You were criticised for going too far in the Lauren Harries incident. I remember the week after you said, 'For those of you that didn't notice, this is a performance.'*[11]

DH: Yes, it's a performance. I don't have any regrets. I like the idea of going 'too far' of course. It's a funny idea, isn't it? It's like you must always be reined in, as an artist – like a child on a rein, who someone has to yank, and pull back in. Too far? You can't go far enough as far as I'm concerned.

DJ: *I've got some questions about your early days. You mentioned Blackpool. How did growing up in Blackpool in the 1960s and 1970s make you who you are, as a person and as an artist?*

DH: Well, I think my life grew out of films like *A Taste of Honey* and *Saturday Night and Sunday Morning*.[12] Life was in black-and-white in

the 1960s. Then, going into the 1970s, life came into colour – probably around the same time that colour television happened. I can
remember life before colour. I can remember the old money, when
pennies were the size of cartwheels. I know I might not look old
enough. I guess growing up in Blackpool taught me a work ethic. I
had two paper rounds from the age of ten. In the 1960s and 1970s,
even for children, work was just what you did. In Blackpool there
were lots of temporary jobs, and they weren't bothered about how
old you were, as long as you fitted up the chimney [*laughs*]. I delivered papers from age 10 to 14, and then I washed up in a hotel from
14 to 17. I did all the washing up myself – in a 65-bed hotel!

I think you've got to have a sense of humour to come from
Blackpool. There are always people on holiday, acting out and having
a great time, so it isn't really representative of the rest of the country.
If you're from Blackpool, and you go to another town as a child,
you're surprised and nonplussed that people aren't wearing 'Kiss-Me-
Quick' hats and eating candy-floss and laughing, or lying in the
gutter, or rolling around in their own vomit on the tram tracks. That's
how it was in Blackpool. You're surrounded by people on holiday. But
in a way you're encouraged not to tune into them. It was an *apartheid*
situation. There were people living in the town, like me, and then
there were the holidaymakers. You were just meant to ignore them
and pretend there weren't tens of thousands of strange new people in
your home town, outnumbering the ones that are there legitimately.

Just talking about Blackpool makes me want to laugh, but in a
hysterical way that's not all to do with fun or happiness. Blackpool
contains lots of scary statistics about poverty, deprivation, and drug
addiction. There's a lot of dysfunction in Blackpool. I think
Blackpool is an education in the superficial, because the Golden
Mile, to me, is like a set. The holidaymakers see it as three-
dimensional reality, but it's a screen. I know about life behind the
façade. Similarly, when Catherine the Great would do her Grand
Tour, she'd visit artificial Russian cities and towns that were built to
create a false impression that the peasants were living in beautifully
designed neoclassical towns and cities, in luxury and not in squalor.
It was all an illusion.

Blackpool was brutal, but it also gave me a lot of pleasure, because
of the Blackpool Tower – and the circus, particularly. We went to the
Tower every year – our birthday present was to see the circus. I
absolutely loved it. I lived for it. It was an escape. You've got everything in the circus: chaos, anarchy, colour, costumes, people sending

up gender, everything. It's a free-for-all, very liberating, and I really connected with all that – and, of course, the make-up of the clowns. The magic of Blackpool Tower Circus was that in the finale, ingeniously, slats of wood would fall over here and over there, then magically it would fill up with water and there would be fountains and everything. It was just incredible and enchanting. I owe the circus a lot. I'm very lucky because we got to see Charlie Cairoli, probably the greatest clown who ever lived. He had the ability to connect with every single person in the audience. I think we genuinely loved him, and trusted him, and of course he was anarchic, as clowns are. I saw him at an impressionable age. He was a great teacher.

DJ: *Being a queer child in Blackpool was also very difficult for you, personally.*

DH: Yes, definitely. In those days, in the 1960s and 1970s, no one could have imagined that within a lifetime there would be acceptance for lesbian and gay people, or such a thing as gay marriage. In those days, people who loved you thought that they were helping you by encouraging you to conform. There was no indication there was going to be real progress, let alone equality. If you were a homosexual, it went without saying that you were completely worthless. You were null and void. You were told you were an abhorrence, a waste of space, a mistake of nature, and that it probably would've been better if you'd been aborted. I took that very, very personally, and I've needed a lot of help over the years to get over it.

It was tough and depressing because, even as a child, you *know* you're valid, as a *living person*. Whatever I was feeling felt very natural, but you've got adults telling you your feelings are bogus, that you're bringing evil into the world. You're a manifestation of Satan. The evangelical church played a big part in my childhood. There are some zealots in religion, but there are also some open-minded people within Christianity. It all had a huge impact on me. A lot of us spend the whole of our adult lives picking out all the lies and all the garbage, however well-intentioned, that our minds were filled with as children. It's like removing very thin shards of glass, with tweezers, out of a piece of liver. I feel that's what I'm constantly doing.

DJ: *You began performing in Blackpool. Where did you perform first?*

DH: The Belle Vue in Blackpool [in 1979]. It was a working-men's pub. I knew the manager, Barry. He built an extension onto the pub, a cabaret room, and I approached him at 17. I was quite shy. I said,

'I'd love to be on your stage, Barry', and he said, 'What would you do?' I said, 'I don't know, I just want to get on it.' He went, 'Well, if you come on Sunday I'll give you five minutes.' So, on the Sunday, I got on stage; he had an accordionist and a drummer, so I sang a couple of songs. I think I did *Hey Big Spender*, and *The Lady is a Tramp*, and just told ridiculous stories. As luck would have it, it went down very well. He said I could come back. I did every Sunday after that – and there was no looking back.[13]

DJ: *Did you dress up?*

DH: No, not really. I might have played around with a long scarf – there was a bit of flamboyance, for sure – but that would be my only prop. I would treat the scarf as, say, a feather boa, particularly during the numbers.

DJ: *How did you progress from the Belle Vue?*

DH: When I was doing cabaret in Blackpool, I was very lucky to work at the cheese counter at British Home Stores, because in my lunch hour they would allow me to go to the pubs where the holidaymakers were; there'd be a band, and they'd let you get up and do a song. At the Blackpool Tower lounge there was at least an eight-piece band, there at your disposal. I'd also perform at the Merrie England bar, on North Pier. Blackpool's a great place to learn. Holidaymakers went there to enjoy themselves, so there were a lot of venues where people could get up and do a song. Invariably people would be singing either *Danny Boy*, or *Ave Maria*, or an Elvis number. Of course, I like to think that I was the person who introduced Shirley Bassey to Blackpool [*laughs*].

DJ: *Where did you go from Blackpool?*

DH: I moved to London when I was 21 [in 1983]. I like to say that after I arrived in London, I went out one night, and stayed out for three years. I lived very intensely whilst I was in London. Very much so.

DJ: *Were you performing?*

DH: Yes, I was very fortunate. I got involved in a fringe production of *The Rocky Horror Picture Show*. I played Riff Raff [the alien butler], so my big song was *The Time Warp* – you can't really go wrong with that. I'd got my Equity card in Blackpool, and in those days you had to have one to work in the business. Then, when I was about 24 [in

1986], I found myself in hospital with acute hepatitis. I was a mess. The life I was living would have had long-term implications for my health, both mentally and physically, so I chose to relocate. I left London for Manchester, and I've been there ever since.

DJ: *When did you begin to identify as an artist?*

DH: I always identified as an artist. I didn't know what it was to *not* be an artist – I thought everybody was. I think I did it because as a child, and as a teenager, I had a lot of time on my hands. I was lonely. My grandparents had a business [they owned a chemist's shop], which meant they always had a lot of invoices knocking around, so there were tonnes of paper for me to draw on. I just created conveyor belts of drawings. I was drawing my own company. Or I'd write signs and put them in my grandparents' back window – signs like 'Hello birds, please come into the garden.' I could put that sign in the window and within seconds there would be, like, 20 or 30 starlings, fluttering about in the garden. Drawings can work like magic. You don't see that many starlings usually [*laughs*].

DJ: *In Manchester, how did The Divine David come about?*

DH: In the late 1980s, I got a gig as the quizmaster at the Old Steam Brewery, a student pub in Manchester. In those days, nobody was doing quiz nights – it was very early days for the pub quiz, believe it or not. To start with, I did it in jeans, trainers and a T-shirt. As the weeks went by, a little nail varnish crept in, a bit of lipstick maybe, some eye make-up. It built up, until eventually it was *kilos* of make-up, war paint, a mountain of wigs, and ridiculous outré costumes. Because I'd always drawn, and always painted, I'd created all these characters that wore tonnes of make-up on. I wondered what it would be like to become one of the paintings. That's what I did. The name was an accident. If you just put 'Quiz Night with David' on the blackboard outside a pub, it would sound dreary. I needed something that sounded a bit more impressive and ambitious. So I put, 'Quiz Night with *The Divine David*'. Yeah! It was distinctive. The Divine David was born, and it created its own momentum. I became a known *personality* in Manchester. I was invited to be the host of Paradise Factory, which I did for two years.[14] It was the 'Madchester' era, and it was a great time. People were mostly off their heads, of course, but everybody was having a ball.

DJ: *What have you learned about performance from working in clubs?*

DH: I think sustained performance, at some level, can brutalise you. I'm a very sensitive person, but as a performer I had to *toughen up*. I have very different relationships with people when I'm on stage, I think, to how my relationships are in so-called 'real life'. Maybe I'm more 'real' on stage than I am in 'real' life. As I say, I don't interact with that many people outside of performance. Invariably, at home, I'm reading or painting, and these are isolating, lonely pursuits. I'm constantly trying to be more sociable, though, but it's not always easy. I don't like the idea of judging people, but I think I have been a very bad judge of character with some of the people I've allowed into my life. I like to say I'm *the patron saint of paranoid schizophrenics*. It's not an easy cross to bear, I can tell you. But, I think everything happens for a reason – namely as an opportunity to learn.

DJ: *What have you learnt from performance more generally?*

DH: I think performance has given me a lot of confidence. I've been cursed with very low, if not non-existent self-esteem – that's blighted my life from time to time. Performance has counter-balanced that, because I can think: Well, at least I can do something. I came out of childhood feeling completely useless, an anomaly, a source of shame, guilt, valueless, worthless, better off dead, you know. I have had a few botched attempts at suicide over the years. It's sad, really. But I've still retained my sense of humour. Even in my darkest moments, I've never lost my ability to laugh. I never will. I hope I go laughing into the grave – and into your readers' graves [*laughs*].

DJ: *Did other artists influence you? I'm thinking of Lily Savage, for example.*

DH: Totally. I love the Royal Vauxhall Tavern [RVT], and one of the reasons is because of Lily Savage. The RVT became my 'spiritual home'. In the early 1980s, Lily was on at the RVT every Thursday night, doing *Stars of the Future*. I used to stand at the absolute back, where the magazines are, and I was terrified she would point at me, or speak to me. I would have died! It's ironic now, if you think of what I do at the RVT. But people like Lily Savage – of course, you take your hat off to them. Nowadays, people are famous overnight. A truly talented performer like Paul O'Grady [who performed in drag as Lily Savage in the 1980s] got there through determination, dedication, and he really worked, and worked, and worked. That was such an inspiration to me.

I learnt that whatever's going on in your own life, you've got to carry on. *The show must go on.* I know what it's like to lose your father on a Wednesday, and then go on stage and make people laugh on Thursday, Friday, Saturday. I wasn't going to cancel. Everything that I've been booked to do, I have done. Always. I have never bailed, or not turned up. I've always done what I've said I'd do. I've got to have some sort of self-respect and pride, because there are so many people telling me I *shouldn't* have any. Well, *I do.* I reckon, looking back, it's been an interesting life, but not always very easy. It's not over yet. I'm in my early fifties, and I'm from a generation that thought we would be dead in our twenties or thirties. I've survived, so maybe I'm here for the long haul.

DJ: *Were there artists that you learnt from in terms of style, or process? Was Bette Bourne influential to your work, for example?*

DH: Yes, absolutely. Somebody took me to see Bloolips when they were at the Green Room in Manchester in the 1980s.[15] Of course, it was revolutionary, sensational. The influence still goes on to this day. Bloolips taught me how to decorate the stage for less than five quid. They were into recycling way before it became trendy. It looked like they created their costumes themselves, from stolen fabric, thrift-shop clothes, and trash. They taught you there's nothing you can't do. You can do your own make-up, create your own costume, and do your own set, using sheer grit and imagination. Bette has given me consistent support throughout my so-called career, and is often there in the audience at the RVT. Working with Lavinia Co-op recently was also sensational. What wonderful lives these people have led. They weren't ego-driven, and they didn't say 'look-at-me', the isolated performer. They were concerned with the collective, the communal, and the utopian. Bloolips were fantastic.

DJ: *We've talked a bit about The Divine David. Tell me about* The Divine David Presents *and* The Divine David Heals.

DH: Channel 4 used to have a programme called *Takeover TV.* I worked with a friend of mine, Ben Oliver, in the north of England and, invariably, whatever film we made would be shown on the programme [in 1995 and 1996]. Channel 4 asked to meet with me. It took years to get *The Divine David Presents* commissioned and made. I was offered all sorts of vehicles prior to that, but I wasn't interested. Around the same time, my friend Gary Reich got me onto the BBC's

Comedy Nation [1998] show – he has always been committed to facilitating the avant-garde.

  If people are offering you fame, and you don't want to be famous,
well, where do you go in television? Fame is the only currency in
television, so they assume that's what you want. I didn't want fame.
Even now I find it really uncomfortable. The work comes first, and
fame is an inconvenience that accompanies it. What inspires you to
perform shouldn't be fame; it should be the work itself. That's what
I believe. With *The Divine David Presents* I was trying to get avant-
garde performance art onto the telly. Eventually, I think I succeeded.
It was a battle though. They should make a film of the making of that
series, really.

DJ: *If the imperative was to put performance art on television, what were
the effects?*

DH: Well, it was good for some of the artists, though I've got a feeling some of them weren't paid. They were all tip-top people, but I
don't think they were really as valued as they should have been. But,
at least it got it on the television, and it became popular. I don't think
people thought it would, but when you've had a few drinks and you
watch Stacy Makishi be ravished by a cabbage and give birth to a
Brussels sprout, or Ernst Fischer turn into a fish, it's going to make
you smile – it has to make you think – somewhere along the line.

DJ: *When* The Divine David Presents *was shown on TV, I was 18 …*

DH: Bless!

DJ: *I remember you could turn on the television, after a night out, and
there was this strange little pocket of imaginative possibility on late night
TV.*

DH: I'm very proud of that. I love it when people in their thirties
come up to me and say, 'When I was a teenager …'. When I was a
child, in the late 1960s and early 1970s, it was naughty and surrep-
titious to listen to Radio Luxembourg, FAB 208, with headphones on
in bed under the covers. Similarly, I think people felt they'd trans-
gressed by watching me on Channel 4 in the 1990s. When people
say, 'I used to watch *The Divine David Presents*' and you ask what
they're doing now, invariably they have creative careers. I think
most of them are far more successful than I've ever been, though
[*laughs*]. Sometimes it's difficult when you're in the eye of the storm,
isn't it?

DJ: The Divine David On Ice *(19 July 2000) staged the death of The Divine David. Why did The Divine David have to die?*

DH: By the end of the 1990s, I was completely burnt out. Television had definitely, completely, annihilated me. I knew I was out of my depth working in TV, but I also knew not to betray the fact. That was hard. I just wanted a break from it, really. An additional level of fame was offered to me in 2000, and I realised I had to abandon the directions I was being enticed towards. I think if fame happens by accident, as a by-product of what you're doing, that's fair enough, and you just have to go with it. But I felt so fragile within myself that the kind of fame Channel 4 was offering me – which was to become an anarchic figurehead – well, it would have been destructive. I would have found the press intrusion absolutely *murderous*. There's no way that I would want my life to be held up to that sort of scrutiny. It terrified me. They made a very serious offer, but I knew that if I accepted it I'd be dead in six months. The money alone, I would have converted that into drink and drugs. At that time I was very reliant on drink and drugs to cushion me from everything going on around me.

I met some lovely, interesting people, but I wasn't happy in that environment. I liked it creatively, but the life around it, I found it very lonely. The late 1990s was a nihilistic time for me. I'd pushed myself to my limits on stage – slashing myself across the chest with broken glass, getting Marisa Carnesky to take a piss on me … what next? (See **Figure 11.3**.) I was scared by feeling that the only thing left for me to do, as The Divine David, would be *literally* to kill myself on stage. *The Divine David On Ice* was a way out. It had all been very exciting and interesting, but I felt I'd had enough. I'd forgotten what life was like without performance. As it turned out, for six years or so, life without performance meant I didn't really do *anything* – but it seemed to go by in five minutes.

DJ: *What happened in* The Divine David On Ice*?*

DH: It was at Streatham Ice Arena, in South London. I had two professional ice-dancers dressed identically to myself and my *avant-gardeian angel*, Jay Cloth.[16] The idea was to make me and Jay look like virtuoso ice-skaters, but I subverted the illusion, right from the word go, because we all came on together, including the lookalikes. We also had two little children dressed as miniature versions of me and Jay; they were exquisite. The show opened with one of the dancers

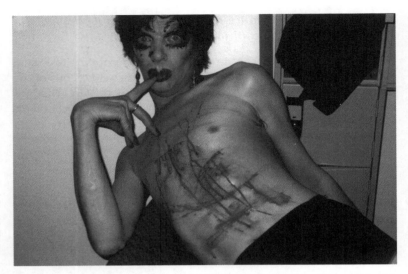

Figure 11.3   The Divine David, aka David Hoyle, after a performance with Marisa Carnesky at *Cinergy* (Fierce Festival, Birmingham, 1999). Polaroid photograph by Jay Cloth

from the Featherstonehaughs (one of Lea Anderson's dance companies). The lights went down, and he came on as an old crone, to a track from the album *Tilt* [1995] by Scott Walker – it was very atmospheric and slow, with this witch character weaving around on the ice. The death march was played for me on a xylophone, which I think then went into *Hello Dolly*. I died to *Rock 'n' Roll Suicide*. What else happened? I remember we blew up a television, on the front of which somebody had put a picture of Graham Norton ... I know there was a lot of invective directed at Channel 4 from me. I just wanted to be away from it all, I couldn't cope with it. People understood I was removing myself from the scene. I'd literally put myself *on ice* – as if I was dead, or had been cryogenically frozen.

DJ: *Why did you return to performance as David Hoyle, rather than The Divine David?*

DH: I think The Divine David was a finite phenomenon. I decided that when I came back I'd perform under my own name. I'd done a few little things, building up to it, but I returned to performance in 2006, for one night at the Royal Exchange Studio Theatre, directed by Sarah Frankcom.[17] It was a wonderful experience, and the show –

David Hoyle's SOS – travelled to the Soho Theatre, and then to the Sydney Opera House. I haven't worked under the name 'The Divine David' since 2000 – except for a one-off show last year [2013], for a event organised by [the designer] Rick Owens. I've reclaimed the name that's on my birth certificate, a yellowing document turning into dust. It has the name David Hoyle on it in elaborate script. Why not use that? What's in a name, really?

DJ: *You've mentioned painting. Not only do you paint in isolation, but you also paint in performances.*

DH: Yes. In the shows I think it brings me together with the person I'm painting. I get to meet somebody new, and they get a tangible souvenir of the evening, which they can take home with them, if they wish. I like to show how easy it is to be expressive, and to demonstrate your creative freedom. Why not get a piece of paper and some paint, and make a few marks? Don't *worry about it*. Enjoy yourself. I think it's a very liberating thing to do, painting, and we don't have to be neurotic about a portrait being a photographic representation. It's just the joy of the colours, and the pleasure of dripping paint. I imagine I've painted you, Dominic?

DJ: *Yes, twice.*

DH: And have you still got the paintings, or have you donated them to the National Portrait Gallery?

DJ: *I was never given them, actually. I left them both at the RVT to dry.*

DH: Yes, well, I think the RVT just rips them up and puts them in the bin.

DJ: *My final question is about a phrase you've already said: 'We're all going to die.' It's another catchphrase …*

DH: Yes, a friendly reminder.

DJ: *It seems to me that you seek comfort in that idea.*

DH: If we're not going to get equality through democracy, then let's get it through our mutual mortality. If we can't achieve it through democratic means, then we'll just have to do it through our own built-in obsolescence.

DJ: *It emerges as a strategy in your shows. I remember you did a series in 2008 punctuated by playing Joan Baez's* We Shall Overcome, *which led up to you distributing Kool-Aid and guiding us in a mock mass suicide.*

DH: Yes. We re-enacted the Jonestown Massacre.[18]

DJ: *And I also remember your show on gay men for World AIDS Day, which was called* The Biggest Suicide Cult in History *(2007).*

DH: It's a great one-liner.

DJ: *What do you enjoy about the idea of 'mutual mortality'?*

DH: Well, I think it puts us in check. I've yet to meet a humanoid organism that is literally going to live forever on earth, in one perpetual lifetime. It's not going to happen. Death is a great equaliser. We live on a tiny planet crammed full with highly individualised organisms. I believe this is hell. We live in hell. The challenge is for us to connect, to communicate, and to realise that we're stronger together than we are as ego-driven cunts. Some of what I do is occupational therapy, some of it is displacement activity, and sometimes it's just filling the time. But the birth and death bit? We've all got that in common, and the question is what we choose to do in between. My suggestion? *Don't be obedient.* How do we do it? *Kill all in authority!* What happens as a result? Let's find out.

Notes

1. David Hoyle, 'Nationalism', *Dave's Drop-In Centre* series (Royal Vauxhall Tavern, London, 2009).
2. 'Shut that door' was the catchphrase of Larry Grayson, a camp entertainer on British television in the 1970s.
3. Hoyle cites from the closing verse, which reads in full: 'Rise like lions after slumber / In unvanquishable number; / Shake your chains to earth like dew / Which in sleep had fallen on you – / Ye are many, they are few.' Percy Bysshe Shelley, 'The Mask of Anarchy' (1819), in *Romanticism: An Anthology*, 2nd edn, ed. Duncan Wu (Oxford: Blackwell, 1998), pp. 930–40 (p. 940).
4. Arcade tells a young artist, 'You need to experience your life without trying to make a product out of it.' See Penny Arcade, 'Letter to a Young Artist No. 1', 8 April 2014, http://pennyarcade.tv/letter-to-a-young-artist-1/#.VBw_OUiLaGh [accessed 28/06/14].
5. Beachy Head is a notorious suicide spot in England.
6. Hoyle has a number of longstanding verbal affectations, including use of the word '*unt*' for 'and'. Others include his peculiar pronunciation of the suffix '-ation', such that a word like 'conversation' becomes 'convers-*aa*-tzion'. These usages are bizarrely funny in performance.

7. David Hoyle and Gerry Potter performed together in the late 1990s as Bitz 'n' Bobz, aka Rachel Cleansing and Nancy Germany, and parodied the racism and anti-feminism of traditional club drag.

8. See Valerie Solanas, *SCUM Manifesto* (Edinburgh and San Francisco: AK Press, 1997). Solanas calls for an apartheid against men, genocide, and the enslavement of a surviving minority of men as a women's SCUM auxiliary force.

9. *You Made Me Love You (I Didn't Want To Do It)* was written by James V. Monaco and Joseph McCarthy in 1913 and revised for Judy Garland as the B-side for *Over the Rainbow* (1939). *Maybe This Time* was written by Kander and Ebb and recorded by Liza Minnelli for the film *Cabaret* (1972). *Where Have All the Flowers Gone?* was written by Pete Seeger in 1955, with new verses by Joe Hickerson in 1960. Marlene Dietrich performed the extended version regularly from 1962.

10. Hoyle does improvised dances, often very short, and consisting of a single movement – he calls these 'abstract shapes'.

11. In *Magazine* (RVT, 2007), Hoyle interviewed Lauren Harries, a transsexual media celebrity. Harries got exceedingly drunk in the interview and audience members felt Hoyle baited her unduly, and mistreated her as a guest. She returned for a second encounter in Hoyle's *Lauren Harries Sober* (2008).

12. The films *A Taste of Honey* (dir. Tony Richardson, 1961) and *Saturday Night and Sunday Morning* (dir. Karel Reisz, 1960) both depict grubby or antisocial couplings between young people in England, and familial repudiations.

13. Hoyle's persona at the time was called Paul Monery-Vaine, a wordplay on 'pulmonary vein'.

14. The Paradise Factory opened in Manchester in 1993. It was the first gay club in Manchester (previously there were only pubs and bars). It closed in 2003.

15. Bloolips was a legendary British drag troupe, founded in the 1977 by Bette Bourne, Lavinia Co-Op and others living in a gay commune in Notting Hill, London.

16. Jay Cloth was The Divine David's creepy, zoned-out assistant/sidekick in live performances in the 1990s, as well as on both television series.

17. At the invitation of John McGrath, Hoyle created *Pixels at the Bottom of the Garden* (2006), a communal garden installation for Queerupnorth, Contact Theatre, Manchester in May 2006; and an interactive reconstruction of his living room in the theatre, later in the same year.

18. Hoyle refers to the mass suicide at the People's Temple in Jonestown, Guyana in 1978, led by cult leader Reverend Jim Jones.

12   Held: An Interview with Adrian Howells

The last letter Adrian Howells sent me ends with a personal encouragement 'to jump beyond yourself'. It was a birthday letter. His was an upbeat injunction, yet tinged with something like sadness. At least, it looks that way now, as I read over the letter, every now and then, in the months since his death on Sunday 16 March 2014. *Jumping beyond oneself* typifies the kind of gesture Howells sought in his intimate performances, many of which were staged for an audience of one. What is one's self, and how can one jump beyond it? How does an individual take the leap to a subject-position outside the confines of biography, of physical or emotional limitation? How does one seek to become more than the sum of one's own known parts – through performance, friendship, love or work? And how might scholarship follow Howells's injunction, *to the letter*, towards a broader engagement with what may be available for critical and writerly engagement? These are the provocations of Howells's practice, which felt so urgent, so alive, in the interview undertaken between us – yet, which also seems too far away, now, so delicate and immaterial in his absence.

Howells was much admired, prolific, pioneering – an obituary in the *Guardian* described him rightly as a 'theatre legend'.[1] In the 1980s and 1990s, he worked primarily in more traditional theatrical contexts, including as an actor and assistant director with the Citizen's Theatre in Glasgow, and then as a performer in experimental theatre productions, the most influential of these being his work with Stewart Laing and Nigel Charnock.[2] His own solo performances – his signature works – often centred on caring interactions. In *Held* (2006), first performed in a private apartment in Glasgow, one-to-one encounters lasted one hour, and involved Howells holding the participant's hand across a kitchen table, then the two hugging or otherwise sitting in close quarters on a sofa in the living room, and finally the artist holding the participant from behind ('spooning') while lying on a bed. These encounters were not straightforwardly convivial. The experience of Howells's work could be joyful, mundane, awkward, upsetting or transformative. He could also explore more explicitly the dark aspects of his psychic life. For example, in *Adrienne: The Great Depression* (2004) at the Great Eastern Hotel in London, Howells inhabited a hotel room for one week, and lived as his drag alter ego, Adrienne, according to self-devised rules: he could not leave the room or open the curtains; he retained the food and crockery delivered by room service; and having put Adrienne's make-up on at the beginning of the week, he wasn't allowed to remove it, shower, or shave. Throughout, Adrian/Adrienne received guests, and conversed with them, in a mounting state of physical and mental dishevelment.

In late 2012, I was invited to contribute to a special issue of the journal *Performing Ethos*, on the topic of one-to-one performances. I proposed an interview with Howells. We'd undertake the interview in two parts: Part I would be published in the journal, and would focus on one-to-one performance; Part II could range more freely. Parts I and II would be published together in this book, which had then recently been contracted. We undertook the interview at my flat in London, in the first weeks of March 2013. A year after the interview, almost to the day, I received author's proofs for *Performing Ethos*, and prepared to return corrections to the publisher. In the midst of rereading the insights shared in this interview, I received the sudden news that Adrian had died.

The published version of Part I was accompanied by a long, detailed contextual introduction. The proofs arrived in the weeks after his death, and it was too late to revise my introduction, so I added an 'In Memoriam' notice, and stated that the terms upon which I approached Howells's work now seemed frivolous to me. I'd missed the points that matter now. Otherwise, I left the original content and language intact (including the painful inaccuracy of the present tense), suspending my friend and his work in wishful animation.

All performance is ephemeral, but Howells's robust work seems *particularly* negligible in its materiality, because the substance of each encounter is categorically singular, intimate, fleeting and resistant to archiving. Many artists have refused to document their performances, but some of these artists, at least, leave individual works that were experienced by more than one spectator, such that memories, manifestations and intimations may be canvassed, and a cumulative experience can be imagined by the critic or historian. This is not possible for much of Howells's work, and the *exemplary* transience of

his work is confirmed, profoundly, sadly, by his suicide. Our interview assuages a fragment of this sadness.

Below, Howells is generous in his detailed analysis of his own
process, and he explains his early attraction to the one-to-one
format, and his development of the form from a fairly impromptu
usage in 2001 to a much more considered and committed investment in subsequent years. He explains key ideas and imperatives,
including the ways audiences appreciate but also resist the apparent
requirements of the format. Throughout, Howells is sensitive to the
debts his recent work maintains to his earlier work in devised and
ensemble theatre. In Part II, published here for the first time, we
discuss his apprenticeship of sorts in traditional theatre, and its radi-
calisation in collaboration with Leigh Bowery. The interview culmi-
nates in his plans for the future, in terms of his work, and his
personal circumstances.

For those who knew Adrian as a friend, the final pages might be
difficult to read. For those who may be new to his work, I hope the
interview will prompt attentive retrospective inquiries and loving
reconstitutions. The hard work of honouring his commitments, and
securing his posterity, will have begun.

Part I

Dominic Johnson: *What was your first experience of making a one-to-
one performance? How did you come to use the form?*

Adrian Howells: In late 2001, I was approached by a collective called
Area 10 Project Space that was based at a disused timber warehouse
behind the library in Peckham, South London (incidentally, the
library Damilola Taylor had left the night he was murdered in 2000).
Area 10 hosted a monthly cabaret night called *Bob's Punkt*, and I was
invited specifically to do 'radical drag', after a member of the Area 10
collective saw me perform in drag in Nigel Charnock's *Asylum*
[2001].[3] I wasn't sure I knew what 'radical drag' was. More importantly, since the run of *Asylum* I was feeling nervous about doing
shows with large audiences. I felt I had reached a stage in my life
where I wasn't sure I wanted to *wash my dirty laundry in public* (as I
identified it then) in front of a group of people who didn't necessarily care about me. In the work I did with Nigel Charnock, we did
improvisations during the devising process, which Nigel recorded
and made endless notes on, and he would be using our personal

information and our life histories to create scripts and scores. In those pieces I was talking about my relationship with my mother, and seven years of bedwetting, and other really personal stuff that I'd also been talking about in therapy. I realised there was never anybody after a show waiting for me at stage door, and asking if I was all right, or offering me company for the night. The work was self-lacerating, and I was ripping myself apart, in the spoken sections, and in the visceral nature of Nigel's choreography, and I would have to go back to a hotel room each night and carefully stitch myself together again for the next day and the next performance.

I explained this to the Area 10 collective, but agreed to go to one of the nights and see what I thought. When I went, I loved the highly experimental, off-the-cuff, spontaneous works artists were doing. One was an angular, bizarre movement piece to loud radio interference, performed in a small, disused office space, with an audience of about a dozen of us seated on boxes around the space. I loved the close proximity between the performer and the audience, and I was aware that the performer had made no attempt to tidy up the space. It was still littered with paper and remnants of its function as an office space. I decided I wanted to do something in the same room, for one, two, or three people at a time, with me talking about my life but involving a kind of meaningful engagement that offered the audience an opportunity to do the same thing. Because I was still responding to the brief of 'radical drag', I wore an outfit I had worn for Russell Barr's play *Sisters, Such Devoted Sisters*, where the two of us had a catfight in drag (for a video that was cut from the final version of Russell's show).[4] Russell had given me a dark wig, a long black leather coat, serious stilettos, and lots of bling, so that's what I wore for the performance for Area 10, as it was all I had. It was quite an intimidating look! I also used lots of stuff from my flat, which I carried in suitcases and installed in the warehouse. I dragged in an old battered sofa, and a counter that I turned into a shrine. The space was covered in trinkets, souvenirs, memorabilia, pictures, vinyl album covers and boxes of photographs and letters. The audience would come in, I'd offer them tea and biscuits, and we'd sit down and have a chat. They could look through my stuff, and ask me about it, and I would talk honestly and openly about my life. Another important factor was that the events started after midnight, but there was no electricity in the whole warehouse, so the spaces had to be lit with candles. As it would happen late at night, by candlelight, in this intimate space, the conditions seemed conducive to a confessional performance.

As it turned out, people were champing at the bit to tell me dark and dirty secrets, and it was very clear that I was perceived as some sort of agony-aunt figure. Interestingly, my friend Linda Dobell [the late director and choreographer] was my timekeeper in the performance, and every 30 minutes she'd pull back a dirty curtain and say, 'Adrienne, your next guests are here.' Linda made up my drag name on the spot, and it stuck. So the intimidating look I had at that time developed into the more developed 'Adrienne' look, with peroxide blonde hair, wearing a tabard, and looking like someone in the service industry.

DJ: *Since 2001, the one-to-one format has evolved into your* modus operandi. *How did it develop from that first, tentative experiment at Area 10 – using the opportunities that were available – to a more sustained engagement with the form?*

AH: The next major development of my use of the one-to-one was in response to a commission from The Arches [a venue in Glasgow], for the gay and lesbian festival, Glasgay. I wanted to work with dirty laundry – literally washing audience members' dirty clothes while inviting them to share their metaphorical dirty laundry – and the idea dictated what kind of space I could use in the building, as a washing machine would need to be plumbed into a sink. I used a small basement space, and converted it into a launderette-cum-living-room. *Adrienne's Dirty Laundry Experience* [2003] became a much more formalised version of the one-to-one for me. And as it was programmed in Glasgay and had plenty of marketing, I think it placed my work, and the one-to-one as a form, on the cultural landscape at that time. (See **Figure 12.1**.)

I became really imbued with an awareness of the opportunity for qualitative connections that this dynamic of the one-to-one could engender. I really felt I could get to know somebody, and they could get to know me. I was very attracted to the fact that it became an opportunity for unburdening – *a problem shared is a problem halved*. It felt useful, not just as an aesthetic experience, but as an interaction that might be emotionally and psychologically beneficial, both for me and for an audience participant.

I also became very interested in how a performance could be co-authored. The audience member and I could share the crafting of a performance, moving away from the convention of the artist having the power and control. Although I would structure the piece, the conversation itself is not scripted. I could allow for flexibility, and for

Figure 12.1 Adrian Howells, *Adrienne's Dirty Laundry Experience* (Home, London, 2005). Photograph by Manuel Vason

the audience to take the performance in another direction, or share something they felt was important. The conversation would have some forethought put into it, in terms of structure, or general themes and directions, but this was never set in stone as a script on my part.

DJ: *How aware were you of the history of the one-to-one as a form at that point? Had you been a participant in other artists' one-to-one performances, for example?*

AH: I wasn't aware of a history of one-to-one performances at that time, and am hard-pushed to think of any that I had experienced before making these two early pieces. After 2003, when I made *Adrienne's Dirty Laundry Experience*, I remember going to more and more one-to-ones. Prior to that time, I can't think of a similar work that was particularly influential upon my decision to work with the form.

As I said earlier, I had become exasperated with working for other practitioners, who were often using my personal history and experience for their work. But I was also imbued with frustration with an idea directors often used – in my time as a jobbing actor, for want of a better term – where they'd say that although you're performing to, say, 700 people, a performer should try to have an intimate connection with each and every person in the collective audience, as though you're performing uniquely for just that one individual. I seriously tried to engage with that sentiment, but of course it's impossible. I never really got how the tangible distance – between the actor on stage, and the audience in rows of seats looking at the back of someone else's head – could be resolved to establish a real sense of intimacy. I understand that this is a question of physical proximity, of spatial awareness, which is different to intimacy. But it was still a problem for me. And how do you have an intimate relationship with 700 people at the same time? So I thought, what if we just chuck the 699 other people out of the room, and try to focus on one person at a time. That struck me as an exciting idea to explore. I became very interested in one-to-one performance as an opportunity to sit really close to somebody – and then, eventually in my work, not just sitting next to someone, but touching them, by washing their feet, or bathing them.

So it wasn't really connected to seeing other artists struggling with the same problem in their work. Interestingly, Daniel Brine [then associate director at the Live Art Development Agency], had told me about Oreet Ashery's use of Marcus Fisher as a distinct performance persona, which did indeed directly influence my creation of Adrienne, but I was not aware of *Say Cheese* [2001] as a one-to-one at that time; I also subsequently found out about Franko B's *Action 398* [1998–2003], but I hadn't experienced it at that time either.[5] Moreover, I was highly suspect and uncomfortable about live art – my background was very much in traditional theatre.

DJ: *Speaking as an artist and also as an audience member, what do you think makes an effective performance? What do you look for in performance?*

AH: I think I look for an experience in which I am touched, moved and transported. I am immediately aware that I am using the word 'touched'. I am excited when a performer physically touches me in a performance, and I suppose that's because I am so often the one instigating the touching and I'm looking for a little bit of tactile nurturing in return. But I am also interested in being touched emotionally and energetically, as if by an invisible hand. I really like it when I am seriously and devastatingly moved, break down uncontrollably in tears, or experience a moment of acute rage or anger, or inconsolable sadness or melancholy. It can feel like being transported for the moment to a different 'realm' of emotional or sensorial experience that is other than the everyday – I know I'm in danger of sounding a bit mystical here – and yet is simultaneously connected to and rooted in it. But touch is also an extremely powerful facilitator of deep connection with the self and with another. It can and frequently does engender an experience of transcendence or catharsis. When I performed *The Pleasure of Being: Washing/Feeding/Holding* [2010] in Milan, I was bathing a naked 30-something-year-old man and he started to cry uncontrollably and said, 'What I can't get over is that this is absolutely extraordinary and ordinary at one and the same time.'[6] I feel that increasingly I value an opportunity – even for a moment – to experience the extraordinary within the ordinary. The other way round can also be interesting, but certainly I'm fascinated by a slippage between the two. (See **Figure 12.2.**)

DJ: *There's a suggestive ambiguity in your valuation of being 'touched, moved, and transported'. How does your work engage with the similarities and differences between being 'touched' emotionally, and 'touched' physically?*

AH: In *Foot Washing for the Sole*, which I have performed hundreds of times, the structure, content, spaces, activities, and so on are very familiar to me, but each person that enters into the performance is

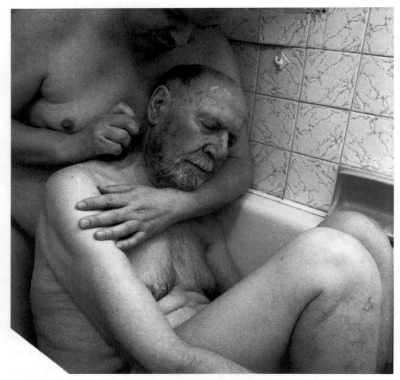

Figure 12.2 Adrian Howells, *The Pleasure of Being: Washing/Feeding/Holding* (2010). Photograph by Hamish Barton

completely different.[7] I'm excited by the fact, in this piece of work, if I think I can predict an emotional response from the next person coming through the door, I am usually wrong-footed. In the moments when I am physically touching somebody – and I have touched many other people in the same way on the same day – suddenly within that actual touch there can be a heightened awareness of the way that skin feels, what it is to touch and be touched in return. Part of the allure is that the experience of touching another human being is a unique thing in and of itself. In skin-to-skin contact, a chemical called oxytocin is released – a hormone that promotes well-being. Babies grow physically and emotionally stronger the more they are handled and touched, because of the release of oxytocin. It makes sense to me that a performance that incorporates these experiences of touching, which can make you feel very aware, very sensitised, operate in similar ways to the more traditional ways that a performance might induce emotional experiences.

DJ: *A sceptical audience member might think that it's easier – or somehow manipulative – to achieve an emotional effect by physically manipulating, moving or touching the audience member, as opposed to achieving the effect through more abstract, elliptical means, such as through text, or image, atmosphere, or other techniques in the traditional theatrical apparatus.*

AH: I think that would be an intellectualisation, which is important in some respects, but in an experiential sense the performance provides different information. It's also important for me to point out that I'm not interested in coercing individuals into having experiences that they're really not 'up' for having. What fascinates me is the number of individuals who sign up for my performances and proudly tell me that they did so because they feel they have 'issues with intimacy', 'don't like being touched', or felt they really wanted to 'challenge themselves'. Of course my audience participants – like those of Kira O'Reilly or Franko B in their challenging one-to-ones – tend to be self-selecting, but it never ceases to impress me that so many individuals, from so many different backgrounds, are seeking out what they perceive to be *real, immediate* and *urgent* experiences.[8] I think there is a sense that people are a little disillusioned with the traditional theatrical apparatus – and, of course, I'm delighted that this includes work that is about mutually deeply nurturing and profoundly *tenderising* ourselves through touch and intimacy.

DJ: *Your training or apprenticeship was in traditional theatre, where a key principle is the production of fakery. Your solo work has in some ways overcome this principle, or at least you have distanced yourself from the prevalence of artificiality, towards what might be called a more 'authentic' experience. What is at stake in the departure from theatrical pretence?*

AH: I used to be somebody that was much more involved in 'traditional' theatre. My more clearly theatrical work comes out of that – like *An Audience with Adrienne*, which was performed for 25 people at a time [between 2007 and 2010], or *May I Have the Pleasure ...?* [2011], which also has a collective audience. I am very aware of those pieces being 'shows'. But I love the fact that with my particular kind of background I have been embraced by live art. I think that intellectually and conceptually, the discussion in and around live art works is much more interesting than the discussions around traditional theatre. Marina Abramović makes a useful distinction between acting and performing: 'Theatre is fake ... The knife is not real, the blood is not real, and the emotions are not real. Performance is just the opposite: the knife is real, the blood is real, and the emotions are real.'[9] I am proud to be identified with a group of people who might be working to achieve the real, rather than artifice, pretence and fakery.

In *Foot Washing for the Sole*, or *The Pleasure of Being: Washing/Feeding/Holding,* however, I know that I can slip into being mechanical or habitual, or fall into acting, or become self-conscious. The interaction loses something when that happens – a sense of the 'real' is lost – because I don't feel I'm really engaging with that individual, in terms of the key principle of my work, which is often connectivity. On the whole, though, I don't conceive of individual interactions in terms of success or failure. It's not helpful for me to polarise encounters in that way, or think about particular connections in pejorative terms.

DJ: *Earlier you used the image of distilling the 700 members of the collective audience down to the singular participant. This must have financial implications for institutions seeking to programme your work, unless you are expected to perform a run of 700 consecutive performances, each for an audience of one. Do you have to deal with the apparent impracticalities of the one-to-one performance, or is this kind of consideration outside the work?*

AH: I do, but I am not burdened by it as a consideration. I am sometimes told that if a festival is going to programme a work of mine, they call it a 'loss leader' – they accept they are not going to make a profit from it, as I can only present, say, 24 performances in the three days of the festival. But the festival accepts that it's culturally important that the work is part of the programme, as it has another 'currency' that will not necessarily translate into making money. What is an issue is that because of that fact, a festival will sometimes argue that they don't need to pay me a going rate in terms of what the festival pays other artists – and that isn't good enough. They'll sometimes try and persuade me to do a lot more performances to help them break even. If I say I can only do 12 performances in one day, a festival might ask me to add another four, and make it up to 16 performances a day. But over the last decade, I've got used to having those conversations, even if I do find it a bit exasperating to have to argue that I should not be paid substantially less than another artist in the same festival.

DJ: *Are there instances when an audience participant will explicitly question, resist, or even reject the conditions of the one-to-one performance, from within their participation? How do you respond to these situations?*

AH: While some interactions do begin with a wrestle of some kind, I've never had an experience where it hasn't moved forward in some way, towards a kind of resolution. For example, I'm thinking of an elderly woman in Munich, who was really quite resistant to the concept of *Foot Washing for the Sole*. She was definitely what I might call 'cantankerous', and literally asked where the rest of the audience was, and was shocked at having to remove her shoes and socks (despite the information in the title and brochure). She said, 'No, I don't want to do this performance', which was fine, and I encouraged her to go back to the box office and ask them to refund her ticket. She stayed, and asked, 'But is this art?' I explained that I didn't know, and that I hoped it was, but that I could definitely claim that it was an experience. She sat there for more time, and eventually said, 'I will do your "experience"', as though she was doing me a great favour. But I could understand her being elderly, and having to go through the rigmarole of taking off her shoes, and then having to remove bandages and plasters from her very damaged feet. I realized that I'm not just dealing with a 'cantankerous' older woman, but a fearful or embarrassed person. The deal I make with myself is that I will always try to dig deeper for the compassion.

In that performance, I am kneeling in front of the participant, and offering my services, and it's important that I am connecting with humility. It was interesting that the moment I got that, she did enjoy me very respectfully and tenderly washing her feet, she melted, and the experience changed for both of us, and she left the space saying she was pleased she'd decided to stay for the experience. Whether it's because of me – the deeper learning and shift of understanding she engendered in me – or the alchemy of the pleasurable feeling of her feet being washed in warm water, I'd like to think it's a combination of those things. I don't think I'm being coercive. I think I'm also quite practiced at being patient and accommodating and I often offer people the opportunity to leave the experience, but I've never had a situation where a resistant person hasn't seemed to have a change of heart in some way.

DJ: *You mention one resistant audience member, but do you have to deal frequently with uncertainties about the status of your work as art, or as theatre, for example from programmers? Have you yourself been concerned* *that the departures you undertake might make the works unrecognisable as aesthetic projects?*

AH: It's not an issue for me from the point of view that 'the proof of the pudding is in the eating'. I feel very committed to what I do. There's a place for it, and I feel that it's culturally and artistically significant. But I feel that what's more important is the interactions between performer and participant, what happens organically, chemically in the experience. It doesn't so concern me to then have to make an argument for its status as art, or to argue its place in the cultural landscape, or that it should receive arts funding, or be taken seriously. I feel committed to what happens in the performances. I believe we live in increasingly brutal and brutalising times, and we need to find ways of physically connecting more. I probably sound like I have some sort of missionary zeal, but I guess there is some kind of zeal about me. I'm not interested in having an argument about where we locate this piece of work, just in order to put it in a pigeon-hole or a category.

DJ: *There is a qualitative difference between the experience of a one-to-one performance and a commercial interaction – between, say, participating in* Foot Washing for the Sole *and receiving a high-street pedicure. A key difference, for me, is the aesthetic staging of the situation in your work. Can you tell me about how you develop and refine the aesthetic aspects of your work?*

AH: When I first started working with one-to-one performances, I was more general about how things worked in the space. In *Adrienne's Dirty Laundry Experience*, for example, there was a pictorial representation of my 'dirty laundry', including photographs of me from a baby to the present day, and I was very keen to include images of me in drag, at parties, or in compromising situations that would paint me as being a person who gets down and dirty in life. I think of that as a key aspect of the performance. However, when I did the performance at The Arches, I supplemented the memorabilia on display with props from The Arches' storeroom, which I thought looked kitsch, or 'Adrienne-y'. I don't think I would do that now – I wouldn't include something that wasn't 'of' me – from my home, or something that I haven't specifically chosen and bought for the performance. I'm really careful now to make sure that the objects have associations, and are things I have an attachment to. Now I would also be incredibly careful about placement. In *Foot Washing for* *the Sole*, for example, I painstakingly work out where the soap dish should sit in relation to the essential oils, and it's those details that take up my time when I'm going to a festival to do a one-to-one performance. I'm really careful about colours, proximity and the space around things, lighting, temperature, and the way objects and arrangements might be read.

So much of this attention to detail comes from having the creative fellowship at University of Glasgow.[10] I was really encouraged to ask and answer the 'why?' question all the time. Why does the bowl I mix the frankincense and sweet almond oil in have to be this particular piece of ceramic? Being in that environment of questioning – especially with Dee Heddon [a scholar of theatre and performance] as my academic mentor – was important in this respect. Before that, I never really thought it was important to answer the 'why?' question. I assumed I worked from instinct, but not only is that not good enough, it's not really the answer.

As a very practiced audience member in other people's work I also learn from my experience of this as well. At the PAZZ Festival [in Oldenburg, Germany] in 2012, I went to Rotozaza's auto-performance piece *Etiquette* [2007], which I thought was beautifully executed – but I had an adverse experience because they decided to locate it in a container that was open to the elements, and I was freezing cold. This completely impaired my enjoyment of it – it didn't affect my appreciation of it as a fantastic piece of work, but as an audience participant I found it hard to really engage. In *Foot Washing for the Sole*, for example, it wouldn't matter if I got everything else right if I was asking somebody to put their feet in tepid or cold water. It would no longer be caring and kind, and would sabotage the performance, as well as my intention and integrity as an artist.

DJ: *Cold water might be interesting, if the piece was potentially geared towards a difficult or uncaring encounter. I think intimacy can have a broad range of possible textures or affective qualities, from the agreeable and comfortable to hostile or abusive interactions. A work like* Foot Washing for the Sole *clearly engages with the genial end of this continuum, yet the possibility of difficult encounters arises – like the person you described who was fearful of showing her feet. How do you engage explicitly with less palatable or pleasurable intimacies in your one-to-one performances?*

AH: There's a difference between, on the one hand, making a performance that is discomforting and challenging, and, on the other, those situations in which a participant might have an adverse response to an experience that might be seemingly and purposefully very caring. I created a piece called *The 14 Stations of the Life and History of Adrian Howells*, which is not as well known as *Foot Washing for the Sole* or *The Pleasure of Being*, as it has only been performed twice [The Arches, Glasgow, 2007; and Battersea Arts Centre, London, 2008]. I take individuals on an escalation of uncomfortable experiences because I wanted that to mirror in some way the idea that Christ carrying the cross to Golgotha became a much more intense and painful experience before he reached the ultimate pain and suffering, namely the crucifixion. In the biblical narrative the centurions force Jesus to strip, and give him a sponge soaked in vinegar and gall.[11] In a very confined space I stripped off in front of the participant, who was induced to be complicit, and when I was naked the participant had to pour out a glass of cider vinegar, which looks like urine. It's vile and bitter, but I drink it. In the commentary afterwards, participants said they felt very uncomfortable, and saw the actions as confrontational. I am aware that I have deliberately used opportunities and experiences to put people in a place of discomfort, which I hope leads them to question what it is in the action that makes them feel challenged. But the problem with *The 14 Stations* is that it is unrelenting. I do think there's a payoff at the end, but because it was literally one thing heaped onto another, the participant ceases to have a perspective on the individual actions, or their own complicity in the performance. One of the stations include me naked on all fours in a paddling pool full of freezing water and I ask the participant to pour a bucket of ice over my back. Some refuse to do it. If they refused I did it to myself.

In another section I stand next to a projected film image of a gorgeous man – a former student of mine who was the object of my unrequited love – and the audience participant watches me as I break down and cry, from the pit of my gut, while I'm listening to a piece of music that takes me back to that particular time in my life. Some people would come over and put their arms around me, or pass me a tissue; three people removed the headphones to stop me listening to the music. Dee Heddon agreed to have her participation in the piece documented, and in the video she stands there helpless, and seemingly doesn't know what to do.

In terms of whether or not participants have negative experiences of works that are intended to be more caring, I think it's really difficult to know if someone has gone away with a negative experience, as I don't always get to hear about that. In *The Pleasure of Being: Washing/Feeding/Holding*, which I do intend to be a loving experience, a student emailed me a year after the performance to tell me that she was experiencing feelings of guilt and shame about what she had done as a participant. She felt it was akin to a one-night-stand, and she regretted having the experience with me. In quite accusatory terms, she said that at no point I had made it clear to her that we could talk during the performance, and that if we could have talked she wouldn't have felt as complicit in her own disempowerment. Interestingly, it says very clearly in the printed guidelines for participation – before you even enter a cubicle to change – that it is entirely up to the participant if we talk or remain silent. But perhaps she was in such a place of anxiety or apprehension that she didn't digest the information. When I got the email I was very concerned for her. She said that she gave herself to me, but felt that if I passed her on the street I wouldn't even recognise her. I thought it was awful that a year later she felt ashamed and dirty, and was wrestling with the experience. I knew it was important for me to really engage with her, and reassure her about what my intentions were for the piece. It wasn't my place to say, 'Well, I never held a gun to your head and forced you to do the piece', or to engage her with the idea that there might be something valid in her feeling uncomfortable. I felt she shouldn't be giving herself such a bad time, but I could sense she was suffering, and that was what I needed to address at the time.

I'd want to distance my work from the attitude that one-to-one performances – including my own – are only fluffy, warm and genial, and to be clear that prickly or uncomfortable experiences do indeed take place. In *The Pleasure of Being*, there are unexpected or difficult interactions, including if male participants get an erection and seem to suggest that we're going to have an erotic encounter. It's fine to get an erection. Why wouldn't you? The participant is lying in a really warm bath, with rose petals and milk products, and there's rose oil burning and it's candlelit, and I'm touching his body in a tender way. It's a physiological reaction, and it doesn't faze me, but in some instances it's clear from a participant's energy that he may be expecting or wanting this to be a sexual experience, especially if they touch me back. If I think of specific instances, I ask myself, why shouldn't that happen? Why should the participant know all the parameters? I don't have to go along with it. I can move his hand and continue, and I feel proud that it doesn't become sexualised, and that I can say something else through the piece – that two men can have a qualitative experience of intimacy and that it can remain tender and platonic, and that we can both learn from that. There are conflicts and negotiations, and these may be tricky.

DJ: *What is the place of the contract – social or written – in your perform-ances? How do you deal with unwritten agreements or limitations, which all performances potentially entertain?*

AH: I think there does have to be a level of protection, for the artist and the participant. Partly that comes from my engagement with the university's research ethics committee while a creative fellow. At first I assumed they would be merely prohibitive, but I realised that they were genuinely protecting individuals, including me. I deliberately work with a psychologist, Lisa Mayall, and seek advice from her. In *The Pleasure of Being*, she was adamant that the guidelines needed to be written down – a physical document that the participant could read – as she pointed out that if the guidelines are just spoken to the partic-ipant as they enter the space they won't hear me and process the infor-mation especially as they may well be anxious, nervous or apprehensive. I state, for example, that while I invite the participant to be naked, at no point will I wash or go near their genitals, to remove some of the anxiety from the performance. It makes it clear that sexual contact is not on the cards – although participants will sometimes not acknowledge this. The guidelines protect the audience, but also protect me – and the commissioning festival – from legal problems. The bullet points might look like dos and don'ts, but they try to make it clear what the experience is trying to be, and not something else.

I'm very mindful of the parameters of the experience, and it's important to make these clear and transparent. But I also know that as an audience participant I love to go to performances where the parameters are blurred. However, I feel with the work that I do, I am trying to create safe environments where we feel protected because that is the most likely climate for the work to thrive and be appropri-ately impactful. But that doesn't mean there can't be some difficult and challenging negotiations too.

Part II

DJ: *You performed in Stewart Laing's production of Copi's* The Homosexual, or The Difficulty of Sexpressing Oneself *(1993). Can you tell me about the production?*

AH: *The Homosexual* was hugely important to me. We did it first at Bagley's Studio, behind King's Cross Station, and we toured it to Manchester and Glasgow.[12] When I was at college [at Bretton Hall, Leeds, 1980–84], I was a born-again Christian – indeed I was president of the Christian Union. I was incredibly cautious about what I would get involved in, in terms of productions – I guess I didn't want to offend the Lord! I met Stewart Laing, and he showed me the script of Copi's play. I thought it was the most radical thing I had ever encountered. He offered me the role of the Madre, and told me he was going to ask Leigh Bowery to play Madame Garbo. I'm not sure I really knew who Leigh Bowery was at that time, other than a vague awareness of Taboo [the legendary 1980s club venue off Leicester Square in London], and the 'Blitz Kids' scene. I really like the fact that Stewart wanted to cast Leigh – with his excessive approach to performance; me, from what I call the 'Dora Bryan School of Performance';[13] and Ivan Cartwright, who used to do Myra Hindley drag and get beer cans thrown at him by enraged queens at the Two Brewers [a traditional drag club in South London]. Ivan had a scandalous show where he'd come out onto the stage covered in leprous sores, ringing a bell to the sound of Donna Summer's *Love's Unkind* – because she said AIDS was a punishment from God. I thought Ivan was fantastic. It was really inspired of Stewart to get the three of us together to do Copi's disgusting play.

The process was really satisfying. For the first three days of the rehearsal periods we sat and read the play together, and put every single word and line under the microscope. Leigh was fucking clever – I don't know if people realise that about him. It was a joy for us to discuss and argue over our readings of the play. Leigh and I fell in love with each other. I was the epitome of old-school Danny La Rue camp, and I'd never come across someone as brilliantly radical as Leigh. We gelled. He worked very hard, and I respected that. Even after a long day we would sit and go over lines together, and laugh and laugh. It was a marriage made in heaven.[14]

I could say what I wanted. The whole experience was new to me. Before that, particularly working with the Citizen's Theatre [as Assistant Director, 1990–2000] – with Giles Havergal, Philip Prowse and Robert David MacDonald – my experience had been of working with powerful but intimidating people. As an actor you can sometimes feel ridiculed for your ideas. I never felt like that working with Leigh, even though he *certainly* had a reputation that preceded him. And Stewart was completely liberating, too. He loved that I could be camp, and ridiculous, and tasteless. I learnt to celebrate queerdom. We were radical queers, and I learnt that about myself being involved in that show, and particularly from spending all that time with Leigh. *Time Out* called our production 'a hymn to tastelessness', and we all enjoyed that very much. I can't remember if they meant it kindly or not, but it did sum up our process. We'd ask how tasteless and offensive we could be, and go for it. *It gave me license to go beyond myself.*

The play opens with Irina and myself on a sofa. I was blacked-up, and I played the Madre as an Asian transsexual on speed. I guess you couldn't get away with that any more. Leigh applied my body make-up every night, and I wore a sari, tracksuit top and trainers. I had a *Carry On Up the Khyber* cockney accent. Ivan played Irina as a complete slut, who gets banged by soldiers on the steps of the Russian Palace, in a miniskirt that was practically a belt, with plat-form shoes, and an amazing cleavage. In the opening of the play, I give Irina an abortion, and out comes a skinned rabbit wrapped in cling film, attached to an umbilical cord. People were appalled, and it was very funny. Leigh would walk in wearing 36 fox furs stitched together as a huge coat – he'd see the aborted rabbit-foetus, and barf a load of vegetable soup onto the floor. It was all really distasteful. I loved it. It brought out violent reactions in people. Copi is too much to begin with – his plays are rarely staged in the UK – and Stewart took it to another level of offensiveness.

It was all very liberating, and my permission to 'go there' was initiated by working with Stewart, Leigh and Ivan. I think a lot of people, nowadays, think I'm too 'pure'. There is that side to me, and to what I choose to do in performance. But, at times, I want to get my hands dirty. I am drawn to the darker, seedier side of things, to impropriety. I still choose to get my hands dirty, not just artistically, but in terms of going places in my imagination, my fucked-up rela-tionships, and my research.

DJ: *Sexuality and sexual identity are central to Copi's play, from the title to the text and performed images, and the working relationships you've described. How important is sexuality to your own practice?*

AH: I've been thinking about doing a performative walk, which will look at night-time experiences of sexual contact that I've had. Some of them have been hilarious. It feels important for me, now, to remind everyone – and myself – that I'm a gay man. I don't feel that it's necessary to do so in *Foot Washing for the Sole*, or *The Pleasure of*

Being, but it still comes up. After *Garden of Adrian* [2009], for example, after we spooned, a straight guy commented that he'd never had an intimate experience with a gay man before, and he was surprised I didn't 'come on' to him.[15] I don't want to get too carried away by saying this, but I think it's important that I'm a gay man – not a straight man, in case you didn't know this about me [*we laugh*] – saying we can have experiences of intimacy, and *tenderisation*. I feel pride that I can own the responsibility for doing that.

DJ: *To what extent is the work therapeutic for you, and to what extent do you set out to undertake a therapeutic function for your participants?*

AH: I'm very comfortable with the idea of performance as therapy, and about admitting that my work can often have a therapeutic benefit for others. I know it's not fashionable to say that. I've become less comfortable with talking about how the work may have a therapeutic benefit for *me*. I think the dynamic of nurturing someone else is very different to the dynamic of nurturing someone else and being nurtured in return, at the same time. I used to say that if I was nurturing and nourishing another human being, of course I am going to be nurtured and nourished in return. It's not necessarily the case. In *The Pleasure of Being*, for example, it's labour-intensive – someone gives me their body weight, and I'm lifting the arms and legs to wash them – at the end of the day my back is killing me from all the heavy work of bending over a bath and lifting their limbs. Actually, the focus of my attention is on *giving* care and pleasure to that individual. They're not giving it back to me at the same time. I experience *something* of a nurturing nature in return, but it's not the same. That person is surrendering, with their eyes closed, and I'm doing all the work rather than being treated in the same way. That doesn't negate the beneficial experiences that come from the feel of flesh on flesh – but to say that the act of nurturing brings an experience of nurturing in return, well, I think I was simplifying things.

It's poignant and timely that before we started recording, Dominic, you asked me how I'm doing, and I told you I was starting to go on some dates, and that I'm trying to get myself out there again. I've given a lot to people, and I think I've reached a point where I would like to get something back. I want to be bathed or stroked, or caressed, or held, the way I've been doing all these things for other people. My psychotherapist said a very interesting thing to me. I told her I felt reluctant to create a dating profile, but that I didn't think I'd be worried about responding to one. She told me she wasn't surprised I was reluctant – I've been putting myself out there for quite a few years, trying to say 'This is who I am', but I don't necessarily feel that a lot has come back in return. You know what? I think that if someone else if prepared to give and give, well, the recipient will just keep taking. Earlier we talked about contracts, and sometimes it feels like my performances do not involve a mindful contract, in the sense that we agree that the other person must give me something back. The problem is that I'm not even doing the work to get something back, or not consciously. But I think I've reached a point where I do want something in return, in performance, or elsewhere.

DJ: *This makes me think of the economy of the gift. You want performance to be closer to this economy, where a gift warrants something in return, even if this compensation is immaterial, and the thing that is given comes at a cost – albeit an emotional or psychic cost.*

AH: What I think I've done is to realise the degree to which my continual giving has been a mask for feeling like I do not need to receive. Speaking of masks, when I started my fellowship at Glasgow, after talking with Dee, I made a conscientious decision to dispense with the mask of Adrienne – the make-up, hair, and costume. I wanted to be much more open and honest about risk, and vulnerability – and the *cost*, I guess, of an engagement with another person. I am not very good at receiving. I want to get better at it.

DJ: *If the gift is one economy you seem to work with, another is a sacrificial economy, where you set yourself up as a martyr. I think you're saying that the sacrificial aspect means you give too much of yourself in the encounter.*

AH: Yes. I identify with what you've just said. I think I have had a tendency – not on a conscious level – to *play the martyr*. I guess I've been comfortable with that, as it's all I've ever known. Now I'm conscious of it, I don't want to play the martyr anymore.

My other concern is that if I'm not prepared to receive, *I invalidate my giving.* Surely, for there to be equanimity, I also need to be willing to receive, beyond taking on the burden of another's sadness, joy, or the weight of their transcendence. It's not good enough when – sometimes, only sometimes – the other person has offered, say, to give me a bath during *Washing/Feeding/Holding*, and I've said, unthinkingly, 'no, it's not about me, the experience is about you'. What's interesting to me, now, is how quick I've been to say that. Why can't the experience *include* me?

DJ: *Finally, what's the difference between you the person and you the artist? It strikes me that it's difficult to distinguish where the work ends and you start.*

AH: I do get confused between the inside and the outside of the work. For example, I have become very aware that I'm virtuosic at *performing* intimacy. I am not so good at letting it happen in everyday life, of *having* intimacy without performing. It's cyclical, though, as that is one of the reasons I want to make sure I can explore intimacy in performance. The less intimacy I get, the more I want to perform it; and the more I perform it, the less I feel capable of finding it in my life. I'm willing to *'fess up* about this.

When I had a breakdown in 2011, I went into a very serious depression. It was after I performed *May I Have the Pleasure ...?*, and my psychotherapist said that I terrified myself, because I gave so much of myself to the performance that I have nothing left of myself to fall back on, or to hide behind, when I tried to return to everyday life. That's true. Hence, I put myself in a place of terror. There was no foundation for living, because I had given it away. Interestingly, that show was about me being 49, gay, still single, and having never been in a serious committed relationship, and talking openly and honestly about my isolation, my loneliness. I was in the grip of this knowledge when I made that show. I had no distance – historical or emotional – from what I was looking at. My psychotherapist said – and I love this expression – it was 'too much risk for a risk-taker'. So, yes, I find it very difficult to navigate between performance and 'real life', whatever that might be.

The breakdown was precipitated by a startlingly cruel review of the performance, which, of course, I took to be a demolition of *me* – of my life and my choices. The few bad reviews devastated me. But I *chose* not to separate my self from the work. I think I'm getting much clearer about these things now. How can I make sure I'm safe? How can I be a risk-taker and not take on too much risk to bear? In the future, I should try to work with feelings and experiences that are in the past, and can create narratives in which my memory – my confession – is *fudged*, in order to protect myself. This worked in *Lifeguard* (Govanhill Baths, Glasgow, 2012), where I didn't find myself in such a position of emotional self-exposure. I became a mouthpiece for my own biographical material, but also for other people's experiences, which were muddled together, and the audience never knew which stories were mine, and which belonged to other people. That way, *criticism can't cut so deep*. I'm conscious that I said earlier that with *Adrienne's Dirty Laundry Experience*, the fudging of my possessions and found ones was suspect. However, it's not the same thing. That was accidental, or unthinking – in *Lifeguard* it is a strategy of *self-preservation*.

I realise I'm driven to go to a place of self-exposure, risk and pain so much so that I have to put obstacles in place, to protect myself. I put my hand into the fire. I've been burnt. I put my hand back into the fire. When I do so, I know I'm alive. That's the power of performance. But it can also feel like a fatal attraction to getting burnt.

Notes

1. Nancy Groves, 'Theatre legend Adrian Howells dies aged 51', *Guardian*, 19 March 2014, http://www.theguardian.com/stage/2014/mar/19/adrian-howells-glasgow-theatre-legend-dies [accessed 06/08/14].

2. Laing directed Howells in Copi's *The Homosexual, or the Difficulty of Sexpressing Oneself* (1993), discussed below; TV Production's devised portrait of Michel Foucault, titled *Brainy* (1995); Samuel Beckett's *Happy Days* (1996); and *Myths of the Near Future* (1999), based on a short story by J. G. Ballard. Between 1996 and 2003, Howells performed in six stage works by Charnock, and his film *Are We Not Gods* (2003).

3. Nigel Charnock was a dancer and choreographer, and co-founder of DV8. He died of stomach cancer on 1 August 2012. After *Asylum*, Howells and Charnock collaborated on *Stupid Men* (The Place, London, 2008).

4. Russell Barr is a playwright whose work in the early 2000s included solo monologues, often performed by him, which drew upon and extended the visceral content associated with 'In-Yer-Face' theatre.

5. In *Say Cheese*, Ashery's Hasidic alter ego received guests on a bed in a domestic gallery, Home, in South London. Ashery/Fisher agreed to do anything the participant asked, apart from inflicting pain. In *Aktion 398*, Franko B was installed naked except for a dog's protective cone, with a bloodied gash in the flesh of his abdomen; he received audience members for three-minute encounters.

6. *The Pleasure of Being: Washing/Feeding/Holding* was first performed in a specially installed bathroom space at Battersea Arts Centre (BAC), South London in 2010. Howells bathed each participant in a bath and dried them with a towel; the participant was cradled in his arms, fed chocolate, and held.

7. In *Foot Washing for the Sole*, Howells performed the tasks of washing, drying, anointing, massaging and kissing the participant's feet.

8. Kira O'Reilly's most challenging one-to-one is likely *Untitled Action* (2005–06), in which audience-participants are invited to make an incision in her skin; after cutting (or not cutting) her, one holds her naked body in a *pièta*.

9. Sean O'Hagan, 'Interview: Marina Abramović', *Observer Magazine*, 3 October 2010, p. 32.

10. Howells was the recipient of an Arts and Humanities Research Council (AHRC) Fellowship in the Creative and Performing Arts in the Department of Theatre, Film and Television Studies from 2006 to 2009. He was subsequently an Honorary Research Fellow in the department.

11. Howells has frequently appropriated the images and rituals of Christianity, both indirectly (in pieces such as *Foot Washing for the Sole*) and explicitly in *The 14 Stations*. This was influenced by his religious upbringing, and by a period as a 'born-again' Christian at university.

12. Copi was Raúl Damonte Botana (1939–1987), an Argentine playwright and satirical cartoonist active in Paris in the 1970s and 1980s. See Copi, *Plays, Vol. 1*, trans. Anni Lee Taylor (London: John Calder 1976). Laing's production of Copi's greatest play *The Homosexual* (1971) toured to Tramway in Glasgow, in June 1993, and as part of the Queerupnorth festival at Green Room, Manchester in September.

13. Dora Bryan was an actress in Ealing comedies of the 1950s, in which she invariably played fruity characters including fallen women.

14. Leigh Bowery died of an AIDS-related illness on 31 December 1994, just over a year after the play ended its tour.

15. *The Garden of Adrian* was performed in June 2009 at the University of Glasgow. In each half-hour encounter, the artist led participants through a garden (designed by Minty Donald), and engaged in a series of contemplative interactions.

Epilogue

The Art of Living has brought together the anomalous, disparate, spirited voices of artists working in performance. As a partial oral history of performance art, the preceding pages should not be taken as an attempt to provide a new anti-canon, or to replace one list of pioneers with another, while leaving the evaluative and valuing structures of the canon undisturbed and unreconstructed. Rather, in constructing a kind of oral *Wunderkammer*, I ask that we shift the collective vantage, and refocus one's critical perspective on a different chain of unsatisfied dreams, to see *what possibilities and promises might be afforded by looking elsewhere* for a story of what happens in performance, from the 1970s to the present day.

An artist enters a museum and steals the favourite painting of the century's most reviled despot. Another hugs, treats, bathes, massages and consoles an army of civilian casualties, one by one. A pair of artists obliterates their individualities, merging themselves, in life and in performance, via the name, body and language. An artist becomes a Goddess, a silhouette, and a channel for the passage of dead legends, less a shaman than a creature of the night. Another turns his asshole into a tribute, temple, target, totem and tomb. An artist slathers her husband in food, and feeds him through a tube, after secreting him in bondage in the darkest basement of her love. It goes on.

What has happened *matters*. It has been profound, unfamiliar, important, reckless, half-mad even, sublime, and on the brink of full life. It is always so, and it is always senseless – for there can be no sense in *hope*.

Further reading

The following is a preliminary guide to substantial critical writings and commercially available audiovisual resources on each artist.

Penny Arcade

Penny Arcade is the subject of a monograph, namely Penny Arcade, *Bad Reputation: Performances, Essays, Interviews* (Los Angeles: Semiotext(e), 2009). She is interviewed in Zora Von Burden, *Women of the Underground: Art – Cultural Innovators Speak for Themselves* (San Francisco: Manic D Press, 2012), pp. 22–33. Her own writings include Penny Arcade, 'The Last Days and Last Moments of Jack Smith', in *Flaming Creature: Jack Smith, His Amazing Life and Times*, ed. by Edward Leffingwell, Carole Kismaric and Marvin Heiferman, exh. cat., Institute for Contemporary Art, P.S.1 Museum (London and New York: Serpent's Tail, 1997), pp. 192–5; and 'On David Wojnarowicz's *In the Shadow of the American Dream*', in *East Village USA*, ed. by Dan Cameron (New York: New Museum of Contemporary Art, 2005), pp. 109–10. There are currently no commercially available audio-visual recordings of Arcade's work.

Joey Arias

Arias published a book of interviews, namely Joey Arias, *The Art of Conversation* (Berlin: MaasMedia, 2002). There are frequent discussions in catalogues and surveys of Downtown art, especially: Steven Hager, *Art After Midnight: The East Village Scene* (New York: St. Martin's Press, 1986), pp. 31–7; and Dan Cameron, 'It Takes a Village', in *East Village USA* (New York: New Museum of Contemporary Art, 2005), pp. 41–64 (pp. 57–8). Early performances are featured in: the cult movie *Mondo New York* (dir. Harvey Keith, International Harmony, 1988); and the documentary, *Wigstock* (dir. Barry Shils, MGM, 1995). Commercially available audio recordings include *The Lost Record* (Moonfire Tower Records, 2013).

Ron Athey

Ron Athey is the subject of an edited collection: *Pleading in the Blood: The Art and Performances of Ron Athey*, ed. by Dominic Johnson (Bristol and London:

Intellect and Live Art Development Agency, 2013), which also includes Athey's own writings. Scholarly writing on his work includes: Patrick Califia, 'The Winking Eye of Ron Athey', in *Speaking Sex to Power: The Politics of Queer Sex* (San Francisco: Cleis, 2002), pp. 357–64; Amelia Jones, 'Holy Body: Erotic Ethics in Ron Athey and Juliana Snapper's *Judas Cradle*', *TDR*, 50 (2006), 159–69; and Jennifer Doyle, *Hold It Against Me: Difficulty and Emotion in Contemporary Art* (Durham and London: Duke University Press, 2012). See also Athey's own reflective essay 'Reading Sister Aimee', *Live: Art and Performance*, ed. by Adrian Heathfield (London: Tate, 2005), pp. 86–91. Audio-visual resources on DVD include: a biographical documentary, *Hallelujah! Ron Athey: A Story of Deliverance* (dir. Catherine Saalfield Gund, Aubin Pictures, 1998); and a performance document, *Monster in the Night of the Labyrinth* (Unbound, 2007).

Julia Bardsley

The key publication on Bardsley's work is a self-published artist's book: Julia Bardsley, *'u' see the image of her 'i': Pinhole Photographs* (London: ear eye gym books, 2014). For a critical overview of her early work, see Helen Manfull, *Taking Stage: Women Directors on Directing* (London: Methuen, 1999). For a thematically focused conversation, see Dominic Johnson, 'The Subtle Aggressors: An Interview with Julia Bardsley and Simon Vincenzi', in *Return, Rewrite, Revisit: Theatre and Adaptation*, ed. by Margherita Laera (London: Methuen, 2014), pp. 107–20. A transcript of her performance *Trans-Acts* (2003) is published in *Theatre in Pieces: Politics, Poetics and Interdisciplinary Collaboration: An Anthology of Play Texts 1966–2010*, ed. by Anna Furse (London: Methuen, 2011), pp. 155–98. Her video series *Foolish Suicide Attempts* (Unbound, 2006) is available on DVD.

Anne Bean

The key monograph is Anne Bean, *Autobituary: Shadow Deeds* (London: Matt's Gallery, 2006), which includes a DVD of selected documentation. Key writings on her work include: Chris Millar, 'Profile: Anne Bean – A Portentous Event in Earshot of Braying Donkeys', *Performance Magazine*, 20–21 (December/January 1983), 4–8; and Kathy Battista, *Renegotiating the Body: Feminist Art in 1970s London* (London: I.B. Tauris, 2013). Bean's own writings include 'Lifelines', *PAJ: A Journal of Performance and Art*, 107, 36.2 (May 2014), 26–29. Audio recordings of Bow Gamelan Ensemble include nine works in *Audio Arts Supplement* (1985): http://www.tate.org.uk/audio-arts/supplements/bow-gamelan-ensemble [accessed 13/08/14].

BREYER P-ORRIDGE

Genesis BREYER P-ORRIDGE has been the subject of several monographs, including Simon Ford's *Wreckers of Civilisation: The Story of COUM Transmissions and Throbbing Gristle* (London: Black Dog, 1999); and Genesis P-Orridge, *Painful but Fabulous: The Life and Art of Genesis P-Orridge* (New York: Soft Skull, 2002). On pandrogeny, see Dominic Johnson, 'Psychic Weight: The Pleasures and Pains of Performance', in *ORLAN: A Hybrid Body of Art Works*, ed. by Simon Donger with Simon Shepherd and ORLAN (Abingdon and New York: Routledge, 2010), pp. 84–99. Their published writings include: *Esoterrorist: Selected Essays, 1980–88* (San Francisco: MediaKaos and Alecto, 1994); and *Thee Psychick Bible: Thee Apocryphal Scriptures*, ed. by Jason Louv (Port Townsend: Feral House, 2010). Audio-visual documents include the cinematic portrait, *The Ballad of Genesis and Lady Jaye* (dir. Marie Losier, Adopt Films, 2012); and a vast discography of audio releases by COUM Transmissions, Throbbing Gristle, Psychic TV, and Thee Majesty.

Adrian Howells

Scholarly articles and book chapters include: Jon Cairns, 'Ambivalent Intimacies: Performance and Domestic Photography in the Work of Adrian Howells', *Contemporary Theatre Review*, 22.3 (2012), 355–71; Deirdre Heddon, Helen Iball and Rachel Zerihan, 'Come Closer: Confessions of Intimate Spectators in One to One Performance', *Contemporary Theatre Review*, 22.1 (2012), 120–33; and Helen Iball, 'My Sites Set on You: Site-specificity and Subjectivity in 'Intimate Theatre', *Performing Site-Specific Theatre: Politics, Place, Practice* ed. by Joanne Tompkins and Anna Birch (Palgrave Macmillan, 2013), pp. 201–18. Howells' work is also addressed in: Fintan Walsh, *Theatre & Therapy* (Palgrave Macmillan, 2013); and (on Copi's *The Homosexual*) in Sue Tilley, *Leigh Bowery: The Life and Times of an Icon* (London: Hodder and Stoughton, 1997). Howells' writings include: Deirdre Heddon and Adrian Howells, 'From Talking to Silence: A Confessional Journey', *PAJ: A Journal of Performance and Art*, 97, 33.1 (2011), 1–12; and Adrian Howells, 'Foot Washing for the Sole', *Performance Research*, 17.2 (2012), 128–31. There are no commercially available audio-visual documents.

David Hoyle

Scholarship on Hoyle's work includes Daniel Oliver, ' "You're Funnier When You're Angry": Affirmation, Responsibility and Commitment in David Hoyle's Live Performance Practice', *Performance Research*, 19.2 (2014), 109–15; and Gavin Butt, 'Just a Camp Laugh? David Hoyle's Laden Levity', in Gavin

Butt and Irit Rogoff, *Visual Cultures as Seriousness* (Berlin: Sternberg Press, 2013), pp. 39–60. Audio-visual resources on DVD include: David Hoyle, *Magazine: The Reprint* (Unbound, 2008); *Revelations: The Films of David Hoyle and Nathan Evans* (Unbound, 2011); and the feature film *Uncle David* (dir. Mike Nicholls and Gary Reich, Peccadillo, 2011).

The Kipper Kids

Substantial commentaries include: C. Carr, 'The Kipper Kids in Middle Age', in *On Edge: Performance at the End of the Twentieth Century* (Middletown: Wesleyan University Press, 1993), pp. 148–53; Cary Levine, *Pay For Your Pleasures: Mike Kelley, Paul McCarthy, Raymond Pettibon* (Chicago: University of Chicago Press, 2013), pp. 33–4; and Karen Finley, 'Sheis Fleis', in *A Different Kind of Intimacy: The Collected Writings of Karen Finley* (New York: Thunder's Mouth, 2000), pp. 1–7. Interviews include: Andrea Juno and V. Vale, 'Harry Kipper', in *Pranks!* (San Francisco: RE/Search Publications, 1987), pp. 219–25; and Linda M. Montano, *Performance Artists Talking in the 80s* (Berkeley and Los Angeles, University of California Press, 2000), pp. 314–6, 430–4, 431–3. Commercial DVD releases include the cult movie *Forbidden Zone* (dir. Richard Elfman, Hercules Films, 1980).

Ann Magnuson

Critical writings on Magnuson's performances include: C. Carr, 'Am I Living in a Box?', in *On Edge*, pp. 229–31; and Rebecca Schneider, *The Explicit Body in Performance* (New York and London: Routledge, 1997), pp. 108–12. Published interviews include: Denise Sullivan, 'Artists Without Limits: Ann Magnuson', in *Rip It Up!: Rock & Roll Rulebreakers* (San Francisco: Backbeat, 2001), pp. 219–29; and Linda M. Montano, 'Ann Magnuson', in *Performance Artists Talking in the 80s*, pp. 386–90. Magnuson's writings include: 'Excerpts from *You Could Be Home Now* and *Pretty Songs*', in *Extreme Exposure: An Anthology of Solo Performance Texts from the Twentieth Century* ed. by Jo Bonney (New York: Theatre Communications Group, 2000), pp. 135–44; and 'Grandma, Tell Me About the Eighties', in Richard Marshall, Carlo McCormick and Ann Magnuson, *Kenny Scharf* (New York: Rizzoli, 2009), pp. 259–66. Magnuson is discussed in surveys of Downtown performance, including: Dan Cameron, 'It Takes a Village', in *East Village USA*, pp. 41–64; Peter Frank and Mike McKenzie, *New, Used and Improved: Art for the 1980's* (New York: Abbeville Press, 1987); and Steven Hager, *Art After Midnight*, pp. 73–85. CD releases include three Bongwater albums; and four solo albums including *The Jobriath Medley* (Pink Fleece, 2012).

Sheree Rose

On Rose's collaborations with Bob Flanagan, see Amelia Jones, *Body Art / Performing the Subject* (Minneapolis and London: University of Minnesota Press, 1998); and Linda S. Kauffman, *Bad Girls and Sick Boys: Fantasies in Contemporary Art and Culture* (Berkeley and Los Angeles: University of California, 1998). Rose's own writings include: 'In Semi-Sickness and in So-Called Health: I'm Still in Love with You', in Bob Flanagan, *The Pain Journal* (Los Angeles: Semiotext(e), 2000), pp. 174–8; and 'Fighting Sickness with Sickness', in *Access All Areas: Live Art and Disability*, ed. by Lois Keidan and CJ Mitchell (London: Live Art Development Agency, 20112), pp. 94–5. Interviews include: Klare Scarborough, 'Coffins and Cameras: A Conversation with Sheree Rose', *Performance Research*, 15.1 (2010), 123–30; and Tina Takemoto, 'Love is Still Possible in this Junky World: Conversation with Sheree Rose about her Life with Bob Flanagan', *Women and Performance*, 19.1 (2009), 95–111. The key audio-visual resource is the documentary *Sick: The Life and Death of Bob Flanagan, Supermasochist* (dir. Kirby Dick, BFI, 2003/2012).

Ulay

Ulay is the subject of a monograph: Maria Rus Bojan and Alessandro Cassin, *Whispers: Ulay on Ulay* (Amsterdam: Valiz Foundation, 2014). The most sustained writer on Ulay's solo work was Thomas McEvilley; see his *Ulay: The First Act* (Ostfildern: Canst Verlag, 1994); and *Art, Love, Friendship: Marina Abramović and Ulay – Together and Apart* (New York: McPherson, 2010). On Ulay/Abramović, see Kathy O'Dell, 'My Mirror', *Contract with the Skin: Masochism, Performance Art and the 1970s* (Minneapolis and London: University of Minnesota Press, 1998), pp. 31–44. The sole scholarly article on Ulay's own works is Mechthild Fend, 'Emblems of Durability: Tattoos, Preserves and Photographs', *Performance Research*, 14.4 (2009), 45–52. For photographic works, see Ulay, *Portraits 1970–1993* (Amsterdam: Basalt, 1996). Audio-visual resources include the documentary *Project Cancer: Ulay's Journal from November to November* (dir. Damjan Kozole, Emotionfilm, 2013); and *The Great Wall Walk: Lovers at the Brink* (dir. Murray Grigor, Contemporary Art Foundation, 1989).

Bibliography

Acconci, Vito, 'Some Notes on Activity and Performance' (1970), in Jennifer Bloomer, Mark C. Taylor and Frazer Ward, *Vito Acconci* (London: Phaidon, 2002), pp. 88–92.

Allen, Steven, *Cinema, Pain and Pleasure: Consent and the Controlled Body* (Basingstoke: Palgrave Macmillan, 2013).

Als, Hilton, 'Critic's Notebook: Arcade Fire', *New Yorker*, 86.4 (15 March 2010), 12.

Arcade, Penny, 'Letter to a Young Artist No. 1', 8 April 2014, http://penny arcade.tv/letter-to-a-young-artist-1/#.VBw_OUiLaGh [accessed 28/06/14].

—, 'The Last Days and Last Moments of Jack Smith', in *Flaming Creature: Jack Smith, His Amazing Life and Times*, ed. Edward Leffingwell, Carole Kismaric and Marvin Heiferman, exh. cat., Institute for Contemporary Art, P.S.1 Museum (London and New York: Serpent's Tail, 1997), pp. 192–5.

—, *Bad Reputation: Performances, Essays, Interviews* (Los Angeles: Semiotext(e), 2009).

Arias, Joey, *The Art of Conversation* (Berlin: MaasMedia, 2002).

Artaud, Antonin, *The Theatre and its Double*, trans. Victor Corti (London: Calder & Boyars, 1970).

Athey, Ron, 'Reading Sister Aimee', in *Live: Art and Performance*, ed. Adrian Heathfield (London: Tate, 2005), pp. 86–91.

Bardsley, Julia, 'Trans-Acts', in *Theatre in Pieces: Politics, Poetics and Interdisciplinary Collaboration: An Anthology of Play Texts 1966–2010*, ed. Anna Furse (London: Methuen, 2011), pp. 155–98.

—, *'u' see the image of her 'i': Pinhole Photographs* (London: ear eye gym books, 2014).

Battista, Kathy, *Renegotiating the Body: Feminist Art in 1970s London* (London: I. B. Tauris, 2013).

Bean, Anne, 'Lifelines', *PAJ: A Journal of Performance and Art*, 107, 36.2 (May 2014), 26–9.

—, *Autobituary: Shadow Deeds* (London: Matt's Gallery, 2006).

Berger Gluck, Sherna, 'What's So Special About Women?: Women's Oral History', in *Women's Oral History: The 'Frontiers' Reader*, ed. Susan H. Armitage with Patricia Hart and Karen Weathermon (Lincoln and London: University of Nebraska, 2002), pp. 3–20.

Berryman, John, *Collected Poems 1937–1971*, ed. Charles Thornbury (New York: Farrar, Straus & Giroux, 1989).

Beuys, Joseph, *Energy Plan for the Western Man: Joseph Beuys in America*, ed. Carin Kuoni (New York: Four Walls Eight Windows, 1990).

Bradby, David, ed., *Bernard-Marie Koltès: Plays 1* (London: Methuen, 1997).

Brett, Guy, *Exploding Galaxies: The Art of David Medalla* (London: Third Text Publications, 1995).

BREYER P-ORRIDGE, Genesis, 'Excerpts from a Dialogue with Dominic Johnson', in *Everything You Know About Sex Is Wrong: Extremes of Human Sexuality (and Everything In Between)*, ed. Russ Kick (New York: Disinformation Press, 2005), pp. 345–8.

—, *Thee Psychick Bible: Thee Apocryphal Scriptures*, ed. Jason Louv (Port Townsend: Feral House, 2010).

Bürger, Peter, *Theory of the Avant-Garde*, trans. Jochen Schulte-Sasse (Minneapolis: University of Minnesota Press, [1974] 1984).

Butt, Gavin, 'Just a Camp Laugh? David Hoyle's Laden Levity', in Gavin Butt and Irit Rogoff, *Visual Cultures as Seriousness* (Berlin: Sternberg Press, 2013), pp. 39–60.

Cairns, Jon, 'Ambivalent Intimacies: Performance and Domestic Photography in the Work of Adrian Howells', *Contemporary Theatre Review*, 22.3 (2012), 355–71.

Califia, Patrick, *Speaking Sex to Power: The Politics of Queer Sex* (San Francisco: Cleis Publications, 2002).

Cameron, Dan, ed., *East Village USA* (New York: New Museum of Contemporary Art, 2005).

Carr, C., *On Edge: Performance at the End of the Twentieth Century* (Middletown, CT: Wesleyan University Press, 1993).

Clothier, Peter, 'The Kipper Kids: An Endless Ritual', in *Performance Anthology: Source Book for a Decade of California Performance Art*, ed. Carl E. Loeffler with Darlene Tong (San Francisco: Contemporary Arts Press, 1980), p. 165.

Copi, *Plays, Vol. 1*, trans. Anni Lee Taylor (London: John Calder 1976).

Cotter, Holland, 'Nothing to Spend, Nothing to Lose: "Rituals of Rented Island", Performance Art at the Whitney', *New York Times*, 31 October 2013, p. C25.

Danto, Arthur C., *Unnatural Wonders: Essays from the Gap Between Art and Life* (New York: Farrar, Straus & Giroux, 2005).

Delgado, Maria M. and Paul Heritage, *In Contact with the Gods?: Directors Talk Theatre* (Manchester and New York: Manchester University Press, 1996).

DeLillo, Don, *Mao II* (London: Vintage, 1992).

Doyle, Jennifer, *Hold It Against Me: Difficulty and Emotion in Contemporary Art* (Durham, NC and London: Duke University Press, 2013).

Fend, Mechthild, 'Emblems of Durability: Tattoos, Preserves and Photographs', *Performance Research*, 14.4 (2009), 45–52.

Finley, Karen, *A Different Kind of Intimacy: The Collected Writings of Karen Finley* (New York: Thunder's Mouth, 2000), pp. 1–7.

Flanagan, Bob, *Slave Sonnets* (Los Angeles: Cold Calm Press, 1986).

—, *The Pain Journal* (Los Angeles: Semiotext(e), 2000).

Ford, Simon, *Wreckers of Civilisation: The Story of COUM Transmissions and Throbbing Gristle* (London: Black Dog, 1999).

Foucault, Michel, *Fearless Speech*, ed. Joseph Pearson (Los Angeles: Semiotext(e), 2001).

Frank, Peter and Michael McKenzie, *New, Used and Improved: Art for the 80's* (New York: Abbeville Press, 1987).

Frank, Peter, 'The Kipper Kids', *Performance Magazine*, 1 (1979), 43–5.

Furmanski, Jonathan, 'The Kipper Kids', *California Video: Artists and Histories*, ed. Glenn Phillips, exh. cat., J. Paul Getty Museum (Los Angeles: Getty Research Institute, 2008), pp. 134–7.

Genet, Jean, 'Interview with Madeleine Gobeil', in *The Declared Enemy: Texts and Interviews*, ed. Albert Dichy, trans. Jeff Fort (Stanford, CA: Stanford University Press, 2004), pp. 2–17.

Georges-Lemaire, Gérard, '23 Stitches Taken', in William S. Burroughs and Brion Gysin, *The Third Mind* (London: John Calder, 1979), pp. 9–24.

Greenberg, Clement, '*Partisan Review*, Art Chronicle: 1952', *Art and Culture: Critical Essays* (Boston: Beacon Press, 1961), pp. 146–53.

Groves, Nancy, 'Theatre legend Adrian Howells dies aged 51', *Guardian*, 19 March 2014, http://www.theguardian.com/stage/2014/mar/19/adrian-howells-glasgow-theatre-legend-dies [accessed 6 August 2014].

Gurdjieff, G. I., *Beelzebub's Tales to his Grandson: An Objectively Impartial Criticism of the Life of Man* (London: Routledge & Kegan Paul, 1950).

Hager, Steven, *Art After Midnight: The East Village Scene* (New York: St. Martin's Press, 1986).

Hattenstone, Simon, 'Love Hurts', *Guardian*, 13 February 1998, p. 2.

Heddon, Deirdre and Adrian Howells, 'From Talking to Silence: A Confessional Journey', *PAJ: A Journal of Performance and Art* 97, 33.1 (2011), 1–12.

Heddon, Deirdre, Helen Iball and Rachel Zerihan, 'Come Closer: Confessions of Intimate Spectators in One to One Performance', *Contemporary Theatre Review*, 22.1 (2012), 120–33.

Henige, David, *Oral Historiography* (New York: Longman, 1982).

Hoberman, J., ' "Like Canyons and Rivers": Performance for Its Own Sake', in Jay Sanders with J. Hoberman, *Rituals of Rented Island: Object Theater, Loft Performance, and the New Psychodrama – Manhattan, 1970–1980*, exh. cat, Whitney Museum of American Art, New York (New Haven, CT and London: Yale University Press, 2013), pp. 9–24.

Hollway, Wendy and Tony Jefferson, *Doing Qualitative Research Differently: Free Association, Narrative and the Interview Method* (London and Thousand Oaks, CA: Sage, 2000).

Howells, Adrian, 'Foot Washing for the Sole', *Performance Research*, 17.2 (2012), 128–31.

Iball, Helen, 'My Sites Set on You: Site-specificity and Subjectivity in 'Intimate Theatre', *Performing Site-Specific Theatre: Politics, Place, Practice* ed. Joanne Tompkins and Anna Birch (Palgrave Macmillan, 2013), pp. 201–18.

Iles, Chrissie, 'Taking a Line for a Walk: Interview with Ulay and Marina Abramović', *Performance Magazine*, 53 (April/May 1988), 14–19.

Johnson, Dominic, 'Psychic Weight: The Pleasures and Pains of Performance', in *ORLAN: A Hybrid Body of Art Works*, ed. Simon Donger with Simon Shepherd and ORLAN (Abingdon and New York: Routledge, 2010), pp. 84–99.

—, 'The Subtle Aggressors: An Interview with Julia Bardsley and Simon Vincenzi', in *Return, Rewrite, Revisit: Theatre and Adaptation*, ed. Margherita Laera (London: Methuen, 2014), pp. 107–20.

Johnson, Dominic, ed., *Pleading in the Blood: The Art and Performances of Ron Athey* (Bristol and London: Intellect and Live Art Development Agency, 2013).

Jones, Amelia, 'Holy Body: Erotic Ethics in Ron Athey and Juliana Snapper's *Judas Cradle*', *TDR: The Drama Review*, 50 (2006), 159–69.

—, *Body Art/Performing the Subject* (Minneapolis and London: University of Minnesota Press, 1998).

Juno, Andrea and V. Vale, 'Harry Kipper', in *Pranks!* (San Francisco: RE/Search Publications, 1987), pp. 219–25.

—, *Angry Women* (San Francisco: RE/Search Publications, 1991).

—, *Bob Flanagan: Supermasochist* (San Francisco: RE/Search Publications, 1993).

Kaprow, Allan, *Essays on the Blurring of Art and Life*, ed. Jeff Kelley (Berkeley and Los Angeles: University of California Press, 1993), pp. 1–9.

Kauffman, Linda S., *Bad Girls and Sick Boys: Fantasies in Contemporary Art and Culture* (Berkeley: University of California Press, 1998).

Kaye, Nick, *Art into Theatre: Performance Interviews and Documents* (London and New York: Routledge, 1996).

Keighley, Geoff, 'The Phantasmagoria Factory', *CNN Money*, 1 January 2004: http://money.cnn.com/magazines/business2/business2_archive/2004/0101/359604/ [accessed 19/02/14].

Kelley, Mike, 'Foreword: Utopia is a Space Outside the Market', in John Miller, *The Ruin of Exchange and Other Writings*, ed. Alexander Alberro (Zurich: JRP/Ringier, 2012), pp. 7–10.

—, *Minor Histories: Statements, Conversations, Proposals*, ed. John C. Welchman (Cambridge and London: MIT Press, 2004).

Kvale, Steinar and Svend Brinkmann, *InterViews: Learning the Craft of Qualitative Research Interviewing*, 2nd edn (Los Angeles and London: Sage, 2009).

Levine, Cary, *Pay For Your Pleasures: Mike Kelley, Paul McCarthy, Raymond Pettibon* (Chicago: University of Chicago Press, 2013).

Magnuson, Ann, 'Excerpts from *You Could Be Home Now* and *Pretty Songs*', in *Extreme Exposure: An Anthology of Solo Performance Texts from the Twentieth Century* ed. Jo Bonney (New York: Theatre Communications Group, 2000), pp. 135–44.

—, 'Grandma, Tell Me About the Eighties', in Richard Marshall, Carlo McCormick and Ann Magnuson, *Kenny Scharf* (New York: Rizzoli, 2009), pp. 259–66.

Manfull, Helen, *Taking Stage: Women Directors on Directing* (London: Methuen, 1999).

McEvilley, Thomas, *Art, Love, Friendship: Marina Abramović and Ulay – Together and Apart* (New York: McPherson, 2010).

—, *Ulay: The First Act* (Ostfildern: Canst Verlag, 1994).

Millar, Chris, 'Profile: Anne Bean – A Portentous Event in Earshot of Braying Donkeys', *Performance Magazine*, 20–1 (December/January 1983), 4–8.

Montano, Linda M., *Performance Artists Talking in the 80s* (Berkeley and Los Angeles, University of California Press, 2000).

Murphy, Tim, 'Loud and Colorful, with Total Recall: The Performance Artist Penny Arcade, Now an Actress', *New York Times,* 31 October 2013, www.nytimes.com/2013/11/03/theater/for-penny-arcade-a-new-role-onstage.html [accessed 28/09/14].

Nietzsche, Friedrich, *The Gay Science*, trans. Walter Kaufmann (New York: Vintage, 1974).

—, *Twilight of the Idols, or How to Philosophize with a Hammer* (London: Penguin, 1990).

O'Brien, Martin, 'Action with Sheree Rose', in *Access All Areas: Live Art and Disability*, ed. Lois Keidan and CJ Mitchell (London: Live Art Development Agency, 2012), p. 92.

O'Dell, Kathy, *Contract with the Skin: Masochism, Performance Art and the 1970s* (Minneapolis and London: University of Minnesota Press, 1998).

O'Hagan, Sean, 'Interview: Marina Abramović', *Observer Magazine,* 3 October 2010, p. 32.

Oliver, Daniel, '"You're Funnier When You're Angry": Affirmation, Responsibility and Commitment in David Hoyle's Live Performance Practice', *Performance Research*, 19.2 (2014), 109–15.

P-Orridge, Genesis, *Esoterrorist: Selected Essays, 1980–88* (San Francisco: MediaKaos and Alecto, 1994).

—, *Painful but Fabulous: The Life and Art of Genesis P-Orridge* (New York: Soft Skull, 2002).

Phillips, Adam, *Houdini's Box: On the Arts of Escape* (London: Faber & Faber, 2001).

Pollock, Della, ed., *Remembering: Oral History Performance* (New York and Basingstoke: Palgrave Macmillan, 2005).

Riley, Robert R., 'Concept, Art, and Media: Regarding California Video', in *California Video: Artists and Histories*, ed. Glenn Phillips, exh. cat., J. Paul Getty Museum (Los Angeles: Getty Research Institute, 2008), pp. 274–8.

Roms, Heike, *What's Welsh for Performance: An Oral History of Performance Art in Wales* (Cardiff: Trace/Samizdat Press, 2008).

Rus Bojan, Maria and Alessandro Cassin, *Whispers: Ulay on Ulay* (Amsterdam: Valiz Foundation, 2014).

Sacher-Masoch, Leopold von, *Venus in Furs*, trans. Joachim Neugroschel (Harmondsworth: Penguin, 2000).

Sade, Marquis de, *Justine, or the Misfortunes of Virtue*, trans. John Phillips (Oxford: Oxford University Press, 2012).

Scarborough, Klare, 'Coffins and Cameras: A Conversation with Sheree Rose', *Performance Research*, 15.1 (2010), 123–30.

Schneider, Rebecca, *The Explicit Body in Performance* (New York and London: Routledge, 1997).

Shaar Murray, Charles, 'David Bowie: Who Was That (Un)Masked Man?', *NME: New Musical Express* (November 1977), http://www.bowiewonderworld. com/press/press70.htm [accessed 17/01/14].

Shawn, Wallace, *The Designated Mourner* (London: Faber & Faber, 1996).

Shelley, Percy Bysshe, 'The Mask of Anarchy', in *Romanticism: An Anthology*, 2nd edn, ed. Duncan Wu (Oxford: Blackwell, 1998), pp. 930–40.

Smith, Jack, 'Capitalism of Lotusland' (1977), in *Wait For Me at the Bottom of the Pool: The Writings of Jack Smith*, ed. J. Hoberman and Edward Leffingwell (New York and London: High Risk Books, 1997), p. 11.

Smith, Marquard, *Visual Culture Studies: Interviews with Key Thinkers* (Los Angeles and London: Sage, 2008).

Smith, Patti, *Just Kids* (London: Bloomsbury, 2010).

Solanas, Valerie, *SCUM Manifesto* (Edinburgh and San Francisco: AK Press, 1997).

Sullivan, Denise, *Rip It Up!: Rock & Roll Rulebreakers* (San Francisco: Backbeat, 2001), pp. 219–29.

Sylvester, David, *Interviews with American Artists* (London: Chatto & Windus, 2001).

Takemoto, Tina, 'Love is Still Possible in this Junky World: Conversation with Sheree Rose about her Life with Bob Flanagan', *Women and Performance*, 19.1 (2009), 95–111.

Thompson, Paul, *The Voice of the Past: Oral History*, 2nd edn (Oxford: Oxford University Press, 1988).

Tilley, Sue, *Leigh Bowery: The Life and Times of an Icon* (London: Hodder & Stoughton, 1997).

Ulay, *Portraits 1970–1993* (Amsterdam: Basalt, 1996).

Vale, V., ed., *Modern Primitives: An Investigation of Contemporary Adornment and Ritual* (San Francisco: RE/Search Publications, 1989).

Von Burden, Zora, *Women of the Underground: Art – Cultural Innovators Speak for Themselves* (San Francisco: Manic D Press, 2012).

Walsh, Fintan, *Theatre & Therapy* (Palgrave Macmillan, 2013).

Welchman, John C., *Mike Kelley* (London: Phaidon, 1999).

Wengraf, Tom, *Qualitative Research Interviewing: Biographic Narrative and Semi-Structured Methods* (London: Sage, 2001).

Index

The letter 'n.' followed by a number indicates an endnote. Numbers in **bold** indicate images of artists.